Contemporary Industrial/
Organizational Psychology

Contemporary Industrial/ Organizational Psychology

L. N. JEWELL, Ph.D.

University of South Florida

WEST PUBLISHING COMPANY

St. Paul • New York • Los Angeles • San Francisco

Copyeditor: Kathleen C. Massimini

Compositor: Master Typographers

Cover photograph: © 1984 Chris Grajczyk

Library of Congress Cataloging in Publication Data

Jewell, L. N.
    Contemporary industrial/organizational psychology.

    Includes index.
    1. Psychology, Industrial.   I. Title.
HF5548.8.J48   1985   158.7   84-25693
ISBN 0-314-85252-2

Photo Credits

7 John Coletti/Stock, Boston, Inc. **11** Robert George Gaylord/Jeroboam, Inc. **34** Bohdan Hrynewych/Stock, Boston, Inc. **38** Richard J. Baljer/Stock, Boston, Inc. **51** Hazel Hankin/Stock, Boston, Inc. **55** Rose Skytta, Jeroboam, Inc. **110** Frank Siteman/Jeroboam, Inc. **118** B. Kliewe/Jeroboam, Inc. **148** Christopher Morrow/Stock, Boston, Inc. **153** Ellis Herwig/Stock, Boston, Inc. **189** Bell & Howell, Mailmobile® Operations 1984 **192** Courtesy of *EPRI Journal* **197** Jane Scherr/Jeroboam, Inc. **201** Emilio A. Mercado/Jeroboam, Inc. **223** James Holland/Stock, Boston, Inc. **230** Greg Mancusco/Jeroboam, Inc. **235** Richard Baljer/Stock, Boston, Inc. **251** Robert George Gaylord/Jeroboam, Inc. **263** Emilio Mercado/Jeroboam, Inc. **284** David Glaubinger/Jeroboam, Inc. **298** Jane Scherr/Jeroboam, Inc. **317** Barbara Alper/Stock, Boston, Inc. **329** Peter Menzel/Stock, Boston, Inc. **352** Fredrik D. Bodin/Stock, Boston, Inc. **363** Frank Wing/Stock, Boston, Inc. **389** Peter Southwick/Stock, Boston, Inc. **393** Emilio Mercado/Jeroboam, Inc. **426** Peter Menzel/Stock, Boston, Inc. **442** Phyllis Graber Jensen/Stock, Boston, Inc. **453** Elizabeth Hamlin/Stock, Boston, Inc. **461** Owen Franken/Stock, Boston, Inc. **475** Kent Reno/Jeroboam, Inc.

To my Mother

Contents

Preface

Contemporary Industrial/Organizational Psychology is written out of the deepest respect for tradition and for those who laid the foundation for I/O psychology as it exists today. I took my own introductory I/O psychology course over twenty-five years ago. My professor not only knew I/O history, he personally knew many of those who made it and his knowledge and enthusiasm had a considerable influence on my career choice. In the subsequent quarter-century, I have watched things change. The scope and knowledge of the field have changed, the world has changed, organizations have changed, colleges and universities have changed, and students have changed.

Today the subject matter of I/O psychology attracts students from a variety of backgrounds and interests. How can one write a book that meets the needs of psychology majors, business majors, and students from other areas, who believe some knowledge of this subject will help them in their chosen careers? How can one write at a level that is meaningful to students who have never worked, students who have worked part time and students who have been working for years in various positions in organizations of all kinds?

There are as many solutions to this predicament as there are authors of introductory I/O psychology textbooks. My approach stems from the conviction that the purpose of such a book is to *introduce* this field of study. By this, I mean that the first priority is to provide students with an understanding of the topics, the issues, and the methods of I/O psychology.

To introduce a field as rich and complex as I/O psychology, some choices must be made regarding the balance of coverage given to its several facets—application, theory, and research. With respect to the applied side of I/O psychology, my goal is to acquaint students with objectives, decisions to be made, alternatives available, and issues involved in choosing among these alternatives. The section that begins each chapter—"I/O Psychology at Work"—adds the flavor, if not the specifics, of applying I/O to the problems in today's organizations.

Theory is handled similarly. The major theories are summarized or discussed in context as alternative explanations and foundations for studying certain phenomena; they are not treated as subject matter in and of themselves. Every effort has been made to put these theories in a perspective accurately reflecting a consensus of their standing with respect to research support and practical utility in the mid-1980s.

While this is not a theory-oriented text, it *is* a research-based text. Whenever possible, points are made and illustrated through the empirical literature of I/O psychology; margin notes aid the student in linking this material to the introductory discussions of research and testing in Chapters 3 and 4. As appropriate, recent review of the topic's research literature is cited for further reference. Finally, the role of research in I/O psychology is further emphasized by "Spotlight on Research," a feature of Chapters 3–15 that summarizes a recent or classic study in a topic area relevant to the subject matter of each chapter.

These research-oriented features continually reinforce the point that the body of knowledge we are accumulating about human behavior in organizations is both the heritage and the future of I/O psychology. A view of this future is presented at the end of each chapter in a special "At Issue" section. The "At Issues" provide a forum for the new, the speculative, and the controversial.

Some "At Issue" topics are so new that their implications for our field are now only beginning to be explored. Genetic screening for employees is one such issue. In other cases, this feature presents the views of those who are questioning mainstream or traditional approaches to topics of established importance, such as leadership. The advancement of knowledge requires the courage to question and I believe students will benefit from a glimpse of this process. I also believe that discussions and debates of these questions are a valuable aid to learning.

In summary, I have tried to write a book for today, one that gives balanced coverage to the past and the present while keeping an eye toward the future. I have tried to present this material in such a way that students may see the big picture as well as the details, the "why" as well as the "what." I hope I have succeeded and that the reader will find few occasions to question the relevance of a topic or discussion.

PLAN OF THE BOOK

Part I is an introductory section. It presents background material about the field of I/O psychology and prepares the way for understanding the material to follow. Chapter 1 introduces I/O psychology as a field and as a profession. Chapter 2 continues this introduction with a brief review of I/O psychology's basic subject matter—the causes of human behavior. In Chapter 3, the methods by which human behavior in organizations is studied are examined and important terminology that appears frequently in subsequent discussions is introduced.

Parts II, III and IV cover the theory, research, and practice of I/O psychology, each focusing on a different set of variables that determine behavior in organizations. Part II centers on the individual, Part III on jobs and working conditions, and Part IV on the organization system. Part V examines the outcomes of the interaction of individuals, jobs, and organizations from various perspectives.

Acknowledgments

Anyone who writes a textbook is aware of the critical role that reviewers play in the process. I have been fortunate; each person who commented upon this manuscript made useful contributions that added to the insights and suggestions of the others. I am sincerely appreciative of the efforts of Terry Beehr, Leonard Berger, John Bernardin, William Farrar, Larry Froman, H. Joseph Reitz, William Sauser, Lois Smith, William Wooten, and Elizabeth Zoltan-Ford. Robert Haygood must have a line to himself because he accomplished a minor miracle—reviews that were not only thorough and useful, but also fun to read.

I also would like to acknowledge the fine work of the editorial staff of West Publishing Company. Acquiring Editor Gary Woodruff has guided this project with care and has been an invaluable sounding board. Developmental Editor Phyllis Cahoon has coped with the practical problems and, it must be admitted, listened to my complaints for over two years with unfailing courtesy and efficiency. Production Editor Deanna Quinn is, in my opinion, outstanding in the performance of her exacting duties. Last, but not least, is the important role played by Copyeditor Kathy Massimini.

My sincerest thanks also are due to those who helped with the many tedious tasks necessary to preparing a manuscript. Thank you Scott Busbee, Jennifer Jewell, Carl Russell, Marc Siegall, Mary Tippens, and, most particularly, Barbara Smith.

Contemporary Industrial/
Organizational Psychology

PART I

Introduction and Basic Concepts

Part I of *Contemporary I/O Psychology* provides an overview and a foundation for the material that follows. Chapter 1 gives a brief introduction to the field of industrial/organizational (I/O) psychology, its subject matter, development, training requirements, and career opportunities available. Chapters 2 and 3 introduce major concepts, terminology, and principles basic to understanding the theory, research, and practice of I/O psychology.

An Overview of Industrial/Organizational Psychology

CHAPTER CONTENTS

I/O PSYCHOLOGY AT WORK

A Quick Walk through Hawthorne

In the relay assembly test room, as Roethlisberger wrote in *Management and Morale,* "the idea was very simple. A group of five girls were placed in a room where their condition of work (assembly of a telephone relay) could be carefully controlled, where their output could be measured, and where they could be closely observed. It was decided to produce at specified intervals different changes in working conditions and to see what effect these innovations had on output. Also, records were kept, such as the temperature and humidity of the room, the number of hours each girl slept at night, and kind and amount of food she ate for breakfast, lunch, and dinner." Over a two-and-one-half-year period, tons of material were collected and analyzed.

What did the data show? The key point was that with each variable —shorter rest periods, longer but fewer rest periods, the five-day week, introduction of group incentive pay, reversion to original working conditions—production increased period after period in an almost unbroken line. This confirmed the puzzling—to the researchers—result of an earlier illumination experiment in which either raising *or* lowering the light levels had consistently positive impact on productivity, except for one phase in which employees were compelled to work in semidarkness. . . .

One reason for the continuing rise in productivity lay in the changing social environment. An ordinary group of workers, performing routine, low-status jobs with little or no recognition, had been transformed into important people. "Their physical health and well-being became matters of great concern. Their opinions, hopes, and fears were eagerly sought," observed Roethlisberger.

Nor was this all. They were questioned by investigators—frequently in the superintendent's office—sympathetically and at length about their reactions to working conditions. They traded an oppressive production-centered supervisor for a trained observer sympathetic to their needs. They could chat as they wished, and they set their own productivity quotas.

A change in morale occurred with the development of feelings of group responsibility. All labor turnover stopped, and casual absences fell to a fraction of the rate in·the department outside the test room. The "layabout" girl, for example, who had been absent 85 times in the 32 months before the experiment, went for 16 months thereafter without an absence.

The excerpt describes one phase of some of the most famous experiments in the field of I/O psychology. The Hawthorne Experiments, conducted at Western Electric's Hawthorne plant, have been the subject of an extraordinary number of publications over the years. Among these are several books, including Roethlisberger's *Management and Morale* (1941). The original report of these studies, which were conducted by Fritz Roethlisberger along with Elton Mayo, William Dickson, and others was also reported in book form (Roethlisberger & Dickson, 1939).

Although the Hawthorne Experiments took place over 50 years ago, I/O psychologists still disagree about what caused the dramatic production, attendance, and morale improvements among the employees of the relay assembly room. Some believe these effects were a natural consequence of singling out these individuals for attention. This phenomenon often is referred to as the *Hawthorne Effect*. Others believe the improvements were due to the increased participation in work-related decisions that the experiments gave to the employees.

Whatever the differences among those who debate the "true meaning of Hawthorne," the historical significance of these studies for I/O psychology is not in question. The results of the relay assembly experiments and the bank wiring room experiments (see Chapter 11) had a great impact on the study of human behavior at work, on the conduct of research, and on the practice of management. Nevertheless, Hawthorne was only one milestone in the development of I/O psychology.

THE DEVELOPMENT OF INDUSTRIAL/ORGANIZATIONAL PSYCHOLOGY

Psychology is the study of human behavior. As a formal scientific discipline, it began in experimental laboratories in the 1800s. There, early psychologists attempted to discover the laws that govern behavior through systematic observation with experimental methods borrowed from the physical sciences. Gradually, this new science broadened and diversified and developed its own methodologies; psychologists moved out of the laboratory to conduct experiments and study behavior in natural settings as well.

Today, a large number of specialities and subspecialities make up the discipline of psychology. Each has its own interests and characteristic approaches to the study of behavior. The coordinating professional society, the American Psychological Association (APA), was founded in 1892 and now has over 40 specialty divisions; Division 14 is the Society for Industrial and Organizational Psychology, Inc.

The *"Specialty Guidelines for the Delivery of Services by Industrial/Organizational Psychologists"* (APA, 1981) defines this specialty as follows:

> Industrial/organizational psychological services involve the development and application of psychological theory and methodology to problems of organizations and problems of individuals and groups in organizational settings (p. 666).

The definition clearly reflects the status of I/O psychology today. Members of this particular speciality have a dual allegiance to research and practice. As part of a recognized scientific discipline, they *develop* psychological theory and methodology. As practicioners, they *apply* what is developed to solving the problems of organizations.

The Early Years of Industrial Psychology

Relative to other sciences and to psychology in general, I/O psychology has a short history. Like the formal study of organizations themselves, it dates back to the turn of the century (Wren, 1979). In its early stages, I/O psychology was called *industrial psychology* and its scope was considerably narrower than the definition in "Specialty Guidelines" (APA, 1981).

The approach of the mainstream of industrial psychology in the first third of this century might be summed up by the title of one of the earliest textbooks: *Psychology of Industrial Efficiency* (Münsterberg, 1913). As this title suggests, the early industrial psychologists were concerned with efficiency in the work place. Selection (particularly by means of testing), training methods, and job design/work layout were considered to be of major importance in achieving this efficiency.

The work of the early industrial psychologists tended to cross with and be influenced by the work of industrial engineers because of the psychologists' concern with efficiency. Of particular importance were the principles of time analysis and motion study developed and refined by Frederick Taylor, Frank and Lillian Gilbreth, and others. As will be seen in Chapter 7, this engineering approach to the problems of the work place is still very much a part of I/O psychology today.

The practical concerns of the early industrial psychologists were emphasized by this country's entry into World War I in 1918. The army's sudden need to classify and assign large numbers of new personnel to jobs in a short time period led to an application of personnel testing on a new scale. The intelligence, psychomotor, and personality test data collected during this time gave those interested in the measurement of human characteristics material for test development for years to come.

The Years Between the Wars: 1920–1940

A number of things were happening in the 1920s and 1930s that changed the world of work and ultimately expanded the scope of I/O psychology. This period saw the rapid development of unionism in this country. It also brought the Great Depression and Hawthorne.

The impact of the 1920s and 1930s on I/O psychology was felt only gradually. Labor union activities were of more interest to managers than to psychologists in the early years, and unemployment problems were considered to be a more appropriate matter for charitable organizations. The implications of the Hawthorne Experiments, far reaching as they turned out to be, did not receive widespread attention at first. The complete report of these experiments came out in 1939. The United States entered World War II in 1941.

Industrial Psychology and World War II

Like the First World War, the second put an enormous strain on military personnel functions. Large numbers of new recruits had to be sorted out and sent to jobs that they could perform satisfactorily. Many had to be trained to use highly sophisticated equipment in a short time. At home, women entered the work force in unprecedented numbers to fill the gaps left by men. Civilian organizations cried for help in training this inexperienced group to do jobs seldom performed by women prior to this time.

World War II challenged the resources of industrial psychology as never before. Selection, placement, and training problems—both military and civilian—were bigger, more complex, and more immediate. In addition, technology was advancing at an accelerating rate; the demand for more human factors engineering psychologists to help make machines compatible with human capabilities became pressing.

Not all industrial psychologists in the first half of this century were involved with the applied personnel problems created by wars. That

The personnel requirements of the armed forces have played a significant role in the development of I/O psychology.

these problems were a significant stimulus to the advancement of knowledge in this specialty, as well as to its growth, cannot be denied. In his interviews with 13 well-known I/O psychologists, for example, Stagner (1981) found war to be the most frequently-cited influence on choice of career.

I/O Psychology Today

Since the end of World War II, the three main roots of I/O psychology that were developing somewhat separately prior to that time have come together to create a discipline with a broad base. To industrial engineering and related selection/placement issues have been added human factors engineering and human psychological aspects brought into prominence by the Hawthorne Experiments. These issues include worker motivation, job satisfaction, leadership, and group influence on worker behavior.

Today there are few areas that touch on either human behavior or on organizations that have not captured the interest of I/O psychologists somewhere. In addition to the mainstream questions, they study such questions and problems as drug abuse in organizations, behavior of consumers, special problems of minority-owned businesses, and career patterns.

Robert Perloff, the I/O psychologist who is the 1984 president-elect of APA, provides one example of the wide-ranging interests of those in this field. Perloff currently is interested in the subject of self-interest versus altruism—helping others at no benefit and some cost to oneself. Some of Perloff's ideas on the future of APA are summarized in Exhibit 1–1.

EXHIBIT 1–1

APA's 1984 President-Elect: I/O Psychologist Robert Perloff

Perloff Chosen as President-Elect

The most important part of any association is its members, according to Robert Perloff, 1984 president-elect of APA. And it is to these members the APA should pledge its allegiance, he said.

"We have got to disabuse them of the feeling that some people in the governance structure are recklessly making decisions on their own," he said.

Perloff, a professor of business administration and of psychology at the University of Pittsburgh, defeated Logan Wright in a close election this spring, Gregory Kimble finished third in the balloting, followed by Virginia Staudt Sexton and Joseph Grosslight. There were 14,518 ballots cast, representing about 28 percent of the eligible membership. Perloff will serve as president in 1985.

An industrial/organizational psychologist, Perloff anticipates several challenges for the APA and psychology in the 1980s.

Because of his belief in the importance of individual members, Perloff wants to strengthen the link between them and the governance structure. He suggests a "membership panel" that would be polled by questionnaire every six months on issues coming before the Council of Representatives.

"People may be less against a decision when the reasons for it have been explained to them before implementation," Perloff said. "There has been quite a bit of concern about getting involved in things that are not our business. There is a great concern on the part of a large number of our members that we're squandering our resources and our time, and decreasing our credibility."

Recent controversial subjects before the Council, according to Perloff, have included gun control, nuclear arms freeze and the Equal Rights Amendment.

Mindful of the need to broaden the association's economic base, Perloff would like to see the creation of a development officer to develop additional sources of funding for the organization.

"Find an expert who would know how to scout around to find out how to reach those who would like to do something with their money." Perloff said. "A lot of people would like to think their money was being used for all kinds of worthwhile research or training. All institutions have development officers; as resources become available we ought to earmark some to hire one ourselves."

Third, he supports a suggestion offered by past president William Bevan for a commission on the intellectual foundations of psychology, which would produce articles on the state of the art in various branches of psychology. Perloff believes this would aid scholarship, research and policy formation.

"We could say this is our knowledge base, this is why we feel certain things should be written into the legislation," Perloff said. "We could be much more effective and raise fewer hackles if we actually had codified in one place an authoritative state of the art in the major areas of psychology.

Who better than the APA to put out a set of volumes, saying, 'This is what informed psychologists have to say about psychology in 1985'?"

Perloff also hopes to put together a task force to study productivity, noting that these findings could not only help improve employee productivity but call attention to the contribution psychologists can make to national problems.

Noting that "the blood and guts of the APA are the journals and the convention," Perloff, a member of the Publication and Communications Board, believes the APA should introduce new journals periodically and eliminate those which have outlived their usefulness.

Perloff sees his election as a symbolic win for the applied psychologist, and hopes his success might help indicate to others that industrial/organizational psychologists are respected within the field.

Like many I/O psychologists, the 1984 president-elect of APA is associated with an academic institution. This choice, which became increasingly common after World War II, may be one reason behind the expanded interests of I/O psychologists in general. Those in academic settings receive stimulation, not only from the practical problems of organizational settings, but also from the theoretical interests of colleagues pursuing other lines of research. This stimulation has both assisted and strengthened the dual theoretical-applied nature of I/O psychology.

Today, most I/O psychologists recognize that theory, research, and practice cannot be separated. Theories are useless unless they are tested, and the test of a work behavior theory must sooner or later be carried out in a work setting. Practice, on the other hand, is a valuable source of information and insight, but it is not science if it stops there. Science carries with it a responsibility for communicating knowledge to others.

The demands that a scientific approach to knowledge make on those who seek to understand human behavior are discussed further in Chapter 3. Here the place of I/O psychology in the academic world is explored, then attention is given to a more general overview of I/O psychology as a career.

INDUSTRIAL/ORGANIZATIONAL PSYCHOLOGY AS AN ACADEMIC DISCIPLINE

As a formal academic discipline, I/O psychology is one possible area of student concentration in a psychology department. It is a small field, however, and not all psychology departments offer this specialty. Students interested in graduate work in I/O psychology can discover which schools have such programs by consulting *Graduate Study in Psychology and Associated Fields.* *

Industrial/organizational psychology has the same goal as other special interest areas in psychology—to achieve greater understanding of the causes of human behavior. Thus, I/O psychologists share with all psychologists a fundamental and central focus on the characteristics, development, and behavior of the *individual.* What sets I/O psychology apart is its specific interest in human behavior in organizations. This interest, in turn, gives it something in common with the study of management, particularly with those managerial specialties called organizational behavior and personnel management.

Industrial/Organizational Psychology and Organizational Behavior

Organizational behavior (OB) is a speciality area within the study of management. The difference between I/O psychology as a subject for study and organizational behavior is not difficult to define conceptually. Industrial/organizational psychologists are interested in human behavior in general and human behavior in organizations in particular. Organizational behaviorists are interested in organizations in general and in the people component of organizations in particular.

The basic distinction between I/O psychology and organizational behavior as academic areas of study is often difficult to maintain in applied organizational settings. The American Psychological Association formally recognized the interrelatedness of these two approaches to the same basic problems in 1973. At that time, the old designation of *industrial psychology* was replaced with the term now in standard use, *industrial/organizational psychology.*

---

*Published in 1983 by APA. Write: American Psychological Association, Order Department, 1200 17th Street NW, Washington, DC 20036.

I/O psychologists today are interested in every aspect of the interaction between individuals and organizations from recruiting through performance and employee satisfaction and well-being.

Industrial/Organizational Psychology and Personnel Management

The term *personnel* refers to the body of employees of an organization. These employees are the focus of I/O psychology. They are also the focus of those aspects of management that concern the people in an organization; it is usual to find one or more courses in *personnel management* in a formal management program. These courses cover such topics as compensation, government regulations affecting personnel, union-management relations, and human resource management.

In addition to these listed topics, personnel management courses also cover areas central to the subject matter of I/O psychology—selection, training, health and safety, and performance appraisal. Accordingly, these courses are sometimes called *personnel psychology,* and they may be taught in the psychology department instead of (or in addition to) being offered in the management curriculum.

Clearly, it is becoming increasingly difficult to draw firm lines that set off the subject matter of I/O psychology from related areas. Industrial/organizational psychology remains a separate and identifiable academic discipline, but those who are interested in this field are not confined by rigid boundaries either in research or in applied practice.

INDUSTRIAL/ORGANIZATIONAL PSYCHOLOGY AS A CAREER

In this section, the training, work settings, and activities of I/O psychologists are reviewed briefly. An overview of employment in this field is given; however, the statistics available are based on surveys by the APA of APA members. This means that people who are not members of APA, but are performing work that is I/O psychological in nature, are not represented in the data.

Employment in I/O Psychology

On a percentage basis, I/O psychologists are one of the smallest groups in psychology, representing 10% or less of all psychologists according to most estimates. Many reasons have been advanced for this relatively small number. A major one is undoubtedly the variety of other career paths open to people interested in organizations or in business. There is also considerable competition for graduate-level students from the rapidly growing management area of organizational behavior. All indications are that the demand for I/O psychology programs in colleges and universities is on the rise, however (Stoup & Benjamin, 1982).

No figures are available for college graduates with a bachelor's degree in I/O psychology, but those holding advanced degrees have few problems in finding employment. Almost 400 Division 14 members responded to the most recent APA survey of employment (Stapp & Fulcher, 1983). Of this number, less than 1% at either the master's or the doctoral level reported being involuntarily employed, that is, unemployed and seeking employment.

Results from the 1983 APA report of employment are consistent with earlier surveys as far as the I/O specialty is concerned. Selected results from an earlier survey are shown in Exhibit 1–2. These figures, unlike those reported in 1983, are divided by sex within each specialty. Note that a general trend toward higher unemployment for women in most specialties is given little support by I/O psychology.

Additional analyses of the results of past and present APA employment surveys suggest that there is probably more work for I/O psychologists than there are advanced degree holders in this specialty. For example, in the 1979 survey, almost one-quarter of the master's level respondents reported having regular part-time employment in addition to a full-time job (Gottfredson & Swatko, 1979). Full-time employment

Specialty	Men	Women	Total	
	Doctoral Degree (N = 198)			
Clinical	.5	2.4	1.0	**EXHIBIT 1–2**
Community	.0	2.2	.3	
Counseling	2.5	4.7	2.9	Percentage of APA
Developmental	.0	4.3	1.9	Members Who Are
Educational	.3	3.0	1.0	Unemployed and
School	.0	4.1	1.7	Seeking Employment
Experimental	2.3	2.2	2.3	by Degree Level, Sex,
Industrial-organizational	.0	.0	.0	and Specialty
Personality	1.2	.0	.9	
Physiological	4.5	.0	4.0	
Psychometrics	.0	.0	.3	
Social	.0	4.2	.9	
General systems	.0	.0	.0	
Other	1.9	6.6	2.8	
	Master's Degree (N = 173)			
Clinical	4.0	5.2	4.5	
Community	.0	6.5	2.4	
Counseling	3.1	8.9	5.4	
Developmental	.0	12.7	7.6	
Educational	.0	3.6	2.8	
School	.2	3.4	2.0	
Experimental	10.0	20.7	13.1	
Industrial-organizational	1.3	2.0	1.4	
Personality	—	—	.0	
Physiological	.0	—	.0	
Psychometrics	—	3.7	2.2	
Social	8.7	5.4	7.4	
General systems	3.8	3.2	3.7	
Other	1.9	2.5	2.3	

Note. From "Employment, Unemployment, and the Job Search in Psychology" by C. D. Gottfredson and M. K. Swatko, *American Psychologist,* 1979, *34* (11), pp. 1047–1060. Copyright 1979 by the American Psychological Association. Page 1053 adapted by permission of the authors and the publisher.

of those with advanced degrees suggests that general employment prospects are good. This is usually a positive sign for those seeking employment without advanced degrees in any field.

Training for I/O Psychology

The statistics quoted concerning I/O psychology employment are based on surveys of members of APA Division 14. Certain criteria must be met to obtain membership in APA, and most of these relate to training. Full membership requires a PhD (an individual with a master's degree may hold associate status). While not all members have PhDs in psychology, all have demonstrated interest and competence in this discipline through their doctoral research. Today, most I/O psychologists are in agreement that they are psychologists first and psychologists with an interest in organizations second. Most also agree that training should be carried out accordingly. In a fascinating report of his study of the careers of 13 former presidents of APA Division 14, Stagner (1981) notes a repeated emphasis on practical experience; but he believes that this experience should come after psychologists have basic grounding in psychological principles and theories.

> . . . it seems to me that the consensus of these distinguished psychologists is in favor of broad general training as opposed to professional schools or to completely segregated curricula within a department of psychology. I don't like to see young clinical psychologists get into psychotherapy before they learn about emotion and motivation; and I don't like to see young industrial/organizational psychologists get into their practical activities without the same kind of broad background (p. 505).

There seems little doubt that the opinions of Stagner and the well-known people whom he has interviewed with respect to training are consistent with the consensus of other I/O psychologists, at least those in APA. Exhibit 1–3 gives the APA-recommended components of a doctoral study program in I/O psychology. Both broad training and specific experience are included; bachelor and master programs are modified accordingly.

EXHIBIT 1–3

APA Standards for Doctoral Training in I/O Psychology

A fully qualified *I/O psychologist* has a doctoral degree earned in a program primarily psychological in nature. This degree may be from a department of psychology or from a school of business, management, or administrative science in a regionally accredited university. Consistent with the commitment of I/O psychology to the scientist-professional model, I/O psychologists are thoroughly prepared in basic scientific methods as well as in psychological science; therefore, programs that do not include training in basic scientific methods and research are not considered appropriate educational and training models for I/O psychologists. The I/O psychology doctoral program provides training in (a) scientific and professional ethics, (b) general psychological science, (c) research design and methodology, (d) quantitative and qualitative methodology, and (e) psychological measurement, as well as (f) a supervised practicum or laboratory experience in an area of I/O psychology, (g) a field experience in the application and delivery of I/O services, (h) practice in the conduct of applied research, (i) training in other areas of psychology, in business, and in the social and behavioral sciences, as appropriate, and (j) preparation of a doctoral research dissertation.

Note. From "Specialty Guidelines for the Delivery of Services by Industrial/Organizational Psychologists" by the American Psychological Association, *American Psychologist*, 1981, *36* (6), pp. 665–666.

Activities and Work Settings of I/O Psychologists

The dual nature of I/O psychology stressed throughout Chapter 1 also is reflected in career opportunities. Industrial/organizational psychologists may be found doing purely theoretical work in research organizations or doing exclusively applied work as self-employed consultants to organizations. Most, however, are employed in settings that require a mixture of research and practice.

Career Opportunities for Those with Advanced Degrees

Available figures suggest that the majority of I/O psychologists with master's or doctoral degrees are currently employed by either industry or academic institutions in about equal numbers. Typical activities of I/O psychologists in *academic settings* include:

- teaching various courses
- supervising student research
- conducting own research
- publishing research reports or other articles in professional journals
- attending conferences, presenting papers, and/or being on panels or symposia at professional meetings

Many I/O psychologists in academic settings also do independent management consulting with private industry, local, state, or federal government agencies, hospitals, and military services.

The activities of I/O psychologists in *industrial settings* vary according to the size and type of industry, but these activities typically include work related to:

- selection and placement of employees
- training and development
- personnel research
- work environment design
- affirmative action programs
- motivation and production improvement activities
- client- and consumer-related activities

Many I/O psychologists in industrial settings also publish the results of their research and participate in professional meetings.

Career Opportunities for Those without Advanced Degrees

Most students with undergraduate training, but no advanced degree in I/O psychology, may expect to find employment in government or private-sector organizations of various kinds. Personnel managers most often mention three work areas among the employment opportunities available at this level of training.

1. Personnel departments: Employees with I/O training often perform such activities as selection testing, job analysis, and equal employment opportunity (EEO) documentation research.

2. General management: Many companies see I/O training as an advantage for managers.
3. Customer relations: The general psychological training of an undergraduate with a degree is often considered good background for this function.

Students with an I/O psychology degree also report finding employment in large companies that have one or more full-time advanced-degree psychologists, in marketing research, advertising agencies, and a variety of government agencies.

The Regulation of I/O Psychologists

People in the field of psychology have a tradition and a preference for self-regulation. Concern for consumer protection, however, which has led to many external regulations regarding consumer goods, has now spread to consumer services as well. As suppliers of services to the public, applied psychologists have been drawn with other professionals into the issues and debates raised by this development.

The kinds of services I/O psychologists offer to the public are generally less controversial than those offered by other applied psychologists. As a result, they rarely generate the intense heat of debates in which some of these others (most notably psychologists in public mental health) find themselves involved. Nevertheless, those interested in a career in I/O psychology should know that they may be expected to have a license or certificate if they plan to offer certain applied services to the public at large. The basic difference between licensing and certification is defined by Howard and Lowman (1982) as follows:

> Licensing is a legal process which regulates the use of a title and defines the activities that constitute the practice of a particular profession. . . . Certification . . . involves . . . a regulation designed only to limit the use of a title, such as ''psychologist''; it does not define the scope of the practice (p. 1).

At present, the licensing and/or certification of psychologists is done on a state-by-state basis. A summary of state laws as of January, 1983 is shown in Exhibit 1–4. Note that only a few states offer the relatively less stringent certification option. Most require licensing, and every state except Kansas and Wisconsin has a mandatory examination for psychologists to acquire a license.

EXHIBIT 1–4				

A Summary of State Laws Regulating I/O Psychologists

State	Law	Coverage	Degree	Examination
Alabama	L[a]	Practice of Psychologist	Doctorate	Yes
Alaska	L	Psychologist	Doctorate	Yes
		Psychological Associate	Masters	Yes
Arizona	C[b]	Psychologist	Doctorate	Yes
Arkansas	L	Psychologist	Doctorate	Yes
		Psychological Examiner	Masters	Yes

State	Law	Coverage	Degree	Examination
California	L	Psychologist	Doctorate	Yes
		Psychological Assistant	Masters	No
Colorado	L	Psychologist	Doctorate	Yes
Connecticut	L	Psychologist	Doctorate	Yes
Delaware	L	Practice of Psychology	Doctorate	Yes
District of Col.	L	Practice of Psychology	Doctorate	Yes
Florida	C	Psychological Services	Doctorate	Yes
Georgia	L	Practice/Applied Psychology	Doctorate	Yes
Hawaii	L	Practice of Psychology	Doctorate	Yes
Idaho	L	Practice of Psychology	Doctorate	Yes
Illinois	C	Psychologist	Doctorate	Yes
Indiana	C	Psychologist/Private Practice	Doctorate	Yes
		Clinical Psychologist	Doctorate	
		Psychologist (Basic)	Doctorate	
Iowa	L	Practice of Psychology	Doctorate	Yes
			Masters	Yes
Kansas	L	Psychologist	Doctorate	No
Kentucky	L	Practice of Psychology	Doctorate	Yes
		Certificand	Masters	Yes
Louisiana	L	Psychologist	Doctorate	Yes
Maine	L	Psychologist	Doctorate	Yes
		Psychologist Examiner	Masters	Yes
Maryland	L	Psychologist	Doctorate	Yes
Massachusetts	L	Psychologist	Doctorate	Yes
Michigan	L	Psychologist	Doctorate	Yes
		(Limited License)	Masters	
Minnesota	L	Consulting Psychologist	Doctorate	Yes
		Psychologist	Masters	Yes
Mississippi	L	Psychologist	Doctorate	Yes
Missouri	L	Psychologist	Doctorate	Yes
			Masters	Yes
Montana	L	Practice of Psychology	Doctorate	Yes
Nebraska	L	Practice of Psychology	Doctorate	Yes
Nevada	L	Practice of Psychology	Doctorate	Yes
New Hampshire	L	Psychologist	Doctorate	Yes
		Associate Psychologist		
		Psychological Assistant	Masters	Yes
New Jersey	L	Practice of Professional		
		Psychological Services	Doctorate	Yes
New York	L	Psychologist	Doctorate	Yes
North Carolina	L	Practicing Psychologist	Doctorate	Yes
		Psychological Associate	Masters	Yes
North Dakota	L	Psychologist	Doctorate	Yes
Ohio	L	Psychologist	Doctorate	Yes
Oklahoma	L	Practice of Psychology	Doctorate	Yes
Oregon	L	Practice of Psychology	Doctorate	Yes
		Psychologist Associate	Masters	Yes
Pennsylvania	L	Practice Psychology	Doctorate	Yes
			Masters	Yes
Rhode Island	C	Consulting Psychologist	Doctorate	Yes
South Carolina	L	Practice of Psychology	Doctorate	Yes

State	Law	Coverage	Degree	Examination
South Dakota	L	Practice of Psychology	Doctorate	Yes
	L	Psychologist	Doctorate	Yes
		Psychological Examiner	Masters	
Texas	L	Psychologist	Doctorate	Yes
	C	Psychological Assistant	Masters	Yes
Utah	L	Practice as Psychologist	Doctorate	Yes
Vermont	L	Psychologist-Doctorate	Doctorate	Yes
		Psychologist-Master	Masters	Yes
Virginia	L	Psychologist	Doctorate	Yes
Washington	L	Practice of Psychology	Doctorate	Yes
		Psychological Assistant		
West Virginia	L	Practice of Psychology	Doctorate	Yes
		Practice of Psychology	Masters	Yes
Wisconsin	L	Practice of Psychology	Doctorate	No
Wyoming	L	Practice of Psychology	Doctorate	Yes

[a]L = Licensure.
[b]C = Certification.

Note. Data from the American Psychological Association, 1200 Seventeenth Street N.W.; Washington, D.C. 20036

State licensing of applied psychologists is not unlike the process of state bar exams for attorneys or real estate board exams for real estate brokers. Certain basic educational and/or training requirements must be met before individuals are eligible to take the licensing exam. Once granted, licenses must be renewed periodically, in some states every year. Some idea of the subject matter and scope of questions applied psychologists face in acquiring or renewing a license is provided in Exhibit 1–5.

EXHIBIT 1–5

The Curriculum of a Licensing Exam Review Program

Statistics and Research Methodology

Descriptive and inferential statistics; hypothesis testing and significance testing; normal and skewed distributions; measures of central tendency; measures of variation; normalized standard scores; regression and correlation; parametric and nonparametric tests; experimental and statistical controls; standard error of estimate; standard error of the mean; conditional probability.

Test Construction and Interpretation

Reliability; internal consistency; standard error of the measure; content, criterion and construct validities; item difficulty; item analysis; factor analysis; power and speed tests; multiple regression; personnel selection tests; cut-off scores.

Learning

Classical and operant conditioning; reinforcement schedules; acquisition and extinction; drive-reduction learning; latent learning; social learning; learning sets.

Cognition

Memory and forgetting; proactive and retroactive inhibition; encoding and retrieval; language and psycholinguistics.

Experimental Social Psychology and Research in Personality Psychology

Attribution theory and consequences for therapy; attitude change; interpersonal attraction; group processes; experimenter effects; achievement motivation; research methodology in personality and social psychology; trait theories; cognitive theories of personality; androgyny and sex sterotyping.

Behavior Therapy

Counter-conditioning; flooding; aversive therapies; token economies; modeling; Premack principle; cognitive behavior therapy; behavioral medicine; biofeedback.

Clinical Psychology

Etiology and treatment of major affective disorders; diagnosis and DSM III; therapies for specific disorders—sexual dysfunctions, eating disorders, suicide, hypertension; drug therapies and psychopharmacology.

School Psychology

Issues in assessment of intelligence; definition and categories of mental retardation; standard assessment measures—Stanford-Binet and Wechsler Scales, infant and early childhood assessment scales, standardized measures of adaptive behavior, nonverbal tests; test bias.

Development Psychology

Cognitive and moral development; gender role differences; adult development and aging; career development and counseling.

Industrial and Engineering Psychology

Job analysis and job selection procedures; validating job selection tests; rater contamination; predictive and differential validities of job selection tests; decision theories; multiple regression and multiple cutoff scores; motivation at work; job satisfaction and dissatisfaction; work scheduling; accidents; effects of noise and illumination; occupational classification systems; training and evaluation of training programs.

Neuropsychology and Physiological Psychology

Central and autonomic nervous system functioning; psychopharmacological action and effects; perception and the visual system; memory systems and storage; cortex and subcortical localization and functioning; neuropsychological assessment.

Ethics and Professional Practice

Ethical Principles; Standards for Providers of Psychological Services; Specialty Guidelines; court cases relevant to psychologists; clinical judgment issues; confidentialty and privilege.

The complete set of reading materials is included. It is recommended that participants read the relevant chapters before attending the lectures. Practice exam taking with feedback/discussion is also stressed throughout the Workshops.

Note. Printed through courtesy of Academic Review, Inc., Educational Services, 3 West 73rd Street, New York, New York 10023.

Exhibit 1–5 lists the workshop material covered by one of several organizations now offering license exam review programs to psychologists. Notice that the number of topics under the heading "Industrial and Engineering Psychology" exceeds those of any other specialty.

External Regulation: Pros and Cons

State regulation of applied psychologists is not new; Connecticut has had a licensing law since 1945. It has only been within the past 10 years, however, that such laws have come to exist in every one of the fifty states. In their comprehensive review of the background and issues involved in licensing I/O psychologists, Howard and Lowman (1982) identify three major points on which the rationale for such regulation rests.

The primary reason advanced by supporters of external regulation for applied psychologists is protection for the public. Dramatic incidents, such as that in which a psychologist's pet hamster was found to be registered as a psychologist in one state, often are cited as examples of what can happen when there are no checks on who can lay claim to the title "psychologist."

Another reason for licensing applied psychologists is to protect the field itself. Untrained or unqualified people (or hamsters) calling themselves psychologists are not only a potential hazard to the public; they also can damage the reputation of the profession as a whole. Finally, many believe that licensing strengthens the field of psychology from within as well as protecting it from without. The necessity for acquiring and periodically renewing a license to practice, they believe, serves to strengthen identity with the values, ethics, and goals of the profession.

There are arguments against external regulation for psychologists. The most frequently heard one is that regulation simply does not serve its purpose well enough to offset its negative effects. Danish and Smyer (1981) have summarized the more important of these disadvantages. First, since only those holding PhDs can be licensed (see Exhibit 1–4), regulation increases the cost of services to the public. These increased costs stem from (a) the longer training required for a doctorate and (b) the cost of providing supervision (by a licensed psychologist) for those performing applied services without a PhD.

The second problem noted by Danish and Smyer is that the same factors making applied psychological services cost more also reduce the total availability of such services. Finally, since licensing laws specify the activities that psychologists can offer to the public, these laws may decrease the likelihood of innovation in services.

Despite arguments that it does not work and that it has detrimental side effects, there seems little doubt that external regulation of applied psychologists, including I/O psychologists, is here to stay. All indications are that the public is becoming more, not less, concerned about the nature of services being offered by professionals in all fields.

SUMMARY

Industrial/organizational psychology is a relatively small speciality within the discipline of psychology. Its history goes back some 85 years. Today the field is a broad-based discipline concerned with an impressive variety of questions and problems about organizations and the people in them.

Industrial/organizational psychologists work in a variety of academic and applied settings. Most of those holding advanced degrees in this speciality have employment that reflects the dual commitment of I/O psychology to research and application of psychological knowledge. Recommended training for this work is rigorous, stressing both the theoretical and applied aspects of the field. In addition, every state now requires that those who offer applied I/O services to the public be licensed or certified or work under the supervision of a licensed I/O psychologist.

REFERENCES

AMERICAN PSYCHOLOGICAL ASSOCIATION. Specialty guidelines for the delivery of services by industrial/organizational psychologists. *American Psychologist,* 1981, *36*(6), 664–669.

DANISH, S. J., & SMYER, M. A. Unintended consequences of requiring a license to help. *American Psychologist,* 1981, *36*(1), 13–21.

GOTTFREDSON, G. D. & SWATKO, M. K. Employment, unemployment, and the job search in psychology. *American Psychologist,* 1979, *34*(11), 1047–1060.

HOWARD, A. & LOWMAN, R. L. Licensing and industrial/organizational psychology: Background and issues. Prepared for the Executive Committee of the Division of Industrial/Organizational Psychology, American Psychological Association, Washington, DC, 1982.

MÜNSTERBERG, H. *Psychology of Industrial Efficiency.* Boston: Houghton Mifflin, 1913.

ORGANIZATIONAL DYNAMICS. Hawthorne revisited: The legend and the legacy. 1975, *3*(3), 66–80.

ROETHLISBERGER, F. J. *Management and Morale.* Cambridge, MA: Harvard University Press, 1941.

ROETHLISBERGER, F. J., & DICKSON, W. J. *Management and the Worker.* Cambridge, MA: Harvard University Press, 1939.

STAGNER, R. Training and experiences of some distinguished industrial psychologists. *American Psychologist,* 1981, *36*(5), 497–505.

STAPP, J., & FULCHER, R. The employment of APA members: 1982. *American Psychologist,* 1983, *38*(12), 1298–1320.

STOUP, C. M., & BENJAMIN, L. T., Jr. Graduate study in psychology, 1970–1979. *American Psychologist,* 1982, *37*(11), 1186–1202.

WREN, D. *The Evolution of Management Thought* (2nd ed.). New York: John Wiley & Sons, 1979.

CHAPTER 2

Understanding Human Behavior

I/O PSYCHOLOGY AT WORK

Executive Retreads

It can happen anywhere, even in the most civilized and sensible organization. An executive, otherwise intelligent and productive, goes a little haywire, or loses enthusiasm or becomes intolerably overbearing. In times past, after a warning or two, many such executives would simply be shown the door. Now, increasingly, management is calling in an executive rehabilitation consultant . . . There are about 150 consultants in the country now counseling troubled executives . . . Typically they are industrial psychologists with experience at large corporations. . . .

How does rehabilitation work? With one outfit, BeamPines Human Resource Consultants, the first step in the process is to meet with the troubled individual's boss and find out why [he/she] is upset with the executive. . . . Next [the executive] comes to Beam's Manhattan offices for a full day of interviews and written psychological and other tests. That information forms the basis of a 10-to-15 page report which the executive sees and discusses with Beam.

The executive . . . shows the report to [the] boss and the two of them meet with Beam soon afterward. . . . A series of coaching sessions between Beam and the executives follows, and these three-way meetings take place as needed. . . . Fifty executives . . . have gone through the BeamPines program, including people from such companies as Warner-Lambert, Time, Inc., Pepsi Co., and Cahners Publishing.

Excerpted from K. McManus, "Executive Retreads." *Forbes*, 1983, July 18, pp. 140–142. Reprinted by permission.

The behavior of others is often difficult to understand especially when, as in the case of the "otherwise intelligent and productive" executive, it seems to change suddenly for the worse. The use of I/O and other psychologists to help such people is not new. But it is increasing as greater importance is being placed on understanding rather than judging the behavior of people in organizational settings.

Psychologists who are trying to understand and help executives in trouble know that they must look closely at the individuals involved, thus the extensive personal testing. They also know, however, that executives' work environments—jobs, superiors, subordinates, and co-workers—play a role in their behavior. They try, therefore, with help from the individuals' immediate superiors, to bring about changes in behavior within the settings in which executives work.

The premise that all behavior (which includes problem behavior) is caused by an interaction of personal and environmental factors was put forth some years ago by psychologist Kurt Lewin (1951). The statement is straightforward but not simple because (a) there are many relevant personal and environmental factors and (b) the interactions among these factors are complex.

In Chapter 2, the fundamentals of understanding human behavior are discussed. Some of the more important personal and environmental variables that cause people to behave as they do are reviewed, and the significance of how the interactions of these variables affect human behavior is emphasized.

THE STUDY OF HUMAN BEHAVIOR

There are four levels at which the study of human behavior might be approached. At the simplest level, behavior merely is *observed*. For example, I/O psychologists might observe that a large number of a company's workers who frequent a particular candy vending machine appear to be overweight.

The second level of behavior study is *understanding*. Why do workers who are overweight eat more candy than those who are not? Do they get hungrier? Do they have more of a "sweet tooth"? Or are they simply caught in a vicious circle created by poor eating habits?

If behavior is understood, it can be predicted, at least in a general way. *Prediction* is the third level of behavior study. It serves as a check on understanding. For example, if overweight employees get hungrier than others, it might be predicted that they also would eat more of other vending machine products if candy were unavailable. This prediction could be checked out by observing what happens if the candy machine were allowed to run out of candy while a health food machine was kept well stocked.

The most sophisticated level of behavior study is *control*. If behavior is understood well enough to predict it, then its causes are understood well enough to bring about desired changes. If psychologists found that consumption of less fattening vending machine items went up among overweight workers when the candy machine was empty, there would be a guide to action. Removing the machine to an out-of-the-way location (or perhaps altogether) would be one way to help these employees bring about positive changes in their eating habits.

Most likely there would be objections to moving or removing the candy machine even if the action were taken with the interests of the employees in mind. The example is not intended to illustrate either a scientific study of eating habits or a practical solution to the problem of excessive candy consumption among overweight employees. Its purpose is to show the progression through, and relationships among, the four levels of the study of human behavior—observation, understanding, prediction, and control.

All psychologists are concerned with advancing *understanding* of the behavior they *observe*, and they check this understanding by investigating *predictions* about behavior; but applied I/O psychologists must confront behavior at the *control* level as well.

To I/O psychologists, control means helping organizations arrange conditions and solve problems so that they and the people in them can be successful. To accomplish this, I/O psychologists must be able to identify some of the more important variables that cause the behaviors they observe. It is not necessary to be a psychologist to acquire such understanding, but it is necessary to be committed to understanding behavior to be a psychologist. On the professional level, this commitment means being able to differentiate between *understanding* behavior and the *reasons* for and *evaluation* of behavior.

Understanding Behavior Versus Reasons for Behavior

The common sense way to understand behavior is to ask people why they do what they do, that is, to determine the reasons people have for their behavior. For example, a supervisor might ask an employee why he or she is so often late to work and be given the reason, "My car is always breaking down."

To psychologists, the tardy employee's reason for this behavior raises more questions than it answers. Why does the employee not make other arrangements for getting to work if unreliable transportation is a chronic problem? Why does he or she not leave home earlier? Why has this behavior continued when getting to work on time is a basic worker responsibility; in other words, how does the employee continue to "get away with" being late?

There is more to the explanation of why a particular employee is chronically late to work simply than the fact of an unreliable car. Both the employee's personal characteristics and certain aspects of the work situation play a part as well. For example, further investigation might reveal that nothing happens when this employee is late except an occasional irritated remark from the supervisor. This employee, therefore, who is not much of a long-range planner, decided to buy a new videotape machine instead of a better car. At best, then, expressed reasons for behavior usually will be only one piece to understanding the puzzle.

Understanding Behavior Versus Evaluating Behavior

Evaluating behavior is making judgments about its rightness or wrongness, its appropriateness or inappropriateness. Such judging is human, but has no bearing on *understanding* behavior. By the same token, understanding behavior does not imply anything about the evaluation of behavior. A psychologist who wants to understand why employee theft in a particular organization is high no more approves of theft than trial lawyers who defend accused murderers approve of murder.

The natural tendency of people to evaluate the behavior of others can create problems for I/O psychologists in applied settings. Organizations, like the world in general, tend to expect people to do what it is believed they should do. "He should get to work on time." "She should try to be nicer to people." "They should work more and talk less." Efforts to understand why he does not get to work on time, she is not nicer to people, or they talk more than they work can be interpreted as looking for excuses for these behaviors.

When efforts to understand behavior are interpreted as making excuses for behavior, it is difficult to get the support and help needed to solve organizational problems. For I/O psychologists, then, part of the task of helping organizations control behavior often will be convincing them of the necessity for understanding behavior first.

THE CAUSES OF BEHAVIOR

Psychology is the study of behavior, but it is difficult to find a definition of the word *behavior* that satisfies all psychologists. Some believe the terms should be restricted to actions that can be observed by others, such as work performance. Others believe it should include unseen mental activities, such as decision making, and unseen mental states, such as attitudes.

All **behavior** is the result of interaction between individual characteristics and characteristics of the environment in which the behavior occurs.

Fortunately, it is not necessary here to resolve differences of opinion about the precise definition of behavior. Industrial/organizational psychologists study the responses of people to a work environment. Some of these responses may be observed directly. Other responses, such as decision-making processes and attitudes, can be observed only indirectly in terms of results or of how people describe them verbally. As long as this distinction is kept in mind, it is satisfactory for present purposes to refer to all such responses as *behavior*. Understanding all behavior starts with the same basic premise.

The principle is set forth by psychologist Kurt Lewin (1951). It states that *two* sets of factors must be considered if behavior is to be understood—individual characteristics and environmental characteristics (sometimes called *situational variables*). Any explanation that relies on only one set of factors will be incomplete. Conceptually, the issue can be expressed as follows: An explanation based only on individual characteristics cannot explain *inconsistencies* in behavior. An explanation based only on situational characteristics cannot explain *consistencies*. An example helps to clarify this point.

Suppose that a supervisor is observed taking considerable time to help an employee who has been making many errors in work previously performed with no difficulties. One explanation for the supervisor's behavior is that he or she is a kind person who tries to understand and help others whenever possible. This individual characteristic explanation, "kind person," does not explain why another employee whose work was slipping was given a verbal reprimand instead of assistance, however.

The supervisor acted differently in two cases where employees were making work errors although it is safe to assume that his or her personal traits did not change in the time between the two incidents. What *was* different was the characteristics of the two ''work slipping'' situations. In the first case, the employee was one with a stable work history who was trying to do the work of two people while the company found a replacement for a coworker who had quit without notice. In the second case, the employee was one who had been doing exactly the same work for years and who openly admitted getting ''careless once in a while.''

When the situation is examined, the inconsistency in the behavior of the supervisor is more understandable. If behavior were caused solely by the situation in which it occurred, however, the behavior of a different supervisor, who tried to help *both* employees (behaved consistently), becomes difficult to explain. Clearly, it is necessary to examine both individual and situational factors if the behavior of either supervisor is to be understood.

INDIVIDUAL VARIABLES THAT AFFECT BEHAVIOR

The basic unit of observation in the field of psychology is the individual. Every such individual is a unique combination of characteristics. Some of these characteristics are present from birth; others develop over time. It is convenient to refer to these two sets of factors as *inherited* and *learned* characteristics, respectively.

Inherited Characteristics

The term **inherited characteristics** refers to individual characteristics whose basic nature is determined by genetic structure at birth.

The genetic structure of a person is a mixture of those genes carried by both natural parents as passed on from *their* parents, and so back into time. Among the more important of the characteristics basically determined by genes are:

- physical attributes
- physiological functioning
- basic intellectual capacity
- sex

Although characteristics such as those listed above are inherited, they can be modified considerably by what happens to a person after birth. Some people's environment, for example, may help to develop their intellectual capacity while others' would retard that development. The result is that two people with the same basic capacity may appear to be of very different intelligence levels.

Inherited characteristics also might be modified by deliberate intent. Muscles can be developed by weight training, the shape of a nose changed by surgery, and eye color changed by contact lenses. There are limits to such modifications however, and it is these limits that set inherited characteristics apart. Short people can wear high-heeled shoes and "stand tall," but neither strategy will make them tall people.

Consistent differences in behavior between groups of people who differ markedly on some inherited characteristic long have been of interest to psychologists. Some recent studies of this type with respect to the behavior of people at work are summarized in Exhibit 2–1.

Three important points should be kept in mind concerning Exhibit 2–1. The first is that each example is only one study. It would be necessary to have much more evidence before drawing any conclusions about these relationships. The second important point is that these findings are based on *group* data. The relationship might or might not hold for particular individuals. It must be kept in mind always that many other factors are involved. For example, Czaja and Drury (1981) found that performance on the task of work inspection tended to decline with age. Results of another study (Giniger, Dispenzieri, & Eisenberg, 1983) suggest that this tendency may be offset by experience; in that study, experienced workers performed better regardless of age.

The final point is critical with respect to understanding behavior. The results summarized in Exhibit 2–1 are *associations*. There is no information about what lies behind them, that is, about what causes the observed relationships.

Inherited characteristics affect behavior in ways that are both direct and indirect. The finding that men can lift more weight than women (Ayoub, et al., 1978) is a good example of both effects. Certain structural and muscular differences between men and women do indeed tend to make women in general the physically "weaker sex." There also are,

Characteristic	Behavior	Relationship Found
Age	Speed/errors on work inspection	Errors up and speed down for older workers[a]
Sex	Weight lifted to various levels	Males lifted significantly more to all levels[b]
Intelligence	Turnover on simple jobs	Higher turnover associated with greater intelligence[c]
Memory	Signal detection	Better performance associated with better short-term memory[d]
Physical Condition	(Truck) driver negligence-related property damage	Better physical condition associated with less damage[e]
Race	Expressed job expectations	Blacks had higher expectations for managerial jobs than whites[f]

EXHIBIT 2–1

Inherited Characteristics and Behavior at Work: Recent Research Findings

[a]Czaja and Drury, 1981.
[b]Ayoub et al., 1978.
[c]Behling and Schriesheim, 1976.
[d]Forbes and Barett, 1978.
[e]Drory, 1982.
[f]Brenner and Tomkiewicz, 1982.

however, long-standing differences in the emphasis given to physical training and development for girls and boys that add an indirect effect to the direct influence of physical differences between the sexes.

Attempts to separate the direct and indirect influences of inherited physical characteristics on behavior have a long tradition in psychology, and the "nature versus nurture" question still is being debated in some areas (e.g. Konner, 1982). The important point is that research into behavioral differences associated with inherited characteristics provides clues to understanding behavior. The results of such research must be kept in perspective however. There are many other factors involved, among them the learned individual characteristics to be discussed.

A Note on Employees, Inherited Characteristics, and Equal Employment Opportunity

Relationships between inherited characteristics and work behavior, especially work performance, have been of particular interest to many I/O psychologists because such traits are relatively easy to observe or measure. This can be a substantial advantage in an activity such as selection. For example, if women seem to perform better than men on a particular job, then hiring only women would seem to be a simple, effective selection policy. Although most psychologists would not recommend such a procedure, many companies have long followed selection policies of this sort. In the past 25 years, however, this approach has been moderated considerably by equal employment opportunity (EEO) laws and court decisions.

Although stimulated originally by unfair racial discrimination, fair employment laws prohibit discrimination on the basis of age, sex, country of national origin, and religious affiliation as well. With the exception of religion, all of these characteristics fall within the province of inherited characteristics. Such characteristics, unlike knowledge and skill, are basically beyond individual control.

As a result of EEO legislation and the rulings that have gone into enforcing it, modern I/O psychologists cannot stop with demonstrating a relationship between inherited characteristics and work behavior. They also face the challenge of finding ways to help organizations develop the skills and talents of those who are not "naturally" suited to particular kinds of work.

Learned Characteristics

Learned characteristics are acquired as people grow, develop, and interact with their environments.

Many of the traits that make people different are not inherited but learned. Among these are personality traits, attitudes, skills, values, perceptual sets, and interests.

The process by which individuals acquire their particular learned characteristics is complex, but a critical aspect is what happens when individuals have new experiences or "try on" new behaviors. These results, or *outcomes*, can be classified as generally positive, negative, or

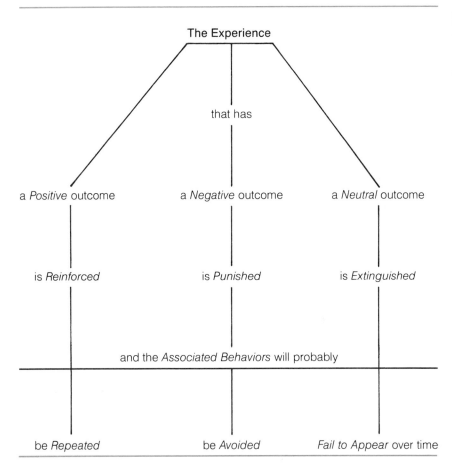

EXHIBIT 2–2

Learning and the
Outcomes of
Experience

neutral. As shown in Exhibit 2–2, each type of outcome has a predictable effect on the associated behaviors.

As seen in Exhibit 2–2, if the outcome of an experience is perceived by the individual involved to be *positive*, associated behaviors are said to be *reinforced*. This means that these behaviors are likely to be repeated in the future.

When behaviors are positively reinforced by what follows them, the individual is changed. The shy child who gets a laugh when he or she suddenly makes a funny face behind the teacher's back has learned something. If such behavior continues to be reinforced, the child is on the way from ''shy'' to ''class clown.'' If, on the other hand, the outcome is perceived to be punishing in some way (no one laughs, and he or she gets caught in the act and has to stay after school), the child is more likely to continue in the pattern of behavior described as shy.

The outcome of the face-making student's behavior may be less dramatic than the possibilities described. Perhaps no one even noticed. The learning that takes place following such a *neutral* outcome tends to be slower. The student may try this behavior change a few more times, but sooner or later will give it up if there is no reinforcement. Behavior that is followed consistently by outcomes perceived as neutral simply ceases to occur after a while; that is, it is *extinguished*.

The process described above by which a particular person comes to be shy or extroverted is accurate but oversimplified. Such learning usually takes place slowly, and the nature of relevant experiences is influenced considerably by other factors. Nevertheless, it is in this way that people acquire the patterns of individual characteristics that make each different in some way from everyone else on earth.

Although each person is unique as a complex whole, most share certain traits with others. Thus, in any work setting, "friendly people" and "unfriendly people" are found, as are people who seem to like to work and people who do not. Some recent research findings with respect to work response differences between groups of people who differ significantly on some learned characteristic are summarized in Exhibit 2-3.

The cautions made with respect to the research findings in Exhibit 2-1 also must be applied to the material in Exhibit 2-3. In fact, greater care must be taken to avoid carrying the possible implications of such research too far. Learned characteristics are subject to continual modification and change. The limits for this change are far less confining than those for inherited characteristics. No matter how young he or she looks or acts, for example, a person cannot change actual chronological age. But a timid person can become an aggressive one, a "lazy" person a hard worker, and a "liberal" can turn "conservative" at almost any stage in life.

As seen in Exhibit 2-3, the most heavily-researched learned individual characteristics in I/O psychology are personality traits and attitudes/values. The history of this research is interesting. With some

EXHIBIT 2-3	Characteristic	Behavior	Relationship Found
	Tolerance for conflict	Perceived role conflict	Less role conflict with greater tolerance for conflict[a]
Learned Characteristics and Behavior at Work: Recent Research Findings	Relative importance of extrinsic versus intrinsic job rewards	Expressed job satisfaction	"Extrinsic managers" expressed less job satisfaction[b]
	Value on work ethic	Attendance	Stronger work ethic associated with greater attendance[c]
	Diversity of interests	Salary-based measure of performance	High general interest diversity associated with better performance[d]
	Locus of control	Experienced job stress	More stress with emphasis on external locus of control[e]

[a]Randolf and Pozner, 1981.
[b]Gorn and Kanungo, 1980.
[c]Ilgen and Hollenback, 1977.

[d]Arvey and Dewhirst, 1979.
[e]Kyriacon and Sutcliffe, 1979.

exceptions (e.g., Argyris, 1957), personality characteristics have been treated as if they were inherited traits, that is, as if they were fixed and unlikely to change.

The idea that personality traits are firmly established by the time a person reaches employment age may be seen in the popularity of personality tests as selection devices in the late 1950s and 1960s. Either people had the characteristics believed to be associated with job success or they did not. By contrast, attitudes, acquired in the same way as personality traits, long have been subjected to the most widespread and intensive change efforts.

The use of personality tests as selection devices faded as the difficulties of validating such instruments became increasingly obvious to psychologists. Preoccupation with changing attitudes also has decreased for different reasons. Test validation is discussed further in Part II, and the attitude called *job satisfaction* is examined in Part V.

ENVIRONMENTAL VARIABLES THAT AFFECT BEHAVIOR

The second major group of factors that influence behavior lies in the situation, or environment, of individuals. Psychology distinguishes between two aspects of this environment. One aspect is physical—this is the aspect that comes closest to the common use of the word *environment*. The second aspect is social. While the term *social environment* is less familiar, its influence on behavior is extensive.

The Physical Environment

Among the familiar aspects of the physical environment are:

- weather
- noise
- lighting
- odors
- altitude
- physical objects

All aspects of the physical world that can be seen, heard, felt, smelled, or touched are part of the **physical environment** of behavior.

The influence on behavior of the kinds of factors listed receives little attention in everyday life unless conditions are extreme or unusual in some way. Most people simply adapt their behavior to their physical environments. They wear more clothes when it is cold, or move the tennis game to an indoor court if it is too windy to play outside. Alternatively, they may alter some aspect of this environment to better suit themselves and their accustomed behavior patterns. They move a desk nearer a window, turn up the air conditioning or the heat, or move from the city to a suburb. Both adaptation and change are clear instances of the effects of the physical environment on behavior.

Both the physical and social environments of the job have important effects on employee behavior and attitudes.

The influence of physical aspects of the environment on behavior at work is an area of traditional interest to I/O psychologists. Among the variables that have been studied are:

- noise
- temperature
- lighting
- wall color
- worker density (crowding)
- spatial arrangements of furniture

The nature of the materials, tools, machines, and other aids used by employees also are aspects of the physical environment studied by I/O psychologists, along with engineers and others interested in improving work settings. The physical environment is examined in detail in Part III.

The Social Environment

In Chapter 1, the influence on I/O psychology of a series of field experiments conducted at Western Electric's Hawthorne plant is discussed briefly. These studies often are cited as the benchmark for formal appreciation of the influence that employees' social environments have on their behavior at work. The experiments turned attention to such social environmental factors as peer groups, the importance of worker communication, and the effects of being singled out for special attention.

As used in the definition, the term *social* goes far beyond the usual meaning of that word. The social environment of an individual includes relationships with family, friends, coworkers, supervisors, and subordinates, and membership in groups, such as unions. The behavior of others (as distinct from the individual's relationship with them) is also part of an individual's social environment. In addition, any norms, rules, laws, or reward systems that originate with other individuals or groups help to form an individual's social environment.

The influence of the social environment on behavior within organizations or outside of them is enormous. Some of the social variables that play a part in determining what people do, where they do it, and how they do it, are shown in Exhibit 2–4.

The **social environment** includes all of those aspects of an individual's situation that stem from other people and his or her relationship to them.

Hawthorne experiments: See pages 4 to 5.

Variable	Example of Influence
Presence of other people	Not talking loudly in a movie
Group membership	Wearing a T-shirt with group name on it
Laws of society	Driving a prescribed speed
Rules of an organization or group	Getting to work at 8 A.M.
Norms of culture, group or organization	Calling new acquaintances by first names (American society norm)

EXHIBIT 2–4

Influence of Variables in the Social Environment on Behavior

The examples in Exhibit 2–4 come more from everyday life than from organizations. These familiar examples were chosen to introduce what is an unfamiliar concept to many people. Several aspects of an organization's social environment are explored in detail in Part IV.

PERCEPTION: THE BRIDGE BETWEEN THE INDIVIDUAL AND THE ENVIRONMENT

The discussion of environmental variables may have carried an implication that such factors are objective in nature. With respect to their effects on behavior, nothing could be farther from the truth.

Temperature, one aspect of the physical environment that can be measured reliably and objectively, will illustrate this point. Despite general concensus as to the temperature reading at any particular time, this measurement is not related in any consistent fashion to behavior. One person may be bundled up in heavy clothing when the thermometer reads 55°F while another walks around comfortably in shirt sleeves. As far as either the physical or the social environment is concerned, it is individuals' *perceptions* of it that affect their behavior.

Individual Differences in Perception

Since people are different with respect to their individual characteristics, it follows that their perceptions of the environment are likely to differ. Such differences may be seen in every sphere of life. One pleasure-craft sailor perceives the day as too windy to be safe for sailing and goes to a baseball game instead, while another perceives it as challengingly brisk. One movie critic calls a film a "great slice of life," while another labels it "trash." One employee views the boss as friendly and fair while another sees the same person as aloof and inclined to play favorites.

The role that perceptual differences, such as those described, play in responses to a work environment appears many times in this text. A preview of how substantial these different perceptions can be is provided in a study by Sonnenfeld (1981). Sonnenfeld investigated executives' perceptions of reasons for the involvement of four companies in a price-fixing conspiracy charge. He found that top executives perceived the involvement of their companies as:

> . . . a consequence of the uncontrollable variation in human morals, obedience, and intelligence. The widespread criminal offenses were seen as isolated incidents of human weakness tempted by the prevailing low morals of a few isolated industry subcultures (p. 195).

By contrast with the perceptions of the corporate-level executives interviewed for Sonnenfeld's report, divisional executives viewed the price-fixing convictions more in terms of a few people "taking the rap" for what the industry in general was doing to cope with various business and political pressures. In terms identified at the beginning of Chapter 2, these executives explained the price-fixing behavior as being caused by the *environment;* the top executives attributed the cause to the *individuals* involved.

Perceptual differences, such as those found in the study described, create problems for an I/O psychologist in an applied setting. Since people act on the basis of their own perceptions of reality, the steps different people believe should be taken to solve a problem will not necessarily be the same. In addition, there will be differences in perception of the change efforts instigated by others. The potential problem is described in Exhibit 2–5.

The implications of the remarks in Exhibit 2–5 are far reaching in the practice of I/O psychology. Applied psychologists can never lose sight

This difference between the objective and perceived environments poses a real dilemma for management and for management consultants. It is fairly easy to recommend, and to introduce, *objective* changes in the work environment. But none of us can guarantee that we shall thereby change the *perceived* environment.

Note. From R. Stagner, "Training and Experiences of Some Distinguished Industrial Psychologists." *American Psychologist*, 1981, 36(5), p. 502.

EXHIBIT 2–5

Organizational Change and Perceived Versus Objective Environment

of the fact that what they intend to accomplish and what they actually accomplish when they initiate change may be two different things. A convenient example may be found in the administration of employee attitude questionnaires. Without careful preparation, such questionnaires may be perceived as a sneaky way to ferret out malcontents instead of as a genuine attempt to find out how employees feel about their work situations.

The Perception of People

People are the most important part of an organization's social environment and the influence of employees' perceptions of others on their own behavior can be substantial. Some important organizational activities also are, to a considerable degree, exercises in perception. Among these are screening, selection, and performance appraisal.

Differences in perceptions of people extend also to differences between an individual's perception of himself or herself and others' perceptions of the individual. For example, people who view themselves as normally ambitious may be surprised to learn that others perceive them as overly aggressive. Again, the important point is that people act according to their own perceptions. "Overly-aggressive" individuals are unlikely to make any effort to change unless that behavior starts blocking their personal goals.

THE INTERACTIVE NATURE OF THE VARIABLES THAT CAUSE BEHAVIOR

Human behavior is highly complex, far more complex than the methods available for studying it. Psychologists concentrate much of their effort on establishing simple relationships between behaviors and single variables known to affect behavior, such as those discussed in Chapter 2. They know, however, that these relationships really are not simple because the variables that cause behavior interact with one another. This is seen in the relationship between age, experience, and work performance described earlier. The variables that influence behavior also influence one another. For example, job performance is influenced by personal ability and motivation. As will be seen, however, level of motivation also can be affected

Behavior at work is the result of a complex interaction of individual and situational factors.

by ability. To complicate things still further, perceptions of ability are affected by the degree of success achieved in performance.

If the reciprocal interaction of individual characteristics, environmental characteristics, and behavior described above complicates the task of understanding behavior, it also opens up multiple channels for bringing about changes. For example, behavior modification techniques seek to bring about desired behavior change through the environment. Most traditional psychotherapy methods approach the same goal by focusing on the individual. Both approaches recognize that changing even one small factor can bring about relatively large changes in behavior.

Given the complexity of the causes of human behavior, it is remarkable that organizations function as smoothly as they do. It also is not surprising that there are problems or that organizational changes to bring about one set of outcomes have unanticipated consequences. All of these complexities are the reality of the study of behavior. Although this reality is segmented into pieces that are manageable for purposes of study here, it should never be forgotten that this segmentation is artificial.

SUMMARY

The study of human behavior can be accomplished at four levels—observation, understanding, prediction, and control. All psychologists are involved with behavior at the first three levels; applied psychologists also must deal with behavior at the control level. For I/O psychologists, this means using knowledge acquired through the scientific study of behavior to (a) solve problems in organizations and (b) create conditions in which organization employees can be successful.

To control behavior, it is necessary to understand it. To understand it is to appreciate the nature of the variables that cause it. There are two broad sets of variables—individual and environmental. Individual variables include both inherited characteristics, such as sex, and learned characteristics, such as attitudes. Environmental variables that influence behavior include physical variables, such as lighting, temperature, and space. Social environmental variables include membership in groups, norms, rules, and relationships with others. The nature of the influence of any particular environmental variable on behavior depends on an individual's perception of that factor. It also depends upon the interaction of this factor with other environmental and personal variables.

AT ISSUE

Genetic Screening for Employees

The term *genetic screening* refers to a variety of tests for detecting individual susceptibility to certain diseases or illnesses in advance. It also includes techniques for identifying *carriers*—healthy people who are capable of transmitting a disease to others (particularly their unborn children) even though they themselves will never contract it. Genetic screening is a tool for acquiring information. In some settings, its use is applauded by all. Routine screening of newborns for a condition called phenylketonuria (PKU), for example, is saving hundreds of babies a year. Other uses, or proposed uses, of genetic screening are highly controversial. One of these is the use of genetic screening in employment settings.

A few organizations report that they are currently using genetic screening; more have used it in the past or expect to use it in the future (Murray, 1983). The rationale for this use revolves around employee health and safety. A great many work environments are hazardous to some degree, but many people work in them for years with no adverse effects. Genetic screening offers the potential for identifying, in advance, those workers more likely to be in the other group—those who *do* suffer ill effects.

The information that people are likely to be adversely affected by a particular work environment may be used in two ways. First, it may exclude such people from employment. Second, it may help individuals make their own decisions about being exposed to the risks. The benefits of either strategy could be substantial. Among these are:

- better health for individuals
- lower illness-related costs for organizations
- fewer disease-related lawsuits in the courts
- increased worker productivity

Despite the potential advantages, routine genetic screening for employment is extremely controversial. In the first place, the kind of strong scientific evidence needed to back the procedure has not been accumulated to date, although research is making great progress. In addition, both the ethics and the legality of using genetic screening for exclusion (the use preferred by organizations) have yet to be examined; nor are these the only problems.

In terms presented in Chapter 2, genetic screening is focused on inherited individual characteristics; but unlike other such characteristics—age, sex, race, and so on—the individual concerned usually is not aware of having or not having a trait. A policy of genetic screening in a particular organization would give those who apply for work this information whether they wanted it or not. In many cases, such information will generate anxiety, most of it unwarranted. Susceptibility to a disease does not mean that the individual involved will ever contract it. Nor does being a carrier mean that the individual will necessarily transmit it.

In summary, genetic screening for employment is an issue that is coming. Its potential benefits are substantial, but once the scientific evidence to back it is available, the associated problems must be faced. The courts will bear the burden of the legal aspects, but it is organizations that must confront the ethical and human considerations.

REFERENCES

ARGYRIS, C. The individual and the organization: Some problems of mutual adjustment. *Administrative Science Quarterly,* 1957, *2*(1), 1–24.

ARVEY, R. D., & DEWHIRST, H. D. Relationships between diversity of interests, age, job satisfaction, and job performance. *Journal of Occupational Psychology,* 1979, *52*(1), 17–23.

AYOUB, M. M., BETHEA, N. J., DEIVANAYA-GAM, S., ASFOUR, S. S. BAKKEN, G. M., LILES, D., MITAL, A., & SHERIF, M. *Determination and modeling of lifting capacity: Final report* (HEW Grant No. 5, Rol, OH-00545-02). Washington, DC: National Institute of Occupational Safety and Health, September 1978.

BEHLING, O., & SCHRIESHEIM, C. *Organizational Behavior: Theory, Research, and Application.* Boston: Allyn & Bacon. 1976

BRENNER, O. C., & TOMKIEWICZ, J. Job orientation of black and white college graduates in business. *Personnel Psychology,* 1982, *35*(1), 89–103.

CZAJA, S. J., & DRURY, C. G. Aging and pretraining in industrial inspection. *Human Factors,* 1981, *23*(4), 485–494.

DRORY, A. Individual differences in boredom proneness and task effectiveness at work. *Personnel Psychology,* 1982, *35*(1), 141–151.

FORBES, J. B., & BARRETT, G. V. Individual abilities and task demands in relation to performance and satisfaction on two repetitive monitoring tasks. *Journal of Applied Psychology,* 1978, *63*(2), 188–196.

GINIGER, S., DISPENZIERI, A., & EISENBERG, J. Age, experience, and performance on speed and skill jobs in an applied setting. *Journal of Applied Psychology,* 1983, *68*(3), 469–475.

GORN, G. J., & KANUNGO, R. N. Job involvement and motivation: Are intrinsically motivated managers more job involved? *Organizational Behavior and Human Performance,* 1980, *26*(3), 265–277.

ILGEN, D. R., & HOLLENBACK, J. H. The role of job satisfaction in absence behavior. *Organizational Behavior and Human Performance,* 1977, *19,* 148–161.

KONNER, M. *The Tangled Wing.* New York: Holt, Rinehart, & Winston, 1982.

KYRIACON, C., & SUTCLIFFE, J. A note on teacher stress and locus of control. *Journal of Occupational Psychology,* 1979, *52*(3), 227–228.

LEWIN, K. *Field Theory in Social Science.* New York: Harper, 1951.

McMANUS, K. Executives retreads. *Forbes,* 18 July 1983, pp. 140–142.

MURRAY, T. H. Thinking the unthinkable about genetic screening. *Across the Board,* 1983, *20*(6), 34–39.

RANDOLF, W. A., & POSNER, B. Z. Explaining role conflict and ambiguity via individual and interpersonal variables in different job categories. *Personnel Psychology,* 1981, *1,* 89–102.

SONNENFELD, J. Executive apologies for price fixing: Role biased perceptions of causality. *Academy of Management Journal,* 1981, *24*(1), 192–198.

STAGNER, R. Training and experiences of some distinguished industrial psychologists. *American Psychologist,* 1981, *36*(5), 497–505.

CHAPTER 3

The Scientific Study of Human Behavior

I/O PSYCHOLOGY AT WORK

The Bell Laboratories

Placing a phone call activates a system designed with the help of thousands of psychological studies and experiments. The studies were performed by psychologists employed at Bell Labs, which serves the AT&T communications conglomerate, the largest corporation in the world.

Bell Labs employs about 250 psychologists, which makes it one of the largest employers of psychologists anywhere. The Bell Labs system is one of the largest research organizations in existence with 22,000 employees spread over 18 locations.

Bell Labs psychologists conduct research of vast diversity on everything from the design of telephone equipment, through the ability to call anywhere at any time, to the efficiency of the Bell system. . .

Edmund Klemmer has worked for Bell Labs as a human factors psychologist for about 20 years. . . . Klemmer cited one applied research project in which he was involved as an example of work that often has important payoffs for AT&T.

"When our Dimension PBX (a multi-lined console operated by secretaries or receptionists) came out, it was clear there would be problems instructing the person at the desk to use the system," he says. . . . "It was conventional wisdom that customers had to have hands-on training. We suspected that hands-on training wasn't necessary. Our laboratory studies confirmed our suspicion. We then conducted a comprehensive field study comparing training with and without the hands-on. Interviews found no significant difference in people's knowledge or use of the features. The hands-on training did nothing for customers' knowledge or skill and it was very expensive; so it was dropped. We earned our entire salary for many years just on the basis of that one finding."

The Bell Laboratories spend a large amount of money each year in pursuit of knowledge about human behavior that is relevant to the use of telephone communication systems. Much of this work is of the type described by Edmund Klemmer; it is designed to answer a specific question about a particular problem. Other work is of a more basic type, designed to answer questions about human perception, memory, learning, and communication. All of these efforts have one thing in common: They are carried out within the context of the scientific method.

THE SCIENTIFIC METHOD

The scientific method has four important characteristics.

The **scientific method** is the investigation of phenomena by an orderly process of observation, inference, and verification.

1. It requires a precise *vocabulary.*
2. It has *rules* for collecting and organizing observations.
3. It is based on a *system of logic* for making decisions or inferences about the meaning of observations.
4. It requires *verification* of these inferences.

As shown in Exhibit 3–1, the scientific method is a cyclical research process; theoretically, the verification phase has no limits. Even apparently fixed physical laws are subject to continual study, revision, and refinement. For example, by all known physical laws, a bumblebee cannot fly. Despite the sophistication of today's scientific world, there is clearly more to learn.

EXHIBIT 3–1

The Scientific Method

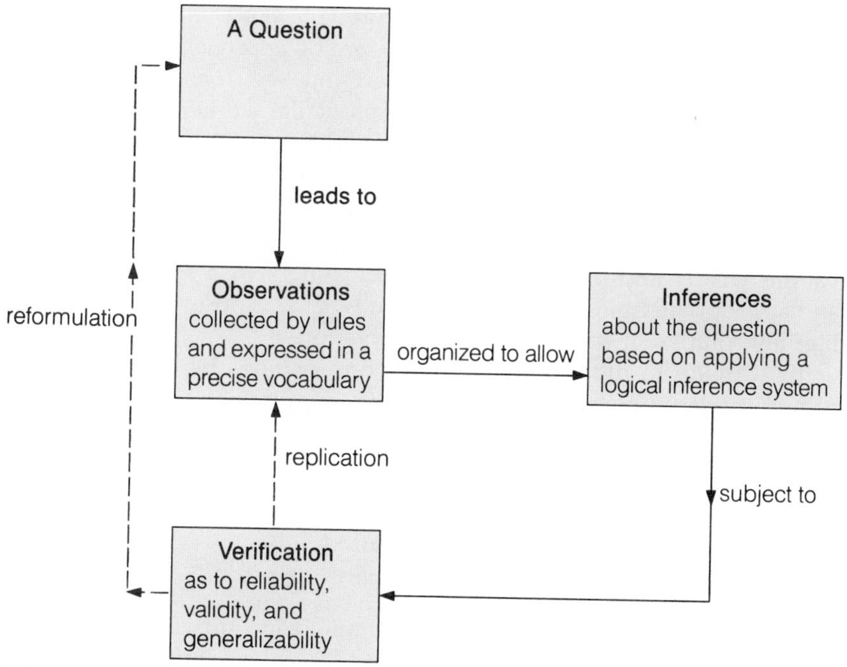

The psychologists at the Bell Labs, like most psychologists, are committed to the scientific method as an approach to acquiring knowledge about human behavior. In practice, this means that *research* is the way psychologists prefer to investigate questions about that behavior. In the investigation cited by Klemmer, for example, Bell psychologists carried out a comprehensive set of laboratory and field experiments to answer what seemed to be a relatively simple question: Was hands-on training required to give customers the necessary knowledge to make use of a particular piece of equipment?

An alternative to the research described by Klemmer would have been to put into practice what "everybody already knew" about training: Hands-on training is necessary to get the job done right. The result of this conventional wisdom approach to human behavior would have cost Bell millions of unnecessary dollars.

Research, such as that being carried out at the Bell Laboratories, is the foundation upon which this book rests. Some familiarity with the vocabulary and methods of research in I/O psychology is therefore necessary. The discussion in Chapter 3 is organized around the three cornerstones of the scientific method—observation, inference, and verification.

OBSERVATION: RESEARCH DESIGN

Laying out a plan for making observations consistent with the rules of the scientific method is called **research design.**

All knowledge starts with the immediate conscious experience of an individual, that is, with *observation*. A scientific approach to knowledge requires a precise vocabulary for describing such observations. For example, a supervisor might note that a particular worker is "good with his hands," while an I/O psychologist would describe the same observation of the person as, "He has a high level of manual dexterity."

A common scientific vocabulary serves an important function in research. It allows those doing the research to communicate their observations clearly and precisely. As a result, others with similar interests and appropriate training can understand what was observed and meaningfully compare it with their own observations.

In addition to the requirement that observations be expressed in a common scientific vocabulary, a scientific approach to knowledge also means that observations must be made systematically according to certain rules. These are rules about:

- the nature and number of observations needed;
- the way these observations are measured;
- the conditions under which observations are made.

The rules that the scientific approach to knowledge imposes on research serve to control sources of error that could (a) make it difficult or impossible to infer answers to the questions under investigation, or (b) allow a variety of equally-likely explanations for what is observed. Thus these rules serve as a source of assistance for scientists in planning research as well as in setting standards against which the conclusions can be evaluated.

Four important questions with respect to research design are considered: What is to be observed? Who is to be observed? Where are observations to be made? How are observations to be made?

What Is to be Observed?

All scientific research starts with a question. Sometimes the question is as general as: "I wonder what would happen if. . . ." Often, however, research is carried out to answer a specific question that has been raised by a theory or a particular problem or just plain curiosity. "I wonder if longer rest periods would reduce worker stress symptoms?" is an example of the kind of specific question investigated in I/O psychology.

Research Hypotheses

To answer a question, such as that of longer rest periods to reduce stress, by means of scientific research, the investigator starts with re-stating it in the form of an hypothesis.

*An **hypothesis** is a statement of a predicted answer to a research question.*

An hypothesis about the question of worker rest periods and stress symptoms might read: "Workers given longer rest periods will show significantly fewer symptoms of stress at the end of six months than workers given shorter rest periods." An example of an actual research hypothesis taken from a recent journal article is shown in Exhibit 3-2.

In the study from which Exhibit 3-2 was taken, Dalton and Perry (1981) were investigating the *question* of the relationship between wages and absenteeism in union companies. Their *hypothesis* about this rela-tionship was that it would be a positive one—higher wages would be associated with higher rates of absenteeism.

Hypotheses, such as the one shown in Exhibit 3-2, come from theories, published research on similar or related questions, experience, or "edu-cated guesswork" based on general knowledge. Research is conducted to determine whether or not such predictions hold up under actual observation. This process is called *hypothesis testing*.

Hypothesis testing is based on statistical analysis, which will be dis-cussed in the section on inference. First, it is necessary to finish design-ing the study. With respect to the current question of what is to be observed, psychologists must specify the variables to be observed and how they are to be measured.

Variables

One of the advantages of stating a research question as a formal hy-pothesis is that it highlights the variables to be observed in the research. The variables specified by the hypothesis in Exhibit 3–2 are (a) peak wages and (b) absence rates. Other examples of variables studied frequently in I/O psychology research are:

*A **variable** is some as-pect of the world that can take on at least two different measured values.*

"A positive association, therefore, is hypothesized between peak wages as defined by the (union) agreement and the absence rates of sample organizations."

EXHIBIT 3–2

Note. From D. R. Dalton and J. L. Perry, "Absenteeism and the Collective Bargaining Agree-ment: An Empirical Test." *Academy of Management Journal*, 1981, *24*(2), 425–431.

A Research Hypothesis

- work performance
- motivation
- test scores
- length of time on a job
- work experience

The theoretical opposite of a variable is a *constant*. When the subject is human behavior, there are few, if any, real constants. Many variables may be *held constant* for research purposes, however. For example, sex is a constant only if a research design calls for one subject. But sex can be held constant in a study by using only male or only female subjects. In such a study, sex, which is a variable in the world, would be a constant.

Although an hypothesis provides a clear and visible statement of the variables to be observed in a research investigation, it must be remembered that the scientific method imposes certain rules on the observation of variables. One of these rules is that what is observed must be defined unambiguously in order for others to understand and to repeat the observations if they desire. In scientific research, this is accomplished by means of what is called an operational definition.

Operational Definitions

An **operational definition** defines a variable to be observed in terms of how it will be measured.

As might be supposed from the term itself, an operational definition differs from the usual conceptual definition. Among the operational definitions used frequently in I/O psychology are:

- *intelligence*—a score on a particular intelligence test;
- *work performance*—a supervisor's evaluation;
- *turnover rate*—the percentage of newly hired employees who leave voluntarily within six months.

Each of the variables listed—intelligence, work performance, and turnover rate—can be and often are operationally defined in a different way. This is true of many research variables. In the Dalton and Perry (1981) study, for example, *absence rate* was defined as the ratio of absent hours to all hours worked, but there are other possibilities.

Operational definitions of absenteeism that differ from that of Dalton and Perry include (a) a flat count of days absent from work and (b) a count of absence incidences in a given time period (three successive days missed would be one incident). Without specific operational definitions of variables, understanding and evaluating research reports would be difficult, and *replicating* (duplicating) a study would be impossible.

To recapitulate, one aspect of research design for psychologists to decide is what to observe in the research. This requires that psychologists frame the question of interest to identify the relevant variables and specify how these variables will be measured. Since the focus of attention in I/O psychology is the behavior of human beings, the next step is to decide who these people will be; that is, who will be the *subjects* of the research?

Who Is to be Observed?

Although there are exceptions (e.g., when organizations are the "subjects"), most research in I/O psychology uses human subjects. Given that the focus of researchers is on organizations, it might appear that the best subjects would be employees of these organizations. Unfortunately, it is not always possible to gain access to such subjects. Finding an organization willing to allow the possible disruption of its normal activities can be a problem. In addition, many variables cannot be controlled in real-life settings. The problems created when such variables affect research is discussed further into Chapter 3.

Population and Samples

Even when it is possible and desirable to use employees as subjects, other issues remain. How many employees in what jobs in what organizations? What characteristics must these subjects (the sample) have to be representative of those to whom research findings are intended to apply (the population)?

Population refers to all of the people (organizations, departments, or other units) that have the characteristics relevant to the research question under investigation.

A **sample** is some defined portion of a population.

In the Dalton and Perry (1981) study mentioned, employees of all union organizations constituted the population of relevance. Few researchers have the resources to study an entire population, however. Like most, these authors selected a sample of their population (see Exhibit 3-2).

In I/O psychology, one of the most important criteria to be met in the choice of subjects from a population is that the sample be *representative* of the population. For example, if the population is all employees of Company X, then the sample should include employees representing the full range of jobs, experience, age, sex, salary, and rank of those in the organization.

The way in which a sample is chosen has important consequences for research results. It affects both (a) confidence in observations and (b) extent to which conclusions about these observations can be extended to people who were not actually in the study.

Because the nature of a sample is important, it is now usual for those who publish the results of their research to describe their subjects in detail. Whether subjects have been drawn from an organization, an introductory college class, an advertisement in a local newspaper, or another source, this description assists readers in evaluating the research. One such description from a recent publication is shown in Exhibit 3-3.

Green, Blank, and Liden (1983) used organization employees in their research. In the description of their sample (Exhibit 3-3), they report the number of subjects by (a) job position, (b) average length of time subjects had been on the job, and (c) sex composition of the sample.

Exhibit 3-3 also contains a description of the organizations in which subjects worked with respect to important variables, such as location and policies. These are the kinds of variables that often make the difference when psychologists decide where to carry out a particular research investigation.

EXHIBIT 3-3

Describing the
Subjects of Research
Observation

Subjects

The sample consisted of 160 employees located at 23 branch offices of a large midwestern bank. The 23 branches were geographically dispersed throughout a large metropolitan area. Each branch had the same organizational structure and policies. . . . The nature of the surrounding environment varied considerably from inner city to affluent suburb to small town locales. The sample of respondents was composed of 19 branch managers, 37 assistant branch managers, and 104 staff members (i.e., tellers—77%—, clerks, secretaries, and receptionists.) The average amount of time spent working at current branch and position was 2.6 years for managers and 2.4 years for staff employees. The manager sample was predominantly male (78%), whereas the staff sample was mostly female (82%).

Note: From S. G. Green, W. Blank, and R. C. Liden, "Market and Organizational Influences on Bank Employees' Work Attitudes and Behaviors. *Journal of Applied Psychology,* 1983, *68*(2), p. 300.

Where Are Observations to be Made?

There are two basic ways in which research observations may be made. Researchers may go to subjects and make observations in their usual surroundings or subjects may be brought to researchers and be observed in surroundings that researchers have created. These two choices of where research observations are to be made are called *field settings* and *laboratory settings,* respectively.

The decision as to whether to conduct research in a field setting or a laboratory sometimes is determined by the nature of the question being investigated. If the behavior of people involved in wildcat strikes is of interest, for example, researchers go to the site of a wildcat strike (i.e., field setting) to make observations.

Not all research questions define the setting in which observations will be made. The assembly of watches, for example, could be observed in a watch factory (field) or in a laboratory. As mentioned in connection with choosing subjects, there are trade-offs in making this decision.

In general, the use of laboratory settings maximizes control of variables that are not being studied at the expense of reality while the opposite is true for field settings. Although some of the variables that cannot be controlled in a field setting have little effect on a particular research investigation, others may affect both the observations and the conclusions substantially. Such variables are called confounding variables.

A **confounding variable** is an extraneous variable that can affect conclusions from research because it has an important effect on a variable that is being investigated.

Confounding Variables

Suppose that the researcher who is interested in watch assembly wants to find out if different kinds of magnifying instruments have predictable effects on individuals' work performances. If this question is investigated in a factory (field setting), varying conditions of lighting, noise, social interaction, and supervision could confuse the issue considerably.

Because these variables affect the vision and concentration of the subjects, they could make it impossible for the researcher to determine how much the different magnifying instruments have to do with observed human performance differences.

If the researcher interested in watch assembly moved the site of the investigation to a laboratory, he or she could control all of the possible confounding variables mentioned. It then would be possible to get a clearer picture of the actual performance differences associated with various types of magnifying instruments. On the other hand, "working conditions" now would be very different from real ones. Thus, there might be some doubt as to whether or not the conclusions reached in the laboratory could be applied in the watch factory.

Because the advantages and disadvantages of laboratory and field settings are sharply contrasted, the choice between them traditionally has been an "either/or" one; however, the argument for using a combination of settings in order to take advantage of the strengths of each has been appearing more and more frequently in recent years (e.g., Flanagan & Dipboye, 1981). For example, an I/O psychologist might observe watch assembly in a factory, then move to a laboratory setting to compare results under controlled conditions. This is exactly the kind of strategy described by the Bell psychologist in "I/O Psychology at Work," although that research began in the laboratory instead of in the field.

Employees' social surroundings can introduce significant confounding variables into I/O psychology field research.

How Are Observations to be Made?

The classic way to make scientific observations is by performing experiments in a laboratory, but experiments also may be conducted in field settings. Nor are experiments the only way to make research observations. A scientist also can go into a particular setting and simply record the observations of interest. Alternatively, observations can be collected by questionnaires or from records of others. In the present discussion, these basic ways of making scientific research observations will be called *experimentation, field observation, survey rearch,* and *historical studies.*

Experimentation

In **experiments,** observations of subject behavior are made under different states of the environment that are **manipulated** by the experimenter.

Industrial/organizational psychologists frequently prefer to conduct research in field settings because that is the focus of their special interest. As discussed however, there can be problems with field research that make the laboratory a better choice for some questions. But the basic process of experimentation is the same whether it occurs in the field or in the laboratory.

The manipulated variables in experiments are called *independent variables,* and the particular states created by the manipulations are called *treatments* or *conditions.* The subject behavior of interest is called the *dependent variable.* In the watch assembly example, the different types of magnifying instruments are the various experimental treatments, and the subjects' work performance is the dependent variable.

The great advantage of using experiments over other ways of observation to answer questions about human behavior is that experiments make the strongest case for inferring *cause-effect* relationships. If predicted changes in a dependent variable are observed consistently to follow specified manipulations of an independent variable, there is evidence that the manipulation is indeed a causal factor in the observed effects.

To illustrate the concept of experimentation, a summary report of a recent laboratory experiment in I/O psychology is presented in ''Spotlight on Research.'' This report also outlines decisions made about the other research design questions relevant to this point. For clarity, only one of the eight research hypotheses actually investigated in the study is discussed.

The laboratory experiment summarized in ''Spotlight on Research'' deals with work motivation in general and with the level of performance goals workers set for themselves in particular. Theoretically, it would have been possible to carry out a similar experiment in a field setting. Work goals usually are set by organizations, however, and the kind of manipulation carried out in this experiment would be unacceptable in most companies.

SPOTLIGHT ON RESEARCH

Influence of Ability, Assigned Goals, and Normative Information on Personal Goals and Performance: A Challenge to the Goal Attainability Assumption

Research hypothesis: "Individuals assigned a very difficult performance goal will set higher personal performance goals than those assigned a relatively easy goal" (p. 22).

Type of study: Laboratory experiment.

Subjects: Fifty-eight male and female undergraduate business students.

Independent variables:
- Objective difficulty of goal set by experimenter. Operational definition: Very hard (12 nouns); or Moderately easy (5 nouns).
- Subjects' beliefs about goal difficulty. Operational definition: Subjects told standard (a) "well below," (b) "the same as," (c) "well above" what most subjects can do.

Dependent variable: Performance goals set by subjects. Operational definition: Number of nouns that subjects are expected to be able to think of in connection with a certain adjective.

General procedure: After the task was explained, each subject was assigned a particular performance goal to meet in a one-minute trial. Before beginning each trial, they also were asked to set their own personal performance goals for that trial. Each subject was assigned randomly to one of the following six experimental treatment conditions:

1. Subjects were given goals that were objectively *very hard* and were told that the goal was *well below* what most students could do.
2. Subjects were given *very hard* goals and were told the goals were *about average*.
3. Subjects were given *very hard* goals and were told that the goals were *well above* what most students could do.
4. Subjects were given goals that were objectively *easy* and were told that the goals were *well below* what most students could do.
5. Subjects were given goals that were *easy* and were told that the goals were *about average*.
6. Subjects were given goals that were *easy* and were told that the goals were *well above* what most students could do.

Presentation of Experimental Treatment Conditions

Information Given to Subjects About Goal Difficulty	Hard Objective Goal Difficulty	Easy Objective Goal Difficulty
Well Below Average	#1	#4
About Average	#2	#5
Well Above Average	#3	#6

Results: Hypothesis supported.

Conclusion: "The results of this experiment are entirely consistent with those of numerous other studies that have found that specific, hard task goals motivate higher performance than do easier goals" (pp. 28–29).

Summarized from H. Garland, "Influence of Ability, Assigned Goals, and Normative Information on Personal Goals and Performance: A Challenge to the Goal Attainability Assumption." *Journal of Applied Psychology*, 1983, *68*(1), pp. 20–30.

Garland (1983) carried out a traditional laboratory experiment and used a controlled task bearing little resemblance to any real work task. A compromise between this approach and a field experiment that works for some research questions is called a *simulation experiment*.

A simulation experiment reproduces certain important aspects of the real world, while maintaining control over the more critical potentially confounding variables. In some simulation experiments, subjects are aware of the experimental nature of the situation. In others, they are not. For example, Ilgen, Nebeker, and Pritchard (1981) conducted such an experiment to study the effects on task performance (dependent variable) of manipulating (a) task difficulty and (b) method of pay (independent variables).

Subjects in this simulation experiment were hired through a newspaper advertisement and worked at what they believed to be an actual short-term job. In other words, a fairly common employment situation was *simulated* by the authors. The difference was that they "hired" only those subjects with certain desired characteristics. In this way, potentially confounding variables, such as sex, age, and scores on selection tests, were controlled. In a field setting, Ilgen and his colleagues would have been limited to using subjects already employed by a particular company.

Whatever the setting, researchers who want to carry out experiments must be able to *manipulate* one or more independent variables—give subjects tasks of different, but controlled difficulty, for example. In some cases, however, the independent variables specified by a research question cannot be manipulated. Sometimes this problem arises for practical reasons. For example, a researcher interested in the effect of work force size on employee turnover cannot manipulate the size of a work force in a company.

Some variables that could be manipulated are not subject to experimentation for ethical reasons. For example, it would be possible to manipulate job stress by giving people impossible work goals or by implying that their jobs were in jeopardy. Such strategies, however, are entirely outside the bounds of ethical research practices in I/O psychology. In such cases, one of the field observation research methods may be a useful alternative.

Field Observation

Other examples of variables in I/O psychology that cannot, or should not, be manipulated by researchers include employee morale, organizational structure, volume of business, and employee friendship patterns. These *are* variables, however; that is, they exist in different amounts or states in the world. One way for researchers to study these variables is to seek out groups of subjects for which the variables already exist at different levels. These subjects then may be used in what is called a field study.

A *field study* often is referred to as a quasi-experiment (Cook & Campbell, 1976). This means that it resembles, or is to some degree like, an

Naturally-occurring events, such as strikes, offer I/O psychologists opportunities to conduct useful field and observational studies.

experiment. For example, an I/O psychologist might make a field study of the effects of the degree of decision-making authority given to managers on their job satisfaction. To do this, he or she would make systematic observations of managerial job satisfaction in several companies with measureably different policies about managerial decision making.

The briefly-described procedure resembles an experiment, but there are two important exceptions. First, the decision-making variable is not *manipulated*; it is observed in different natural states. Second, the experimenter cannot assign subjects randomly to the different conditions; he or she must use those people currently employed as subjects.

In addition to serving as a way to get around the problem of variables that cannot be manipulated directly, field studies are useful to psychologists in their study of the effects of certain naturally-occurring events on their human participants. Among these events are strikes, massive layoffs, company mergers, and so on. For example, psychologists might study worker attitudes in two plants belonging to the same company, one of which has full employment and one of which is experiencing large numbers of layoffs.

An alternative to a field experiment or a field study as a way for psychologists to collect observations in a field setting is simply for them to record what happens with respect to some aspect of the situation that is of interest. These observations frequently appear in the form of the familiar *observational* or *case study.*

Observational studies are time consuming, and they are difficult to write in such a way that those not present can share in what the researcher observed. If they are done carefully, however, they can be especially rich sources of experimental research hypotheses. On the other side of the coin, they can provide verification of observations that were made in the laboratory. Finally, observational studies can help both I/O psychologists and organizations avoid the pitfalls into which others have stumbled. This is illustrated by the observational study excerpted in Exhibit 3–4.

EXHIBIT 3–4	When Tom Watson, Jr. made what he called "the most important product announcement in company history," he created quite a stir. International Business Machines is not a corporation given to making earth-shaking pronouncements casually, and the declaration that it was launching an entirely new computer line, the System/360, was headline news. . . .
An Observational Study	

By 1963, with the important decisions on the 360 being implemented, excitement about the new product began to spread through the corporation. . . . But this rising pitch of interest by no means meant that the struggle inside the company was settled. . . .The System 360 Concepts plunged I.B.M. into an organizational upheaval. . . .The General Products Division [for example] really bristled with hostility. Its output, after all, accounted for two-thirds of the company's revenues for data processing. It had a popular and profitable product in the field, the 1401, which the 360 threatened to replace. . . .

Production of the 360 line was . . . held up by a maddening series of shortages. There were, for example, critical shortages of epoxy glass, copper laminate, and contact tabs. . . . I.B.M. representatives suddenly began appearing at tab plants late in the evening or early in the morning with suitcases. They would pack all the tabs they could and then fly back to Endicott to keep the production line moving.

Around mid–1965, however, the company gradually became aware that production problems were not its only, or even its greatest, obstacle to getting the 360 program on schedule. While there had been no disposition to underrate the technical difficulties in preparing the programming, no one, it appears, foresaw the appalling management problems that would be associated with them. . . .

Note. Excerpted from T. A. Wise, "The Rocky Road to the Market Place." *Fortune,* 1966, *74*(4), pp. 138–212. Reprinted by permission from *Fortune* Magazine.

In Exhibit 3–4, the quotations are from T. A. Wise's (1966) report of IBM Corporation's experiences in marketing and manufacturing an entirely new computer line. The System/360 consisted of six new computer models of a sophisticated technology not previously tested in the marketplace. As may be seen, however, selling this equipment was one of the least of IBM's problems. The corporation also encountered internal resistance to change, production problems, and management problems.

Observational studies, such as the one from which the excerpt in Exhibit 3–4 is taken, field studies, and experiments are all methods of making observations in which the researcher interacts with the subjects in some fashion. But much research in I/O psychology is more impersonal in nature; in many cases, subjects are not seen at all. The two most common forms of such research may be described as historical studies and survey research.

Historical Studies and Survey Research

In a historical study, research observations are made from records kept by others. For example, a researcher may use company records to investigate the question of the relationship between sex and absenteeism. In this case, it would be necessary for the researcher only to obtain the appropriate information from each employee's file.

In most survey research, observations are made by means of written questionnaires. Subjects may be chosen on the basis of membership in some group (as in the APA survey of employment reported in Chapter 1). Alternatively, they may be chosen on the basis of some particular characteristic. For example, a researcher may use a company's files to select subjects on the basis of length of time on the job.

Both historical studies and survey research offer I/O psychologists the advantage of being able to collect large amounts of data in less time and with less disruption to the normal activities of individual subjects and/or organizations than other methods. There are, however, drawbacks. In historical research, for example, the researcher is dependent on the accuracy and completeness with which records have been kept.

Working from the records of others in historical study research can be a frustrating experience; one supervisor has forgotten to record absenteeism or production figures for a crucial period, for example, or the abbreviations of a long-departed personnel assistant cannot be deciphered.

Similar problems can arise in survey research—some questionnaires are not returned, some questions are left unanswered, or a respondent's handwriting is illegible.

Despite problems, both historical studies and survey research remain popular approaches, and a number of examples of such research will be encountered throughout this text. A related procedure, called *field survey research*, also is discussed. In field survey research, observations consist of the responses of subjects to questions as in basic survey research. These questions are asked in personal interviews, however, rather than in written questionnaires.

Concluding Remarks on Research Design

The purpose of this section was to provide an overview of the issues involved in designing research to collect observations within the context of the scientific method. For more detail on research design, many excellent texts, such as that by Anderson and Borkowski (1978), are available. At this point, the discussion is turned to how investigators make inferences from observations that they have made.

INFERENCE: STATISTICAL ANALYSIS

Inference is the process by which scientists derive conclusions from observations.

Research design can be a long complex process. Scientists put in all of this "up-front" time for one purpose—so that they can infer answers to the research question of interest with some confidence after the observations are made.

In I/O psychology, the means for making inferences based on observations is usually some form of statistical analysis that allows one or more hypotheses about the research question to be tested. Although analytical procedures vary, the concept central to all is that of *significance*.

Statistical Significance

Statistical significance means that it is very unlikely that results obtained from a defined procedure were due to chance.

The simplest way to illustrate the concept of significance is by the example of the familiar coin toss. Suppose a coin is tossed into the air 30 times and comes down "heads" 17 times and "tails" 13 times. Is this a *significant* departure from the expected results of 15 heads and 15 tails or was it obtained by chance?

One way to answer the question posed is to repeat 30 tosses of the coin over and over, and note how many times a ratio of 17:13 is observed. Statistical analysis makes this tedious process unnecessary. By applying the appropriate procedures, a *probability statement* can be made after the first 30 tosses as to the likelihood that the 17:13 result was obtained by chance. The concept of probability statements will be illustrated with one of the most common statistics in the I/O psychology literature—the correlation coefficient.

A typical probability statement in an I/O psychology research report will read: "$r = .31, p < .01$." The symbols are shorthand for the verbal statement: "A correlation coefficient of .31 was obtained. A coefficient this large would be obtained by chance less than once out of 100 repetitions of this set of observations." This statement often will appear in research reports in a shorter form: "Results were significant at the .01 level."

Correlation is a measure of association. Thus, the inference to be drawn from the probability statements above would be that the two variables observed were related. If r had *not* been significant, the inference would have been that obtained results were most likely due to chance.

Statistics

The r in the example is a *statistic*. It is the result of a specific set of mathematical computational procedures. The significance of r is obtained if it is compared with published statistical tables. Other computational procedures yield other statistics.

Examples of statistics encountered frequently in I/O psychology research include F, t, χ^2 (chi square), and R (multiple r). In each case, the statistic (one number) obtained from a statistical analysis of a set of observations may be compared with numbers in a table. It then is possible to form a probability statement about the likelihood that results of a study were due to chance factors.

Although there is some difference of opinion, the commonly-accepted standards for significance long have been the .01 level and the .05 level. In other words, results that would be obtained by chance more than 5 times out of 100 are usually *not* considered significant.

It is not necessary to comprehend how to calculate the statistics mentioned in order to understand the research in this book as long as the concept of significance is clear. It is useful, however, to review an assumption that is common to all of these procedures—that the variables observed are distributed so as to approximate a normal curve. Two other statistical concepts also are discussed because they form the basis for many I/O psychology research inferences. One is the concept of correlation. The other is the concept of "variance explained."

The Normal Curve

Most of the statistical analysis procedures in common research use are based on the assumption that the variables observed have what is called a *normal distribution* in the population at large. If a variable is normally distributed, a graph with a large number of measurements on it will have a particular shape. For example, if a large number of people were measured as to height, a relatively small percentage of them would be very short or very tall. The rest would bunch up in between. Graphically, this produces the bell-shaped curve shown in Exhibit 3–5.

All normal curves, such as that shown in Exhibit 3–5, can be described in terms of two statistics. One is the *average measurement* of the scale

EXHIBIT 3–5

The Normal Curve

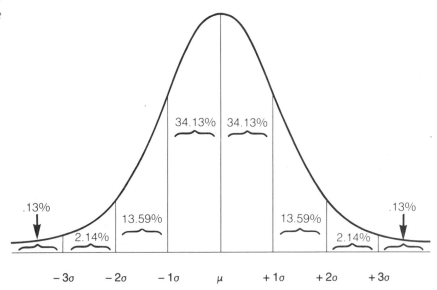

being used. This measurement is called the *mean* (μ) of the distribution. As shown in Exhibit 3–5, it lies at the center of the curve.

The second normal curve descriptive statistic is a measure of the *variability*, or *spread*, of the curve around the mean. By a process of mathematical transformation, the variability of all normal distributions can be described in standard units called *standard deviations* (σ). As noted in Exhibit 3–5, 68.26% of all observations in a normal distribution lie within one standard deviation of the mean (34.13% on each side).

The normal curve has many uses other than serving as a foundation for formal statistical analysis. One of the more important is helping individuals to understand the meaning of test scores. For example, suppose the mean for a standardized test of mathematical ability is 50 and the standard deviation is 10. In this situation, a person who scores 75 has done better than approximately 98% of the people who take the test. There is more discussion of this subject in Chapter 4.

There are variables studied in I/O psychology research that are not distributed in the normal fashion depicted in Exhibit 3–5. Sex, for example, has a *bimodal distribution*. This means that observations of this variable have only two measurements—male or female.

Other research variables have what is called a *skewed distribution*—one in which observations tend to pile up at a point of the scale that is not the middle. For example, in the United States, body weight has a skewed distribution. When height is controlled, there are more people at the higher ends of the distribution than there are people at the lower ends.

Special statistical procedures are necessary for bimodal, skewed, or other non-normal variable distributions. Such variables are encountered rarely in I/O psychology. A particular observed *data* distribution may be non-normal due to design decisions or sampling error, however.

Correlation and Correlates

A familiar example of a correlational relationship is that between height and weight. These two variables tend to be *positively correlated;* that is, in general as height increases, so does weight. Age and hearing ability, on the other hand, tend to be *negatively correlated.* In the general population, as age increases, hearing ability decreases.

> **Correlation** refers to a relationship between variables such that they change in a predictable manner with respect to one another.

There is a variety of procedures for determining whether or not two variables, such as height and weight, are correlated, but all share the same basic technique. A measurement is taken for each subject on each variable and a computational procedure is applied to the resulting set of scores. This procedure yields a *correlation coefficient,* the r discussed earlier.

A correlation coefficient, regardless of the method by which it is calculated, ranges between -1.00 and $+1.00$. The minus sign indicates a negative correlation and the plus sign a positive correlation. (The convention of omitting the plus sign for positive coefficients will be followed in this text.) The actual number indicates the *strength* of the relationship; the closer the number is to 1.00, either plus or minus, the stronger the relationship.

A correlation coefficient is calculated mathematically, but it often is depicted graphically. The two variables are plotted on a two-axis graph and a dot representing each subject's position with respect to the two variables is placed accordingly. The result is called a *scattergram,* an example of which is shown in Exhibit 3–6.

Exhibit 3–6 depicts the position of 18 subjects with respect to two sets of test scores—an English test and a vocabulary test. Subject 5, for example, made a score of 60 on both tests. Although most of the other subjects had different scores on the two tests, it is clear that there is a definite tendency for high scores on one to go with high scores on the other. For these data, $r = .94$. That this is a positive correlation may be seen in the fact that the pattern of dots slants from the lower left corner of the graph to the upper right corner. If it were a negative correlation, the slant would be from upper left to lower right.

Correlational Relationships

The relationship between the variables shown in Exhibit 3–6 is a *linear relationship;* that is, the line that best fits the data is a straight line. Not all correlational relationships between variables are linear, however. For example, research suggests that the relationship between level of education and reported job satisfaction is probably *curvilinear.* This means that

EXHIBIT 3–6

A Scattergram
of Scores on an
English Test and
a Vocabulary Test

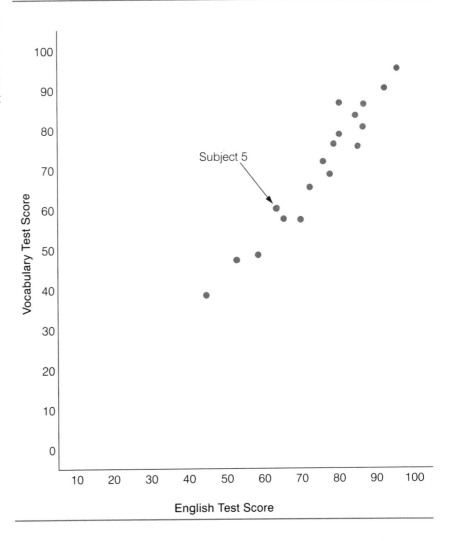

higher job satisfaction is associated with *higher and lower* levels of education. Lower job satisfaction is associated with middle levels of education. This relationship is shown graphically in Exhibit 3–7.

The application of standard correlation procedures to variables (such as those in Exhibit 3–7) that are curvilinearly related can make it appear that there is no relationship at all; that is, it can lead to *incorrect inference*. As analysis in the behavioral sciences has become more sophisticated, therefore, it has become more or less standard procedure for researchers to test for curvilinearity before inferring that there is no relationship between two variables.

A Note on Cause and Effect

Correlation is a basic concept that is encountered frequently. But corre-

EXHIBIT 3–7

A Curvilinear
Relationship:
Education and Job
Satisfaction

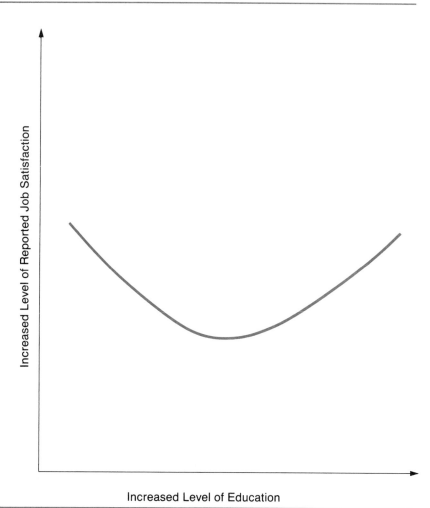

Increased Level of Reported Job Satisfaction

Increased Level of Education

lation is a measure of *association* only. No matter how obvious it may seem that one of two highly correlated variables is causing the other, such an inference cannot be made on the basis of the usual procedure for measuring correlation. If this procedure results in a high positive correlation between two variables, X and Y, the true cause-effect situation may be any of the following:

- X causes Y;
- Y causes X;
- both X and Y are caused by a third variable, Z.

The various causal possibilities underlying an obtained correlation between two variables mean that it is not accurate (on the basis of this procedure alone) to refer to "causes" and "effects." The correct term for X and Y in this case is *correlates*.

The term **correlates** refers to variables found to be associated (correlated) with one another in a predictable fashion.

Much I/O psychology research uses correlational analysis as the basis for inference about observations, and the term *correlate* is encountered many times in this text. There is also reference to the *antecedents* of some behavior or attitude. Antecedents are variables (or groups of variables that are used to define *antecedent conditions)* believed to lie at the causal end of cause-effect relationships.

Some variables that are called antecedents of some behavior or attitude have been found to have causal effects in experiments. It is not uncommon, however, to find the term used in connection with certain kinds of correlational relationships. The positive correlation often found between absenteeism and turnover (see Chapter 14) serves as an example.

As discussed, a correlation between absenteeism and turnover means only that they are correlates, not that one causes the other. Absenteeism always comes before turnover, however, so even if analytical procedures do not allow for a specific cause-effect statement, it is known that turnover does not cause absenteeism. In this case, absenteeism may be referred to as an *antecedent* of turnover.

The Concept of Variance Explained

Inferring cause and effect where two variables are concerned is a matter of determining *which of the two* has the effect on the other. For example, when examining the causal factors behind the positive height/weight correlation, it is the height that "causes" the weight. Weighing more cannot make people taller, but being taller gives them more skeleton to cover, so they tend to weigh more, other things being equal.

When it comes to height and weight, other things are not equal. There are many other important factors that determine what a person weighs. Among these are:

- heredity
- metabolism
- amount of food consumed
- activity level

Together, the listed factors, plus many not listed, *explain the variance in observed differences* in individual body weights. A complete list of these factors would be a list of the *determinants* of human body weight.

Predictor Variables

A **predictor variable** is a variable that explains a significant portion of the variance in another variable.

There are many situations in I/O psychology in which researchers are interested in finding as many of the determinants of observed differences among people on some variable (such as weight) as possible. The general approach to answering this question is to draw on experience, theory, and previous research relevant to this variable to form an hypothesis about the factors that determine it. These factors are called predictor variables.

In research, predictor variables resemble independent variables in that (a) they are variables of interest (not irrelevant or confounding) and (b) they are not dependent variables. Predictor variables are not manipulated (as in experiments), however, nor are they sought at particular levels (as in a field study); they are measured as they exist for particular subjects in a sample. By appropriate methodology, it is then possible to determine the amount of variance in a dependent variable explained by these predictor variables.

As an example of the use of predictor variables, consider the dependent variable of *job involvement*. The research question is: What other variables account for the observed differences (variance) among people on measures of job involvement? In one study (Jewell, 1977), the following four predictor variables were hypothesized to be relevant:

- level of education;
- amount of work experience;
- level of work performance;
- a personality-type variable called *locus-of-control* (Rotter, 1966).

When data on the variables described had been collected and analyzed, it was found that all of the variables except level of work performance were related significantly to a measure of job involvement. Together, the other three variables accounted for 23% of the variance in job involvement for subjects in this study. Clearly, some important determinants of this variable were missing from the hypothesis; a large percentage (77%) of the variance was *not* explained.

Part of the unexplained, or missing, variance in the job involvement study is accounted for by unidentified determinants of job involvement, but part comes from error. Some of this error is measurement error; some stems from the particular subjects chosen for the study. *Both types of error are present in all I/O psychology research.*

There are a number of ways to reduce error in carrying out research. There is also a way to estimate how much of the variance in a particular set of observations is due to such error. This procedure is called analysis of variance.

Analysis of Variance

There are a number of ways to carry out the statistical computations called analysis of variance (ANOVA), but all are based on the concept of "variance explained". In ANOVA, interest is on the amount of variance explained by experimentally manipulated variables versus the amount explained by error. This idea is illustrated by the graph in Exhibit 3–8.

The large circle in Exhibit 3–8 represents the total observed variance in the dependent variable—the average number of errors made by pilot subjects in reading an instrument panel. The circle sectors represent the proportions of variance explained by:

- the independent variable—different instrument panel configurations;
- error associated with the particular characteristics of the subjects in the sample;
- error stemming from other sources, such as measurement problems.

EXHIBIT 3–8

A Graphic Illustration
of Simple Analysis
of Variance

Subjects: Helicopter Pilots

Type of Experiment: Simulation

Dependent Variable: Average number of reading errors

Independent Variable: Arrangement of instrument panel

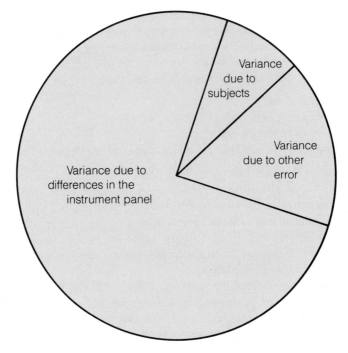

Total Observed Variance in Average Number of Reading Errors

Note. Data from R. E. Kirk, *Experimental Design: Procedures for the Behavioral Sciences.*
Belmont, CA: Brooks/Cole, p. 134.

Even without the computational figures, the graph in Exhibit 3–8 illustrates that more of the variance in pilot instrument reading performance was explained by differences in the instrument panels than by error. Nevertheless, that error is there, and in some experiments it may be significant.

Concluding Remarks on Inference

This section provides the basic understanding of the process of scientific inference—the drawing of conclusions about a particular question on the basis of a set of observations. In I/O psychology, this inference usually is based on statistical analysis, and it rests on the concept of significance. Achieving significant results is not enough, however, if research is carried out within the context of the scientific method. It is also necessary that these results be verified.

VERIFICATION: RELIABILITY, VALIDITY, AND GENERALIZABILITY

As shown in Exhibit 3–1, the third pillar of the scientific method of acquiring knowledge is verification. Verifying the results of a particular study means answering three questions.

Verification means to confirm or substantiate results.

1. Is the inference *reliable?* If the study were repeated exactly, would the observations allow for the same inference?
2. Is the inference *valid?* Did the study indeed measure the variables it intended to measure, control for the more important confounding variables, and use appropriate techniques for inference? If so, there should be no obvious plausible alternative inference (or explanation) for the observations.
3. Is the inference *generalizable?* Does it hold for subjects other than the particular ones used in the study?

To illustrate the concepts of reliability, validity, and generalizability, consider a conclusion from a recent study:

> *The results of this study suggest that flexitime significantly reduces employees' unpaid absences in general (Kim & Campagna, 1981, p. 739).*

Kim and Campagna (1981) conducted a field experiment in which they manipulated a particular aspect of working conditions (independent variable) and observed employee absenteeism rates (dependent variable). The following can be said of their conclusion.

- If this inference is *reliable,* the same or different researchers would reach the same conclusion if the experiment were repeated under the same conditions.
- If this inference is *valid,* an examination of the methods, observations, and analysis of the experiment would allow obvious alternative explanations for the lower absenteeism rate to be ruled out. Among such alternative explanations are statistical problems, biased measures of absenteeism, or uncontrolled relevant differences between employees observed under flexitime and those observed under normal working hours.
- If this inference is *generalizable,* similar inferences could be drawn if the observations were made with different subjects, in different kinds of organizations, or perhaps even in different countries.

Some of the aspects of verifying the inferences made from research can be evaluated by a close scrutiny of research design, execution, and data analysis. Generalizability can only be approximated in this way, however. The real test is to conduct further research of a similar nature with different subjects. Such replication, with and without changes, is an important way for scientists to increase their confidence in any research findings.

The standards discussed for evaluating inferences made about observations should reinforce again the importance of following commonly-accepted rules and using known and understood analytical procedures in research. Without them, there could be no basis for agreement as to reliability, validity, and generalizability. Each researcher could bring his or her own individual methods and biases to the process; there would be no basis for combining these individual efforts so as to build a solid body of knowledge.

To recapitulate, the scientific method is an orderly, cyclical process of observation, inference, and verification guided by rules and logic and characterized by a precise common vocabulary. It is a deliberately conservative method because it seeks to guard against premature or erroneous conclusions. Although some philosophers argue that nothing can be proven absolutely, scientists seek to obtain as much proof as possible.

SUMMARY

The scientific method, within which the study of human behavior in psychology is conducted, is characterized by commonly understood and accepted terminology and methods. In the course of conducting research that is consistent with these criteria, psychologists must make a number of decisions involving research design and procedures on which inferences about research observations are to be built.

Decisions about research design are decisions as to what is to be observed (variables) and how it is to be measured (operational definitions); who is to be observed (subjects); where observations are to be made (setting); and how observations are to be made (experimentation or other). Among the issues involved in making such decisions are the nature of the question to be investigated and the predicted answer to that question—the hypothesis.

In I/O psychology, making inferences from observations collected in research studies usually is accomplished by means of statistical tests of significance. Such analysis allows researchers to conclude that hypotheses about questions are or are not supported by the data, but even when results are significant, the job is not done. The scientific method requires verification of this inference—an evaluation of the reliability, validity, and generalizability of the scientist's conclusions.

AT ISSUE

"Inspirer or Perspirer—Who Gets the Glory When the Study Ends?"

A characteristic of all science is the sense of community among the mainstream of its practitioners. Scientists in any field see themselves as a group dedicated to the accumulation of knowledge in their discipline. Professional meetings serve as one mechanism for maintaining and strengthening this bond and aid scientists in sharing the results of recent work. Professional journals extend this communication to all interested parties as well as to those who cannot attend the meetings.

Because they are accessible to everyone, professional journals are the lifeblood of any science. They allow busy practitioners to "keep current," provide newcomers to the discipline with a "feel" for what is going on, and form the backbone of research progress. With few exceptions, reports in professional journals will begin with a review of previous research and thinking relevant to the topic under discussion. In this review, the author(s) of the report will show how current work builds on or connects to that done previously.

Because of its importance, most universities some years ago began to encourage their faculty members to publish in professional journals. It was expected that this activity would benefit students as well as the university and the various sciences themselves. Encouragement most often took the form of reduced classroom loads and/or more rapid advancement through the academic ranks for those who devoted some part of their time to research and publishing.

The policy of rewarding people for publishing in professional journals has been successful insofar as keeping faculty active and enhancing the reputations of their universities and departments. This success has not been without costs to individuals who are not inclined toward research, as "publish or perish" has gone from being an in-group catch phrase to hard reality.

Although there are no known data to support the position, it seems likely that most scientists believe the benefits of publish or perish to outweigh the problems it creates for some individuals. But one aspect of the issue seems to have implications that go far beyond the careers of individuals. This may be illustrated by the case in which the idea for research comes from someone other than the researcher who carries it out. As Webb (1983) states in the article from which the title of this issue was borrowed: "Who get the credit, the inspirer or the perspirer?" (p. 5)

In studies of team research discussed by Webb, as few as 6% of questionnaire respondents believed that coauthorship should be given to the person who had the original idea if he or she did not take part in the research itself. Even when it was stated that the idea included specific design and methodology, only 54% would give the "inspirer" coauthorship.

Many authors of journal articles now give acknowledgments, if not coauthorship, to those who helped in some way with the research being reported. The number who do not, even though such credit is due, is unknown, but this is not the issue. The issue is that in making credit matter so much, there is risk of wholesale "idea guarding" to the ultimate detriment of the entire discipline.

Title taken from article by W. B. Webb. *APA Monitor,* 1983, *14*(2), p. 5.

REFERENCES

ANDERSON, D. C., & BORKOWSKI, J. G. *Experimental Psychology: Research Tactics and Their Applications*. Glenview, IL: Scott, Foresman, 1978.

COOK, T. D., & CAMPBELL, D. T. The design and conduct of quasi-experiments and true experiments. In M. D. Dunnette (Ed.), *Handbook of Industrial and Organizational Psychology*. Chicago: Rand McNally, 1976.

DALTON, D. R., & PERRY, J. L. Absenteeism and the collective bargaining agreement: An empirical test. *Academy of Management Journal*, 1981, 24(2), 425–431.

FLANAGAN, M. L., & DIPBOYE, R. L. Research settings in industrial and organizational psychology: Facts, fallacies, and the future. *Personnel Psychology*, 1981, 34(1), 37–47.

GARLAND, H. Influence of ability, assigned goals, and normative information on personal goals and performance: A challenge to the goal attainability assumption. *Journal of Applied Psychology*, 1983, 68(1), 20–30.

GREEN, S. G., BLANK, W., & LIDEN, R. C. Market and organizational influences on bank employees' work attitudes and behaviors. *Journal of Applied Psychology*, 1983, 68(2), 298–306.

ILGEN, D. R., NEBEKEN, D. M., & PRITCHARD, R. D. Expectancy theory measures: An empirical comparison in an experimental simulation. *Organizational Behavior and Human Performance*, 1981, 28(2), 189–223.

JEWELL, L. N. Some determinants of job involvement for manufacturing managers. Unpublished study, 1977.

KEARSLEY, G. Think tanks: Bell Laboratories. *APA Monitor*, 1981, 12(11), 1, 4–5.

KIM, J. S., & CAMPAGNA, A. F. Effects of flexitime on employee attendance and performance: A field experiment. *Academy of Management Journal*, 1981, 24(4), 729–741.

KIRK, R. E. *Experimental Design: Procedures for the Behavioral Sciences*. Belmont, CA: Brooks/Cole, 1968.

ROTTER, J. B. Generalized expectancies for internal versus external control of reinforcement. *Psychological Monographs*, 1966, 80(1).

WEBB, W. B. Inspirer or perspirer—who gets the glory when the study ends? *APA Monitor*, 1983, 14(2), 5.

WISE, T. A. The rocky road to the marketplace. *FORTUNE*, 1966, 74(4), 138–212.

The Individual Employee

Part II focuses on finding, hiring, and helping individuals fit into jobs within organizations. Chapter 4 introduces the basic principles of testing that lie behind many organizational screening and selection methods. Chapter 5 examines recruitment of applicants and screening for the purpose of selecting and placing new employees into jobs. Chapter 6 focuses on job training and socialization—the processes by which newcomers to an organization become productive "insiders."

The Foundation of Testing in Organizations

I/O PSYCHOLOGY AT WORK

The Money Test

Tests have been used in making employment decisions in the United States for over 50 years. Although occasional use has been made of personality tests, and content-validated job knowledge and job sample tests have been used with some frequency, the most commonly used employment tests have been measures of cognitive skills; that is, aptitude or ability tests. . . . In the middle and late 1960s certain theories about aptitude and ability tests formed the basis for most discussion of employee selection issues and, in part, the basis for practice in personnel psychology. . . .

One such theory—The Theory of Low Utility—holds that employee selection methods have little impact on the performance and productivity of the resultant work force. . . . The basic equation for determining [if this were true] had been available for years, but it had not been employed because there were no feasible methods for estimating one critical equation parameter: the standard deviation of employee performance in dollars (SD_y). SD_y indexes the magnitude of individual differences in employee yearly output of goods and services. The greater SD_y is, the greater is the payoff in improved productivity from selecting high-performing employees.

During the 1970s, a method was devised for estimating SD_y based on careful estimates by supervisors of employee output. Applications of this method showed that SD_y was larger than expected. For example, for entry-level budget analysts and computer programmers, SD_y was $11,327 and $10,413, respectively. This means that a computer programmer at the 85th percentile in performance is worth $20,800 more per year to the employing organization than a computer programmer at the 15th percentile. Use of valid selection tests substantially increases the average performance level of the resultant work force and therefore substantially improves productivity. For example, use of the Programmer Aptitude Test in place of an invalid selection method to hire 618 entry-level computer programmers leads to an estimated productivity improvement of $54.7 million . . . over a 10-year period if the top 30 percent of applicants are hired. . . .

Excerpted from F. L. Schmidt and J. E. Hunter, "Employment Testing: Old Theories and New Research Findings." *American Psychologist*, 1981, *36*(10), pp. 1128–1137. Copyright 1981 by the American Psychological Association. Title "The Money Test" excerpted from F. L. Schmidt and J. E. Hunter. *Across the Board*, 1982, *19*(7), p. 35. Title used through courtesy of the Conference Board, New York.

For some years, federal government pressures on companies to undertake expensive test validation programs led many organizations to abandon selection testing; they just were not convinced of its worth. Industrial/organizational psychologists were not happy about this state of affairs. When carried out properly, testing programs for selection give organizations employees better suited to their jobs. Such programs also benefit individuals by making it more feasible for them to achieve job success and the rewards that go with it. Thus the development of a way to demonstrate to organizations that selection tests are worth the costs of development and validation was a welcome event.

To demonstrate the cost-effectiveness of selection testing, I/O psychologists had to understand principles of testing as well as selection. For example, to show the productivity improvement associated with using the Programmer Aptitude Test, psychologists had to show the test's *criterion-related validity*. This concept, along with other fundamental testing principles, is discussed in Chapter 4. Selection itself is examined in Chapter 5.

TESTS AND TESTING IN ORGANIZATIONS

Tests are used for many purposes in organizations, but in general these uses fall into one of three categories. There is testing for purposes of *prediction*, as discussed by Schmidt and Hunter (1982) in "The Money Test." There is testing for the purpose of *assessment*, as in performance appraisal that is carried out on a regular basis. Finally, there is testing to generate a *criterion* against which to make some evaluation, such as using performance ratings to validate training methods.

Testing for each of the purposes listed appears in various discussions in this text. Chapter 4 is intended to provide a background for those discussions. For convenience, many of the examples involve testing for selection since this is the topic to be covered in Chapter 5.

What Is Testing?

Tests have been used in organizational settings for at least 50 years and have been used in other contexts for far longer. In the course of this history, many have offered definitions for both *test* and *testing*. Some of these definitions are specific and are tied to the purpose for which the tests are used. For present purposes, however, a broad definition is needed.

Note from the definition that *testing* is an activity. The immediate result of this activity is an estimate of a person's position on some scale of measurement—the *test*. This estimate is usually called a *test score* or, in some cases, a *measurement*.

Testing is the process of making an estimate of an individual's relative or absolute position on some physical, psychological, or behavioral scale of measurement.

Individual characteristics: See pages 28 to 33.

Tests come in a variety of forms, but all attempt to measure some individual physical, psychological, or behavioral characteristic. Examples of *physical characteristics* of interest to I/O psychologists are:

- eyesight
- hearing
- reflexes
- manual dexterity
- manipulation speed (of hands)
- strength

Among the *psychological characteristics* of interest may be:

- personality traits
- perceptions
- attitudes
- needs

Behavioral characteristics often assessed include:

- work history
- job performance
- skills
- communication ability

There are any number of ways for I/O psychologists to go about estimating, or testing, the amount or state of the kinds of individual variables listed. A person's typing skill, for example, might be estimated in absolute terms on the basis of number of words typed in 60 seconds. It might be estimated in relative terms on the basis of ranking as to amount of material typed relative to a group of typists. While some ways of measuring are better than others for particular testing purposes, all contain measurement error.

Error in Testing

The concept of error in testing implies that there is some difference between the *true* level of what is measured and the *obtained* measurement. Because of such error, the definition of testing reads "making an estimate" rather than "determining" an individual's position on a scale of measurement. Although it is theoretically possible for a true score to be obtained, a basic assumption underlying the principles of testing is that all measurement contains error.

Error in testing stems from three sources—the measurement scale (the test), the person taking the test, and the conditions under which the test is given. Any of these sources may produce constant error, unpredictable error, or both. *Constant errors* affect everyone taking a test in the same way (or the same individual all the time). *Unpredictable errors*, as the name suggests, have differential effects—who they will affect and how is not known in advance.

Any student who has taken classroom exams is familiar with a variety of constant and unpredictable errors that affect performance. Three examples of each stemming from the three possible sources are shown in Exhibit 4-1.

Together, constant and unpredictable errors, such as those shown in Exhibit 4-1, combine with "the truth" to give a particular score on a particular test. This may be represented as $X = s + e$ where X is the obtained score, s is the individual's true score, and e is the unpredictable error (Guidon, 1965). Constant errors are combined with the true score since they are conceptually inseparable. The test-anxious student's score, for example, will always reflect the student's fear of tests until he or she is able to overcome that fear. At that point, it will cease to be a source of error.

Since most tests are used to make decisions about individuals (or to help individuals make decisions for themselves), it is important to reduce error in test scores as much as possible. Unpredictable errors cannot be avoided; by definition, they are not known in advance. In fact, they often are not known at all, although the examples in Exhibit 4-1 are obvious ones. Similarly, there is little to be done about constant errors that originate in the person taking the test; these sources of error are rarely known to those who give tests.

Those who develop and those who give tests have the greatest control over constant errors stemming from the test and from the situation under which it is given. This measurement error may be reduced by (a) careful attention to test construction and (b) standard and pleasant testing conditions.

To recapitulate, testing is a process that results in an estimate of an individual's position on some scale of measurement. This result is an estimate rather than a determination because all measurement is subject to error. This error stems from the test, the person being tested, and/or the conditions under which the test is given. Those who use tests can help to reduce error by giving careful attention to the testing situation. Those who develop tests reduce it to the extent that they produce scales of measurement that are both reliable and valid.

Source of Error	Type of Error	
	Constant	Unpredictable
Test	Typographical error	Uneven reproduction; some tests not clear
Person	Fear of tests	Temporary loss of memory; mind "goes blank"
Situation	Crowded room	Uneven desk top makes it difficult to write

EXHIBIT 4-1

Examples of Constant and Unpredictable Errors in Classroom Testing

THE RELIABILITY OF A TEST

If a test is **reliable**, the estimate of an individual's score will be consistent from one time to the next or when different people make the estimate.

Reliability: See page 67.

Reliability refers to consistency. It is a general criterion for any measurement situation, and the term will appear many times in connection with such topics as job analysis, performance appraisal, and training evaluation. The discussion of test reliability provides a foundation for analysis, appraisal, and evaluation as well as for the examination of selection.

If a reading test is reliable, a job applicant should receive about the same score on the test no matter who administers it provided the applicant is tested in a standard way. This individual also should receive about the same score if he or she takes the test twice within a short time interval, with some allowance for practice (a possible positive effect on second score) and fatigue (a possible negative effect on second score).

A **construct** is a term that defines a pattern of observations.

Although the meaning of test reliability is generally agreed upon, reliability is not a *thing* but a *construct*. One familiar example of a construct is *intelligence;* another is *attitude.* Neither intelligence nor attitudes may be observed directly. They are inferred from observations. In other words, the definitions of both intelligence and attitude are *constructed* on the basis of certain behavior patterns. In similar fashion, the definition of reliability is constructed on the basis of observed consistency, in this case consistency of measurement.

Operational definition: See page 48.

Both intelligence and attitudes are complex constructs, and people do not always means the same thing when they use these words. This problem is avoided in I/O psychology research by the use of operational definitions. Intelligence, for example, often is operationally defined as a score on a particular intelligence test.

Like other constructs, test reliability also is defined operationally in research. There are three such definitions, or procedures, commonly used to assess the degree to which a test yields consistent measurements. This consistency is critical to the assessment of test error stemming from the measuring instrument.

Correlation: See pages 61 to 63.

The three basic methods for estimating the reliability of a test are all correlational procedures. They differ, however, in what is correlated with what. As a result, they can yield quite different results because the sources of error included in the calculations differ. Measurements of reliability, therefore, like test scores themselves, should be regarded as estimates.

The Test-Retest Reliability Estimate

One of the more frequently used operational definitions of reliability usually is called *test-retest.* As the name suggests, the variables correlated with this procedure are two measurements from two administrations of the same test to the same people. The resulting correlation coefficient, like all correlation coefficients, is written as r, but is called a *coefficient of stability.* The closer this coefficient is to 1.00, the more reliable the test.

The test-retest procedure for estimating test reliability is quick and easy from the viewpoint of the person interested in the test's reliability. Understandably it is less popular with those who take the test, and it is a safe assumption that some error is introduced into the second test administration by subject impatience or boredom.

Test-retest reliability estimation procedures also can raise practical questions as to the length of time between test administrations. If the time period is too short, the coefficient of stability can be affected by memory, or a *practice effect*, as well as by reduced subject interest. If the time period is too long, subjects may change in some way relevant to the test (have training, gain experience, study the material, and so on).

If practice or changes in subjects affected all of the subjects in a reliability study in exactly the same way, these effects would present no major problem; but it is extremely unlikely that this would happen. Some subjects will have a good memory, others a poor one. Some subjects will have their curiosity aroused by the test and study what they missed, even if they do not know that the test will be given again; others will not bother. The effect of these uneven subject responses is to add error to the reliability estimate of the test involved.

Subjects: See pages 48 to 50.

Because of the potential problems created by the necessary time interval between test and retest, McCormick and Ilgen (1980) suggest that this method will be most useful for estimating the reliability of tests relevant to skills that (a) are not enhanced from the brief practice of the first test administration, and (b) have little connection with memory skills. For example, the reliability of a test of finger dexterity (a psychomotor skill), hearing ability (a sensory skill), or problem solving (a cognitive skill) might be estimated by the test-retest procedure without time-interval problems.

The Internal Consistency Reliability Estimate

Some of the problems of subject motivation, memory, and practice raised by the test-retest method of estimating test reliability can be avoided by using an *internal consistency* estimation. In this procedure, subjects take one test. Afterwards the test is divided, for purposes of estimating reliability, into two parts; now each subject has two scores, and these are correlated with one another.

The most common way for researchers to divide a test to estimate its reliability is to use the odd-numbered items as one test and the even-numbered items as the other. When the two are correlated, the resulting coefficient is called a *coefficient of internal consistency* or a *split-half coefficient*.

Although the split-half procedure circumvents the problems raised by the same test being given twice, it has problems of its own. Unless a test is very long, the coefficient of internal consistency is likely to yield a conservative (low) estimate of reliability. This problem is illustrated in "Spotlight on Research."

Dreher and Mai-Dalton (1983) used the historical study approach to investigate the question of the internal consistency of a test being used in I/O psychology research. They went one step farther than the usual procedure for estimating reliability and estimated the internal consistency of the four *scales* of the test. Part of their explanation for the unacceptable

Historical study: See pages 57 to 58.

SPOTLIGHT ON RESEARCH

A Note on the Internal Consistency of the Manifest Needs Questionnaire

Research question: Does the internal consistency of the four scales of the Manifest Needs Questionnaire (MNQ) meet acceptable reliability standards?

Type of study: Historical.

Subjects: The eight studies reviewed included (employed) management students, managers, hospital employees in various jobs, production workers, administrative workers, state/county government employees, and new employees in a British financial organization.

General procedure: Data from eight published studies of the reliability of the MNQ were analyzed. (The authors also administered the questionnaire themselves. This study is not reported here.)

Results:

MNQ Scale	Range of Estimates	Median
Need for Achievement	.31 — .66	.40
Need for Affiliation	−.17 — .56	.09
Need for Autonomy	.31 — .68	.42
Need for Dominance	.46 — .83	.60

Conclusion: "Only the n Dom *(Need for Dominance)* scale demonstrates a minimally useful degree of internal consistency across all reported studies" (p. 196).

Summarized from G. F. Dreher and R. R. Mai-Dalton, "A Note on the Internal Consistency of the Manifest Needs Questionnaire." *Journal of Applied Psychology,* 1983, 68(1), pp. 194–196.

reliability of three of these scales centers around the fact that each has only a few items. The authors suggest that researchers interested in using the Manifest Needs Questionnaire (MNQ) should consider the development of additional items in order to make the test longer.

In addition to the effect of test length on the internal consistency estimate of test reliability, there also can be problems in getting a test split that results in two tests of the same difficulty. Unequal halves are more likely if a test is split first half/last half than if it is split odd/even. Nevertheless, the careful test evaluator will use one of the statistical formulas available that yields an *average* reliability coefficient based on all possible splits of the test. The best-known of these are the K-R formulas 20 and 21 (Richardson & Kuder, 1939) and the Alpha coefficient (Chronbach, 1965).

The Equivalent Forms Reliability Estimate

An alternative to (a) lengthening or (b) using one of the formulas for estimating all possible splits of a test as ways around the potential problems of using equivalent forms to estimate reliability is to begin with two tests. If the tests cover the same material and are equivalent in form and difficulty, reliability of the test may be estimated by means of the equivalent forms procedure. Each subject takes each form of the test and the resulting scores are correlated; this is the *equivalent forms* estimate of reliability.

The correlation coefficient resulting from the equivalent forms method of assessing reliability is called a *coefficient of equivalence.* The name of this coefficient provides a clue as to the greatest problem with this procedure —the construction of equivalent forms. The question of reliability is a question of consistency in measuring the same thing. If the different forms of a test are not equivalent, then the same thing is not being measured, and the estimate of reliability will be lowered accordingly.

Equivalent test forms are often difficult and time consuming to construct. In addition, before they can be used to estimate test reliability, the forms themselves must be tested for equivalence on different subjects. Once the test has been shown to have adequate reliability, however, having equivalent forms on hand can be useful. For example, if testing is done in a group, one potential source of measurement error will be reduced if people sitting next to one another have different forms of the test.

To recapitulate, there are three commonly-used ways to estimate test reliability. Each has certain advantages and disadvantages. Administratively, the internal consistency method is the simplest because subjects take one test once. For shorter tests, however, the test-retest method or the equivalent forms method may be preferable.

Interpreting a Reliability Coefficient

The three methods described for estimating the extent to which a test is a reliable measuring scale all yield a single number. This number is expressed as r and varies between 0 and 1.00. The question is: What does this number mean? For example, does a coefficient of .61 indicate acceptable test reliability or not?

Most psychologists would agree that a test reliability coefficient in the high .80s or above is acceptable, with figures in the .90s desirable. There is less agreement as to the *minimally acceptable* figure because psychologists use tests for many different purposes. Recall, for example, the conclusion relevant to the internal consistency of the MNQ in "Spotlight on Research." Dreher and Mai-Dalton (1983) found a median internal consistency reliability estimate of .60 to be "minimally useful." This figure seems low, but the test involved is one that is used most extensively for research purposes, not for making employment decisions.

The considerations involved in evaluating the evidence for a test's reliability are discussed in detail in textbooks on testing. Without such comprehensive knowledge, the safest rule of thumb is probably "the higher the better," because the reliability of a test has a direct bearing on the test's standard error of measurement.

The Standard Error of Measurement

*The standard deviation of a test score for a single individual is called the **standard error of measurement.***

Estimates of a test's reliability are estimates of the error made in assessing an individual's true position on a scale of measurement. Theoretically, if the same person were measured a large number of times, the obtained measurements would be spread around this individual's true score. Some of these estimates would be closer to this true score than others because some test administrations would include less error than others. By using certain statistical transformations, all of the obtained scores could be depicted in the form of a normal curve, such as those shown in Exhibit 4–2.

Normal curve: See pages 59 to 60.

The standard error of measurement relates to the distribution of scores that would be obtained if one person were given the test many times (although it is obtained statistically on the basis of the test being given to many people). The larger the standard error of measurement of a test, the more the test score distribution is spread around the true score. In Exhibit 4–2, the standard error of measurement of Test A is approximately one-half that of Test B. This means that a score obtained from Test A is more likely to be near a person's true score than a score obtained from Test B.

The standard error of measurement of a particular test has important implications for decisions made on the basis of scores obtained with the test. For example, the Scholastic Aptitude Test (SAT) has a standard error of measurement of 30. This means that there is a high probability that an obtained score of 530 on the SAT represents a true score as low as 500 or as high as 560. Thus a school that requires a student to score 550 on the SAT for admission could be rejecting a student with a score of 530 solely on the basis of test measurement error.

There are ways to increase the reliability of a test and thus decrease the standard error of measurement. The most common is to increase the length of the test in order to achieve a more stable sample of the characteristic being measured. This strategy is discussed briefly in connection with the internal consistency method of estimating reliability and may be studied further in courses specifically devoted to testing.

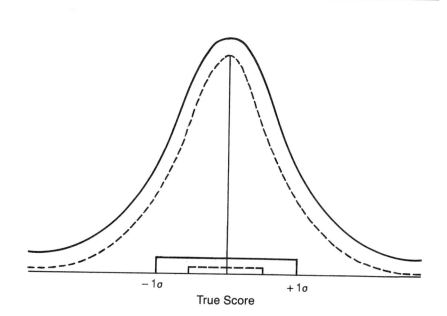

EXHIBIT 4–2

The Standard Error
of Measurement

True Score

−1σ   +1σ

Standard deviation: See
page 60.

– – – Test A
——— Test B

The validity of a test is the topic to be expanded here. This does not
imply however, that validity is more important than reliability in evaluating a test because an unreliable test cannot be valid. *A reliable test is
not necessarily valid, but unless a test is reliable, the issue of validity is irrelevant.*

THE VALIDITY OF A TEST

In its broadest sense, the word *validity* means *truth.* Thus, the validity
of a test may be defined as the extent to which the test yields the truth
about that which is being measured. (Reliability, remember, refers to
how consistently a test measures *whatever* it is measuring.) This definition of validity often is expressed as shown.

This commonly encountered definition is useful for some purposes,
but there are different ways of looking at what a test is supposed to
measure. For example, if the test is an intelligence test, the psychologist
can make a case that it should measure (a) the likelihood of a person
being successful in some future endeavor, such as being a graduate
student, (b) samples of behavior believed to be made possible by higher
intelligence, such as problem-solving ability, or (c) the meaning of intelligence itself. Which of these is of interest in any particular situation
depends upon the reason for testing.

The **validity** of a test is
the extent to which the
test measures what it is
supposed to measure.

Validity: See page 67.

Inference: See page 58.   Because reasons for testing differ, the inferences whose truth is of concern differ. As a consequence, there has grown up a convention of making distinctions between different kinds of validity. Concerning what a test should measure, (a), (b), and (c) listed in the previous paragraph are called *criterion-related, content,* and *construct validity,* respectively.

Like reliability estimates, the validity of a test is assessed by means of correlation and expressed in the form of a correlation coefficient. Unlike operational definitions of reliability, however, the choice of a procedure for estimating validity depends heavily upon the use to which the test will be put. This is the practical basis for maintaining a distinction between kinds of validities.

Many tests in organizations are used for predictive purposes; in this case, the appropriate operational definition is criterion-related validity. Other tests are used for purposes of assessing the current state of an individual's knowledge, skill, or job performance. In such cases, content validity is of primary importance.

Criterion-related validity and content validity are examined further here as a basis for later discussions of organizational selection and performance appraisal. Refer to Messick (1980) or a text on psychological testing for details of the more complex process of establishing construct validity.

Criterion-Related Validity

For a test to have criterion-related validity, it should yield a measurement that is related to some behavioral criterion. Frequently-used criteria in I/O psychology include:

- training progress
- job performance
- absenteeism
- turnover
- rate of job advancement

As an example of criterion-related validity, consider using a test of arithmetic computational ability to predict performance in a training program for bookkeepers. If those who did better on the test also learned the training material more quickly and made fewer errors, the test would have criterion-related validity. The criteria in this case are speed and *Scattergram: See pages 61 to 62.* accuracy. This concept is illustrated graphically by the scattergram in Exhibit 4–3.

Exhibit 4–3 shows the result of graphing the scores made by 16 trainees on an arithmetic computation test against evaluations made by their training instructor at the end of two weeks of training. Note that higher test scores tend to go with higher evaluations; this is a graphic picture of the test's criterion-related validity.

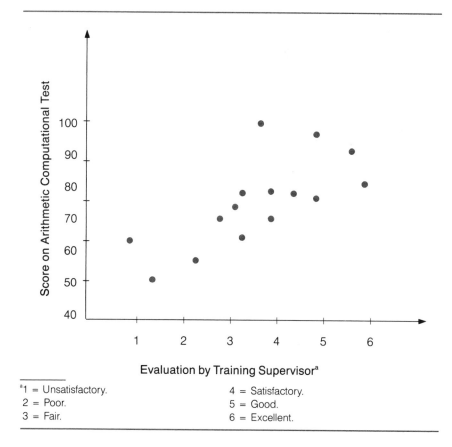

EXHIBIT 4–3

A Graphic Illustration of Criterion-Related Validity

Score on Arithmetic Computational Test

Evaluation by Training Supervisor[a]

[a]1 = Unsatisfactory.   4 = Satisfactory.
2 = Poor.   5 = Good.
3 = Fair.   6 = Excellent.

The Predictive Design for Criterion-Related Validity

Criterion-related validity is an operational definition of validity from which inferences are made about a test's ability to *predict*. Thus the basic model for estimating criterion-related validity is called a *predictive design*. Test scores taken *now* are correlated with scores obtained *later* on some criterion measure for the same subjects. This is the design that is used in Exhibit 4–3. Arithmetic test scores obtained before training were correlated with supervisor evaluations obtained after training.

The predictive design long has been considered the preferred design for estimating criterion-related validity, but it has drawbacks in applied settings. A major drawback has to do with the subjects available. To be carried out correctly, this procedure requires that subjects in the validation sample have a full range of scores on the test being validated. This means that some job applicants with low test scores must be hired, which can be difficult to explain to those who do hiring for a company. An alternative design for assessing criterion-related validity that circumvents this problem is called the concurrent, or current employee, design.

Sample: See pages 49 to 50.

The Concurrent Design for Criterion-Related Validity

The *concurrent design* for estimating a test's criterion-related validity differs from the predictive design in that it uses people already employed as subjects. It is not necessary to hire any new employees with low test scores. The test to be validated is given to current employees, and scores are correlated with the appropriate criterion measures for the same employees.

The concurrent design for estimating criterion-related validity does not affect the hiring of new employees until the test has been validated. It also has the advantage of eliminating the time lag between collecting the test scores and collecting the criterion scores, but this method is not without its drawbacks either. For example, in such a study, it is necessary to assure employees that test results will not affect their jobs. Consequently, since nothing is "riding on the results," many of these subjects will not approach the test in the same way job applicants would; yet job applicants make up the population for which the test is intended.

Population: See page 49.

Restriction of Range

The validation sample used in a concurrent criterion-related validity study may not include subjects from the lower end of the test score range. If the test does have a relationship to some measure of job success, it may be expected that most of those employees who would have scored at the lowest levels already have quit or have been terminated from the organization. A graphic example of the problem that can be created by this *restriction of range* of test scores is shown in Exhibit 4–4.

The graph in Exhibit 4–4 illustrates the relationship between scores on a selection test and six-month performance evaluations for a full range of test scores. The correlation coefficient between these two measures is approximately .40. The boxed portion of the graph shows what a scattergram would look like only for those subjects who scored 60 or above on the test.

Note the almost circular pattern of dots in the boxed portion of Exhibit 4–4. Such a pattern is the classic representation of no relationship between variables. In this case then, a test put to a concurrent criterion-related validity study would be rejected as a selection device if it happened that most of the people still employed scored over 60.

There are statistical procedures for dealing with the problems of range restriction, although a full range of actual scores is preferable. It this is not possible, it may be desirable to use a mixed strategy for determining a test's criterion-related validity. A limited concurrent study could be done to get an idea of the test's potential. If findings are encouraging, the test then could be given to incoming employees who are hired on some *other* basis; over time a sufficient number of cases will be accumulated to carry out the usual predictive study of criterion-related validity.

Validity Generalization

Whatever approach is taken, time is needed to estimate the criterion-related validity of a test. A reasonable question to ask is: Is it necessary

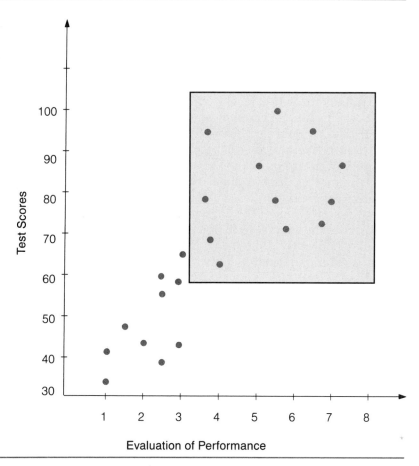

EXHIBIT 4–4

The Problem of
Range Restriction
in Correlation

to conduct a separate study for every job for which the test might be used as a job success predictor? In other words, can evidence of criterion-related validity be generalized beyond the sample on which it is established?

The answer to the question of whether or not a test (or tests) validated for one job may be used for employment decisions about other jobs is "yes," *provided* it can be shown that the various jobs involve ". . . essentially the same work behaviors" (Equal Employment Opportunity Commission, 1978, Section 7B).

Establishing validity generalization on the basis of work behaviors required by a job begins with job analysis—the process of breaking a job down into its components to reveal what job holders actually *do*. Such analysis often reveals that jobs with different titles, such as bookkeeper, bank teller, and customer service clerk, actually require about the same work behaviors from those who perform them. Where this is true, a test validated for selecting employees for one type of job legally may be used

Predictor variable: See pages 64 to 65.

Generalization: See page 67.

EEO: See page 30.

for selecting employees for the other jobs. This validity generalization often is called *job component validity.*

The results of validity generalization research are mixed but encouraging. On the positive side, Pearlman, Schmidt, and Hunter (1980) outright reject the necessity for doing separate validity studies for each job. Their conclusions are based on an analysis of some 700 studies of predictive validity for clerical jobs.

The conclusion of Pearlman and his colleagues was extended by Schmidt, Hunter, and Pearlman (1981) to aptitude testing in general. Some researchers, however, still urge caution. For example, Brown (1981) found that over a third of the variance in predicting the performance of life insurance agents was due to differences in their work situations.

Variance: See page 64.

Validity generalization research offers the most immediately promising hope for a way out of the difficulties created by federal government constraints on the use of tests in organizations. This problem is discussed further in Chapters 5 and 13. It should be noted, however, that the extent to which criterion-related validity can be generalized always will be limited by several factors outside of government regulation. Among these are:

- the type of predictor test;
- the complexity of the job criteria to be predicted;
- the number of validity studies available for a particular test.

Content Validity

The sum total of all of the questions that might be on a test (that are **relevant**) is called the **domain** of the test.

Content validity usually is defined in one or both of two ways. One is the *relevance* of what is on the test to what it is that is to be measured. For example, a multiplication problem is relevant to a test of arithmetic computational ability, but asking someone to spell "multiplication" is not. The second aspect of content validity is the *representativeness* of what is on the test relative to what might be on it.

The concept of a test that is representative of its relevant domain may be illustrated by an example familiar to all college students—the exam. Suppose that the professor of this course gave an exam that was said to cover Chapter 3. Further suppose that all of the questions on the test were about statistical analysis.

In the case just described, it is likely that the halls would ring with the cries of "unfair!" Statistical analysis is only one of the topics presented in Chapter 3; that is, the questions on the test are not a *representative sample* of the relevant domain of questions to evaluate student knowledge of Chapter 3. As a measure of that knowledge, therefore, such a test would have low content validity. Content validity, as defined by relevance and representativeness is illustrated graphically in Exhibit 4–5.

In Exhibit 4–5, the square represents the appropriate domain of the test—the material in Chapter 3, to continue with that example. Dots inside the square are *relevant* test items. The areas labeled A, B, and C represent three possible tests of this material.

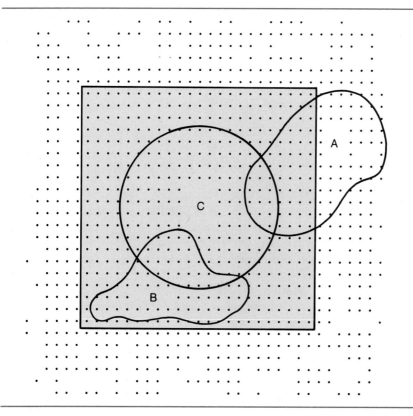

EXHIBIT 4–5

The Concept of
Content Validity

- Test A contains items that are *not domain relevant;* for example, the professor might have included some questions about Chapter 4 on the test.
- Test B contains items that are relevant but *not representative.* All come from one section of the domain. This is the test described in the example; all of the questions were on statistical analysis.
- Test C has the greatest content validity. All of its questions lie inside the square, and it includes questions from all sections of the domain.

Although the example is from an academic setting, the principle of content validity is the same whatever kind of test is involved. For example, a typing test that required job applicants to type only numbers would have low content validity—its "items" would be relevant but not representative of general typing skills. (The test would be appropriate if the job in question involved a person typing only numbers.)

Content validity is more difficult to establish than criterion-related validity because with the latter, the numbers "speak for themselves." In fact, if prediction were the only factor to be considered, it would not matter what was on a test as long as the scores it generated had a high correlation with some criterion. By contrast, what is on a test is exactly the issue when content validity is under consideration.

The establishment of **content validity** rests on judgments about the correspondence between test content and test domain.

Judgments about test content can be made only by human beings, so they are affected considerably by the knowledge, expertise, and biases, of the people involved. Where possible, therefore, it is better to use more than one judge to evaluate the content validity of a test; gaps in one person's knowledge or experience may be filled in by another, and biases of one may be offset by the opposite biases of another. This concept is addressed again in the discussion of performance appraisal in Chapter 13.

Interpreting a Validity Coefficient

Interpreting a validity correlation coefficient is a complex issue involving both theoretical and practical concerns. Content validity interpretation presents particular problems because the process of obtaining the coefficient is so subjective. The current discussion is confined to the more common requirement of interpreting a criterion-related validity coefficient.

In the section on reliability, it is noted that most psychologists will accept a reliability estimate that lies in or above the upper .80 range. Things are not so straightforward with respect to criterion-related validity. Within 70 years of employment testing, these validity coefficients have seldom exceeded .50. Compared with reliability coefficients that routinely lie in the .90 plus range, such a figure seems small indeed.

Although reliability coefficients often come close to a perfect correlation of 1.00, it must be kept in mind that a reliability estimate is a correlation of two measures of the same thing. By contrast, a validity coefficient is an estimate of the correlation between two different things —a test score and some other behavior.

Behavior causation: See pages 27 to 28.

The kinds of behaviors that I/O psychologists are interested in predicting by means of tests are complex ones. As discussed in Chapter 2, they have multiple and complex causes. Whatever a test is measuring, it is unlikely that it can "tap" more than a small number of the factors relevant to the behavior that the test is used to predict. In other words, one test is unlikely to explain more than a relatively small percentage of the variance in the behavior of interest. For a test that correlates .50 with some criterion, this percentage, called the coefficient of determination, is .25.

The **coefficient of determination** is the square of the correlation coefficient between test and criterion.

The ability of one test to account for the variance in any behavioral criterion definitely is limited. Because of this limitation, there might seem little reason to put resources into constructing, validating, and using tests for predictive purposes in organizations; however, the prediction that has been under discussion is *statistical prediction*, which is related to the concept of variance accounted for. The rationale for using tests in organizations is based on *functional prediction*, that is, on the *utility* of a test for adding to effective decision making.

Statistical Validity Versus Utility

Whatever their specific purpose, the use of tests in organizations is not conceptually different from research, as it is discussed in Chapter 3. Observations, in the form of test scores, are used to make inferences. In the case of testing in organizations, the inferences concern such questions as whether or not individuals are likely to perform well if hired, whether or not they will stay with the organization after training, or whether or not they should be promoted or given special educational opportunities.

Observations: See page 46.

As in all research, confidence in inferences made from tests is increased to the extent that the measurements have demonstrated reliability and validity. In an applied setting, however, validity is a very practical issue. A test may account for only a small percentage of the variance in a criterion measure of job success, yet still bring about improvement in selection decisions; that is, it still may have *utility* for the organization.

Testing and Success Rate for Hiring

Utility is relevant to any kind of test for any kind of personnel decision, but it can be seen most clearly in the context of a company's success rate for hiring. There are two types of selection errors that can lower an organization's success rate. Hiring people who do not work out is called a *false positive* error. The opposite error is called a *false negative* error. The relationship between false positive/false negative errors and good decisions in hiring is shown in Exhibit 4-6.

The term **success rate** refers to the percentage of hired employees who measure up to some standard, such as performance, attendance, or tenure.

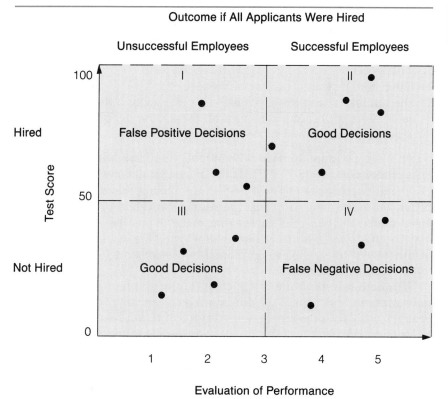

Outcome if All Applicants Were Hired

Unsuccessful Employees   Successful Employees

EXHIBIT 4-6

Errors in the Selection Process

The base of Exhibit 4–6 is a graph showing the relationship between test scores on a selection test (the predictor) and a general evaluation of job performance (the criterion). To illustrate the point, it will be assumed that all new employees hired into this company for a given period of time were given the test. The results of the test were *not* used for selection, however; scores were filed away to be used later when performance evaluations were available for these employees.

To understand the graph in Exhibit 4–6, two more assumptions must be made. The first is that if the test *had* been used for hiring, a score of 50 would have been passing, and applicants who scored below 50 would not have been hired. The second is that employees who receive a performance evaluation above the midpoint on the scale are considered by this organization to be "successful" and the rest to be "unsuccessful."

On the basis of the information given about Exhibit 4–6, the meaning of false positives, false negatives, and good decisions becomes clear. Each dot in the scattergram represents one employee's position with respect to test score and performance evaluation. The employees in Quadrant I had high test scores. It was predicted that they would work out, but they were given low performance evaluations; hence the label "false positives." The opposite holds true for employees in Quadrant IV; on the basis of the test, they would not have been hired, but they are good employees. For these individuals, an incorrect "no" decision would have been made, so these decisions are called "false negatives."

The role that a test can play in improving a selection system (increasing the number of cases in Quadrant II relative to Quadrant I in Exhibit 4–6) depends upon three factors:

1. how good the success rate is without the test;
2. the criterion-related validity of the test;
3. the number of applicants available for every job. If this *selection ratio* is 1:1 (one applicant for every job), there is no decision to be made among applicants and no reason to use a test.

When there *are* more applicants than jobs, there is a selection decision to be made. The question of the utility of a particular test is the question of whether or not the test will help those making this decision to do a better job. Fortunately for busy personnel managers or I/O psychologists, there are published tables that make it possible to answer this question if the three kinds of information listed are available. A portion of the first of these tables, developed by Taylor and Russell (1939) is reproduced in Exhibit 4–7.

Although it is daunting in appearance, the graph in Exhibit 4–7 actually presents a picture of the difference between statistical validity and utility. Consider, for example, a test with a criterion-related validity coefficient of .50. This test accounts for only 25% of the variance in the performance criterion. Now look at the dark lines in the graph.

The success rate for the graph in Exhibit 4–7 is 50% (see top of graph). The dark line indicates that a company only having to hire half of the people who apply (a 50% selection ratio) can push this success rate up to almost 70% by using a test with a validity coefficient of .50. The im-

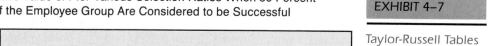

EXHIBIT 4–7

Taylor-Russell Tables

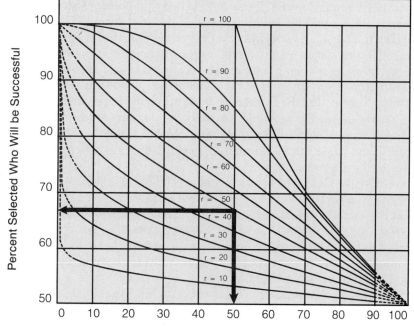

Note. From H. C. Taylor and J. T. Russell, "The Relationship of Validity Coefficients to the Practical Effectiveness of Tests in Selection: Discussion and Tables." *Journal of Applied Psychology*, 1939, *23*, p. 569.

pressive monetary savings that can be effected by such an improvement have been documented by Schmidt and Hunter (1981).

The Taylor-Russell Tables have assisted I/O psychologists and others in evaluating the utility of tests for almost 50 years. It is for this historical value that one of the original graphs was reproduced here. Newer tabular forms of the tables are used more frequently today (see McCormick & Ilgen, 1980). It should be noted also that other sets of tables have been developed for the same purpose (e.g., Naylor & Shine, 1965).

ISSUES IN TEST VALIDATION RESEARCH

The process of validating a test can be a long one, and it ends with a number—a correlation coefficient. On the basis of this number, some important decisions may be made; therefore I/O psychologists constantly are alert to problems that may introduce error into validation research. Two problems are discussed in connection with this research—sampling error and moderator/suppressor variables.

Sampling Error

Sampling error refers to bias that reduces the extent to which a sample is representative of the relevant population.

The theme that all measurement incorporates error has been a recurring one in Chapters 3 and 4. It has been noted that one consistent source of error is the subjects being observed. The term for all of the ways in which the particular subjects of an experiment (including test takers in a reliability or validity study) may differ in some important aspect from other subjects who might have been observed or tested is *sampling error.*

In terms from Chapter 3, the effect of sampling error is to reduce the ability to *generalize* the inferences that can be made on the basis of a set of observations. For example, suppose that for some reason an I/O psychologist could administer an experimental test only to those job applicants who came into a company's personnel office between three and five in the afternoon.

Under the described conditions, any estimate of a test's validity would be based upon a biased sample. The exact nature of the bias is unknown, but the sample almost certainly would include a disproportionate number of (a) "late starters" and (b) job applicants who got going early in the day and have already applied (and perhaps been tested) at other companies. The applicants who got an early start are likely to be tired and perhaps be discouraged as well.

The kinds of bias described almost certainly would result in a sample of test scores that would differ from those that would be obtained by testing applicants who came to the personnel office over the course of a full day. The generalizability of validity estimates based on such a sample is questionable. The coefficients obtained could be significantly different from those that would have been obtained with a more representative sample of job applicants.

The example represents an obvious sampling error that is easy to avoid; but the realities of conducting research, whether to validate a selection test or to achieve some other purpose, are that some kind of sampling error is a foregone conclusion in most cases. This is a reason why the scientific method stresses verification.

Replication: See page 48.

Verification in validity research involves checking the first estimates of validity on another sample, that is, *replicating* the study. Unless there is some reason to suspect that an entire sample is biased, as in the example described earlier, replication frequently is carried out with some portion of the total available sample of subjects. This "sample of a sample" is called a *hold-out sample* because it consists of subjects who are held out of the original data analysis (even though the subjects were tested in the same study).

One replication of a validation study is considered the absolute minimum in acceptable procedure if a test is to be used in an applied setting. If the test is used for any length of time, reevaluation at intervals also is necessary. Jobs change, standards change, and the characteristics of job applicants to a particular organization change.

Moderator Variables

In Chapter 3, the concepts of independent, dependent, and predictor variables were introduced. There are, of course, no real independent and dependent variables in test validation research. This research is for the purpose of establishing relationships between *predictor* and *criterion variables*. An interesting chapter in the history of selection testing was written when it was suggested that another member of the variable family —the moderator variable—might be affecting studies of this relationship.

Although they are seldom labeled as such, moderator variables are known to most people. A familiar example is the "wind chill factor," which moderates the relationship between thermometer reading and perceived air temperature. Other moderator variables will be met frequently in chapters to come.

Moderator variables began to receive widespread attention when selection testing came under fire as a possible means of perpetuating racial bias in organizations. The question arose when it was pointed out that racial minorities were being left out of jobs in disproportionate numbers even when validated tests were being used for selection. It looked as though race might be *modifying* the basic test score-job criterion relationship established by validity studies.

A simple illustration of race as a moderator variable in testing can be seen in Exhibit 4–8. Graph (A) of that exhibit depicts the results of an hypothetical criterion-related validity study that includes both whites (•) and nonwhites (x) in the sample. The trend of these data (a more or less straight line from lower left to upper right) suggests a modest but acceptable correlation; actual calculations would probably show sufficient validity for selection purposes.

Graph (B) depicts the results of the same hypothetical study if only white subjects are used. Graph (C) illustrates the results if only nonwhite subjects are used. Note that the positive correlation shown in (A) holds and looks stronger in (B), but disappears in (C). This is the concept of *differential validity*; the criterion-related validity is *different* for the two groups of subjects. In the graphs in Exhibit 4–8, the criterion-related validity is acceptable (even rather high) for whites but close to zero for nonwhites. In other words, race *modifies* the test-job performance relationship.

The implications of differential validity for equal employment opportunity led to an intense but short revolution in I/O psychology testing research. Moderator variable research, or *subgroup analysis*, became part of every testing program. Sex, education, social class, and various personality traits, as well as race, came under scrutiny as possible moderator variables.

As has often happened in applied psychology, the initial excitement over moderator variables was followed by a more sober examination of the results of this research. The bulk of that evidence suggests that the appearance of differential validity is most often due to chance or to statistical artifacts. In a 1979 review, Hunter, Schmidt, and Hunter concluded that there probably is no true differential test validity.

A variable that has a predictable influence on the nature of the relationship between two other variables is called a **moderator variable.**

EXHIBIT 4-8

The Concept of
Differential Validity

(A) All Subjects

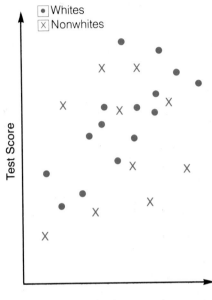

(B) White Subjects

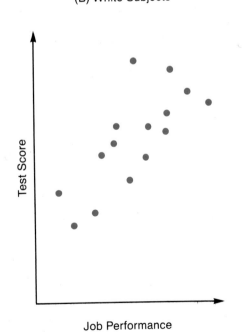

(C) Nonwhite Subjects

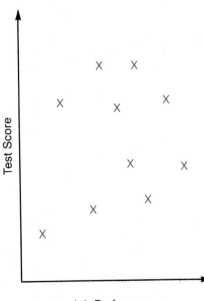

The mainstream of thought in I/O psychology today seems to be that differential validity is not a cause for concern in employment testing. The general issue of white/nonwhite differences in testing still persists, however; today it manifests itself under the label of "test fairness." This concept is explored in the "At Issue" section of Chapter 4.

Suppressor Variables

The most exotic member of the variable family in testing is called a *suppressor variable*. Like a moderator variable, a suppressor variable affects the relationship between other variables; its effect, however, is quite different.

A moderator variable alters a relationship between two other variables. A **suppressor variable** hides it.

In personnel testing, suppressor variables present themselves in the form of abilities required to *take* a test that are not the abilities *measured* by the test. Common examples are (a) the reading skills required to take a personality or arithmetic test and (b) the reasoning abilities required to understand job sample tests. A suppressor variable, in other words, adds error to measurement.

The most widespread effort to deal systematically with suppressor variables in psychology occurred in the 1960s. At that time, considerable effort was devoted to developing culture-fair intelligence tests. A culture-fair test of intelligence is one that measures intelligence not education, exposure to general knowledge, reading ability, and other such experience-related variables. The term *culture-fair* is derived from the fact that these variables are affected strongly by the culture or subculture in which a person grows up.

The development of culture-fair tests of intelligence was not wholly successful. One problem was a lack of consensus as to the "pure" meaning of intelligence. Culture-fair tests also were criticized broadly on humanistic grounds. Many held that such tests approached an important social problem from the wrong end; the point was to eliminate cultural disadvantageousness, not to find ways to construct tests around it.

All-out efforts to find and eliminate suppressor variables from tests used in organizations have been abandoned almost entirely. An easier solution is to include a test of a variable suspected of masking a relationship in the criterion-related validity study. The relationships then may be sorted out statistically. In obvious cases, more practical approaches may be taken. For example, job applicants in certain areas of the country routinely are offered their choice of tests in either English or Spanish.

Concluding Remarks

As a subject matter for study, testing covers a wide area. Many topics are not discussed in Chapter 4, among them test development, test administration, and the ethical issues that can be raised by testing. Chapter 4 provides a basic foundation for understanding such issues as they arise in subsequent chapters.

Those interested in testing as a separate field of study are referred to such readings as that by Kaplan and Sacuzzo (1982) or the excellent summary article by Green (1981). A discussion of testing from the standpoint of social concerns regarding the assessment of individuals may be found in Haney (1981).

SUMMARY

Testing is the process by which an estimate is made of an individual's position on some physical, psychological, or behavioral scale of measurement. In organizations, such testing is used for purposes of prediction, assessment, and generating criteria against which to make various evaluations.

All test results contain error. Some error stems from the subjects who take the test, some from the conditions under which the test is given, and some from the test itself. Errors resulting from the test itself can be reduced by careful attention to test reliability and validity.

In testing, reliability refers to consistency of test results. It is evaluated by a variety of operational definitions of consistency. Each yields a correlation coefficient ranging between zero and 1.00; the closer to 1.00 the coefficient, the more reliable the test.

The validity of a test is best conceptualized as the confidence in making certain inferences on, or about, the test. Criterion-related validity refers to inferences about the relationship between test scores and some other behavior. Content and construct validities are relevant to the internal relationship between what is on the test and what is being measured.

Like reliability, validity is estimated by means of correlation coefficients. Interpretation, however, is a relative matter in applied settings because the utility of a test may be of more concern than its statistical validity.

AT ISSUE

Test Fairness

There are numerous definitions of *test fairness* in the literature and some complex statistical models as well. The essence of the issue, however, has been simply stated by Schmidt and Hunter (1981).

The theory of test unfairness ". . . holds that even if validity coefficients are equal for minority and majority groups, a test is likely to be unfair if the average test score is lower for minorities" (p. 1131).

Schmidt and Hunter go on to note that the theory of test unfairness is based on the assumption that the causal factors lying behind lower test scores for minorities are not related to lower job performance. All available evidence contradicts this assumption. Ability and skill differences that appear on tests are associated with differences in job performance; they are real, not created by "unfair" tests. This suggests that tests revealing such differences are doing what they are intended to do—assessing differences between individuals. Efforts to construct and use tests in order to make these differences disappear in the name of "fairness" destroy both the purpose and the utility of the tests.

Many of those who struggle with the problems currently plaguing test usage in organizations believe that some important issues have become thoroughly confused. Many people in this country have not had or have not taken advantage of educational and cultural experiences associated with better test performance in general. No amount of sophisticated test validation research or legal haggling will change that, however. Thus, many believe that we are not only trying to do the impossible, but also wasting valuable resources in the process. As Tenopyr (1981) expresses it:

> Many of the resources that could be devoted to solving the educational and social problems that underlie the testing issue are being squandered on needless research and legal activities. If the amount of money spent on legal activities alone were used constructively to fund educational programs for the disadvantaged, a great deal could be done both for those who have been excluded from the benefits of our society and for the country as a whole (p. 1125).

Tests, as tests, are neither fair nor unfair. They are simply more or less good at measuring what they are intended to measure; that is, they are more or less reliable and valid. As a result, some are more vulnerable to being *used* unfairly than others are. Neither Tenopyr nor anyone else who has expressed similar opinions suggest that efforts to improve tests and the way they are used should be abandoned. They do challenge the basic assumptions of those who seek to solve a serious social problem by attacking the use of employment tests.

REFERENCES

BROWN, S. H. Validity generalization and situational moderation in the life insurance industry. *Journal of Applied Psychology,* 1981, *66*(6), 664–670.

CHRONBACH, L. J. *Essentials of Psychological Testing.* New York: McGraw-Hill, 1965.

DREHER, G. F., & MAI-DALTON, R. R. A note on the internal consistency of the Manifest Needs Questionnaire. *Journal of Applied Psychology,* 1983, *68*(1), 194–196.

EQUAL EMPLOYMENT OPPORTUNITY COMMISSION. Adoption by four agencies of "Uniform Guidelines on Employee Selection Procedures." *Federal Register,* 1978, *43*, 38290–38315.

GREEN, B. F. A primer of testing. *American Psychologist,* 1981, *36*(10), 1001–1011.

GUION, R. M. *Personnel Testing.* New York McGraw-Hill, 1965.

HANEY, W. Validity, vaudeville, and values: A short history of social concerns over standardized testing. *American Psychologist,* 1981, *36*(10), 1021–1034.

HUNTER, J. E., SCHMIDT, F. L., & HUNTER, R. Differential validity of employment tests by race: A comprehensive review and analysis. *Psychological Bulletin,* 1979, *86*(4), 721–735.

KAPLAN, R. M., & SACCUZZO, D. P. *Psychological Testing: Principles, Applications, and Issues.* Monterey, CA: Brooks/Cole, 1982.

McCORMICK, E. J., & ILGEN, D. *Industrial Psychology* (7th ed.). Englewood Cliffs, NJ: Prentice-Hall, 1980.

MESSICK, S. Test validity and the ethics of assessment. *American Psychologist,* 1980, *35*(11), 1012–1027.

NAYLOR, J. C., & SHINE, L. C. A table for determining the increase in mean criterion score obtained by using a selection device. *Journal of Industrial Psychology,* 1965, *3*, 33–42.

PEARLMAN, K., SCHMIDT, F. L., & HUNTER, J. E. Validity generalization results for tests used to predict job proficiency and training success in clerical occupations. *Journal of Applied Psychology,* 1980, *65*(4), 373–406.

RICHARDSON, M. W., & KUDER, G. F. The calculation of test reliability coefficients based on the method of rational equivalence. *Journal of Educational Psychology,* 1939, *30*, 681–687.

SCHMIDT, F. L., & HUNTER, J. E. Employment testing: Old theories and new research findings. *American Psychologist,* 1981, *36*(10), 1128–1137.

SCHMIDT, F. L., & HUNTER, J. E. The money test. *Across the Board,* 1982, *19*(7), 35–37.

SCHMIDT, F. L., HUNTER, J. E., & PEARLMAN, K. Task differences as moderators of aptitude test validity in selection: A red herring. *Journal of Applied Psychology,* 1981, *66*(2), 166–185.

TAYLOR, H. C., & RUSSELL, J. T. The relationship of validity coefficients to the practical effectiveness of tests in selection: Discussion and tables. *Journal of Applied Psychology,* 1939, *23*, 565–578.

TENOPYR, M. The realities of employment testing. *American Psychologist,* 1981, *36*(10), 1120–1127.

CHAPTER 5

Recruiting, Selecting, and Placing Employees

I/O PSYCHOLOGY AT WORK

What Turns Job Interviewers On—or Off?

A recent nation-wide survey of leading personnel executives should interest anyone about to interview for a job. The study, designed to reveal factors which can determine whether an interview will be successful, was conceived by Robert Half, Inc., the world's largest financial executive, accounting and data processing recruiters. Burke Marketing Research, Inc., an international research firm, conducted the study for the Half organization.

Of the 100 personnel directors and managers surveyed, half worked for Fortune 500 companies, and half were selected from the "Who's Who in the American Society for Personnel Administration" directory. The study revealed the following points:

- Interviewers attach great importance to good grooming and appropriate dress . . .
- Interviewers like candidates who are enthusiastic and responsive . . .
- Ask questions about the job . . .
- Don't ask direct questions about salary or fringe benefits at the beginning of the interview . . .
- Even if you need the job desperately, don't convey it.
- Don't exaggerate your skills or accomplishments . . .
- Interviewers are more favorably impressed by candidates who look them in the eye . . .
- Interviewers prefer the candidate to know about the company . . .
- Candidates who appear to be overconfident are much more likely to favorably impress interviewers than those who act shy . . .

The recruiting firm noted that, while heeding the findings of the survey would not guarantee a position, candidates who keep them in mind during an interview will significantly increase their chances of landing a job.

The employment interview is the single most commonly-used employment screening method. As the survey designed by the Half organization reveals, those who do this interviewing have certain expectations and preferences regarding interviewee behavior. The extent to which a job applicant conforms to these expectations and preferences can bias interviewer evaluations, whatever the applicant's actual job qualifications.

Interviewer bias is only one of the problems that can arise when one person interviews another for a job. The relative advantages and disadvantages of the interview, along with those of other common screening methods, are examined in Chapter 5. Recruiting job applicants and placing people in specific jobs once they have been hired also are discussed. Together, recruiting, screening and selection, and placement bring people to the jobs and working conditions that are the focus of Part III.

RECRUITING JOB APPLICANTS

An organization's recruitment goal is to find some number of qualified job applicants who will take a position in the organization if it is offered. Usually, several applicants per job opening are preferred; the more applicants available, the more selective an organization can be in offering jobs to people who meet its particular requirements.

Recruiting is the process of finding and attracting people to fill the jobs in an organization.

Selection ratio: See page 94.

Establishing Personnel Requirements

Recruiting starts with establishing personnel requirements—the number and type of new employees needed in some defined time period. Sometimes this is in the form of an informal communication to those who need the information. A more systematic approach is to begin with a statement of personnel needs based on formal human resource planning. Human resource planning includes a variety of personnel activities, among which are job analysis, current personnel inventories, and forecasting. Detailed discussion of human resource planning may be found in most personnel textbooks, such as that by Schuler (1984).

Formal human resource planning is a desirable baseline for recruiting, but it is not always feasible. Much recruiting starts with unexpected terminations or with sudden expansion, as when a firm acquires a large contract that cannot be completed with its present employees. Many large companies recruit almost continuously, either to offset turnover or to be prepared for unanticipated personnel demands.

Whatever the stimulus for recruiting, the process will be more efficient if the jobs to be filled are understood. The basis for this understanding are job descriptions and job specifications that result from job analysis (to be discussed in Chapter 9). This information tells those involved in recruiting where to look for job applicants most likely to meet a company's requirements.

Sources of Job Applicants

Job applicants may be sought within the organization—internal recruiting—or from some external source—external recruiting. Each approach has its advantages and disadvantages, and most organizations use a combination of strategies.

Internal Recruiting

There are a number of advantages to seeking job applicants from within the ranks of current employees.

- It is less costly than external recruiting.
- Job applicants have first-hand knowledge of the organization.
- The organization has first-hand knowledge of the job applicants.
- There can be certain motivational consequences of internal recruiting. A policy of recruiting from within expands individual employment opportunities and conveys an organization's commitment to the development and career advancement of its employees. Other things being equal, both factors may increase employee motivation.

Internal recruiting may aid organizations in filling jobs at any level and so may involve either horizontal or vertical employee movement. *Horizontal movement* occurs when an employee moves from one job to another at the same level in the organizational hierarchy. *Vertical movement* occurs when the employee moves up in the hierarchy; most internal recruiting is for this purpose, that is, for *promoting* current employees.

Since most internal recruiting involves promotion, attention to this process is often focused on management and executive jobs. A major issue is the relative benefits to be obtained by internal promotion versus bringing in "new blood."

The responses of many organizations to the internal versus external recruiting problem resembles a seesaw—first they try one policy then the other. For example, both the television and the automobile industries went through a relatively long period of promotion from within. In the best American tradition, Lee Iacocca began his auto industry career as a Ford salesman and ended up as a Ford vice-president. By the late 1970s however, both the television and the auto industry became involved in a flurry of "executive switching" that often baffled outsiders. Fred Silverman was president of two major commercial television networks and held a top position at the third. Iacocca is currently chairman of Chrysler Corporation.

If some companies cannot seem to decide whether to follow an internal or an external recruiting policy for top management, there is a good reason. Too many factors are involved to make any general statements about the effectiveness of either policy. The comparison as to what *did* happen when one strategy was followed with what *might* have happened if the other had been followed can only be made in a speculative fashion after the fact.

An I/O psychologist can assist a company in choosing a strategy based on knowledge of the situation, but a more general use of I/O skills lies in improving both internal and external recruiting processes. One approach to improving internal recruiting by exploiting its particular strengths is outlined in Exhibit 5–1.

Exhibit 5–1 presents a diagram of the process used by Graphic Controls for internal recruitment of upper-level management personnel. This process is noteworthy in four respects.

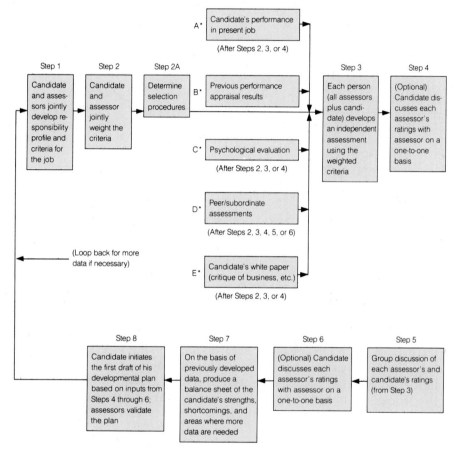

Graphic Controls' Team Selection and Development Process:
Internal Candidates for Division General Manager and
Corporate Department Manager Positions
(August 1979)

EXHIBIT 5–1

Plan for Internal
Recruiting and
Employee
Development

*Need to discuss whether additional Steps A, B, C, D, and E are required or optional.

Note. From E. C. Miller, "Hire in Haste—Repent at Leisure: The Team Selection Process at Graphic Controls." *Organizational Dynamics,* Spring, 1980, p. 8. Copyright 1980 by AMACOM, a division of American Management Associations, New York. All rights reserved. Reprinted by permission of the publisher.

1. Candidates themselves are involved in developing the selection criteria for the new job (Steps 1–3).
2. Candidates as well as company assessors evaluate candidates' positions with respect to the criteria (present job performance, past performance appraisal results, and so on) in Step 3.
3. Candidates have the option of discussing their evaluations with each assessor individually (Steps 4 and 6).

4. Whether candidates are selected for promotion or not, each receives a comprehensive evaluation of personal strengths and weaknesses (Step 7) to be used in making a personal development plan (Step 8) for the future.

The integration of job analysis, performance appraisal, and employee development with internal recruiting is a process that benefits all involved. Such an ambitious program, however, remains the exception rather than the rule in internal recruiting.

External Recruiting

All of the ways by which people who do not already work for an organization are brought in to apply for jobs are referred to collectively as external recruiting. External sources of employees include:

- newspaper advertisements
- private employment agencies
- public employment services
- unions
- colleges and universities
- other companies
- professional associations
- vocational schools

The role of personnel specifications is an important one in external recruiting because it offers psychologists or managers guidelines for spending recruiting money where it will do the most good. For jobs requiring particular combinations of high-level skills and training, for example, the expense of traveling the college or professional meeting circuit to locate job applicants is often necessary and justified. For jobs that require little training and/or experience and basic abilities likely to be possessed by most working people, less expensive external sources, such as newspaper advertisements or public employment agencies, more often are used.

Recruiting Research

Organizational behavior: See page 10.

Traditionally, I/O psychologists have not been as actively involved in external recruiting as in selection, placement, and internal recruiting in the form of promotion. There are some professional recruiters who are trained as psychologists. In general, however, the interest of the field has tended to stop, as it were, at the door of the company. This is changing rapidly as the costs of screening and selection continue to rise. Affirmative action programs also have stimulated applied psychologists to take more interest in the sources that produce job applicants.

As a result of the kinds of pressures mentioned, I/O psychologists, together with personnel specialists and researchers in the field of organizational behavior, have begun to examine some new questions. One of these is: What is the relationship, if any, between the source from which an employee is recruited and various aspects of his or her work behavior? Researchers have investigated this relationship in a variety of contexts.

- Employees recruited by college placement offices were found to have both poorer performance and higher absenteeism rates than employees recruited in other ways (Breaugh, 1981).
- Informal recruiting sources (e.g., ''word of mouth'') were associated with longer tenure for white store clerks. Nonwhites recruited from formal sources (e.g., employment agencies) had longer tenure (Caldwell & Spivey, 1983).
- Former employees (called ''rehires'') were the single best source of applicants in a packing plant (Taylor & Schmidt, 1983).

In addition to their interest in recruiting source, psychologists have been paying more attention in the past few years to recruiting as a two-way process. From this viewpoint, there are two decisions to be made—one by the organization and one by the job applicant if he or she is offered a job.

Available research supports the conclusion that the nature of the recruiting process and the behavior and perceived characteristics of the recruiter(s) do have an effect on whether or not a job applicant takes a position that has been offered. In reviewing this research, Rynes, Heneman, and Schwab (1980) discuss three specific factors that have been found to affect this choice:

- type of job interview and tests given
- company's follow-up policies
- knowledge and personality of the recruiter

Recruiting and screening as opportunities to help job applicants make the best choice for themselves and for the organization to which they are applying is elaborated upon further in Chapter 5.

Recruiting and Equal Employment Opportunity

Title VII of the Civil Rights Act of 1964 is the cornerstone of the equal employment opportunity (EEO) laws in this country that prohibit employment discrimination based on the nonjob-related characteristics of race, color, sex, age, religion, and country of national origin. The major thrust of fair employment policies is to ensure that individuals who are equally qualified on the basis of *job-related* requirements have equal access to employment, promotion, and other opportunities.

EEO: See page 30.

Although EEO laws and associated court rulings are fundamentally concerned with preventing future unfair discrimination, there also has been substantial pressure on organizations to make up for their past shortcomings in this respect. Specifically, organizations have been encouraged in a variety of ways to find qualified members of certain groups currently underrepresented in many jobs.

One of the most prevalent examples of underrepresentation in this country is the very small number of women and blacks in top manage-

The term **underrepresentation** refers to a marked discrepancy between the number of people in the labor force who are available for a job (or occupation) and the number who are actually employed.

Both women and blacks are underrepresented in upper management positions in this country.

ment positions. A formal plan for reducing such an imbalance is called an affirmative action plan (AAP) and it is in conjunction with AAPs that the primary impact of EEO on organizational recruiting is felt.

Affirmative Action

Affirmative action plans are not required by law as is adherence to general fair employment practices. At this time, however, they are mandatory for firms with at least 250 employees and government contracts worth $1 million or more a year. An AAP also may be ordered by a court as part of an EEO-related settlement against an organization, but many plans are voluntary. The Equal Employment Opportunity Commission's (1974) guidelines for an effective AAP are summarized in Exhibit 5–2.

However they are instituted, both informal affirmative action and formal AAPs depend upon vigorous recruiting efforts for success. Underrepresentation has arisen from a number of causes, but the clearest symptom is a shortage of applicants in certain groups for certain jobs. The philosophy behind affirmative action is that this problem has been created by two interacting factors.

1. Social norms have directed women and minorities into certain occupations and certain kinds of jobs believed appropriate.
2. Past organizational discrimination has generally caused women and minorities to expect to be turned down when nontraditional jobs are sought.

Social conditions have changed and discrimination on a personal basis is now illegal, but changes in expectations lag behind. Commitment to

A. Issue written equal employment policy and affirmative action commitment.

B. Appoint a top official with responsibility and authority to direct and implement your program.
   1. Specify responsibilities of program manager.
   2. Specify responsibilities and accountability of all managers and supervisors.

C. Publicize your policy and affirmative action commitment.
   1. Internally: to managers, supervisors, all employees and unions.
   2. Externally: to sources and potential sources of recruitment, potential minority and female applicants, to those with whom you do business, and to the community at large.

D. Survey present minority and female employment by department and job classification.
   1. Identify present areas and levels of employment.
   2. Identify areas of concentration and underutilization.
   3. Determine extent of underutilization.

E. Develop goals and timetables to improve utilization of minorities, males and females in each area where underutilization has been identified.

F. Develop and implement specific programs to achieve goals.
   This is the heart of your program. Review your entire employment system to identify barriers to equal employment opportunity; make needed changes to increase employment and advancement opportunities of minorities and females. These areas need review and action:
   1. Recruitment: all personnel procedures.
   2. Selection process: job requirements; job descriptions, standards and procedures. Pre-employment inquiries; application forms; testing; interviewing.
   3. Upward mobility system: assignments; job progressions; transfers; seniority; promotions, training.
   3. Wage and salary structure.
   5. Benefits and conditions of employment.
   6. Layoff; recall; termination; demotion; discharge; disciplinary action.
   7. Union contract provisions affecting above procedures.

G. Establish internal audit and reporting system to monitor and evaluate progress in each aspect of the program.

H. Develop supportive in-house and community programs.

Note. From Equal Employment Opportunity Commission, *Affirmative Action and Equal Employment: A Guidebook for Employers.* Washington, DC: U.S. Government Printing Office, January, 1974, pp. 16–17.

| EXHIBIT 5–2 |

Steps to an Effective Affirmative Action Plan

---

affirmative action is commitment to active efforts to overcome both of the major perceived obstacles to employment opportunity on the parts of underrepresented workers. Carrying out this commitment requires two special recruiting activities.

1. Developing the potential of current employees for promotion to jobs in which their groups are underrepresented (internal recruiting);
2. Exploring, in an active fashion, nontraditional sources of job applicants (external recruiting). Among these sources are
   - *The Talent Search Skills Bank* (women and minority professionals)
   - *The Directory of Predominately Black Colleges and Universities in the U.S.*
   - *The Listing of Spanish-Surnamed College Graduates*

Addresses for these and related sources of special job applicants may be found in Miner and Miner (1978).

SCREENING JOB APPLICANTS

The process of separating out job applicants more likely to be successful in a job and/or fit into the organization from other applicants is called **screening**.

The purpose of recruiting is to find people to apply for jobs in organizations. In most cases, companies like to have several applicants for a job in order to select the one they believe will be the best. To make this selection decision, they use a variety of screening methods.

To review the major *screening methods* used by organizations, general principles of testing discussed in Chapter 4 are drawn on extensively for two reasons. The first is that various forms of tests long have been used as screening devices.

The second reason testing is important to this discussion is that the Equal Employment Opportunity Commission (EEOC, the enforcement arm of EEO legislation) has been moving rapidly toward the position that *any* source of information used to make a selection decision is legally a test. Thus, application blanks and interviews technically are subject to the same reliability and validity scrutiny as more traditional tests.

Application Blank Information

The first screening information collected by virtually every organization concerning job applicants comes from an application blank, such as that shown in Exhibit 5–3. For certain jobs, a resumé may be substituted for this form; however, such positions are relatively few in most companies.

For some time, the EEOC has been placing constraints on companies relating to the kinds of questions that they may ask legally of a job applicant. These constraints are for the purpose of blocking the use of application blanks as a means of unfair (nonjob-related) employment discrimination. Examples of *suspect questions* include questions about:

- age
- marital status
- religious preference
- home ownership status
- membership in groups
- criminal record
- citizenship
- child-care arrangements

EXHIBIT 5–3

A Sample
Application Blank

LAST NAME_____

FIRST NAME AND
MIDDLE INITIAL_____ DATE_____

SOC. SEC. NO._____   APPLYING FOR_____
TELEPHONE NO._____   MINIMUM ACCEPTABLE WAGE_____

PRESENT_____   PREVIOUS U.S._____
ADDRESS_____   ADDRESS ONLY_____
HOW LONG?_____   HOW LONG?_____

HOW DID YOU HAPPEN TO APPLY FOR WORK HERE?

NEWSPAPER ADVERTISEMENT_____   AGENCY SENT ME_____
FRIEND'S RECOMMENDATION_____   NAME OF AGENCY_____
RELATIVE'S RECOMMENDATION_____   OTHER_____

HAVE YOU WORKED FOR US BEFORE?_____ WHEN?_____
NAME AT THAT TIME_____

ARE YOU UNDER AGE 18?_____
IF YES, DO YOU HAVE A CURRENT WORK PERMIT?_____
DATE ISSUED?_____ DATE OF EXPIRATION?_____

IF YOU ARE NOT A U.S. CITIZEN, DO YOU HAVE: A PERMANENT VISA_____
A TEMPORARY VISA_____

DO YOU HAVE ANY OBLIGATIONS THAT WOULD PREVENT YOU FROM:
WORKING CONSISTENTLY_____ WORKING OVERTIME_____
PERFORMING JOB FUNCTIONS_____ IF YES TO ANY, EXPLAIN_____

The general rule is that such questions may be asked only if they are *not* used in the selection decision, that is, if they are to serve only as a record of information for personnel files or for research purposes.

An important exception to the general rule about application blank questions occurs if it can be demonstrated that the answer to a suspect question has a relationship to some aspect of an applicant's behavior on the job. In other words, if application blank information can be *validated*, it can be used for selection decisions as well as for information or research purposes.

Employment test validation: See pages 86 to 88.

Validating Application Blank Information: The Biodata Approach

A comprehensive approach for organizations in using application blank information as a predictor of various work behaviors is the Biographic Information Blank (BIB) or Biodata approach (Owens, 1976). A BIB is a test in the form of an application blank. Certain questions on the form have "right" and "wrong" answers in the sense that certain answers have been found to be correlated with either desirable or undesirable worker behaviors.

Biographic Information Blanks can be scored just as other tests can be scored. The scoring key assigns the appropriate values to the key

Correlation: See pages 61 to 63.

questions. (Filler and informational items are not scored.) The values of these questions are determined by research into the correlation of the answers with some criterion. In the study summarized in "Spotlight on Research," the criterion was job tenure (Cascio, 1976). Other job criteria predicted by Biodata include training success, attendance, and advancement within the organization.

In the Cascio (1976) study what is called a *weighted application blank* was used as a predictor of tenure. Sixteen questions found in previous research to correlate with job tenure were scored. Those questions that had negative correlations with tenure were given minus weights, those with positive correlations, positive weights. The 16 items then were combined to give each employee one score. This is the score used to calculate the averages shown in the Results section in "Spotlight on Research."

The 16 items used in the Cascio (1976) study included questions about:

- age
- marital status
- children's age
- education
- tenure on previous job
- number of friends/relatives in company
- location of residence
- home ownership
- time at previous address
- previous salary

Significance: See pages 58 to 59.

A number of these questions fall into the EEOC's suspect group, but their use is justified when based on results such as those shown in "Spotlight on Research"; in that study there was a significant difference between Biodata scores of long- and short-tenure employees for both minority and nonminority subjects.

Biographic Information Blanks enjoyed considerable initial popularity, but soon came under attack for being a form of "dust bowl empiricism," that is, for being unconcerned with theoretical relationships between questions and job behavior as long as the answers predicted something. As an example of this issue, one of the strongest predictors of turnover found in a study of a certain company by the author was the question: "Can you swim?" Yet the company was located in an inland state, was not near a lake or river, and no large amounts of water were used in the production process.

Despite criticisms, the Biodata approach often has worked better than available alternatives for predicting certain worker behaviors (e.g., Alker & Owen, 1977). Efforts by Schoenfeldt (1974) and others to develop a sound theoretical basis for the use of Biodata show promise as a way to keep the best of this approach while advancing knowledge of organizational selection.

A recent review of the Biodata literature offers support for continuing work with this screening technique (Reilly & Chao, 1982). The average Biodata criterion-related validity coefficients found in the studies reviewed ranged from .32 to .46. These figures compare well with more

SPOTLIGHT ON RESEARCH

Turnover, Biographical Data, and Fair Employment Practice

Research question: Can selected application blank information be used to predict turnover? Is there a difference in this relationship between minority and nonminority employees?

Type of study: Historical.

Historical study: See pages 57 to 58.

Subjects: One hundred sixty clerical employees from a large insurance company located in the Southeast. All were hired within the same 14-month period.

Variables:

Operational definition: See page 48.

- Application blank score. Operational definition: One score from summing scores on 16 positive and negative items.
- Job tenure. Operational definition: Long tenure equals more than one year; Short tenure, less than one year.

General procedure: Application blank information and job tenure data were acquired from company records. Application blanks were scored according to the predetermined system.

Analysis: Correlation.

Results: In validation and cross-validation, the same 10 items predicted tenure for both minority and nonminority subjects.

Tenure	Minority Subjects		Nonminority Subjects	
	Long	Short	Long	Short
Average Score	− 1.53	− 10.85	− 1.72	− 10.54
Cross-Validation	− 3.41	− 14.73	− 3.24	− 14.22

Conclusion: "In summary, even after satisfying the legal requirements for using biographical data, turnover can still be predicted with an appreciable degree of accuracy. Moreover, the same scoring key can be used for both majority and minority groups, although this must be empirically demonstrated in each instance" (p. 579).

Summarized from W. F. Cascio, "Turnover, Biographical Data and Fair Employment Practice," *Journal of Applied Psychology,* 1976, *61,* pp. 576–580.

traditional types of tests. More detail on the Biodata approach to screening and selection may be found in the monograph by Owens and Schoenfeldt (1979).

In summary, virtually all organizations use application blanks. In some cases, they serve only as a summary of personnel data. Some companies use them for prescreening purposes, for example, to screen out inexperienced applicants who answered a newspaper advertisement for "experienced salesperson."

A few companies use application blanks as tests. To use information legally in this way, the information must be shown to be valid; that is, it must differentiate between good and poor employees in some manner. Finally, application blanks frequently serve as a point of departure for the next major source of screening information—the interview.

Interviews

The oldest and most frequently-used source of information about job applicants is the familiar one-on-one employment interview. This interview may occur early in the screening process or after applicants have been through any other screening procedures. The interviewer may be a recruiter, personnel department employee, manager, supervisor, company executive, or professional interviewer.

Whenever it occurs, and by whomever it is conducted, the most interesting fact that emerges from studies of the interview process is the weakness of this source of information by usual standards. Unless steps are taken to improve interviews, their reliability typically is low (Coleman, 1975). Different interviewers look for different things and interpret interviewee responses quite differently. Nor surprisingly, they also can reach different conclusions about the suitability of a particular job candidate for a job.

Reliability: See pages 80 to 84.

With respect to the validity of the interview, Reilly and Chao (1982) estimated the average criterion-related validity coefficient of 12 studies in which interview evaluations were correlated with supervisor ratings of subsequent performance to be .19. A few higher coefficients were found in another review by Arvey and Campion (1982); however, the trend of this research suggests that interviewers are not as good as might be hoped at "measuring what they are supposed to measure."

Sources of Interview Weaknesses

The typical employment interview is a dynamic, interactive process between two people, each with his or her own individual characteristics. Each brings biases and stereotypes to the situation. In addition, this situation itself has certain characteristics. For example, there is a difference between the situation in which a company is pressured to hire someone to fill an empty position immediately and when it is not. The various components of a typical interview situation are shown in the model in Exhibit 5–4.

Of the various factors listed in Exhibit 5–4, interviewer characteristics have been studied most extensively, especially interviewer biases and stereotypes. In a review of this literature, Arvey (1979) came to some discouraging conclusions with respect to interviewer evaluation of women and older people. Both tend to be evaluated less favorably than their similarly qualified younger male counterparts.

Arvey found interviewer bias to be especially strong when females are applying for traditionally "male jobs." This finding fits in with the more general conclusion of Schmitt (1976) that interviewers tend to measure job applicants against a stereotype of an ideal applicant. In our society, this ideal is still frequently young, white, and male.

Although the possibility of applicant manipulation of job interviews has been given far less attention than interviewer biases and stereotypes, it is likely that this is also a factor reducing the validity of the employment interview as a predictor of job behavior. There is research to suggest that job applicants are becoming increasingly sophisticated with respect to understanding the behaviors and question responses, such as those identified in "I/O Psychology at Work," that put them in a favorable light at interviews (e.g., Harlan, Kerr, & Kerr, 1977).

EXHIBIT 5–4

A Model of the Employment Interview

Applicant	Situation	Interviewer
1. Age, race, sex, etc.	1. Political, legal and economic forces in marketplace and organization	1. Age, race, sex, etc.
2. Physical appearance	2. Role of interview in selection system	2. Physical appearance
3. Educational and work background	3. Selection ratio	3. Psychological characteristics: attitude, intelligence, motivation, etc.
4. Job interests and career plans	4. Physical setting: comfort, privacy, number of interviewers	4. Experience and training as interviewer
5. Psychological characteristics: attitude intelligence motivation, etc.	5. Interview structure	5. Perceptions of job requirements
6. Experience and training as interviewee		6. Prior knowledge of applicant
7. Perceptions regarding interviewer, job, company, etc.		7. Goals for interview
8. Verbal and nonverbal behavior		8. Verbal and nonverbal behavior

Employment Interview

Interview Outcome

Note. From R. D. Arvey and J. E. Campion, "The Employment Interview: A Summary and Review of Recent Research." *Personnel Psychology,* 1982, *35*(2), pp. 281–322. Reprinted by permission of the authors and publisher.

The employment interview is still the most commonly used employment screening method.

Improving the Interview

Although the issue has been highlighted by EEO concerns, the short-comings of the interview have been recognized for many years (e.g. Wagner, 1949). Still organizations have not and will not give them up. Whatever else happens in the screening process, there is no viable substitute for seeing and talking to job applicants. The question is: How can this advantage be retained while the reliability and validity of the interview are improved? Research suggests a number of strategies.

One of the first approaches psychologists took to improving the interview was to change it from the typical free-flowing, or open-ended, conversational form to a structured interaction (Fear, 1958). In a *structured interview,* the interviewer has a predetermined set of relevant topics to cover. The interviewer's job is broadly defined as acquiring and making notes (or ratings) relevant to these topics. A form, usually called an *interview guide,* may be provided for recording this information.

A structured interview does little to offset interviewer bias in *interpreting* information, but it does control the *reporting* of information. To the extent that interview unreliability stems from differences in what interviewers do or do not ask (or report), this procedure should bring about an improvement. There are few direct comparisons of the structured interview with open interviews, but such evidence as is available supports this expectation (e.g., Carlson, Schwab, & Heneman, 1970).

From one perspective, a structured interview may be seen as a form of *interviewer training*. The second major approach to improving the reliability and validity of the employment interview is to train interviewers directly. Training methods vary, but the primary objective of most such efforts is to teach interviewers to be aware of certain aspects of the interview situation that can bias their evaluations of job applicants. Among the specific targets of interviewer training is the bias that can be created by the following:

- *first impressions*—greater weight given by interviewer to what is seen and heard during the early minutes of the interview;
- *contrast effects*—an interviewer's impression of an applicant is influenced by the impression made by the previous applicants;
- *similarity effects*—tendency for interviewers to evaluate applicants perceived as similar to themselves more favorably;
- *negative information*—tendency for an interviewer to give more weight to negative information in arriving at an evaluation.

Perception: See pages 36 to 37.

Findings from research on job interviewer training are mixed, but sufficiently positive to warrant further effort (see Arvey & Campion, 1982).

Two final strategies for improving the interview offer the advantages of simplicity and practicality. The first approach is to *separate the information-gathering function of the interviewer from the evaluation function of the selection decision maker* (Grant & Bray, 1969). In this case, the interviewer makes neither recommendations nor decisions. The results of the interview merely are reported as one more piece of information about the job applicant.

The last approach to improving the interview as a source of job applicant information is to *restrict the agenda of the interview*. More than alternative methods, the interview seems suited to providing information about applicant:

- self-confidence
- interpersonal skills (e.g., communication ability)
- career motivation
- interest in the job and the organization

By contrast, the interview has been shown to be a poor way to assess applicant job skills and abilities (e.g., Guion & Imada, 1981). Background information, such as age and education, can be obtained more efficiently by means of an application form.

Tests

Although the legal definition of a test has been expanded considerably in recent years by the EEOC, the current discussion is based on a more

A **test** is a defined procedure for making an estimate of an individual's relative or absolute position on some physical, psychological, or behavioral scale of measurement.

Testing: See page 77.

traditional definition consistent with the definition of *testing* in Chapter 4.

The use of tests to screen job applicants has a long history in I/O psychology, going back at least as far as World War I. Most of this early testing involved paper-and-pencil tests of intelligence, but the scope has expanded since to include a wide variety of tested characteristics, test forms, and administrative procedures. In this section, the most common types of tests used to provide information about job applicants will be reviewed briefly.

Ability Tests

An ability test is designed to assess the *potential* of an individual for learning something or for performing some activity. For example, the Scholastic Aptitude Test (SAT), which many took while still in high school, was developed to assess a person's ability to master certain academic material at the college level. In organizations, aptitude tests are used to assess the ability to be trained to perform particular jobs. Among those used more frequently are tests of mental, mechanical, and psychomotor abilities.

Assessing mental abilities. The oldest type of ability test in use in organizations is the intelligence test, or test of mental ability. Among the aspects of intelligence assessed by this type of test are:

- verbal ability
- spatial ability
- numerical reasoning
- abstract reasoning
- logical reasoning
- mental adaptability

A sample item from a test used to assess logical reasoning ability is shown in Exhibit 5–5. Such a test might be used to select trainees for jobs in which they would need some degree of judgement to sort or arrange items or materials.

Assessing mechanical abilities. One of the more important abilities needed by a person to perform many jobs in organizations is the ability to be able to acquire and use skills that are mechanical in nature. Psychologists who have studied this ability have found that it has two distinct, but related, aspects: one is a general ability to understand mechanical concepts; the other is the more specific ability to grasp spatial relationships. A sample item from one of the general mechanical aptitude tests is shown in Exhibit 5–6. Such a test might be used to select employees for semi-skilled mechanical jobs.

Assessing other abilities. There are various ability tests used in organizations that do not fall into the categories above. Among these are tests of psychomotor, or physical movement, abilities. These include (a) general manual dexterity, (b) finger dexterity, (c) reaction-time speed, and

Practice Items:

For each item find the picture that goes best with the picture in the first box. Draw a dark line from the upper right corner to the lower left corner in the proper box to show the right answer.

EXHIBIT 5–5

A Test of
Mental Ability

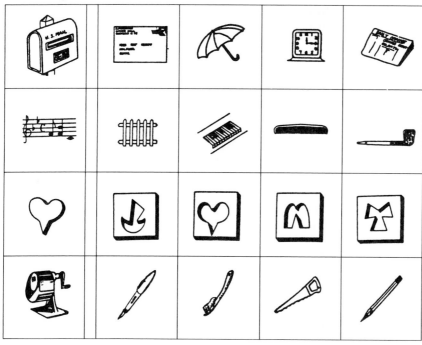

Note. From the *Non-Verbal Reasoning Test* developed by R. J. Corsini, 1957, published by London House Press, 1550 Northwest Highway, Park Ridge, IL 60068. Reprinted by permission.

(d) eye-hand coordination. Psychomotor abilities are important for the successful performance of most operative-level jobs in organizations.

Other ability tests that are used in screening in organizations are tests of perceptual abilities, such as eyesight and hearing. There is also a variety of job-specific ability tests, such as one for the ability to make fine distinctions between colors required in the job of inspecting dye lots in some fabric manufacturing companies.

Personality Measures

Tests assessing various aspects of personality were once popular with organizations for screening applicants for jobs at upper levels. There were two basic purposes behind such tests. One was to screen *out* people who might have difficulty coping with job pressures or getting along with others. The second purpose was to screen *in* job applicants who were highly motivated to work hard and achieve success.

The various personality tests used for both of the purposes above fall into two categories—objective and subjective. Objective tests are paper-and-pencil questionnaires that are scored with special scoring keys.

EXHIBIT 5–6	Use of Tools and Materials
	Times 10 Minutes

A Test of
Mechanical Ability

The five pictures in this sample group include: D. a needle, N. a plumb-bob, M. a thimble, V. a pair of scissors, and A. a spool of thread. The needle, thimble, scissors, and the thread are the most common articles in a sewing kit. The plumb-bob is used mostly in construction work and would be out of place in a collection used for sewing. Therefore, letter "N" is written in the block on the right.

SAMPLE:

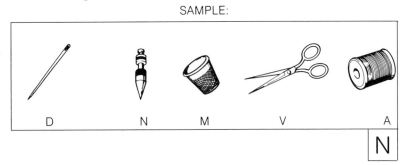

D	N	M	V	A

N

DIRECTIONS: This is a test of ability to identify the proper use of some common tools and materials. Below, there are twenty groups of pictures. In each group of five pictures across the page, there is one item which does not properly belong in the group. Each picture is marked with a letter. Write in the small block on the right in each group, the letter of the picture which does not belong in the group.

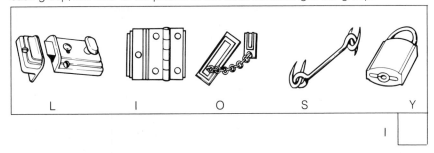

L	I	O	S	Y

I

Note. From the Acorn National Aptitude Tests, Test 4, *Mechanical Aptitude Test: Non-Verbal,* published by Psychometric Affiliates, 1620 E. Main Street, Murfreesboro, TN 37130. Reprinted by permission.

These typically yield measures of several personality dimensions. For example, the Guilford-Zimmerman Temperament Survey (Sheridan Psychological Services, Inc.) gives a profile of 10 personality traits.

Projective personality tests consist of ambiguous stimuli, such as the famous inkblots of the Rorschach Test (Psychological Corporation) or the photographic scenes of the Thematic Apperception Test (Harvard University Press). The person taking the test "projects" his or her personality into what is seen in the inkblots or the story that is told about the pictures. Such tests must be scored by highly-trained specialists, and they are used far less frequently than paper-and-pencil tests.

Interest Tests

Interest tests were developed originally for vocational counseling, but they also have been used considerably as organizational screening and placement devices. The use of such tests for any of these purposes begins with the premise that people in various jobs or professions have interests in common. Thus, one clue to a job applicant's suitability is the extent to which his or her interests are similar to those who are already successful on the job.

The most well-known of the interest inventories are the Strong-Campbell Interest Inventory (Stanford University Press) and the various Kuder interest surveys (Science Research Associates). A sample item from another interest test is shown in Exhibit 5–7.

Part A

- ☐ D. Contact various individuals to find those who wish to purchase an item.
- ☐ A. Prepare plans to improve home decoration or landscaping.
- ☐ C. Compute tax rates, deductions and interest rates.
- ☐ F. Put into practice new methods of conserving and fertilizing soil.
- ☐ B. Study and improve office procedures, and simplify business forms.
- ☐ E. Try to develop in an audience the emotions of humor, sympathy, or excitement.
- ☐ I. Help conduct a recreational center, persuading everyone to participate.
- ☐ S. Analyze products or materials and experiment on possible improvements.
- ☐ M. Test electric or plumbing connections and make needed adjustments.
- ☐ P. Put a smooth finish on manufactured parts or assemblies.

EXHIBIT 5–7

An Interest Test

Part B

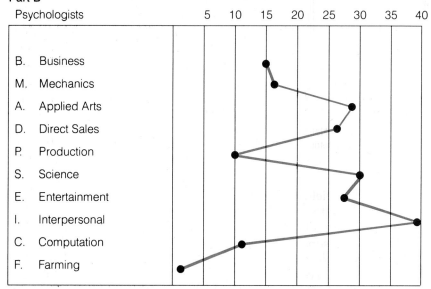

Note. From *The Curtis Interest Scale* developed by J. W. Curtis, 1959, published by Psychometric Affiliates, 1620 E. Main Street, Murfreesboro, TN 37130. Reprinted by permission.

Each of the ten statements in Part A of Exhibit 5–7 is most representative of the interests of people in one of ten particular areas of work. The test is scored as a profile showing the individual's relative interest in each of the ten areas as determined by the rankings within each set of items. (Part A shows one such set). This may be compared with established profiles for certain occupations, such as that for "Psychologists" shown in Part B. Note that psychologists, as might be expected, are higher on interpersonal interests than on any other single scale.

Job Sample Tests

A job sample test is a sample of some behavior that is important for a person to exhibit in a particular job. It is taken under standardized conditions and scored on a defined scale of measurement. The most familiar of these tests are those for typing and shorthand although there are many others in use. American Telephone and Telegraph Company, for example, has developed tests of number transcription, coding, area code usage, and filing (Gael, Grant, and Ritchie, 1975).

Unlike most tests that are used for screening, a job sample test is a *direct* measure of some important behavior that a person needs for a job. A young cooking school graduate recently showed his understanding of the attractiveness of this approach. He walked away with the job of cook in a New Jersey prison by bringing two full-course dinners to his job interview.

Content validity: See pages 90 to 92.

The great strength of job sample tests for screening is that they are *obviously* job related; that is, they have established content validity. In one of the more well-known job sample approaches to screening, the firm of Merrill Lynch, Pierce, Fenner, and Smith puts stockbroker applicants through a three-hour simulation of an account executive's job. Although this "test" is more costly and more complex than the usual pencil-and-paper alternatives, the company is happy with it and has been using it for more than five years. Over 6,000 applicants at Merrill Lynch have been through this final and toughest screening procedure during that time.

The use of job sample tests for screening generally has been confined to applicants with experience or training for the job in question. The Equal Employment Opportunity Commission's pressures for validating screening tests, however, have stimulated interest in the possibility of more general use, and early research reports are encouraging. For example, Cascio and Phillips (1979) report success with job sample testing for inexperienced applicants for the job of concession stand attendant at an amusement park. After the use of the cash register was explained, applicants were required to count change, fill out a revenue report, make several public announcements, and respond to irate customers. The authors report this approach to be less expensive, better liked by job applicants, and as effective as paper-and-pencil tests.

Test Batteries

The term *test battery* refers to a combination of tests given one after the other. Typically, a half or full day is required to administer a full battery, which may consist of one or more tests from any of the test groups. Exxon Corporation's Early Identification of Management Potential (EIMP) battery, for example, consists of the following (Vincino & Bass, 1978):

- two intelligence tests
- a personality test
- a judgment test
- a biographical inventory

Test batteries that consist of combinations of different tests may be used in two ways for screening purposes. One strategy is for administrators to give all job applicants one test, drop the lowest scorers out of the group, give the remainder a second test, drop the lowest scorers, and so on. An alternative is to give all of the applicants all of the tests and combine the results in some fashion; this is then used as *one* piece of screening information. A formalized version of this procedure that has received considerable attention in recent years is the assessment center.

Assessment Centers

An assessment center derives its name from the fact that groups of people are brought to a particular location (center) where specialists guide them through a formal evaluation process. This assessment typically lasts from a day to a week.

The group, multiple-technique assessment center procedure first was used extensively in industry by psychologists at the American Telephone and Telegraph Company. They believed the method had considerable promise as a way to generate information for employee development and internal promotion decisions.

Since the early work by psychologists at AT&T, the assessment center approach has come to be used for screening as well as for evaluation, although this use has been confined almost entirely to upper-level jobs. Among the characteristics most frequently assessed for these managerial and executive jobs are:

- work motivation
- leadership ability
- interpersonal skills
- administrative skills
- career orientation
- ability to perform under stress

In a recent review of the substantial research into the effectiveness of assessment centers, Cascio and Sibley (1979) conclude that there is sufficient evidence as to the reliability and criterion-related validity of this approach to warrant continued research and use. This is an expensive screening tool, however, and it is doubtful that assessment centers will ever see general use for lower-level organizational positions.

Testing and Ethics

The major categories of tests in use for organizational selection purposes have just been reviewed. All of the tests mentioned are commercially available and come with administration manuals, technical reports, updates of relevant data and research, and norms to assist in score interpretation. A comprehensive single source of information about these and other tests in print is the *Eighth Mental Measurements Yearbook* (Buros, 1978).

Not all tests used for organizational personnel decisions are developed by commercial test publishers. Many companies use the services of test specialists and I/O psychologists to develop and validate their own specialized tests. Whatever the source of a test, however, its use raises certain ethical considerations that are an integral part of professional I/O psychologists' approach to personnel testing in any form.

There are a number of published guidelines for the use of tests in industrial, educational, and social settings. For psychologists, the standard *APA: See page 5.* reference on testing ethics is the American Psychological Association's (APA) *Ethical Standards of Psychologists* (1977). References more specific to the use of tests in organizations include the *Standards for Providers of Industrial and Organizational Psychological Services* (1979) and *Principles for the Validation and Use of Personnel Selection Procedures* (1980), both produced wholly or in part by the APA Division of Industrial and Organizational Psychology.

There are many ethical questions raised by the use of tests in organizations. A good introduction to these questions may be found in London and Bray (1980). The clear and concise discussion by these authors has been summarized in Exhibit 5–8.

The brief outline in Exhibit 5–8 describes the nature of the various ethical responsibilities of professional psychologists who use tests in applied settings. It is clear that these responsibilities incorporate the potential for considerable conflict of interest. The matter is further complicated for psychologists by a need to balance these responsibilities with compliance to legal requirements and constraints.

Testing and the Law

As discussed earlier, the aim of equal employment legislation is to ensure that employment decisions (hiring, promotion, special training, educational opportunities, and so on) are based on job-related factors and not on job-irrelevant personal factors. There are many inputs to such employment decisions in organizations, but the EEOC long has focused its efforts on the role of tests in perpetuating unfair discrimination. A brief review of the most relevant court cases is presented by Bersoff (1981).

The standard reference for the use of tests in making personnel decisions is the "Uniform Guidelines on Employee Selection Procedures" (EEOC, 1978). The gist of these guidelines may be summarized as follows: Any procedure (test) used to make an employment decision must have

EXHIBIT 5-8

Ethical Responsibilities
of I/O Psychologists
Using Tests in an
Applied Setting

I. Responsibilities to the profession.
   A. Keep informed of relevant advances in the field.
   B. Report unethical practices.
   C. Educate others to ethical issues.
II. Responsibilities to those tested.
   A. Guard against invasion of privacy.
   B. Keep promised confidentiality.
   C. Explain nature of testing and possible uses to which information might be put.
   D. Impose time limits on organization's use of test data.
   E. Treat all those tested with respect and consideration.
III. Responsiblities to the organization.
   A. Convey accurate expectations about costs and benefits of testing program.
   B. Collect the best test data available within the constraints set by the situation.
   C. Monitor the continuing use of testing and revise where necessary (including tests for training administrators).
   D. Recognize the rights of the organization to ownership of methods and procedures it has funded.

Note. Summarized from M. London and D. W. Bray, ''Ethical Issues in Testing and Evaluating for Personnel Decisions.'' *American Psychologist,* 1980, *35*(10), pp, 890–901.

a demonstrated relationship to a job-related criterion if its use results in adverse impact.

If 6 out of 10 white applicants are hired for a job on the basis of a test, this is a selection rate of 60%. If using the test means that only 2 out of 10 nonwhite applicants are hired, this is a selection rate of 20%. Since this figure is well below 48% (80% of 60%), the use of this test results in adverse impact. Unless the test is validated on the basis of some job-related behavior, such as performance, its use constitutes unfair employment discrimination.

Many people are confused about adverse impact, and many organizations lack the resources and/or commitment to carry out the necessary test validation programs when adverse impact is suspected. One result of this situation has been what is described as a ''flight from testing,'' of which the following three symptoms have been noted:

- a marked general decline in the use of tests for selection (Prentice-Hall and the American Society for Personnel Administration, 1975);
- a decline in the number of new vocational tests submitted for inclusion in the Buros *Mental Measurements Yearbooks* (Mitchell, Reynolds, & Elliott, 1980);
- a decline in the number of test validation studies appearing in the scientific literature (Boehm, 1982).

Many I/O psychologists believe that the flight from testing is unfortunate. No one claims tests to be the single best way to screen all employees. Nevertheless, available data suggest that they are as good or better than many alternative screening methods as far as validity and lack of adverse impact are concerned (e.g. Reilly & Chao, 1982).

Adverse impact occurs when a selection procedure results in a selection rate for any protected group that is less than 80% of the rate with the highest group.

SELECTING EMPLOYEES

In the previous section, the major sources of information about people who apply for jobs in organizations—application forms, interviews, and tests—were reviewed. Screening methods not discussed include reference checks, academic record checks, physical examinations, and such controversial methods as polygraph (lie detector) tests. Organizations collect this information to make a *selection decision:* To which applicant(s) should a job be offered?

Success rates: See pages 93 to 96.

An organization uses screening information in making selection decisions to increase its *success rate* for hiring, that is, to select people who will be productive and satisfied employees. Most people who hire for organizations believe that the more information they have, the less likely they are to make one of the major selection errors—hiring someone who does not work out *(false positive)* or rejecting someone who would have been a good employee *(false negative).*

False positives and negatives: See pages 93 to 94.

The actual extent to which more information will help reduce selection errors depends on whether or not certain conditions hold. There are three of these conditions.

1. The various sources yield different kinds of information. Grades in high school math courses, for example, do not help if the applicant's record in a computer training course is available and computer programming is the job in question.
2. The costs of getting the information do not exceed its usefulness. For example, if a large number of applicants is involved, recommendations and reference checks probably are not worth the time they take. Long experience shows these to be of little use in discriminating among job applicants because they almost always are favorable or noncommittal.
3. The information acquired is relevant to some aspect of job performance. For example, to put all applicants for jobs in a department store through the same standardized battery of tests is likely to generate a lot of information that will never be used. All of the tests in the battery will not be relevant to every job.

Using Screening Information

Assuming that the three conditions outlined above hold true, the question is: How are the various pieces of information about job applicants to be used to make a selection decision? How does the individual sitting there with application blanks, test scores, interviewer remarks, and other information put it all together to mean something? It is possible to distinguish two major ways to answer this question—the clinical approach and the statistical approach.

The Clinical Approach to Selection Decisions

The term *clinical approach* originates in the practice of medicine and clinical psychology. In those areas, the judgments of trained and experienced professionals long have been the primary basis for diagnosis and treatment.

Clinical prediction in organizational selection is also a tradition. This approach comes out clearly in conversations with many experienced personnel interviewers who will state flatly that "There is no substitute for knowing human nature." Many of these individuals are successful at selecting good employees. Available evidence, however, challenges their belief in the *general* superiority of clinical prediction in organizational selection. Reviews of the relevant literature strongly favor the statistical approach (e.g., Wiggins, 1973).

When people use their own knowledge, skills, experience, and values to make a judgment about the combined meaning of several pieces of information about an individual, the process is called **clinical prediction.**

The Statistical Approach to Selection Decisions

Clinical prediction rests on a case-by-case judgment. By contrast, the statistical approach is based on rules.

The simplest decision rule for making use of multiple pieces of information about a job applicant is to turn the situation into a single information one, that is, to use each piece of information once in a sequential fashion that screens out more applicants at each step. This process often is called the *multiple-hurdle* strategy.

An example of the use of a multiple-hurdle approach to selection is provided by a drapery manufacturing concern that recently underwent a long and expensive search for a new workroom supervisor. The "hurdles" set up for the 27 applicants are shown in Exhibit 5-9. On the basis of this multiple-hurdle process, which took some months, the job of supervisor was eventually offered to the top-ranked candidate at hurdle six. This individual turned down the job, and it was subsequently accepted by the candidate ranked second.

The multiple-hurdle screening process shown in Exhibit 5-9 has some unusual features. For example, there was considerable reliance on the judgment of the current supervisor, an individual considered to be superior in every aspect of job performance for the 16 years she had held the job. Another unusual feature was the weight given to the opinion of those to be supervised. While this makes intuitive sense, it is seldom considered and only occasionally feasible.

Despite the deviations of the process from what might be more typical, Exhibit 5-9 illustrates the two most important conditions for using this decision-making process for selection.

When information about an individual is evaluated in an empirical manner according to a predetermined decision rule, the process is called **statistical prediction.**

1. It must be possible to grade the applicant abilities and characteristics assessed in the screening process. The basic, but relatively common, abilities are screened first, then the process moves up through successively less common and more particularly job-related criteria.
2. Each hurdle must have a clear and valid accept-reject standard.

EXHIBIT 5–9

Multiple-Hurdle
Decision Making
in a Drapery
Manufacturing
Company

I. Basic sewing competence (job sample test)
   A. If satisfactory (to current supervisor), accept
   B. If not satisfactory, reject

II. Basic arithmetic skills (job sample test—coverting specification sheets to sewing tickets)
   A. If no more than two errors, accept
   B. If three or more errors, reject

III. Manufacturing problem-solving ability (two work problems from actual experience)
   A. If pass both, accept
   B. If fail one or both, reject

IV. Personnel management skills (recommendations for action on two typical personnel problems)
   A. If satisfactory to supervisor, accept
   B. If not satisfactory, reject

V. Workroom employee evaluations (rankings based on interviews between applicants and workroom staff); three top-ranked applicants to become candidates

VI. Supervisor and management evaluations (rankings based on interviews); combined with those in VI to form new ranking

---

In testing, accept-reject standards are called **cut-off scores.**

A cut-off score is a test score (or percentile ranking) that "cuts off" those below it from further consideration for the job, training, school, or other opportunity. This score is determined on the basis of previously-established statistical probabilities for success. In organizational testing, this probability is obtained by the process of criterion-related test validation. The relationship between test scores and the probability of job success is illustrated by the *expectancy chart* shown in Exhibit 5–10.

As suggested by its name, an expectancy chart provides information about the *expected performance* of individuals with different scores on a particular test. In Exhibit 5–10, for example, this expectation is about 50:50 for job applicants with a test score of 50 (out of 100). In other words, in the past, approximately half of the employees whose test scores at the time of hiring were 50 subsequently received "very good" performance ratings.

It takes time to develop an expectancy chart, such as that shown in Exhibit 5–10; and in a multiple-hurdle procedure, this would be the basis for only one cut-off score for one hurdle. Accordingly, the multiple-hurdle decision-making strategy for selection is time consuming and expensive. Extensive preparation is required to set up and validate the various hurdles and accept-reject criteria. On the other hand, these are the factors that tend to make statistical approaches to selection more successful than clinical prediction.

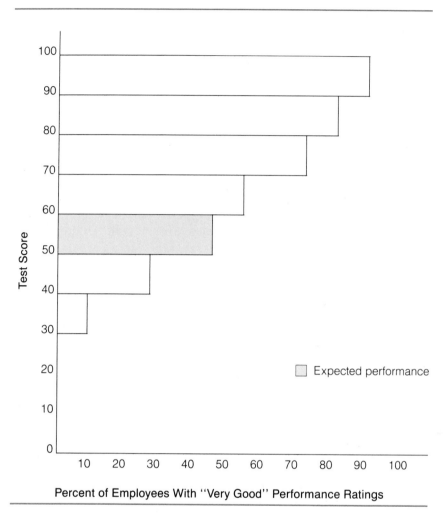

EXHIBIT 5-10

Sample Expectancy Chart: Probability of Job Success for Different Ranges of Test Scores

Percent of Employees With "Very Good" Performance Ratings

The multiple-hurdle approach is not the only type of decision-making rule that may be used by psychologists or administrators in combining screening information to make selection decisions. A variation of this method is called the *multiple cut-off* method. Under this rule, all applicants are given all screening, and those who pass *all* cut-offs become candidates. This variation does not require the various hurdles to be ranked in terms of difficulty, which is a step that can be a problem for some jobs.

It is also possible for those doing selection to take a more purely statistical approach to selection by means of various procedures that ultimately yield a single score for each job candidate. These methods have an advantage in that it is unlikely for more than one person to come out on top. By contrast, in either the multiple-hurdle or the multiple cut-off approaches, ties are quite possible. Psychologists may have difficulty, however, in convincing those who hire for organizations to go quite so strictly "by the numbers." As in all organizational activities, there are trade-offs involved in choosing among the various alternatives available.

Monitoring Selection Procedures

Whatever screening methods are used and however this information is processed to make selection decisions, it is necessary to keep monitoring these procedures. One reason for this is that things change. Jobs change and the characteristics of job applicants change. At some point, "tried and true" tests may no longer be useful and/or sufficient. For example, word processors have replaced standard typewriters entirely in some companies. As a result, standard typing tests may need to be supplemented or dropped for tests more predictive of the skills required by the new machines.

Restriction of range: See pages 88 to 89.

A second reason selection systems must be monitored continously is related to the issue of *restriction of range.* Theoretically, a good selection system gradually raises the performance level of an organization's employees by screening out those less likely to be successful. As this happens, the range of job performance (the criterion) is restricted, and old tests or cut-off scores may no longer be appropriate (Linn, Harnish, & Dunbar, 1981). For both of these reasons, it is necessary that selection methods used by an organization be subject to periodic reexamination. As is true for all scientific research, the job of validation is never finished.

PLACING NEW EMPLOYEES

To this point, the discussion of how screening information is used has been directed exclusively toward selecting one or more individuals for hiring, but this may not be the only decision to be made. It also may be necessary to make a *placement decision:* If there are several jobs for which a newly-hired employee is qualified, where should he or she be placed? This situation arises frequently in large organizations that have a variety of low-skill-level jobs in which turnover tends to be high. A new employee with basic abilities often will be suitable for several of these jobs.

Placement decisions also arise when employees finish basic training programs. For example, many companies have general management training programs into which recent college graduates are recruited. Upon completion of this program, someone must decide where to place the new manager. However the need for placement arises, there is a variety of strategies that might be followed.

- Place the individual in the job that has the highest priority of those for which he or she is judged to be qualified. This strategy puts out the immediate fires as far as filling jobs. However, it can lead to consistent under- or overutilization of employee skills and abilities.

- Place the individual in the job for which the evaluated probability of his or her success is highest. This maximizes the opportunity for individual success, but may limit opportunities for employee development.
- Place the individual in the job that incorporates the potential to which he or she might be expected to grow. This strategy is the opposite of the one above. It can reap the benefits of challenge, but may backfire if the individual's potential has been overestimated.
- Place the individual in the job that he or she favors among those judged to be suitable. This may be the strategy preferred by new employees, but it is likely to lead to a chronic shortage of workers in important, but unattractive, jobs.

The variety of trade-offs suggested in the list illustrates the basic question to be asked about placement decisions.

*Does the organization concentrate on **filling** positions or on **fulfilling** individual expectations and potential?*

Current thinking and research with respect to both selection and placement is that the greatest good for everyone involved will come from a strategy that makes a deliberate and coordinated attempt to accomplish both of these goals. The key to this strategy is the concept of *matching*.

MATCHING INDIVIDUALS TO ORGANIZATIONS AND JOBS

With respect to organizational selection and placement, the concept of matching is not a new idea. Matching individual abilities and skills to job requirements is the essence of screening and selection. What is relatively new is the concept of matching individual needs, values, and expectations to what organizations can offer as well.

There are several pieces of information required to bring about a full matching of individual talents, needs, and expectations with organizational requirements and rewards. Those involved in selection and placement need information about:

- skills and abilities required by the job;
- rewards and opportunities offered by the job and by the organization;
- applicant/new employee skills and abilities;
- applicant/new employee needs, values, and expectations.

Information about job requirements and rewards comes from the job analysis discussed in Chapter 9. The subject of applicant skills and abilities has been addressed. Information as to needs, values, and expectations must be obtained directly from the job applicant or new employee.

A Matching Model and Realistic Job Previews

The concept of matching individuals to jobs and to organizations has been formalized by Wanous (1980) into a Matching Model. The practical cornerstone of this model is the Realistic Job Preview (RJP).

A **Realistic Job Preview** presents job applicants with all pertinent information about the organization and the job in a straightforward, non-selling manner.

The Realistic Job Preview may be accomplished by any combination of interviews, films, day on the job, work samples, or group discussions with current employees. The concept grew out of research findings that organizations and jobs frequently fail to meet expectations set up during the usual recruiting and screening processes.

The difference between expectations for employment and job reality can be substantial. For example, a large-scale study at the Ford Motor Company found significant discrepancies on four of the five job characteristics that employees rated as most important to them (Dunnette, Arvey, & Banas, 1973). If such discrepancies lead to dissatisfaction with the job and with the company, turnover can increase and recruiting, screening, and selection costs can increase accordingly.

Realistic Job Preview Research

If there is a relationship between voluntary turnover and unrealistic expectations set up during the traditional recruiting/screening process, then RJPs might improve things in two ways.

1. Applicants who assess the chances of an organization or job meeting their own needs and desires to be low, could "select themselves out" and seek employment elsewhere.
2. Applicants who decide to accept a job offer would go into the job with more realistic expectations and would experience fewer disillusionments.

If RJPs have the effects listed, then voluntary turnover should decline and employee satisfaction should increase in firms that take this approach to recruiting and screening. Although there has been considerable research into these issues, results are inconclusive. Both Wanous (1980) and Dugoni and Ilgen (1981) report that the evidence strongly supports the hypothesis that RJPs reduce voluntary turnover rates. Others (e.g., Reilly, Brown, Blood, & Malatesta, 1981) disagree. The most accurate statement of the current situation with respect to this research may be the more moderate conclusion of Breaugh (1983).

> *Although it seems clear that RJPs can sometimes have beneficial effects (e.g., reducing turnover), at present empirical data are lacking on why RJPs have the effects they do and in what contexts they are likely to be useful.*

As Breaugh suggests, one of the problems with making statements about the effectiveness of RJPs is that the context, or situation, in which recruiting and selection takes place can confuse the issue. For example, the tendency for organizational personnel to accentuate the positive in these activities is strong, especially when there is a particularly attractive job candidate available or when there is a pressing need to fill a position. Accordingly, there may be considerable variation in the extent to which an RJP conforms to the nonselling ideal.

Another aspect of the situation that affects the utility of the RJP is the job applicant involved. The organizational openness required by RJPs may facilitate greater job applicant openness or it may not. Individuals take jobs for many reasons. Some accept positions they know are likely to be dissatisfying because other considerations are more important at the time.

In summary, Realistic Job Previews are not a panacea for avoiding individual/organization/job mismatches. At the same time, there seems to be sufficient evidence that RJPs can be effective in certain situations to warrant continuing use and research efforts.

SUMMARY

Recruiting is the process of attracting people to consider taking jobs in an organization. These job applicants may be sought within or outside of the organization, with both strategies having advantages and disadvantages.

Screening is the process of separating qualified and/or promising job applicants from unqualified and/or less promising ones. The most common sources of screening information in use in organizations are application blanks, interviews, and tests. All are subject to reliability and validity criteria under equal opportunity laws.

Screening information is collected for the purpose of improving selection and placement decisions. Selection decisions may be based on the use of this information in a judgmental clinical way or by means of some statistical decision-making rule. In either case, continued monitoring and validation of methods is required to offset both built-in reductions in utility and changes in job requirements and applicant population.

Placement decisions raise the basic dilemma of whether to respond primarily to the individual or primarily to the needs of the organization. Current research and thinking suggest a balanced strategy that will allow the organization to fill jobs with people who can do and who will be satisfied with the jobs in which they are placed.

AT ISSUE

Equal Employment Opportunity and Affirmative Action: Catch-22?

There was only one catch and that was Catch-22, which specified that a concern for one's own safety in the face of dangers that were real and immediate was the process of a rational mind. Orr was crazy and could be grounded. All he had to do was ask; and as soon as he did, he would no longer be crazy and would have to fly more missions. Orr would be crazy to fly more missions and sane if he didn't, but if he was sane he had to fly them (p. 47).

The quotation comes from Joseph Heller's famous novel, *Catch-22.* As many know from experience, the unfortunate Orr is not alone in his predicament. Modern life seems full of Catch-22s. One that job applicants long have complained about is the experience requirements for many jobs; applicants must have experience to get jobs, but unless they get jobs, they cannot get experience.

It may be that organizations in this country are now facing one of the biggest Catch-22s of all. In simple terms, the law says that they must offer equal job opportunities to all qualified applicants and employees. But other laws (and/or court orders) say that under certain conditions, they must bend over backwards to give female and minority applicants first crack at these opportunities; that is, they must pursue affirmative action policies.

In 1974, Allan Bakke brought suit against a California university. Bakke, a white male, claimed that he had been rejected twice from the university's medical school, not because he was not qualified, but because he was white. The sought-after medical school places, he claimed, were going to people less qualified than he because these people were members of minority groups.

After a four-year legal battle that went all the way to the U.S. Supreme Court, Bakke was admitted to the medical school. In a majority decision, the Supreme Court justices ruled that the university was wrong to reject him in order to serve an inflexible quota system biased against white applicants. They also ruled that college admission programs should continue to give minorities special advantages —Catch-22.

The way out of Catch-22 for educational institutions is a little gimmick called the "plus factor" system. The courts have told our nation's schools that such variables as age, sex, and race may be considered "plus factors" in competition between equally qualified white males and other candidates for admission. But getting an education and earning a living are two different (if related) things.

Equal employment opportunity legislation was directed specifically at employment situations, not educational ones. The "plus factor" system seems a clear violation of those laws that state that age, sex, race, religion, and national origin are *irrelevant* employment opportunity criteria. Yet is not affirmative action essentially a form of this system? Organizations, like Orr, are coping as best they can and hoping that an Allan Bakke does not appear in their employment offices.

REFERENCES

AMERICAN PSYCHOLOGICAL ASSOCIATION. *Ethical Standards of Psychologists.* Washington, DC, 1977.

AMERICAN PSYCHOLOGICAL ASSOCIATION, Committee on Standards for Providers of Psychological Services. *Standards for Providers of Psychological Services.* Washington, DC, 1979.

AMERICAN PSYCHOLOGICAL ASSOCIATION, Division of Industrial and Organizational Psychology. *Principles for Validation and Use of Personnel Selection Procedures* (2nd ed.). Berkeley, CA, 1980.

AKLER, H. A., & OWEN, D. W. Biographical, trait, and behavioral sampling predictors of performance in a stressful life setting. *Journal of Personality and Social Psychology,* 1977, *35*(10), 717-723.

ARVEY, R. Unfair discrimination in the employment interview: Legal and psychological aspects. *Psychological Bulletin,* 1979, *86*(4), 736-765.

ARVEY, R. D., & CAMPION, J. E. The employment interview: A summary and review of recent research. *Personnel Psychology,* 1982, *35*(2), 281-322.

BERSOFF, D. N. Testing and the law. *American Psychologist,* 1981, *36*(10), 1047-1056.

BOEHM, V. R. Are we validating more but publishing less? *Personnel Psychology,* 1982, *35*(1), 175-187.

BREAUGH, J. A. Relationships between recruiting sources and employee performance, absenteeism, and work attitudes. *Academy of Management Journal,* 1981, *24*(1), 142-147.

BREAUGH, J. A. Realistic job previews: A critical appraisal and future research directions. *Academy of Management Review,* 1983, *8*(4), 612-619.

BUROS, O. K. (Ed.). *Eighth Mental Measurements Yearbook.* Highland Park, NJ: Gryphon, 1978.

CALDWELL, D. F., & SPIVEY, W. A. The relationship between recruiting source and employee success: An analysis by race. *Personnel Psychology,* 1983, *36*(1), 67-72.

CARLSON, R. E., SCHWAB, D. P., & HENEMAN, H. G., III. Agreement among selection interview styles. *Journal of Industrial Psychology,* 1970, *5*(1), 8-17.

CASCIO, W. F. Turnover, biographical data, and fair employment practice. *Journal of Applied Psychology,* 1976, *61*(5), 576-580.

CASCIO, W. F., & PHILLIPS, N. F. Performance testing: A rose among thorns? *Personnel Psychology,* 1979, *32*(4), 751-766.

CASCIO, W. F., & SIBLEY, V. Utility of the assessment center as a selection device. *Journal of Applied Psychology.* 1979, *64*(2), 107-118.

COLEMAN, C. J. *Personnel: An Open System Approach.* Cambridge, MA: Winthrop, 1975.

DUGONI, B. L., & ILGEN, D. R. Realistic job previews and adjustment of new employees. *Academy of Management Journal,* 1981, *24*(3), 579-591.

DUNNETTE, M. D., ARVEY, R. D., & BANAS, P. A. Why do they leave? *Personnel,* 1973, *50*(3), 25-39.

EQUAL EMPLOYMENT OPPORTUNITY COMMISSION. *Affirmative Action and Equal Employment: A Guidebook for Employees.* Washington, DC: U.S. Government Printing Office, 1974.

EQUAL EMPLOYMENT OPPORTUNITY COMMISSION. Uniform Guidelines on Employee Selection Procedures. *Federal Register,* 1978, *43,* 38290-38315.

FEAR, R. A. *The Evaluation Interview: Predictors of Job Performance.* New York: McGraw-Hill, 1958.

GAEL, S., GRANT, D. C., & RITCHIE, R. J. Employment test validation for minority and nonminority clerks with work sample criteria. *Journal of Applied Psychology,* 1975, *60,* 420-426.

GRANT, D. L., & BRAY, D. W. Contributions of the interview to assessment of management potential. *Journal of Applied Psychology,* 1969, *53,* 24-34.

GUION, R. M., & IMADA, A. S. Eyeball measurement of dexterity: Tests as alternatives to interviews. *Personnel Psychology,* 1981, *34*(1), 31-36.

HARLAN, A., KERR, J., & KERR, S. Preference for motivation and hygiene factors in a hypothetical interview situation: Further studies and some implications for the employment interview. *Personnel Psychology,* 1977, *30,* 557-566.

HELLER, J. *Catch-22.* New York: Dell, 1955.

LINN, R. L., HARNISH, D. L., & DUNBAR, S. G. Corrections for range restriction: An empirical investigation of conditions resulting in conservative corrections. *Journal of Applied Psychology,* 1981, *66*(6), 655–663.

LONDON, M., & BRAY, D. W. Ethical issues in testing and evaluation for personnel decisions. *American Psychologist,* 1980, *35*(10), 890–901.

MILLER, E. C. Hire in haste—repent at leisure: The team selection procedure at Graphic Controls. *Organizational Dynamics,* 1980 (Spring), pp. 3–26.

MINER, M. G., & MINER, J. B. *Employee Selection Within the Law.* Washington, DC: Bureau of National Affairs, 1978.

MITCHELL, J. V., REYNOLDS, C. R., & ELLIOTT, S. N. Test news from the Buros Institute. *Measurement News,* 1980, *23*(6), 16.

OWENS, W. A. Background data. In M. D. Dunnette (Ed.), *Handbook of Industrial and Organizational Psychology* (pp. 609–644). Chicago: Rand McNally, 1976.

OWENS, W. A., & SCHOENFELDT, L. F. Toward a classification of persons. *Journal of Applied Psychology Monograph,* 1979, *65,* 569–607.

PRENTICE-HALL AND THE AMERICAN SOCIETY FOR PERSONNEL ADMINISTRATION. PH/ASPA survey probes employee testing and selection procedures. In Authors (Eds.), *Personnel Management Policies and Practices Reports.* Englewood, Cliffs, NJ, Prentice-Hall, Inc., 1975.

REILLY, R. R., BROWN, B., BLOOD, M. R., & MALATESTA, C. E. The effects of realistic previews: A study and discussion of the literature. *Personnel Psychology,* 1981, *34*(4), 823–834.

REILLY, R. R., & CHAO, G. T. Validity and fairness of some alternative employee selection procedures. *Personnel Psychology,* 1982, *35,* 1–62.

RYNES, S. L., HENEMAN, H. G., III, & SCHWAB, D. P. Individual reactions to organizational recruiting: A review. *Personnel Psychology,* 1980, *33*(3), 529–542.

SCHMITT, N. Social and situational determinants of interview decisions: Implications for the employment interview. *Personnel Psychology,* 1976, *29*(1), 79–101.

SCHULER, R. S. *Personnel and Human Resource Management.* St. Paul: West, 1984.

SCHOENFELDT, L. F. Utilization of manpower development and evaluation of an assessment-classification model for matching individuals with jobs. *Journal of Applied Psychology,* 1974, *59*(5), 583–595.

TAYLOR, M. S., & SCHMIDT, D. W. A process-oriented investigation of recruitment source effectiveness. *Personnel Psychology,* 1983, *36*(2), 343–354.

VINCINO, F. L., & BASS, B. M. Lifespace variables and managerial success. *Journal of Applied Psychology,* 1978, *63*(1), 81–88.

WAGNER, R. The employment interview: A critical summary. *Personnel Psychology,* 1949, *2,* 17–46.

WANOUS, J. P. *Organizational Entry: Recruitment, Selection, and Socialization of Newcomers.* Reading, MA: Addison-Wesley, 1980.

WIGGINS, J. S. *Personality and Prediction: Principles of Personality Assessment.* Reading, MA: Addison-Wesley, 1973.

CHAPTER 6

Employee Training and Socialization

I/O PSYCHOLOGY AT WORK

Employees Learn Faster with Computer Instruction

Classroom lectures and guided on-the-job training are taking a back seat at Olin Corp.'s Stamford, CT, headquarters. A computer-based instruction system is being used instead to train the Chemical Group's new hires to process sales orders.

Since using an interactive instructional system (IBM) the time required for customer service representatives to become productive has decreased significantly, say company officials.

"Formerly it took new customer service representatives from three to six months to reach 80 percent efficiency," says Ben Graves, corporate manager of interactive instructional systems. "Now they reach that same level of proficiency in four to five weeks. . . ."

In the past, to teach new customer service representatives the correct way to process sales orders and handle customer inquiries involved four weeks of traditional instruction—a combination of lectures with one-on-one guidance at the computer terminals and on-the-job training.

Today, the new hires are still at the computer terminals, but this time instead of keying orders into the computer, they're using a training system programmed into the computer to learn their new jobs. . . .

Olin's computer-assisted training program is designed to present a modular approach to learning new skills. The course proceeds in a "go at your own pace," covering aspects of the sales order process —taking customer calls, entering orders into the system, correcting data entry errors, and using the system to find out the status of outstanding orders. . . .

As students proceed through the course, the system automatically keeps track of their progress. A history file, kept for each student, shows courses taken, number of hours of computer time, and test scores.

"Evaluation of a student's performance is much more objective," Ms. Murphy [manager of the system for the Chemicals Group] says, "since we are able to measure actual skills. We know a student's weaknesses and can give extra practice in those areas as well as alert management so that additional help can be given to the individual on the job."

Computer-assisted instruction (CAI) is a relative newcomer to the ranks of organizational training methods, but like Olin Corporation, many companies are finding such training both effective and efficient.

Where computer information processing systems are already in place, CAI also is relatively inexpensive because it can be added to existing computer resources.

Training is one of the processes required to turn new members of an organization into productive "insiders." The other process is less clearly defined, but equally important; the newcomer must adapt to his or her work group and to the company. This process is called *socialization.*

Training people to do their job tasks and socializing them to the expectations, procedures, policies, and norms of an organization are interrelated processes, although they are discussed separately for clarity. The training to be examined is formal job training for the relatively inexperienced new employee. Individual development training is discussed in Chapter 15.

TRAINING AND ORGANIZATIONAL FUNCTIONING

In the past 15 years, training has come to occupy an increasingly important place in the activities of organizations. A wide variety of programs now come under the heading of *training program,* but all have the same basic purpose.

Training is a process in which abilities are developed into specific, required, or desired skills, knowledge, or attitudes.

In the definition of training, the term *ability* may be thought of as physical, mental, or psychological potential. *Skill* is a particular use of that potential. People differ with respect to their various abilities, so they differ in the degree of skill they can acquire as the result of training. This is the reason that ability tests, discussed in Chapter 5, long have been among the most commonly used employment tests.

Ability testing: See pages 120 to 121.

In Chapter 6, the development of various abilities into job skills is discussed. *Job training* continues the process of matching individuals to jobs, a process that begins with screening, selection, and placement. For the organization, this training serves three important functions—maintenance, motivation, and socialization.

Making sure that a new employee knows how to do his or her job the way the organization expects it to be done is one important function of training. This function may be seen as one of *maintenance,* a means for *maintaining* employee performance within the limits required for organizations to meet their objectives.

In addition to its maintenance function, training also serves a *motivational* function. Employees' expectations that they will be able to perform successfully are an important factor in how much effort (motivation) they will exert on the job. To the extent that this confidence is increased by training, there should be an associated increase in motivation.

Training and socialization are interrelated processes. One aspect of this interrelationship is that training is an important part of the socialization process; that is, training serves a *socialization* function. Among the features of a training program that send new employees messages about the priorities, values, and norms of an organization are:

• the way the training program is structured

- the content of the training program
- the job goals and procedures emphasized
- the attitudes and skills of the trainers

These issues, as well as more on socialization, are addressed later in Chapter 6. At present, attention is turned toward training itself.

SETTING UP A TRAINING PROGRAM

There are many decisions to be made when the question of how to train people for jobs is broached.

- How much and what kind of training is needed?
- Where should training take place?
- What training methods will be used?
- How will the success of training be evaluated?

Determining Training Needs

The training being discussed in this chapter is initial job training. Assessing training needs, therefore, is a matter of determining (a) how much and (b) what kind of training is needed for new employees.

How Much Training Is Needed?

The extent of initial job training needs depends upon the discrepancy between (a) what new employees already can do and (b) what the jobs for which they were hired require of them. Where discrepancies are slight (the new employee is experienced), training may be limited to familiarizing the individual with the particular work methods, opportunities, and constraints in the new organization. Where discrepancies are larger, more specific job training is required.

In general, there are several factors that affect the extent to which new employees will need training. The most important of these is the organization's *selection policy:* Does the organization hire primarily for potential or for experience? This policy, in turn, is influenced by the size and skill level of the available labor pool and the nature of the jobs for which hiring is done.

When the available labor force is small and/or largely unskilled, it may not be possible to get experienced new employees. The same may be true for organizations that produce highly specialized products or services that require unusual skills. In these cases, hiring is done for potential rather than for experience, and training needs are considerable.

What Should Trainees Be Taught?

Setting up job training requires that psychologists or trainers carefully specify the *task* requirements of a job as well as the desired *outcomes* of training. For example, the job of a movie theater concession stand attendant is to serve customers. This requires taking and filling orders, adding up bills and making change. Most attendants also take inventory and keep the stand clean. The tasks that must be learned in order to carry out these duties are shown in Exhibit 6–1.

As may be seen in Exhibit 6–1, even simple jobs reveal many facets when they are examined from a training standpoint. In many cases, these job tasks also must be accomplished in a particular order or sequence. One such *fixed-procedure* job is described in Exhibit 6–2.

Unlike the tasks required of a movie concession stand attendent, most people already know how to perform the basic tasks of putting a radar set into operation—flipping switches, turning dials, and so on. What is critical in this job is the *sequence* of tasks. Doing Step 5 before Step 4 is not only incorrect procedure, but it may be dangerous. In other words, the real training task here is teaching trainees to perform tasks in the right order.

The jobs described in Exhibits 6–1 and 6–2 are relatively simple ones, but the principles of task analysis for training programs are basic to all jobs. Gagné (1962) describes these three steps.

1. Identify the component tasks of final job performance.
2. Make sure that each of these component tasks is learned.
3. Arrange the total learning situation in the appropriate sequence.

Job: Attendant at movie theater concession stand.

EXHIBIT 6–1

A Training
Task Analysis

Training Objective: Employees who can fill customer orders accurately and quickly so as to maximize stand profits in the time available.

Job Duty	Associated Training Tasks
Take customer order.	Memorize verbal instructions as given.
Fill customer order.	Operate beverage dispensers; fill popcorn containers to specified levels; recognize different prepackaged items; use cardboard carrying trays as appropriate.
Total customer bill.	Memorize stand item prices; calculate sales tax (if appropriate); add customer purchases "in head" or operate equipment provided for addition.
Make change.	Figure correct change from amount tendered or operate equipment provided.
Keep inventory.	Fill in inventory control form correctly on basis of day's sales.
Clean stand and leave ready for next day.	Know required cleaning tasks/standards; deactivate equipment and prepare for next use; remove trash to appropriate location.

EXHIBIT 6–2

Putting a Radar
Set in Operation

This kind of task is typically what is called a "fixed procedure." That is, the individual is required to push buttons, turn switches, and so on, in a particular sequence. Here, for example, is a set of steps in a procedure used by radar operators to check the transmitter power and frequency of an airborne radar. . .

1. Turn the radar set to "Stand-by" operation.
2. Connect power cord of the TS-147.
3. Turn power switch on.
4. Turn the test switch to transmit position.
5. Turn DBM dial fully counter-clockwise.
6. Connect an RF cable to the RF jack on the TS-147.

There are 14 more steps in this procedure. Notice that each of the steps by itself is easy enough; the individual is quite capable of turning a switch or connecting a cable. What he must learn to do, however, is to perform each step in the proper sequence.

Note. From R. M. Gagné, "Military Training and Principles of Learning." *American Psychologist*, 1962, *17*(2), p. 83.

Selecting a Training Location

There are three possible physical locations in which to carry out job training. One is on the job itself (on-the-job), the second is at company's physical location but not on the job (on-site), and the third is somewhere other than the organization's premises (off-site). These three choices all have advantages and disadvantages.

On-the-Job Training

The most frequently-used location for job training is on the job itself. A new employee is put to work immediately and instructed in job duties by a supervisor, experienced coworker, or floor training specialist.

Most organizations use on-the-job training to some extent, either as the main form of training or as a supplement to other training. It has many advantages.

- No special personnel or facilities are required.
- The relevance of what is being taught is obvious to trainees.
- The trainee can begin making some work contribution immediately.

The success of on-the-job training is less certain than its convenience and its economy. Disinterested, rushed, inexperienced, or poor trainers may do an inadequate or incomplete job of training a newcomer. A particular problem can occur if trainers pass on work-method shortcuts that can threaten worker safety or product/service quality instead of training the newcomer by defined procedures.

The potential problems with on-the-job training can be reduced by giving those who do this training some training of their own. One approach to this training is the four-step Job Instruction Training (JIT) method. Job Instruction Training was developed during World War II to help inexperienced supervisors cope with training thousands of new workers, many of whom had never worked before. The four steps of the JIT, as described by Gold, (1981) are shown in Exhibit 6-3.

The JIT method has been used successfully by many supervisors who have little or no experience in giving formal job training. It begins, as discussed in the last section, with supervisors dividing the job into the tasks for which employee training is necessary. The actual instruction combines explanation, practice, and feedback. Finally, JIT includes a formal follow-up phase—the employee is not left to feel awkward about asking for help with any problems encountered in early days on the job.

On-site Training

On-site training does not allow trainees to begin making an immediate work contribution because training is carried out in special facilities on the job. Offsetting this drawback is the fact that both trainee and company are protected from the consequences of slow or incorrect work. In addition, the organization has more control over the quality of employee training because it usually is carried out by one or more full-time trainers.

The major disadvantage to on-site training is that it can be costly, especially when expensive equipment is duplicated in what is called a *vestibule school* (simulated work place). There also can be a certain artificiality attached to training that takes place in a protected environment away from noise and pressures. Experienced trainers report, however,

---

The Four Steps in Training

	EXHIBIT 6-3

I. **Prepare**
  A. Break down the job into tasks
  B. Prepare an instruction plan
  C. Put the trainee at ease
II. **Present**
  A. Tell
  B. Show
  C. Demonstrate
  D. Explain
III. **Try Out**
  A. Have the trainee describe the job verbally
  B. Have the trainee instruct the supervisor on how to do the job
  C. Let the trainee do the job
  D. Provide the trainee with feedback as to performance
  E. Let the trainee practice
IV. **Follow-Up**
  A. Check progress frequently at first
  B. Tell the trainee where to go for help if needed
  C. Gradually taper off progress checks

Job Instruction Training Method for Supervisors

Note. Summarized from L. Gold, "Job Instruction: Four Steps to Success." *Training and Development Journal*, 1981, *35*(9), pp. 28–32.

that if the job is learned well, most trainees adjust to actual working conditions quickly.

Off-site Training

A variety of training programs in organizations takes place somewhere other than on the premises. Much of this training is of the employee development type discussed in Chapter 15, but there is also off-site initial job training.

Some off-site initial job training, such as McDonald's famous Hamburger University, is conducted by the organization. Other such training is carried out by professional trainers or by educational institutions. One parcel delivery company, for example, sends its drivers to a local vocational school to receive training in basic vehicle maintenance and emergency repair.

With the exception of programs like McDonald's, off-site training programs have the advantages of on-site locations without the expense of a permanent facility. For example, the parcel delivery company pays only for maintenance training as needed; when driver turnover is low, some time may elapse before any training costs are incurred in this area.

The two greatest disadvantages to off-site job training are: (a) if the training is conducted by someone else, the organization has little control over its quality; (b) the relevance of off-site training may not be clear to trainees until later when they are on the job. Thus, they may miss some important aspects and require retraining.

The brief descriptions of the three main training locations are concentrated on basic advantages and disadvantages. There are no hard and fast rules for choosing among these alternative sites; each organization must consider its own situation. For example, if an analysis of training needs shows that even inexperienced employees need little training to master a job, then on-the-job training may be the logical choice. There are also other factors to be considered.

1. What is the average number of new employees hired in a time period? If the number is small, the expense of a formal on-site training program is not justified. If on-the-job training is not feasible or satisfactory, trainees can be sent to off-site facilities.
2. What are the resources available for training? Some companies use on-the-job training almost exclusively, not because it is preferred, but because they lack the financial resources required by alternatives. Training costs money, both in direct training costs and in lost productivity during the training period, and these costs can be substantial. For example, the Bell Telephone system's training program for switching maintenance takes six months and costs more than $25,000 per trainee.
3. What are the consequences that might be incurred because of trainee mistakes and/or lack of speed? In some instances, choice of training location is made, not on the basis of job difficulty or training costs, but on the basis of problems that might be created by trainee mistakes or substandard performance.

Training public transit drivers is one example of a situation in which trainee mistakes could be serious. No matter how impeccable the personal driving record of a trainee, no one would seriously consider on-the-job training as the only training for bus drivers. In other cases, sensitive production processes or expensive equipment prohibit the use of on-the-job training. When even a slight error can ruin a machine, prejudice worker health, or require scrapping a day's production, new employees will be trained off the job.

IMPLEMENTING EMPLOYEE TRAINING

Formal job training is for the purpose of giving new employees the skills and knowledge they need to be successful in day-to-day job performance. Deciding what these skill/knowledge requirements are and where to carry out training are first steps. The core of the training program, however, is the training method or methods used.

To some extent, choice of a training method is limited by the nature of the training tasks. This point is pursued as the various methods are reviewed. A more fundamental consideration is the extent to which a training method is consistent with what is known about human learning.

Training as a Learning Experience

As suggested by the story about computer-assisted training in ''I/O Psychology At Work,'' there are some very sophisticated training methods available. Do not forget, however, that it is *people* who are being trained. Changing the behavior of people in a particular way, such as training them for a job, rests on three important principles of human learning—practice, feedback, and reinforcement.

Practice

There is some disagreement among learning theorists about whether active participation in the form of practice is *essential* to learning. Nevertheless, it does appear that practice *facilitates* learning for most people. This principle seems to apply to all levels of training and to most training tasks. Although it is impossible to specify exactly how much practice is optimal for any particular person or task, there are two guidelines to be found in the learning literature.

1. Repetitive practice appears to be most effective for motor skills or any task that requires trainees to commit material to memory. The two jobs described in Exhibits 6–1 and 6–2 would fall into this category.
2. Spread-out, or *distributed*, practice sessions appear to be more effective than an intensive, one-time practice session for all tasks.

The two guidelines are guidelines, not rules. There are a number of difficulties when general learning research findings are applied to a training situation. One of the major problems is that the tasks used in learning research often bear little resemblance to real training tasks. A review of this issue may be found in Gagné and Rohwer (1969).

Feedback

However much trainee practice is involved and however practice periods are set up, learning research leaves no doubt that *feedback* as to trainee progress is vital for learning to take place. Results of a recent field experiment comparing employee training alone with training plus feedback make this point clearly (Komaki, Heinzmann, & Lawson, 1980). Exhibit 6–4 shows a comparison of the percentage of safe work behaviors associated with (a) safety training only and (b) safety training with feedback as to how trainees were performing with respect to specified safety criteria.

In Exhibit 6–4, the safety performance of employees on four jobs in a large city department of public works is shown at three points in time: (a) before training (baseline), (b) after training with no feedback as to subsequent performance, and (c) after feedback for safety performance was initiated.

The dotted horizontal lines in each figure in Exhibit 6–4 represent the average percentage of work incidents that employees performed to safety standards in each period. Note that for each job, this percentage increased with safety training alone, but not to the level attained when training was accompanied by feedback.

The feedback in the study from which Exhibit 6–4 is taken was in the form of a posted graph based on random, timed observations of trainee

Feedback is a critical phase of any training program; people learn from the results of their efforts.

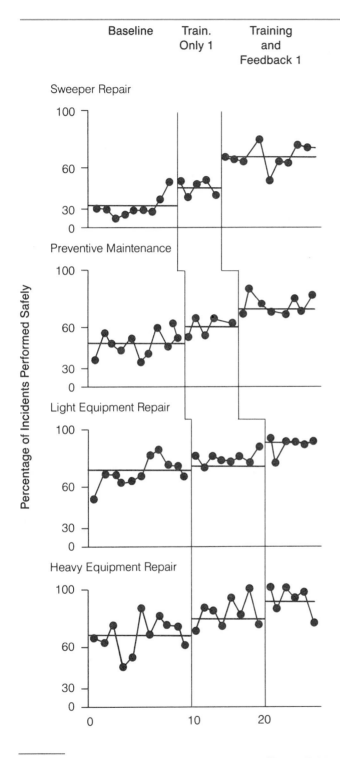

Baseline | Train. Only 1 | Training and Feedback 1

Sweeper Repair

Preventive Maintenance

Light Equipment Repair

Heavy Equipment Repair

Percentage of Incidents Performed Safely

Note. From J. Komaki, T. Heinzmann, and L. Lawson, "Effect of Training and Feedback: Component Analysis of a Behavioral Safety Program." *Journal of Applied Psychology,* 1980, *65*(3), pp. 261–270. Copyright 1980 by the American Psychological Association. Adapted by permission of the authors and the publisher.

behavior. Training feedback also may be built into the training task itself. For example, a student learning a foreign language pronounces a word into a machine, which then pronounces it correctly for comparison (feedback).

The purpose of giving feedback to job trainees is to give them information about their training performance and progress. The nature of the feedback is dictated by the nature of trainee behavior; that is, feedback in and of itself is neither a positive nor a negative concept. When performance is unsatisfactory, "negative feedback" gives the trainee the information to make changes. When performance is good, "positive feedback" helps to *reinforce* or strengthen the associated behaviors.

Reinforcement

A positive outcome **reinforces** the behavior with which it is associated.

Reinforcement: See page 31.

As discussed in Chapter 2, much of what people learn is shaped by what happens to them as a result of experiences. An important aspect of any training program is whether or not it allows for some reinforcement of trainee behavior that is desired—effort, progress, or skill achievement. Positive feedback is one form of such reinforcement—feelings of accomplishment are powerful rewards for some people. Other possibilities for reinforcement include:

- praise from the trainer(s)
- formal recognition, such as a designation of "Trainee of the Week"
- increased training pay as trainees meet certain standards
- faster movement out of training and onto the job for faster learners

Positive reinforcement as a means of strengthening desired behavior is examined in some detail later in the text. In this chapter, positive reinforcement is one of the criteria by which the advantages and disadvantages of various common training methods are evaluated.

Training Methods

The term **training method** refers to the basic instructional technique of the training situation.

Many training methods are available and in regular use. The ones discussed here are among the more common approaches. Some organizations rely on one method, some use a combination of methods, and some vary the method according to the nature of the job. For convenience of discussion, these methods are grouped in three categories—nonparticipative, individual participative, and group participative.

Nonparticipative Training Methods

This group of instructional approaches consists of methods in which trainees take a passive role as recipients of information. The information they need to know traditionally is communicated by means of *lectures*, but *written materials, demonstrations, visual aids,* and *films* also may be used.

When used alone, nonparticipative training methods typically lack all three of the important characteristics of training implementation discussed—opportunity for practice, feedback, and reinforcement of desired learning. Nevertheless, there are situations, such as those described below, in which such methods are necessary and/or appropriate.

- A substantial amount of information must be communicated to a large number of people in a relatively short period of time. This situation occurs frequently when people must be trained to work under unusual conditions, for example, when a union walkout makes it necessary for managers to take over operative jobs. It also can arise when a sudden increase in production demands requires that a large number of temporary employees be put to work as quickly as possible.
- The information to be communicated is not of a nature that allows for trainee participation. Such information usually pertains to the *knowledge* required of employees to do a job rather than to the *skills* required of them. For example, films may be used to demonstrate the dangers of a burning building to firefighter trainees.
- An overview or preview of training plans and activities is necessary; that is, lectures or demonstrations are appropriate ways to communicate to trainees what they will be doing in training and why.

Individual Participative Training Methods

A variety of instructional techniques allow both for active participation on the part of a trainee and for individual pacing of learning. Among the more well known of these methods are programmed instruction (PI), the more recent computer-assisted instruction (CAI), various individual simulation methods, and job rotation.

Programmed instruction. Programmed instruction first gained fame in the form of "teaching machines." These were mechanical devices for presentation of learning stimuli and feedback to students. Pressey (1926) was the first to use such machines, which since have been used extensively in language instruction and in teaching children to spell and to perform simple arithmetic computations. More recently, the use of such devices has been extended to other situations, such as the programmed machines that give what used to be the written part of the examination in many state driving license facilities.

Various forms of teaching machines have been used for training in organizations, but the concept has been applied more in written, or booklet, form. The basic concepts are (a) graduated presentation of material with (b) feedback as to correct or incorrect answers at each step. To illustrate these concepts, a short test of some of the material from this section is presented in PI form in Exhibit 6–5.

Programmed instruction booklets presenting material in the form illustrated by Exhibit 6–5, are a relatively inexpensive way to add elements of trainee practice and feedback to nonparticipative training methods, such as written job instructions. This method also can provide positive reinforcement to the trainee in the form of feelings of mastery and accomplishment.

The reinforcement potential of programmed instruction depends upon trainees who (a) do not "cheat" by looking at the correct response ahead

EXHIBIT 6–5	**Instructions:** Cover the left side of the page and reveal each answer only after you have filled in the blank space with your own response.

A Programmed
Instruction Approach
to Learning

Programmed instruction	_____ _____ first gained fame in the form of "teaching machines."
Pressey	A teaching machine is a mechanical device for presenting stimuli and feedback to students. It was developed by_____.
Graduated	One important aspect of the programmed instruction approach to learning is _____ presentation of material.
Feedback	At each stage in a programmed presentation, the learner makes a response and receives immediate _____ as to whether or not the response was correct.

of time, and (b) *feel* rewarded by getting correct answers. Neither condition necessarily holds true. One employee of a large supermarket chain that uses PI for training new clerks reported: "Everyone I know just went through and copied the answers and turned the books in."

Computer-assisted instruction. Computer technology has developed rapidly since businesses first began to use computers routinely in the 1950s. This expansion has made computer-assisted training a logical extension of the older teaching machines. Computer-assisted instruction has the same advantage of individual pace and instruction and a considerably wider potential range of applications.

The potential training advantages of CAI over standard on-the-job training or vestibule training have been discussed in some detail by Mallory (1981). Among these advantages are:

• standard presentation of materials to all trainees
• standard structured practice
• instant, specific feedback

To illustrate these and other points, Mallory describes the Ford Motor Company's CAI program for industrial maintenance electricians and general troubleshooters.

Trainees in the Ford program must learn to locate complex system malfunctions through an analytical process of identifying and then eliminating suspect components until the one causing the malfunction is isolated. With the CAI program, each step of a trainee's problem-solving process is analyzed by the computer and his or her solution is compared with the optimal solution. Ford reports that trainee reactions to the program have been positive, and tests support its effectiveness.

The major drawback to CAI for most organizations is probably the initial expense. Companies with ongoing training programs, however, may find start-up costs offset by reduced training time and the need for fewer trainers. For example, the Olin Corporation program described in "I/O Psychology at Work" has cut instructor training time by 75%.

Simulation: See page 54.

Simulation techniques.   As the name implies, simulation training is based on a reproduction of some aspect of job reality. The military makes extensive use of simulation, and their flight simulators for training pilots have been in use for many years. The nuclear power industry also uses simulation training as do a variety of other industries with complex, sensitive, and expensive equipment.

As training methods, task simulators have the advantages of giving trainees practice at an individual pace. Many simulators provide built-in feedback as well. For example, when the pilot trainee makes a serious mistake on takeoff, he or she experiences a simulation of the resultant "crash."

The major disadvantage of job simulation training, like the major disadvantage of CAI, is probably the cost of the equipment. Where simulation is concerned, however, there also have been some serious disagreements about the effectiveness of a method that approximates rather than duplicates reality. A well-known study in this line of research is summarized in "Spotlight on Research."

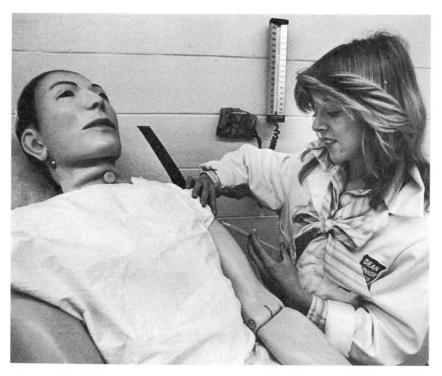

Job simulation training is preferred to on-the-job training when trainee mistakes can have serious consequences.

SPOTLIGHT ON RESEARCH

The Optimal Use of Simulation

Research question: What are the effects of (a) simulator fidelity (approximation to the real-job equipment) and (b) amount of practice on (c) performance on the actual job?

Laboratory experiment: See pages 52 to 54.

Type of study: Laboratory experiment.

Subjects: One hundred males and females with no experience on the task.

Operational definition: See page 48.

Independent variables:
- Simulator fidelity. Operational definition: (a) Three-rack collator (less fidelity), (b) Five-rack collator (closer to real eight-rack equipment).
- Practice time. Operational definition: (a) Overtrained (five trials beyond set speed goal), (b) Trained (to set speed goal).

Independent variable: See page 52.

Dependent variable: Performance on job. Operational definition: Time required to collate paper with real-job eight-rack equipment.

General procedure: There were five groups of 10 males and five groups of 10 females: (1) overtrained on three racks, (2) overtrained on five racks, (3) trained on three racks, (4) trained on five racks, and (5) control. Subjects in each group were given 15 trials collating paper with a real collator after training.

Results: The results for male subjects are shown in the following graph. By the end of the 15 performance trials, *overtrained* subjects were performing significantly less well than other subjects, even those with no training (control).

Weitz and Adler (1973), authors of the study, analyzed the results in a number of ways. They were interested in differences among the various trials on the real task, the different movements used by male and female subjects, and the implications of these findings for different kinds of training. Of particular interest in the present discussion is the finding that lack of simulator fidelity to the real thing did *not* inhibit the transfer of training from the simulator to the actual equipment.

As may be seen in the graph in "Spotlight on Research," the best performance (fewest seconds to task completion) on the first six performance trials was given by subjects trained on the simulator *least* like the real job equipment. The poorest performance (on all but the very early trials) was given by subjects overtrained on the task simulator most like the real thing.

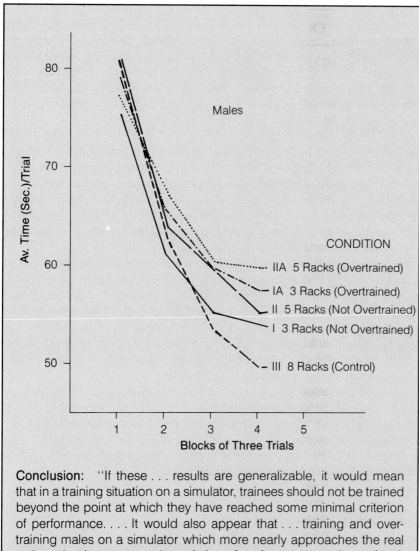

Males

CONDITION

IIA 5 Racks (Overtrained)

IA 3 Racks (Overtrained)

II 5 Racks (Not Overtrained)

I 3 Racks (Not Overtrained)

III 8 Racks (Control)

Blocks of Three Trials

Conclusion: "If these . . . results are generalizable, it would mean that in a training situation on a simulator, trainees should not be trained beyond the point at which they have reached some minimal criterion of performance. . . . It would also appear that . . . training and over-training males on a simulator which more nearly approaches the real task . . . leads to greater degredation of performance on the real task than training on a simulator of less fidelity" (p. 223).

Summarized from J. Weitz and S. Adler, "The Optimal Use of Simulation." *Journal of Applied Psychology*, 1973, *58*(2), pp. 219–224. Copyright 1973 by the American Psychological Association. Graph reprinted by permission of the author and the publisher.

One of the most interesting aspects of the graph in "Spotlight on Research" is that approximately halfway through the 15 job trials, control subjects began to outperform all other subjects. The only training these subjects received was the practice they acquired on the first job trials. This finding lends some weight to the argument that trainees in simulation training "learn the simulator" rather than the job.

The task used in the Weitz and Adler (1973) experiment was not a particularly difficult one, and simulator fidelity may be considerably more important with some of today's complex work equipment. The study does suggest that the issue is not so straightforward as the degree to which the simulator approximates the real thing. For the Weitz and Adler subjects who received simulation training, the amount of practice on the simulator was a more important determinant of final job performance.

Job rotation. All of the individual participative methods of training discussed to this point take place off the job. Job rotation provides trainees with first-hand knowledge and experience of a variety of operations *on* the job. At lower levels, this can serve to strengthen the work force by increasing flexibility. Unless union constraints prohibit the practice, for example, employees so trained can switch jobs to reduce boredom or to perform the work of absent employees.

Despite its advantages to lower levels in an organization, job rotation is traditionally a management training technique. As such, its effectiveness varies considerably. The benefits of highly routinized programs that move all trainees from one job to another in a standard order and at preset time intervals are questionable. Everyone involved knows that time is limited and trainees will be moving on soon to be replaced by others. Many of those who have gone through such programs report having felt more like observers than trainees.

There are ways to structure job rotation training in order to make it an effective way to meet training goals. For example, superiors on each job may have some formal coaching and evaluation responsibilities for trainees that encourage greater commitment on both parts. It also can be helpful to leave the time to be spent in each position open so that trainees may spend more time where they need it.

Group Participative Training Methods

Within the category of group participative training methods is a variety of specific training techniques. The common factor in these methods is that trainees interact with and learn from one another as well as from training methods and trainer. This can enhance learning, but it also injects an element of uncertainty into the training.

However they are selected, every group of trainees will be different from every other group. Exactly what will happen in any particular group training session is not known in advance. The effective use of group methods requires of trainers the ability to work with the dynamics of a group as well as with a method. Considerable skill can be required to keep activities and discussions on the general training course without losing the benefits of trainee interaction.

Discussion techniques. A variety of training techniques are based on group discussions. The most common formal technique is probably discussion for purposes of analyzing case studies or incidents (short cases). Trainees are given the facts of a real organizational problem (or one developed especially for training purposes) and work through the issues and questions together. An example of an incident that might be used for training purposes is shown in Exhibit 6–6.

As training devices, cases and incidents, such as that in Exhibit 6–6, have the advantage of stimulating the development of trainee analytic and problem-solving skills. Trainees learn not only to examine the facts of a situation as given, but also to identify crucial missing information.

Plant Democracy at National Foods

	EXHIBIT 6–6

Part I

The opening of a new pet food processing plant at Omaha, Nebraska, gave the National Food Company (NF) an opportunity to design its organization structure in a manner that incorporates modern design principles. Utilizing the design principles of (1) *participation,* an attempt to distribute power throughout the organization and (2) *autonomy,* creation of independent work teams, NF designed a new factory system aimed at overcoming problems that beset other food processing plants. The specific goals of the new factory system, according to T.K. Nunley, manager of organizational development at NF, included maximum machine utilization, minimum waste, low distribution costs, low productivity costs, and low absenteeism and turnover. Many of the functions traditionally the prerogatives of management were designed to be performed by the workers. The aim of the new system was to have workers make job assignments, interview prospective employees, schedule coffee breaks, and decide on pay raises. Having workers perform these duties was NF's way of attempting "to balance the needs of the people with the needs of the business," according to Nunley.

A Management Training Incident

(This case is based largely on an experience of General Foods Corporation as reported in "Stonewalling Plant Democracy," *Business Week,* March 1977, pp. 78–82.)

Analysis Questions

1. If you were asked by Nunley to react to his design ideas and goals, what would you tell him? Why?

2. Do you think a new structure alone will create the behaviors and outcomes that Nunley expects? Discuss.

3. As an organizational development attempt, is the structural design enough, or is more needed to produce the results desired?

Note. From John Veiga and John Yanouzas, *The Dynamics of Organization Theory: Gaining a Macro Perspective* St. Paul: West Publishing Company, 1979, p. 427. Copyright 1979 by West Publishing Company. Reprinted by permission. All rights reserved.

In addition, the different opinions and problem-solving approaches of the various group members are valuable aids to an important lesson; there is seldom one solution to an organization's problem that everyone agrees is correct.

Group discussion techniques typically are used as training devices at the management level. It is possible that they may come to have broader utility, however. For example, the "quality circles" that are so much in the news basically are discussion groups. Such circles consist of groups of workers (with or without supervisors and managers) who meet regularly to make recommendations about solving production problems and enhancing product/service quality.

A number of companies, including Honeywell and Motorola, now use versions of the "quality circle" concept and are pleased with the results. As more evidence for the effectiveness of such groups is accumulated, group discussion training at other than the management level may go beyond current informal use.

Role playing and behavior modeling.   Two related training methods extend the learning potential of group discussion to a more realistic level. Instead of talking about issues, trainees become involved with them on a behavioral level. For example, instead of talking about the need for better communication in a case, participants would communicate with one another as if they were people in the case (role playing), or watch and emulate effective communication techniques (behavior modeling).

Role playing was developed originally for use in psychotherapy by J. B. Moreno. This technique, which Moreno called *psychodrama*, appears to have been first applied to a business setting in the early 1930s at Macy's Department Store in New York. The great strength of role playing as a training method is that it focuses attention on the human element of dealing with organizational problems.

Those involved in real organizational problems have positions to defend and a stake in the outcome of the situation. Traditional case-discussion training techniques make it too easy for everyone concerned to concentrate on the facts of the case and ignore this human element; yet, it cannot be ignored in an actual work situation. Role playing is one way to make training in problem-solving and interpersonal skills more realistic.

Behavior modeling is a relatively new training technique (Goldstein & Sorcher, 1974) based on the social learning theory of Bandura (1969, 1977). Social learning theory emphasizes the role that watching the behavior of others and observing the outcomes of this behavior play in individual learning. Its premise is that some of what people learn is acquired indirectly by their imitation of behavior they observe to have positive outcomes for others.

Moses (1978) has described the four steps to using behavior modeling in training: modeling, rehearsal, feedback, and transfer of training.

1. *Modeling*—Trainees observe filmed, videotaped, or live actors performing some task or dealing with some problem in a desired or

effective way. Key behaviors for this successful performance are highlighted.

2. *Rehearsal*—Trainees practice the behaviors as modeled.
3. *Feedback*—Both trainer and other participants provide feedback for the rehearsed behavior. The social reinforcement provided by others for successful performance is an important part of the process.
4. *Transfer of Training*—The new behaviors are followed up on the job and reinforced where used appropriately.

Both role playing and behavior modeling have been used most frequently for training at or above the supervisory level, and both have been used more frequently for developmental purposes than for initial job training. This limited usage, however, is more a function of time and cost than of any inherent limits in the method. For example, behavior modeling has been used successfully in a program sponsored by the Philadelphia Retail Council to teach certain new employees the ''people skills'' they need to succeed in a middle-class work environment.

Concluding Remarks on Employee Training

The various training methods discussed have been grouped according to the amount and kind of trainee participation they incorporate. Differences among these three approaches with respect to the opportunities they offer for practice, feedback, and reinforcement of desired training behaviors are summarized Exhibit 6–7.

Exhibit 6–7 illustrates the differences in *potential* of each training method. This potential may be altered considerably by the way a method is used and the skills of the trainer. For example, nonparticipative methods can be made more effective by a highly skilled trainer and/or by supplementing them with other methods. Individual participative methods, on the other hand, can fail to live up to their potential since they guarantee only practice. Unless feedback is built into the training task (as with many applications of CAI), it is up to those who design and carry out the training to add feedback and reinforcement of desired training behaviors.

The greatest difference between potential and actuality with respect to training effectiveness is likely to occur with the group participative methods. These techniques have very high potential for both feedback

Type of Training Method	Opportunity for		
	Practice	Feedback	Reinforcement
Nonparticipative Methods	None	Low	Low
Individual Participative Methods	High	High	High
Group Participative Methods	Low to High	Very High	Very High

EXHIBIT 6–7

Type of Training and Opportunity for Practice, Feedback, and Reinforcement

and reinforcement because these can come from other members of the group as well as from the training task and from the trainer. This potential, however, will not be realized unless the trainer makes sure that all trainees actively participate. As shown in Exhibit 6–7, individual participation in group training methods is not guaranteed.

To the extent that training methods allow for practice, feedback, and reinforcement of desired behaviors, a training program is more likely to be effective. But trainees differ considerably as to both ability and motivation. Those who select people for training can do much to make sure that trainee ability is at least adequate. Those who conduct training programs can try to make them as interesting, challenging, and rewarding as possible. In the last analysis, however, it is the *interaction* of the trainee with the training situation that determines individual training success.

EVALUATING TRAINING EFFECTIVENESS

Training is an expensive undertaking. The costs of training new employees may include any or all of the following:

- equipment, materials, and trainer costs
- wages to trainees who are not yet productive
- replacing employees who are trained and leave the organization shortly thereafter
- mistakes and lack of speed on the parts of on-the-job trainees

Given the variety and size of the costs that may be charged to an organization's training program, some way to evaluate its effectiveness should be part of that program. This evaluation may be made on the basis of internal or external criteria. *Internal criteria* are measures of training effectiveness *during training*. Examples include, formal tests of trainee knowledge and skill and ratings by trainers of trainee progress and performance.

External criteria for evaluating training are measures of training effectiveness in producing the desired *job behaviors* in trainees. The extent to which positive evaluations on internal criteria are matched by positive evaluations on external criteria is the extent to which there is successful *transfer of training*.

In the following discussion, the evaluation of training effectiveness is examined from three perspectives. The first is training as seen from the viewpoint of those who are trained. This is an *internal criterion* approach; trainees are asked to evaluate the training program itself.

The second perspective to be taken in the evaluation of training effectiveness is that of the organization. Two questions are foremost from this viewpoint: Did trainees learn what they were expected to learn? Was the training method cost-effective and/or more cost-effective than alternative methods? Both *internal* and *external criteria* must be considered in answering these questions. Finally, training effectiveness is considered from the perspective of transfer of training—an *external criterion* measure.

Trainee Evaluations of Training

Trainee evaluations usually are made by means of one or more question-naires that ask for (a) trainee *opinions* as to the quality and effectiveness of the training procedures, materials, and methods, (b) trainee *feelings* of satisfaction or dissatisfaction with the training experience, and (c) trainee *evaluations* of the extent to which they personally gained from training.

Trainee opinions and feelings (a and b) about training typically are assessed by means of one-time questionnaires administered at the con-clusion of the training. Self-evaluations of learning (c) may be handled in this way as well. Alternatively, trainees may be given the same ques-tionnaire before and after training about the extent to which they believe they have particular skills. A graph (called a *histogram*) summarizing the results of such a procedure is shown in Exhibit 6–8.

The data in Exhibit 6–8 show that participant ratings of their com-munication skills before and after training were significantly different only with respect to their listening skills. There are a number of problems with evaluating this result, however. A major one is that most trainees were rating their skills in a different light before and after training because they knew more *about* communication after training. This prob-lem, a form of *response-shift bias*, gives such measures of training effec-tiveness limited utility (Mezoff, 1981).

Significance: See pages 58 to 59.

Organization Evaluations of Training

From the viewpoint of the organization, the two most important ques-tions to ask about training are (a) whether or not it accomplished its purpose and (b) whether the benefits were greater than the costs. The ultimate answer to whether or not training accomplished its purpose lies in the job performance of trainees, that is, in external criteria. A number of other factors affect transfer of training to the job, however, so it is usual to check trainee skills and knowledge by means of tests or trainer evaluation at the end of training, that is, by internal criteria.

If organizations decide that post-training tests or evaluations show that trainees have indeed learned what their programs set out to teach, the question arises as to whether or not this outcome was worth the costs. To be cost-effective, a training program must have at least two characteristics. First, training must yield results that are superior in some way to those achieved by employees without training. Second, these benefits must outweigh the costs in either an absolute sense or relative to alternative methods of training.

Is Training More Effective Than No Training?

If training is worth its costs, then new employees who have been through training should be superior in some way to new employees who have

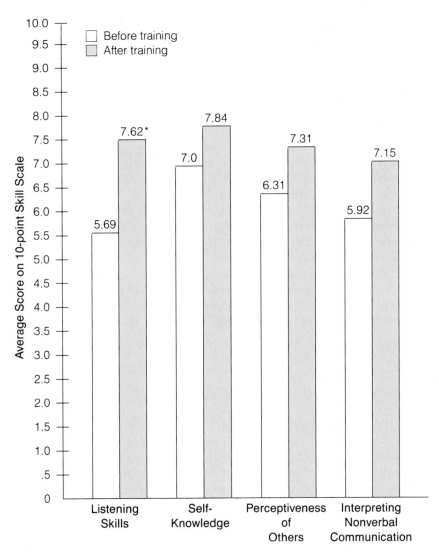

*Difference from Pretraining significant at p < .05.

Note. Data from B. Mezoff, "How to Get Accurate Self Reports of Training Outcomes." *Training and Development Journal*, 1981, 35(9), pp. 56–61.

not been through such a program. As a group, trained employees should exhibit one or more of the following behaviors:

- becoming productive more quickly than those without training
- making fewer mistakes than those without training
- doing work of higher quality than those without training
- having fewer accidents than those without training

The basic strategy for assessing whether training is more effective in some measurable way than no training is to conduct a field experiment or field study. In this research, some aspect of the job behavior of employees with training is compared with that of employees who do not have training. The goal is to set up the investigation so nontraining factors can be ruled out as explanations for observed differences between those who received training and those who did not.

Field experiment: See page 52.

Field study: See pages 55 to 56.

To rule out nontraining explanations for differences between trained and untrained subjects, people chosen for the investigation (the sample) should be assigned randomly to the training/no training groups. The untrained subjects should have any experiences the training subjects have *except* the training; for example, they should receive the orientation to the company (if this is not part of the training) and be given the same *pretests* of job skills and knowledge to establish baselines against which to measure changes.

Sample: See pages 49 to 50.

The reasons for the precautions taken in evaluating the effectiveness of training versus no training were demonstrated clearly in the Weitz and Adler (1973) laboratory experiment summarized in "Spotlight on Research." Without a control group, these investigators would not have known that *untrained* subjects performed better than trained subjects after only a small amount of practice. So important is this control factor, that some believe one control group is not enough. The experimental design for evaluating training that is shown in Exhibit 6–9 has *three* control groups.

The training effectiveness research design in Exhibit 6–9 was proposed by Solomon (1949). Control Group 1 is the standard control group discussed above. The other two control groups allow the researcher to examine separately the possible effects of pretests both on training and on post-test (criterion) measures. For example, if a significant difference were found on criterion measures between Control Groups 1 and 3, but not between Control Group 1 and the experimental group, it would be possible that the pretest was a more powerful influence on post-test performance than training was.

Is Training Cost-Effective?

Even if research shows training of employees to be more effective than no training, the question as to whether or not it is worth the costs still

Group	Pretest	Training	Post-test[a]
Experimental Group	Yes	Yes	Yes
Control Group 1	Yes	No	Yes
Control Group 2	No	Yes	Yes
Control Group 3	No	No	Yes

[a]Post-test is the criterion measure.

Note. Summarized from R. L. Solomon, "An Extension of Control Group Design." *Psychological Bulletin*, 1949, 46(2), pp. 137–150.

EXHIBIT 6–9

The Solomon Design for Training Effectiveness Research

remains. An expensive training program that shows only a small gain over no training, for example, is not cost-effective. If subsequent job performance of employees is about the same, a program that lasts three weeks and costs $4,000 per week is less cost-effective than one that costs $5,000 per week for two weeks.

Evaluating the cost-effectiveness of training versus no training is a matter of monitoring the two groups of employees over time to see if initial differences hold up. Review again the Weitz and Adler (1973) study. If the practice afforded by the job itself closes the gap rather quickly, then it may be that the training program is not earning its way.

Evaluating the *relative* cost-effectiveness of alternative training programs is more difficult. Traditional approaches by researchers to this problem have begun with the assumption that the training provided by these alternatives is equally effective, but this assumption is a weak one in many cases (Kearsley & Compton, 1981). An evaluation that allows for differentially effective training by the various alternatives is based on the following equation:

Amount of Training Accomplished = Number/Skills of Trainers × Training Technology (Kearsley & Compton, 1981).

On the basis of the equation, the cost-effectiveness of alternative methods of training is evaluated in terms of the increased amount of training that can be accomplished with greater expenditures of resources. According to the equation, some level of training can be accomplished with any type of training program (although it may not be more effective than no formal training).

Kearsley and Compton call the model described a *Productivity Model.* In this model, increased training expenses in the form of more trainers, more skilled trainers, and more expensive equipment will add to training effectiveness, but at a diminishing rate. At some point, the increased costs will not reap equal benefits. For example, the Olin Corporation found that adding a particular kind of computer program to their training (an increased expense) brought trainees up to job speed much faster and so saved the company money. Such savings might not be worth the costs to a company that had to buy all of the computer equipment especially for this purpose.

One implication of the Productivity Model for evaluating training cost-effectiveness is that it might pay off to set up training in a graded fashion according to the resources it requires. For example, a training group might begin with lectures and films, move on to behavior modeling, and finally to individual, supervised hands-on training. Each step advances the learning process, but each takes more resources and is more effective once earlier steps have been taken. In addition, resources are not wasted on trainees who decide to drop out of the program.

Transfer of Training and Training Effectiveness

The issue of transfer of training does not arise when training occurs on the job, and for this reason, many people in industry prefer on-the-job training. Admittedly, off-the-job training raises the possibility that employees will leave some of what they learned behind, but the extent of the difficulty varies considerably. Exhibit 6–10 presents a summary of Bass and Vaughn's (1966) well-known evaluation of popular training methods with respect to transfer of training potential.

The term **transfer of training** refers to the generalization of what is learned in training to the job setting.

Bass and Vaughan's evaluation of the potential for transfer of training of various training methods is based on the *most likely* degree of similarity between training and job conditions. It is possible, however, to increase the transfer from any method of training. The two primary tools for accomplishing this already have been discussed—feedback and reinforcement. These principles are used in exactly the same way as they are used during training. Employees are provided with *information* as to how they are doing, and they are given *reinforcement* when they are doing well.

An evaluation of training effectiveness based on transfer of training should be a measure of whether or not skills and knowledge acquired by people in training are used on the job. Any behavior will fail to develop and/or persist without feedback and reinforcement; on the other hand, most behaviors will persist if these conditions hold. In this sense, all job training has an on-the-job component.

Concluding Remarks on Evaluation of Training Effectiveness

Each of the perspectives on training effectiveness reviewed provides a different kind of information about the training program. All of this information can be valuable. Like most decisions in organizations, however, the decision of how to formally evaluate training ultimately rests on the costs versus the benefits of the alternatives.

At this point, attention to training in organizations is brought to a close and is shifted to socialization, a topic that appears to be quite

---

I. Methods more likely to facilitate transfer of training
  A. Simulations
  B. Vestibule schools
  C. Role playing
  D. Case studies
  E. Structured group exercises

II. Methods less likely to facilitate transfer of training
  A. Lectures
  B. Special classes
  C. Films and television
  D. Discussion group techniques
  E. Programmed instruction

EXHIBIT 6–10

The Transfer of Training Potential for Some Popular Training Methods

---

Note. Summarized from B. M. Bass and J. A. Vaughan, *Training in Industry: The Management of Learning.* Belmont, CA: Wadsworth, 1966.

different. As noted earlier, however, training and socialization are interrelated parts of the process by which newly hired people are transformed into productive employees.

Socialization is the process by which newcomers to a group acquire the attitudes, values, and norms necessary to become accepted members of the group.

SOCIALIZATION

In organizations, there are at least two groups to which a newcomer must be socialized. One is the group of people with whom the newcomer works. The other is the "group" of the organization itself. Learning the official ropes of this larger social system is usually called *orientation.*

Organizations with large, formal new-employee training programs often make orientation a part of training. Many others handle it by means of written handbooks. These books typically cover such diverse topics as the rules for coffee breaks and the availability of medical insurance plans.

Orientation is the process by which newcomers to a group are acquainted with its rules, operating procedures, policies, and performance expectations.

Many organizations give orientation responsibility to a new employee's immediate supervisor. This responsibility often is informal, but not always. A formal supervisory orientation checklist is shown in Exhibit 6–11.

EXHIBIT 6–11

A Formal Orientation
Checklist for
Supervisors

Employee's Name	Discussion Completed (please check each individual item)
I. Word of welcome	_____
II. Explain overall departmental organization and its relationship to other activities of the company	_____
III. Explain employee's individual contribution to the objectives of the department and his or her starting assignment in broad terms	_____
IV. Discuss job content with employee and give him or her a copy of job description (if available)	_____
V. Explain departmental training program(s) and salary increase practices and procedures	_____
VI. Discuss where the employee lives and transportation facilities	_____

VII. Explain working conditions:
    a. Hours of work, time sheets
    b. Use of employee entrance and elevators
    c. Lunch hours
    d. Coffee breaks, rest periods
    e. Personal telephone calls and mail
    f. Overtime policy and requirements
    g. Paydays and procedure for being paid
    h. Lockers
    i. Other _____   _____

VIII. Requirements for continuance of employment—explain company standards as to:
    a. Performance of duties
    b. Attendance and punctuality

Employee's Name	Discussion Completed (please check each individual item)

      c. Handling confidential information
      d. Behavior
      e. General appearance
      f. Wearing of uniform   _____

IX. Introduce new staff member to manager(s) and other supervisors.

     Special attention should be paid to the person to whom the new employee will be assigned.   _____

X. Release employee to immediate supervisor who will:
      a. Introduce new staff member to fellow workers
      b. Familiarize the employee with his or her work place
      c. Begin on-the-job training   _____

If not applicable, insert N/A in space provided.

_____	_____
Employee's Signature	Supervisor's Signature
_____	_____
Date	Division

Form examined for filing:

_____	_____
Date	Personnel Department

Note. From J. Famularo, *Handbook of Modern Personnel Administration.* New York: McGraw-Hill, Inc., 1972, pp. 23–24 to 23–25. Reprinted with permission.

As can be seen in the topics covered in Exhibit 6–11, orientation is basically an introductory process. Although it is the first step in socialization, it is usually of brief duration and has received little attention in I/O psychology literature. The broader topic of socialization is addressed in the remainder of Chapter 6.

The Importance of Socialization to the Organization

Katz (1964) lists three types of behaviors that the members of an organization must exhibit if the organization is to function. Employees must:

- stay with the company;
- carry out their jobs dependably;
- engage in innovative and cooperative behaviors that go beyond minimal job descriptions.

There are many factors that influence the extent to which any particular employee exhibits the behaviors discussed by Katz. One is the extent to which the employee feels at home, comfortable with job performance, and motivated to help the organization accomplish its goals, that is, the extent to which he or she is effectively socialized to the organization.

A Model of Socialization

Since the role of socialization in organizational effectiveness first began to attract systematic attention, a number of writers have formulated models of the process. Among the more well known of these models are Buchanan's (1974) three-stage early career model, the Porter, Lawler, and Hackman (1975) three-stage entry model, and Schein's (1978) three-stage socialization model. Drawing on this literature, Feldman (1981) has proposed the three-stage model shown in Exhibit 6–12.

In the model shown in Exhibit 6–12, the three stages of socialization are labeled *Anticipatory, Encounter,* and *Change/Acquisition.* The goals of socialization, or "socialization tasks," at each stage may be summarized as follows.

1. *Anticipatory*—The potential new employee gets information about the organization, the job, and the extent to which his or her own skills, abilities, needs, and values will fit in.
2. *Encounter*—The newcomer learns his or her new job tasks, is included into the work group, defines his or her role within the work group, and deals with any conflicts created by being a member of that particular group (intergroup role conflict) and of the organization (outside-life conflict).
3. *Change/Acquisition*—The new employee masters his or her job tasks and work roles and satisfactorily adjusts to the work group and the organizational culture. At this point, the newcomer is an insider.

As may be seen in Exhibit 6–12, Feldman postulates various direct and indirect relationships between the socialization tasks at different stages and the behaviors described by Katz (1964) as critical to organization functioning. In addition, socialization is seen as having *affective* outcomes for new employees, including feelings of satisfaction and a stronger tendency toward internal work motivation and job involvement.

Feldman (1981) cites a number of studies and writers that have made specific links between the various socialization tasks in his model and the behavioral and affective outcomes. He notes that a number of researchers have found links between effective socialization and job tenure. Support for another relationship also is found in Feldman's own 1976 study. Employees reported feeling that they must demonstrate task competence before they could feel comfortable about making innovative suggestions relative to the work situation.

Other reviews of socialization research support the contention that this is an important determinant of employee behavior and attitudes (e.g., Louis, 1980). Given this importance, what can be done to make the process more effective? There is no quick and easy answer since

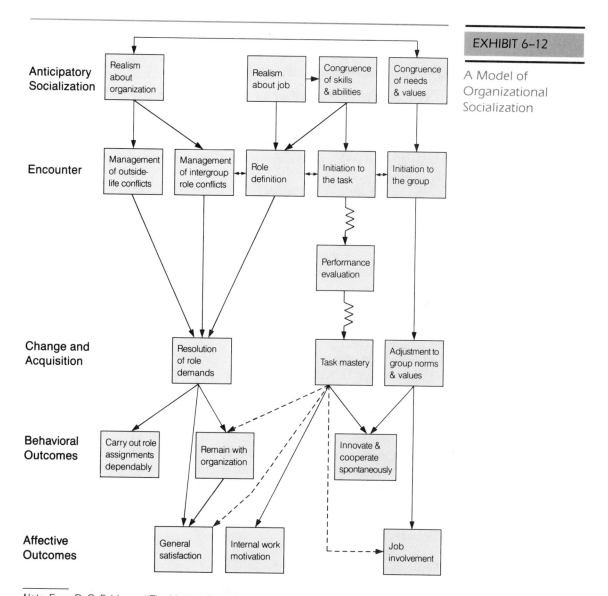

EXHIBIT 6-12

A Model of
Organizational
Socialization

Note. From D. C. Feldman, "The Multiple Socialization of Organization Members." *Academy of Management Review*, 1981, 6(2), p. 311. Reprinted by permission of the author and publisher.

socialization is a multidimensional process that is accomplished through a variety of means, many of which are informal. Certain formal organizational activities, however, do have an impact on the extent to which socialization is successfully accomplished.

Factors That Influence Successful Socialization

Three sets of formal organizational activities have particular impact on the success or failure of socialization—screening/selection, training, and performance appraisal. The effects of these activities are discussed in terms of Feldman's model of socialization for easy reference.

Screening/Selection and Socialization

RJP: See pages 133 to 134. In Chapter 5, the concept of Realistic Job Previews (RJPs) was introduced as one approach to solving certain problems created by individual/organization/job mismatches. The same remarks now may be seen to be relevant to socialization. The more accurate the information provided to job applicants at this phase, the more effective anticipatory socialization should be.

The anticipatory socialization phase is an information-gathering phase. The potential employee must attempt to assess whether or not he or she will fit into an organization. There seems little doubt that candor on the part of those doing screening and selection will facilitate this process. To the extent that this candor stimulates unsuited applicants to ''screen themselves out,'' fewer problems also are likely to occur at later stages of socialization.

Training and Socialization

Becoming familiar with and mastering job tasks are important parts of encounter and change/acquisition socialization in Feldman's model. Job training speeds up this process. Training also affects the process of adjusting to the organization and to future coworkers because it sends messages about the nature of an individual's future work role and the values and standards of the company.

Both anticipatory and encounter socialization are likely to be inhibited if training messages contradict expectations set up earlier. For example, a new employee led to expect that his or her own value on individualism is supported by the organization will find it more difficult to adjust if the training program is a routinized, prepackaged one. Similarly, careless on-the-job training can contradict expressed expectations for high performance standards.

Performance Appraisal and Socialization

With respect to socialization, the major role of performance appraisal, formal or informal, is to move the new employee through to mastery of his or her work role and job tasks. Early and frequent appraisals are important, both to continue the training process and to reinforce performance expectations.

Performance appraisals also can affect a new employee's socialization into a new work group, although the nature of the effect depends upon the nature of the group and its informal performance expectations. For example, a new employee who does not receive outstanding evaluations may not find acceptance in a highly skilled work group that views itself as elite. On the other hand, a highly-motivated ''performance hotshot'' may have difficulty being accepted into a group with indifferent performance standards.

Concluding Remarks on Socialization

Screening and selection, training, and performance appraisal were singled out for discussion as relevant to effective socialization because these activities are under the control of formal organizational policy. Other factors that play an important role can be controlled in a limited way, or not at all.

Among the factors affecting socialization that are beyond formal control are (a) the behavior of a newcomer's coworkers and (b) the newcomer's own perceptions of and ability to deal with the issues of socialization (see Jones, 1983). Successful socialization, like all behavioral phenomena, is best understood as a complex interaction of individual and environmental factors.

SUMMARY

Recruiting, screening and selection, and placement bring new employees into an organization. Training and socialization change them from newcomers to insiders. Training is a structured learning experience intended to transform employee abilities into specific job skills. Among the functions it serves for organizations are those of maintenance, motivation, and socialization.

A number of decisions must be made in setting up an organization's training program. These include how much and what kind of training is needed, where it will take place, and what instructional methods will be used. Both who is available to do training and certain learning principles should be considered in making these decisions.

However a training program is conducted, some way to evaluate its effectiveness should be included. Evaluation may be in terms of the trainees' reactions to the program, the effectiveness of the program in producing demonstrable learning, the extent to which learning transfers to the job, the cost-effectiveness of the program, or some combination of these approaches.

Socialization in organizations is a broad concept covering all of the ways by which newcomers learn about and adjust to procedures, policies, expectations, norms, values, and attitudes of both the organization itself and particular work groups within it. The process of socialization is a multidimensional one that is affected considerably by an organization's policies with respect to screening and selection, training, and performance appraisal. Successful socialization is related to the three classes of behaviors that any organization must elicit from its members if it is to survive and function—job performance, tenure, and cooperation/innovation.

AT ISSUE

Productivity and Socialization

There has been much discussion in recent years about the decline of worker productivity in the United States. For the period 1970–1980, for example, the U.S. Department of Labor's Bureau of Labor Statistics estimated the increase in productivity in the manufacturing industries to be 28%. This figure puts this country well behind other industrialized nations, such as Italy, Germany, France, the Netherlands, and Japan. The record in other segments of American industry has been even poorer, with decreases in productivity being reported in some areas.

The cause of a downturn in America's traditional pattern of increasing man-hour productivity has been attributed to unions, the failure of organizations to meet worker needs, a general shift from a work to a leisure ethic, and the interference of the federal government in organizational personnel policies. More recently, the intense interest generated by Japan's phenomenal postwar industrial and economic development has led to a more complex explanation. Declining productivity is seen as lying at the end of a chain of events that begins with worker alienation and proceeds through an associated lack of commitment to organizational goals and low levels of motivation. Eventually the chain can lead beyond low productivity to such hostile acts as sabotage and theft.

The dismal picture painted has emerged from a causal inference made between two facts: (a) Japan's productivity increases have far outstepped those of the United States in recent years; (b) Japanese management in general differs markedly from American management in general. The most striking aspect of this difference lies in the employee-employer relationships in the two countries. Until recently, this relationship, usually described as a partnership one in Japan, was becoming increasingly adversarial in the United States, particularly in larger companies.

Of the many ways to look at the differences between United States and Japanese labor relations, one is from a socialization standpoint. Employment with a particular company in Japan traditionally has been a lifetime affair for most Japanese workers. Management expects and rewards hard work, self-reliance, loyalty, pride, and cooperation among workers. In return, management takes its responsibilities for the welfare of employees very seriously and sees part of this responsibility as involving employees in most aspects of organizational decision making (Byron, 1981). Conditions, in other words, are impressively conducive to effective worker socialization.

There is no doubt that attributing Japan's industrial successes to the effective socialization of its work force is an oversimplification. At the same time, what is known about socialization and organizational effectiveness makes it impossible to ignore this factor. As a result, interest in "Japanese management" is growing by leaps and bounds. The problem is that Japan and the United States are very different countries. Japanese management simply cannot be tacked on to organizations in a country whose culture does not support the underlying philosophy. The challenge lies in finding ways to make use of the "lessons of Japan" within the context of our own culture—a culture that traditionally values individualism and independence and one whose organizations traditionally have been efficiency-oriented and run by authoritarian decision-making processes (Ozawa, 1980).

REFERENCES

AMERICAN SOCIETY FOR TRAINING AND DE-VELOPMENT. For your information. *Training and Development Journal*, 1981, *36*(8), 8–9.

BANDURA, A. *Principles of Behavior Modification.* New York: Holt, Rinehart, & Winston, 1969.

BANDURA, A. *Social Learning Theory.* Englewood Cliffs, NJ: Prentice-Hall, 1977.

BASS, B. M., & VAUGHAN, J. A. *Training in Industry: The Management of Learning.* Belmont, CA: Wadsworth, 1966.

BUCHANAN, B. Building organizational commitment: The socialization of managers in work organizations. *Administrative Science Quarterly,* 1977, *19*(4), 533–346.

BYRON, C. An attractive Japanese export. *Time,* 1982, (March 2), p. 74.

FAMULARO, J. *Handbook of Modern Personnel Administration.* New York: McGraw-Hill, 1972.

FELDMAN, D. C. A contingency theory of socialization. *Administrative Science Quarterly,* 1976, *21*(3), 433–452.

FELDMAN, D. C. The multiple socialization of organization members. *Academy of Management Review,* 1981, *6*(2), 309–318.

GAGNÉ, R. M. Military training and principles of learning. *American Psychologist,* 1962, *17*(2), 83–91.

GAGNÉ, R. M., & ROHWER, W. D., Jr. Instructional psychology. In P. H. Mussen & M. Rosenzweig (Eds.), *Annual Review of Psychology* (Vol. 20). Palo Alto, CA: Annual Review, 1969.

GOLD, L. Job instruction: Four steps to success. *Training and Development Journal,* 1981, *35*(9), 28–32.

GOLDSTEIN, I., & SORCHER, M. *Changing Supervisory Behavior.* New York: Pergamon Press, 1974.

JONES, G. R. Psychological orientation and the process of organizational socialization: An interactionist perspective. *Academy of Management Review,* 1983, *8*(3), 464–474.

LOUIS, M. R. Surprise and sense making: What newcomers experience in entering unfamiliar organizational settings. *Administrative Science Quarterly,* 1980, *25*(2), 226–251.

KATZ, D. The motivational basis of organizational behavior. *Behavioral Science,* 1964, *9*(2), 131–146.

KEARSLEY, G., & COMPTON, T. Assessing costs, benefits, and productivity in training systems. *Training and Development Journal,* 1981, *35*(1), 52–61.

KOMAKI, J., HEINZMANN, T., & LAWSON, L. Effect of training and feedback: Component analysis of a behavioral safety program. *Journal of Applied Psychology,* 1980, *65*(3), 261–270.

MALLORY, W. J. Simulation for task practice in technical training. *Training and Development Journal,* 1981, *35*(9), 12–20.

MEZOFF, B. How to get accurate self reports of training outcomes. *Training and Development Journal,* 1981, *35*(9), 56–61.

MOSES, J. L. Behavior modeling for managers. *Human Factors,* 1978, *20*(2), 225–232.

OZAWA, T. Japanese world of work: An interpretative survey. *MSU Business Topics,* 1980 (Spring), pp. 45–55.

PORTER, L. W., LAWLER, E. E., III, & HACKMAN, J. R. *Behavior in Organizations.* New York: McGraw-Hill, 1975.

PRESSEY, S. L. A simple apparatus which gives tests and scores—and teaches. *School Sociology,* 1926, *23,* 323–376.

SCHEIN, E. H. *Career Dynamics: Matching Individual and Organizational Needs.* Reading, MA: Addison-Wesley, 1978.

SOLOMON, R. L. An extension of control group design. *Psychological Bulletin,* 1949, *46*(2), 137–150.

VEIGA, J. F., & YANOUZAS, J. N. *The Dynamics of Organization Theory: Gaining a Macro Perspective.* St. Paul: West, 1979.

WEITZ, J., & ADLER, S. The optimal use of simulation. *Journal of Applied Psychology,* 1973, *58*(2), 219–224.

PART III

The Job and Working Conditions

In Part III, the jobs for which employees are recruited, selected, and trained are examined. Chapter 7 gives an overview of job design from both physical and psychological perspectives. In Chapter 8, more general working conditions and worker health and safety are considered. Chapter 9 covers job analysis, the formal process by which the work of an organization is examined. Job evaluation, one of the major uses to which job analysis information is put, also is discussed.

CHAPTER 7

Job Design

I/O PSYCHOLOGY AT WORK

Human Factors Lessons from Three Mile Island

After the automatic shutdown system of a New Jersey nuclear reactor failed twice in February [of 1983]—the most significant nuclear incidents since the Three Mile Island scare—two psychologists were there, helping the government to probe the scene. . . .

At TMI [Three Mile Island], there were no NRC [Nuclear Regulatory Commission] engineering psychologists to turn to as government and utility officials struggled to explain how a series of mechanical and human errors—at a plant in commercial operation just three months—was doused just an hour before igniting a major nuclear tragedy.

In fact, before TMI there were almost no human factors professionals, psychologists or otherwise, on the staffs at NRC, the firms designing and building nuclear plants, or the utilities operating them.

Consequently, human factors engineers' special expertise—the science of how best to integrate people into systems—was all but absent from an industry confronting one of the most complex and potentially hazardous systems in the world.

Humans Ignored

"Before Three Mile Island [NRC] wasn't even aware of the fact that there were any humans in that plant," says Robert Mackie, an experimental psychologist who directs Human Factors Research, a subsidiary of the Essex Corporation . . .

The NRC has hired about 30 psychologists since TMI. It has issued a series of new regulations and guidelines for the nation's 76 nuclear plants licensed for full power to address human factor problems identified by TMI investigators, particularly those of faulty control room design, inadequate training of operators, and emergency operating procedures.

And it has already carried out or approved the implementation of most of the 51 major recommendations in the August, 1982 report of a Human Factors Society study group. The group was commissioned by NRC to draw up a long-range human factors plan for nuclear reactor regulation. All six members on that panel were psychologists. NRC is currently completing a three-year human factors plan which addresses most of the group's concerns.

Excerpted from C. Cordes. "Human Factors and Nuclear Safety: Grudging Respect for a Growing Field." *APA Monitor*, 1983, *14*(5), pp. 1, 13–14. Copyright 1983 by the American Psychological Association.

The Nuclear Regulatory Commission (NRC) hired 30 psychologists to deal with a variety of complex issues raised by the March, 1979 events at Three Mile Island near Harrisburg, Pennsylvania. Many of these issues concern the training of people to work effectively and safely in one of the most recent, most technologically advanced, and most controversial industries in this country. But many issues are more basic, having to do with the initial design of jobs, equipment, and work space.

The evidence that has accumulated since Three Mile Island reveals that the most elementary principles of human factors engineering had been overlooked in many cases. Among the problems found with respect to human use of the control panels for the operation of the plant were the following.

- Display methods for critical information (such as that indicating the stuck valve) were not designed to stand out and get operator attention.
- Almost 30% of the displays were so high that some operators could not read them at all.
- The same colors had opposite meanings on different control panels used by the same operators.

The kinds of problems found in the control panels at TMI are typical of the problems addressed by people who work in *human factors engineering* (usually called *ergonomics* outside of the United States). These practitioners come from a variety of disciplines, including engineering, biology, medicine, and psychology. Their particular specialty is designing jobs, equipment, and work environments so that these elements are compatible with human capabilities and limitations.

Human factors psychologists primarily have experimental or I/O psychology backgrounds. Their professional interest in job design lies in its physical aspects. Other psychologists are more interested in the psychological aspects of job design. In Chapter 7, some of the basic issues of both approaches are considered.

THE HUMAN FACTORS APPROACH TO JOB DESIGN

As it exists today, human factors engineering came into its own around the time of World War II. Prior to that time, the physical aspects of job and work place design had been largely the province of industrial engineers, of whom the best known are probably Frederick Taylor and the husband-wife team of Frank and Lillian Gilbreth. Between them, Taylor (1911) and the Gilbreths (1921) developed the principles of *time analysis* and *motion study* that are still in use today.

Industrial engineer: See page 6.

Time analysis and motion study are complementary strategies for finding the most efficient way to perform a job. They involve studying worker movements to find a way for them to perform a particular task that maximizes speed and minimizes wasted movements. For example, should a person who packs books into boxes for shipping use one hand or two? Should the books be located to the right, the left, or in front of the box? Should this person be seated or standing?

Time and motion study are concerned with the best way to perform a job. Traditionally, it was the role of I/O psychologists to fit the worker to the job (as the job was so designed) through selection and training. In general, this approach worked quite well until the technology leap produced by the emergency conditions of World War II. During this period, technological advances in machinery and equipment began to outdistance available selection and training methods; fitting the worker to the job became increasingly difficult for psychologists.

The problems encountered in World War II led to a new conceptualization of the relationship between worker and job. Person, machines and tools, and the work space came to be viewed as components of a system. As in any system, these components must be compatible if the whole is to work effectively and efficiently. The term *human factors engineering* reflects this emphasis on fitting the job to the worker as well as the worker to the job.

Operator-Machine Systems

The term **operator-machine system** means that human and machine work together to accomplish a job.

In an operator-machine system, the person and the machine together do the job, but they perform different tasks. If the machine is a simple one, the worker operates the controls and the machine does "the work." An ordinary sewing machine is a machine of this sort.

More complex machines require the operators to watch various forms of displays and make adjustments based on what these tell them. For example, a photocopying machine has visual displays that tell the operator when to begin input, when paper must be added, and when service is needed. In addition, the quality of the output provides the operator with information about making other adjustments, such as placement of material to be copied and changes in the light contrast of the copies. This operator-machine system is shown in Exhibit 7-1.

The basic operator-machine system illustrated in Exhibit 7-1 has counterparts in many industrial jobs—the worker operates controls and makes adjustments as various displays and/or machine output dictate. But the advent of the electronic/computer age has given modern organizations machines of a far more complex nature.

The work that many modern machines do is primarily the organizing and display of information. The operator uses this information to make a continuing series of decisions; these decisions constitute the major part of the job. For example, the equipment used by an air traffic controller gives him or her a picture of the skies in a given area. It is the human controller who makes the correct decisions about aircraft movement on the basis of this information.

The increasing complexity of modern machines places increasing demands on the perceptual and cognitive abilities of their human operators. These demands, in turn, place increasing demands on human factors

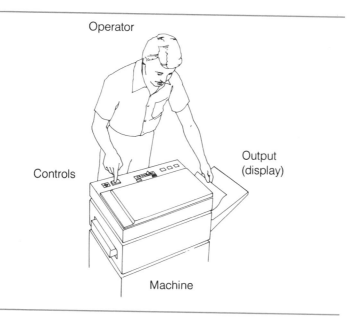

Operator

Output
(display)

Controls

Machine

EXHIBIT 7-1

An Operator-
Machine System

psychologists to help industrial designers make control and display mechanisms compatible with human abilities.

The Design of Controls

Controls are the means by which a machine is activated and operated. They are the first "interface" between human and machine in an operator-machine system. Familiar examples of controls include:

- switches
- buttons
- keys
- levers
- pedals
- wheels

Many machines, such as typewriters, have very simple controls. Others, such as aircraft or machines used in the taping of a television program, have banks of dozens or more controls.

In the design of controls (or in specifications for their design), a large number of decisions must be made. Among these are decisions as to shape, form, and location relative to human capacities, to purpose, and to other controls and/or displays. A comparison of five simple and frequently-used controls on four human operation criteria is given in Exhibit 7-2.

Exhibit 7-2 shows the relative advantages and disadvantages of five controls with respect to (a) the speed with which the operator can use the control to make necessary adjustments, (b) the accuracy with which the operator can use the control, (c) the physical effort required to use

EXHIBIT 7–2

A Comparison of Five
Common Control
Mechanisms

Component	Speed	Accuracy	Effort Required	Working Range
Handwheel 	Poor	Good	Moderate	Moderate
Knob Small (continuous)	Poor	Good	Very poor	Moderate
 Large	Very poor	Moderate	Poor	Moderate
Knob (clock stops) 	Good	Good	Very poor	Very poor
Push-button 	Good	Very poor	Very poor	Very poor
Pedal 	Good	Poor	Good	Very poor

Note. Adapted from E. Grandjean, *Fitting the Task to the Man: An Ergonomic Approach* (3rd ed.). New York: International Publications Service, London: Taylor & Francis Ltd:, 1982. p. 147. Adapted by permission of the author and the publishers.

the control, and (d) the range of responses that the control will accommodate. Clearly, there are trade-offs; for example, the pedal allows for good speed but poor accuracy, while the handwheel has the opposite characteristics.

When a machine has multiple controls, the problems become even more complex. Each control must be compatible with the other controls as well as with its own purpose and with operator capabilities. In addition, each control must be readily *distinguishable* from the others, particularly if operator speed is important or if the operator cannot see all of the controls.

The various issues in designing multiple machine controls may be illustrated by the control requirements of a standard-shift automobile. The basic controls required are for activation (starting the car), steering, accelerating, braking, and changing gears. These controls must be consistent with the following constraints.

- Starting the car is an independent operation.
- It must be possible to steer and accelerate simultaneously.
- It must be possible to change gears simultaneously with steering and accelerating as required.
- It must be possible to brake while simultaneously steering and changing (or disengaging) gears.

These constraints mean that the automobile operator frequently must operate several controls at the same time. As humans have only two hands, some of these controls must be operated with the feet, and feet do not have the same capabilities for movement as hands. In addition, because driving a car requires close visual attention to the road, the operator can look only occasionally at hand controls and not at all at foot controls. All controls, therefore, must be within easy reach, and foot controls in particular must be distinguishable from one another by feel, that is, by size, shape, and relative position.

Today, automobile controls have a fairly standard design; a typical one is shown in Exhibit 7–3. Steering is accomplished by means of a large wheel (for accuracy) placed directly in front of the operator. Gear shifting is done by means of a lever located on the steering column or, as in Exhibit 7–3, to the right of the operator at waist level. Braking, accelerating, and gear disengagement are controlled by foot pedals (good speed) placed in standard positions on the floorboard.

The control setup of the modern automobile is a fair approximation to the requirements of this operator-machine system, but it has not been developed in any systematic way. There are some flaws from a human factors perspective. For example, braking is a function that is frequently

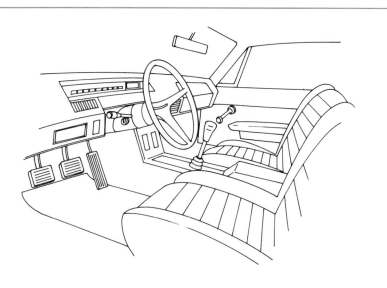

EXHIBIT 7–3

An Automobile
Control System

used in an emergency fashion. Since eye-hand reaction time for humans is faster than eye-foot reaction time, braking logically should be accomplished by hand.

Brake pedals were put on the floor of automobiles in the days before power-assisted braking. The average person at that time was more likely to be able to apply the force needed by foot. Unfortunately, for people to make the switch now would be very difficult. Machine operators become "control dependent" over time as any driver used to a gear shift lever between the seats finds when switching to an automobile with the lever located on the steering column (or vice versa).

The dependency of experienced operators on a particular configuration of machine controls highlights the importance of the human factors research behind controls design. An interesting example of what can happen when the initial research is inadequate is provided by the case of the familiar typewriter keyboard.

EXHIBIT 7–4

Human Factors
Engineering and
Typewriter Keyboard
Control Design

Standard Design

Improved Design

Exhibit 7–4 shows two such keyboards; the one at the top is the standard control layout found on most typewriters. The keyboard on the bottom typewriter is designed from a human factors standpoint—it makes more efficient use of the movements and relative finger strengths of the normal human hand than does the standard keyboard. Although it was developed some time ago, it has never seen general use. Experienced typists simply cannot make the switch, so this improved design (originally called the Dvorak keyboard) remains a little known and seldom seen alternative to the usual keyboard control arrangement.

The Design of Displays

Displays provide the operator of a machine with information. This information may pertain to the machine's operation, or it may be the actual output (work) of the machine. Many machines have displays for both purposes. Whatever the case, displays are subject to the same design decisions—size, shape, location, form, and compatibility—as controls are. They also add new considerations.

Most displays are visual or audio in form. Thus, designing these displays requires knowledge of human visual and hearing processes as well as knowledge of human physical attributes. Displays also provide information that must be used in some fashion by the operator, so their design must incorporate human capacities and limitations in information processing.

The basic question for psychologists in evaluating the design of any display is: Can the machine operator take in, or perceive, the information that the display presents as quickly as the job requires? One determinant of the answer to this question is how the display is actually designed. An illustration of some good and poor visual display designs with respect to human perceptual capacities is shown in Exhibit 7–5.

Perception: See page 36.

There are five types of visual display dials shown in Exhibit 7–5. In each case, the good design makes reading easier and quicker for the operator than the poor design does. For example, when a fixed dial with a moving pointer (similar to the ordinary wall clock) is used, an operator can read it more easily and quickly if the numbers are printed with his or her line of sight. Most operators could read the other dial with the numbers askew, but they would take longer and be more subject to error.

There are factors other than basic design that determine the ease and speed with which display information is perceived. One such factor is placement. Remember the displays placed too high for operators to read at Three Mile Island? Another factor is the extent to which the display stands out from its surroundings. Again, Three Mile Island provides an illustration of poor design; the malfunction of a critical function was displayed to the operator at the control panel only as the absence or presence of a single red light among hundreds of displays.

A detailed list of the principles involved in designing and placing machine displays to avoid the kinds of problems discovered at Three Mile Island may be found in any basic human factors text. One of the

| | | Preferred | Poor |

Visual Dial Display Designs

For fixed dials with moving pointers
  Position numerals horizontal to line of sight, not radially.

For moving dials with fixed pointers
  Position numerals radially. Pointers preferably should be in twelve o'clock position.

If space is not limited, it is desirable to place the numerals beyond the scale markers to avoid having numerals obscured by pointer. (If there is any restriction at all on space, however, it is usually desirable to place the numerals inside the markers in order to have the scale as large as possible.)

For open-window dials
  Window should show numbered scale markers at either side, to indicate direction of scale.

Numerals should be placed to appear right side up when exposed.

Note. From E. J. McCormick, *Human Factors Engineering* (2nd ed.). New York: McGraw-Hill, 1964, p. 139. Reprinted by permission.

classics in this field is that by McCormick (1964). A more advanced discussion of these issues may be found in Howell and Goldstein (1971). A classic piece of research into the placement of displays vis-à-vis their relevant controls is summarized in "Spotlight on Research."

SPOTLIGHT ON RESEARCH

A Reaction-time Study of Four Control-Display Linkages

Research question: What is the nature of the relationship between stove control/burner (display) arrangements and subject reaction time and errors in operating the appropriate control?

Type of study: Laboratory experiment.

Laboratory experiment: See pages 52 to 54.

Subjects: Not described. (This classic experiment predates the current emphasis on describing subjects.)

Independent variable: Arrangement of the stove control/display unit. The four arrangements are shown below.

Independent variable: See page 52.

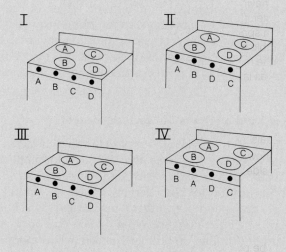

Dependent variables:
- Speed of subject response. Operational definition: Number of seconds between illumination of two lights.
- Errors made by subjects. Operational definition: Number of mismatches between illuminated lights.

Dependent variable: See page 52.

Operational definition: See page 48.

> **General procedure:** When a ready signal was given, the upper light on one of the wooden stove model burners shown was illuminated by the experimenter. The subject's task was to illuminate the matching lower light by pressing the appropriate burner control button (A, B, C, or D). Each subject was tested individually for 80 trials. The order of burner illumination for each subject was random.
>
> **Results:** Reaction times were significantly faster for stove I. No errors were made on stove I. There was no significant difference in the rate of error on the other three stoves.
>
> **Conclusion:** "The results of the experiment show that a control-display arrangement like that in the upper-left corner . . . is clearly superior to the other three. Linkage pattern II is next best while III and IV are about equally bad" (p. 6).
>
> ———————
>
> Summarized from A. Chapanis and L. E. Lindenbaum. "A Reaction-Time Study of Four Control-Display Linkages." *Human Factors*, 1959, *1*(4), pp. 1–7. Copyright 1959 by The Human Factors Society, Inc. Figure reproduced by permission.

In "Spotlight on Research," Chapanis and Lindenbaum (1959) performed a laboratory experiment to determine which of the four stove burner (display)/control designs in common home use was superior in terms of human capacity for processing information. Interestingly, although the superiority of Design I is quite clear, it is rare to find a stove that is so designed. Design II is that most commonly used today.

Robots: A New Kind of Operator-Machine System

Most people think of industrial robots as something modern—a product of space-age technology. It is true that the development and use of robots for industry on any scale has a history of less than 40 years, but robots have been around for considerably longer. A robotlike machine that could write, draw, and play musical instruments was built over 200 years ago by two Swiss craftsmen. What makes "robotics" a hot topic today is the sudden proliferation of such machines in modern factories and offices.

Approximately half of the industrial robots now in use in this country are in the auto industry where they perform a wide variety of tasks from welding to spray painting. Chrysler's Newark, New Jersey, plant currently "employs" about 70 such robots. On the whole, they are homely creatures with none of the endearing qualities of *Star War's* R2D2. But robots can do the same task over and over without getting tired and without getting bored, and they can work in conditions that are unpleasant or dangerous for humans.

An industrial robot: the Bell & Howell Mailmobile®

In their capacity for work, industrial robots are much like old-style machines. But unlike most ordinary machines, they can be programmed to do a variety of jobs, to use tools, and most startling of all, to move around unaided. One such machine is Bell & Howell's Mailmobile, shown in the photograph.

The Mailmobile follows a chemical pathway applied to the floor. The pathway can be changed easily for convenience. This robot moves at a speed of about one mile per hour, beeping and flashing blue lights as it stops at coded mail pick-up and delivery sites. A newer version can be programmed to make choices among alternate routes and board an elevator if necessary.

Their potential for independent movement makes industrial robots a subject for fantasy, but robots still are machines. They must be programmed and/or operated by humans, and the essential operator-machine system relationship still exists. The relationship is not quite the same, however. A number of people who work with such machines reported to the author that they feel more like they have a partner than a machine.

Many give these "partners" names and refer to them as if they are human.

To date, there has been more interest in the training of workers to use industrial robots and in the problem of what to do with those people replaced by these machines (e.g. Ayres & Miller, 1982) than there has been in the effects of this aspect of job design on those who actually work with robots. But "the robots are coming" and such questions are certain to come with them.

Work Methods

The term **work methods** refers to the actual movements by which people carry out job tasks.

To this point, discussion has centered on the machine component of operator-machine systems. The focus shifts now to the actual work to be done by these systems. Whether the "machine" used by a worker is a punch press, a word processor, a shovel, or a pencil, decisions concerning work methods are an important part of the job design.

Work methods were studied extensively by the early industrial engineers, and efforts to find the fastest and most efficient way to perform particular tasks continue today. These efforts are not always appreciated by the workers involved because they usually lead to the setting of *production standards*. Such standards often are perceived as a way for management to get more work out of people for the same money. They also reduce the degree of worker autonomy in making their own work-related decisions and many believe this reduces work motivation.

Although the scientific study of work methods has effects that are not always perceived as positive, the most efficient way for a job to be accomplished is also the least tiring way. If a company benefits from new work methods that allow for greater production, so do its employees. Promoting work efficiency is only one goal of psychologists who study work methods, and promoting efficiency cannot be separated from the other goal—reducing worker fatigue.

Designing work methods in order to increase efficiency and reduce fatigue requires psychologists and engineers to work *with* the human body rather than against it. For example, the pushing power of the average male is substantially greater than his pulling power. Other things being equal, both the work and the man whose job requires shifting heavy loads will benefit from work specifications based on pushing rather than pulling loads.

Those who study work methods use a variety of measures to help them determine the best methods for accomplishing a particular task. Among these measures are energy consumption, heart rate, and the type of muscular effort involved. There are two basic types of muscular effort. One is *dynamic effort* in which muscles alternatively contract and relax. The other is *static effort* in which there is a prolonged state of muscular contraction. Exhibit 7–6 illustrates the critical difference between the effects of these two types of effort.

As seen in Exhibit 7–6, *static* effort produces an imbalance between the blood needed to make the effort and the actual flow of blood to the muscles. By contrast, although *dynamic* effort requires a greater flow of

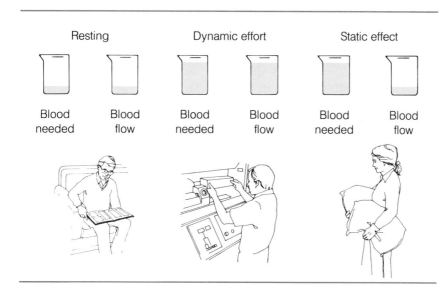

EXHIBIT 7–6

Blood Use and Blood Flow at Rest and at Work

blood than no effort (resting), these greater requirements still can be met by supply. Thus, tasks calling for dynamic effort approximate a natural physiological condition while tasks requiring static effort lead to a higher energy consumption and a raised heart rate.

Because static effort raises the heart rate and burns more energy, workers engaged in such tasks need longer and more frequent rest periods. They also are more subject to joint, ligament, and tendon deterioration (Grandjean, 1982). Therefore, one good general principle to follow in the work methods phase of job design is as follows:

Reduce the amount of static effort required to perform the tasks as much as possible.

Some familiar work activities requiring workers to exert substantial static effort are:

- holding and carrying objects
- sitting with no back support
- standing in one place
- holding the arms in an outstretched position

Even a casual glance around most organizations will reveal workers spending considerable time in one or more of the activities listed above. In many cases, the increased strain of such activities is probably unnecessary. Strain could be reduced or eliminated by some combination of (a) redesigning the work methods, work space, and/or tools and machinery and (b) training the workers to avoid unnecessary static effort.

Although taxing static effort in many jobs could be reduced or eliminated, other jobs containing such components are not changed so easily. One way to offset some of the negative effects of such tasks is to give workers longer rest periods. Another way is to provide a set of alternative tasks that do not require this effort—the workers swap off between tasks. Another way is to employ machines, such as the industrial robots discussed earlier, to perform these tasks.

The Workspace Envelope

A **workspace envelope** is the space assigned to and occupied by an individual worker in the performance of his or her primary job duties.

In Chapter 8, the physical work environment is considered from the perspective of the influence of general working conditions on worker behavior. From a job design viewpoint, the portion of that work environment of greatest interest is the part used by a single worker in performing his or her job. This space is sometimes called the *workspace envelope* to convey the sense of a three-dimensional physical space that surrounds and is unique to an individual worker.

Some workers, such as traveling salespeople, have no actual workspace envelope in the sense that it is defined. For others, such as grounds maintenance workers, their envelope is the great outdoors. More typically, however, the workspace envelope is an office, private or shared, or simply a space, such as that shown in the photograph.

The workspace envelope in the photograph is in the control center of a modern electric power station. The employees who work there make continuing series of decisions about power generation based on information fed in to the various displays from thousands of data points. Time is critical, and the workspace envelope must be designed to enable the operator to see all pertinent displays and to reach controls, such as the telephone and the keyboard, with a minimum of movement.

The workspace envelope in the power station control center illustrates a number of elements that must be questioned concerning this aspect of

A workspace envelope

job design. What kind of chair is best for an employee who is seated most of the time? How high should work surfaces be? Where should displays be placed relative to controls if such equipment is involved? Other questions about workspace envelope design include questions about access, furniture arrangement, and space.

- Where should tools and supplies used regularly, but not constantly, be stored?
- Where should desks and chairs be located relative to shelves, files, doors, and so on?
- How compact can a workspace envelope be without the occupant feeling closed in?

Whatever the kind of job involved and the particular associated design decisions, the goal in setting up a workspace remains promoting efficiency while reducing fatigue. Human factors research to aid in workspace design is an extremely active area. It is possible to find precise recommendations for almost every aspect of the workspace and every situation. For example, Grandjean (1982) lists 10 specific criteria for chair seat designs that will fit the human body and be suited for office workers. Among these criteria are those related to chair back height, chair seat padding, and chair size.

One goal of a human factors approach to designing the workspace envelope is to improve the physical health of workers. This goal could be met best by designing each worker's space individually; unfortunately, this is seldom practical. As a compromise, the following two principles will serve as guidelines:

1. Elements of a workspace, such as chairs, storage racks, and drawing tables should be purchased in an adjustable design if this is available.
2. Those elements of a workspace that cannot be adjustable should be designed for the worker who would incur the greatest discomfort or inconvenience from the alternative arrangements. For example, shelves should be placed for easy access to shorter workers. Non-adjustable work surfaces, on the other hand, should be at a height comfortable for taller people; to stoop over for any length of time frequently produces severe back and neckache. Unusually short workers can be given a raised platform on which to stand while working at such surfaces.

Flexiplace: The Ultimate in Individual Workspace Envelopes

Although most organizations cannot afford to tailor workspace to individual employees, computers and electronic communication advances are allowing a few workers the last word in individual design—their own homes. Just as flexitime (See Chapter 8) gives workers some choice of *when* they will work, "flexiplace" gives some a choice of *where* they work.

Working at home is not new, but working at home doing routine, ongoing office work is. Advances in electronic communication now make it possible for secretaries to take dictation, type copy, and transmit results directly back to the company without ever leaving home. Nor is this *telecommuting* limited to clerical employees.

In a recent report of the issues, advantages, disadvantages, and reactions to flexiplace, Plous (1982) notes that among those currently enjoying the benefits of a regular job without leaving home are stockbrokers, newspaper reporters, market analysts, and computer programmers. Among the companies trying flexiplace are Control Data Corporation, Continental Illinois National Bank, Digital General Corporation, and Blue Cross/Blue Shield of South Carolina.

Flexiplace is still new, and it has not to date been the subject of any systematic scientific research efforts. Evidence as to its effects comes primarily from interviews with participants. Some of them like it, some do not—they miss the social interaction of the office. Some like it at first, then find they have exchanged one set of work place problems for another. One artist's humorous look at some of the special difficulties of home as a workspace envelope is shown in Exhibit 7–7.

The reaction of managers and executives to flexiplace seems to be as varied as that of the participants. According to Plous (1982), some see it as an effective way to utilize human resources that might otherwise be wasted when home pressures create absenteeism or labor-force dropouts. Some believe that allowing people the opportunity to work at their own pace has motivational advantages. Others are not so sure, pointing out that managers cannot manage what they cannot see and flexiplace offers unusual opportunities for abuse of responsibility. Finally, there is no way to enforce health and safety regulations for those who work at home.

The extent to which flexiplace will become a common work place option is unknown. It is clear that making flexiplace available to large numbers of regular employees will create a host of new issues and problems, such as the regulation of health and safety measures. On the other hand, outside sales representatives long have worked a version of "flexiplace," and the problems have not been insurmountable.

Concluding Remarks on the Human Factors Approach to Job Design

The problems and issues addressed by I/O psychologists and their colleagues from other disciplines who are interested primarily in the physical aspects of job design have been reviewed. Whatever the specifics, the core of this approach is harmony among human perceptual, cognitive, and physical abilities, tools and machines, and the work environment. The goal is to allow jobs to be accomplished effectively, efficiently, and with minimal worker strain and fatigue. In the second part of Chapter 7, the psychological approach to job design is considered.

EXHIBIT 7–7

*The Problems
of "Flexiplace"*

Note. From *Across the Board*, 1982, *19*(7), p. 67. Reprinted by permission of The Conference Board and R. Doty.

THE PSYCHOLOGICAL APPROACH TO JOB DESIGN

The criteria psychologists use in evaluating the success of job design are the same as the criteria they use in evaluating any aspect of organizational functioning. These criteria are employee effectiveness, efficiency, and satisfaction. The human factors approach to job design focuses on the first two criteria. By contrast, employee satisfaction is the primary focus of a psychological approach to job design.

The employee satisfaction that is central to this approach is satisfaction with the work itself. Satisfying work is believed by many to be the key to allowing employees to meet needs for self-actualization

The **psychological approach to job design** is characterized by an assumption that effectiveness and efficiency are correlates of satisfaction.

Correlate: See pages 63 to 64.

(Maslow, 1943), that is, for self-fulfillment. In turn, the ability to meet these needs through work is believed to be crucial to work motivation. This basic premise leads many to call the psychological approach to job design the *motivational approach* instead.

Although there are companies in which psychological concerns are formally part of initial job design, it is more common for these concerns to arise when problems surface. Work problems that suggest examination of jobs from a psychological viewpoint include the following:

- chronic lateness
- chronic absenteeism
- wasting of time
- poor work quality
- excess waste of materials
- employee theft
- high turnover rate

Three of the most widely-known psychological job design techniques are examined here. Although such strategies are most often applied to job *redesign*, they are applicable to initial design as well.

Job Enlargement

A basic decision in job design is *how many* tasks to include within the province of the job. At the extreme ends of the continuum of possibilities lie (a) performance of only one task over and over and (b) performance of all tasks that are required to make up a complete job. For example, in some restaurants, the task of serving customers is divided up among a host or hostess, a wine waiter, a waiter who takes the order, a kitchen waiter who serves the food, and another employee who clears away after the customer. In other restaurants, a single individual performs all of these functions.

In the early 1800s, an Englishman demonstrated that 10 workers, each performing only one operation, could produce a pound of straight pins for about one-quarter of the cost incurred when the pound was produced by one worker performing all of the operations (Babbage, 1835). In this country, this *specialization* approach to job design was promoted and used with great success by industrial engineers. So successful was specialization in terms of employee effectiveness and efficiency that it became the basis for virtually all industrial job design.

It is not surprising that limiting the number of job tasks assigned to each employee works well from the standpoint of effectiveness and efficiency. Specialization offers the opportunity for each individual to concentrate on getting very good at one or a few tasks. Performance of the same tasks over and over again, eight hours a day, five days a week, however, is also monotonous; many people find this monotony boring and meaningless. These and other advantages and disadvantages of the task specialization approach to job design are summarized in Exhibit 7–8.

Assembly-line jobs often are the ultimate in the specialization approach to job design.

In Exhibit 7–8, the longest list consists of the disadvantages of job-task specialization for those who perform such jobs. A job redesign strategy that attempts to reduce or eliminate these disadvantages by moving away from specialization is called job enlargement.

As the name implies, *job enlargement* is a plan to make jobs ''bigger,'' or larger. This strategy came to widespread notice in the 1950s with the first significant degree of formal interest in the causes and effects of employee boredom and alienation from a company. It was hypothesized that task specialization frustrates people's needs for variety, for challenge, and for their sense of making a meaningful contribution to group

EXHIBIT 7–8	

Advantages and
Disadvantages of
Task Specialization

Advantages of Specialization

To management:
1. Rapid training of the work force
2. Ease in recruiting new workers
3. High output due to simple and repetitive work
4. Low wages due to ease of substitutability of labor
5. Close control over work flow and work loads

To labor:
1. Little responsibility for output
2. Little mental effort required
3. Little or no education required to obtain work

Disadvantages of Specialization

To management:
1. Difficulty in controlling quality since no one person has responsibility for entire product
2. "Hidden" costs of worker dissatisfaction, arising from
   a. Turnover
   b. Absenteeism
   c. Tardiness
   d. Grievances
   e. Intentional disruption of production process

To labor:
1. Boredom stemming from repetitive nature of work
2. Little gratification from the work itself because of small contribution to each item
3. Little or no control over the work pace, leading to frustration and fatigue (in assembly line type situations)
4. Little opportunity to progress to a better job since significant learning is rarely possible on fractionated work
5. Little opportunity to show initiative through developing better methods or tools
6. Local muscular fatigue due to use of the same muscles in performing the task
7. Little opportunity for communication with fellow workers due to layout of the work area

Note. From R. B. Chase and N. J. Aquilano. *Production and Operations Management* (3rd ed.). Homewood, IL: Richard D. Irwin, 1981, p. 330. Copyright 1981 by Richard D. Irwin, Inc. Reprinted by permission.

goals. To the extent that this is true, job enlargement should help alleviate the problem.

Job Enlargement Research

The results of early job enlargement research are almost all positive. The classic success story is reported by Kilbridge (1960). In that study, enlarging the job of water pump assembler from one operation to assembling, checking, and approving the entire pump produced significant savings for the company involved. When reported job satisfaction, rather than job performance, was the criterion, results were even more favorable.

A bibliography and brief review of this research may be found in Aldag and Brief (1979).

As Aldag and Brief point out in their discussion of job enlargement research, there were a number of methodological problems with the early studies. As this technique became subject to closer examination for applied purposes, a number of practical problems emerged as well. There are at least three major problems.

1. Not all jobs can be enlarged.
2. Not all workers want their jobs enlarged.
3. The ability and skill requirements of an enlarged job may be beyond the capabilities of the present job holder(s). When this happens, employees may have to undergo expensive retraining, and some may have to be replaced.

Even when no obstacles to job enlargement are apparent, problems in application of this technique are present still because there are no guidelines. Should jobs always be enlarged to the maximum (as in the water pump assembly example), or is there some other standard by which to determine the optimal degree of enlargement?

Although the problems encountered by the job enlargement approach to job redesign probably were not insurmountable, this technique suddenly (and apparently permanently) vanished from the I/O literature at the end of the 1960s. Elements of job enlargement are to be found in a more sophisticated form, however, in what is called the socio-technical approach to job design.

Socio-technical Job Design

A socio-technical view of organizations is a systems theory perspective that emphasizes the necessity for a balanced relationship between the human/social and the technological aspects of an organization. This approach has its origins in the work of the British researchers at the Tavistock Institute of Human Relations (see Trist & Bamforth, 1951) and has had a significant impact on the issues involved in designing organizations themselves. For a concise overview of the socio-technical approach refer to Cummings and Markus (1979).

When applied to job design, basic socio-technical principles suggest a work group, or *team*, approach, rather than an individual approach. In this job design strategy, groups of employees are given the responsibility for completing some whole unit of work. They decide among themselves who will perform what tasks at any particular time.

The most famous application of socio-technical principles of job design is that which evolved out of a series of experiments at the Saab-Scania plant at Sodertalje, Sweden, in the late 1960s. As a result of these experiments, Saab switched from the usual continuous assembly line (job specialization) design for assembling automobile engines to a *parallel group assembly design,* similar to that shown in Exhibit 7-9.

EXHIBIT 7–9

*Parallel Group
Assembly Job Design*

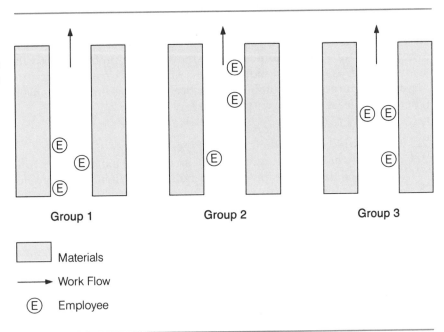

Group 1   Group 2   Group 3

☐ Materials

⟶ Work Flow

Ⓔ Employee

As the parallel group assembly method was used at Saab, teams of workers were responsible for assembling an entire engine. Each team worked at its own rate. Parts and materials were delivered by truck, and assembled engines were carried away by a mechanical conveyor belt that could be reached easily by each group.

Although Saab was pleased initially with the results of its experiments, it later abandoned them. Nevertheless, the success of this, and similar programs at Volvo and other European companies, has led a number of U.S. companies to adopt these job design principles. At the Cadillac engine plant in Livonia, Michigan, for example, 23-member job teams rotate among some 24 assembly, inspection, and housekeeping tasks.

Socio-technical job design most often is cited as a form of job enrichment, which is to be addressed next. However, it also embodies the basic principles of job enlargement—task variety and worker involvement with the job to be done on a level that is meaningful. In team approaches to job design, no one employee is responsible for the whole job, but each can see how his or her effort fits into the accomplishment of that job. Equally important, no one worker is confined to the monotonous repetition of single tasks unless by choice. A complete description of the development of the so-called "new factories" that use a team job design strategy may be found in Katz and Kahn (1978).

Job Enrichment

As a psychological, or motivational, approach to job design, *job enrichment* has much in common with job enlargement. The premise underlying both is that job design should be based on an understanding of human needs for meaningful work. The distinction lies in how this is going to be accomplished. Job enlargement works on the assumption that the primary determinant of meaningfulness is the number and variety of job tasks relative to the whole job.

By contrast with job enlargement, *job enrichment* assumes that the basic determinant of meaningful work is not the number of tasks, but the *kind* of tasks performed. In practical application, job enrichment usually means that jobs are redesigned so that workers have more responsibility and decision-making authority with respect to planning, scheduling, and controlling their own work. For example, in the Saab socio-technical experiments, team members decided who did what assembly tasks and they worked at their own group pace—the usual machine pacing of such work was completely eliminated.

Job Enrichment Research

The early job enrichment literature, like the early job enlargement literature, contains many success stories (e.g., Ford, 1973). In a similar parallel fashion, problems began to emerge. For the most part, they were similar to the problems experienced in the application of job enlargement techniques. Unlike job enlargement, however, job enrichment has remained in the mainstream of I/O psychology.

To some extent, the fact that job enrichment is still around and job

Individual craftspeople perform work high on the characteristics that define enriched jobs.

enlargement is not is explained by the simple fact that enlargement is part of job enrichment. Although the tasks that are added to enrich jobs are usually management-type tasks, job enrichment, like job enlargement, always makes jobs "bigger." Another part of the explanation lies in the better developed theoretical underpinnings of job enrichment (Brousseau, 1979).

Although a number of I/O psychologists have been involved in the theoretical development of job enrichment, its core lies in the work of Hackman and Oldham (1976). These researchers identified five job characteristics that influence the extent to which workers in general report experiencing job satisfaction and internal work motivation—the experiences central to the psychological approach to job design (Hackman & Oldham, 1975).

1. *Skill variety*—Jobs that require a variety of different skills are more meaningful than those that require only one or a few skills.
2. *Task identity*—Jobs that constitute a whole piece of work are more meaningful than those that consist of some portion of the whole job.
3. *Task significance*—Jobs that have an identifiable importance to others are more meaningful than those that do not.
4. *Autonomy*—Jobs that allow the worker independence, freedom, and decision-making authority with respect to job performance are more meaningful than those that do not.
5. *Job feedback*—Jobs that provide built-in feedback as to worker performance are more meaningful than those that do not.

When viewed in the light of these criteria, it is easy to see why assembly line-type jobs usually are described as the ultimate in meaninglessness. Such jobs require only one skill (no task variety); workers do not see the finished product in the course of their work (no task identity); it is difficult to see what importance one tiny function has to others (low task significance); the work is machine paced (not autonomous); and quality control is done by others (feedback does not come from the work itself).

Hackman and Oldham (1975) developed a questionnaire instrument called the Job Diagnostic Survey (JDS) to measure the extent to which a job possesses the five characteristics described. The JDS, together with the Job Characteristics Inventory (JCI) developed by Sims, Szilagyi, and Keller (1976) for the same purpose, did much to support the psychological approach to job design.

Both the JDS and the JCI have been the objects of substantial research (e.g., Brief & Aldag, 1978; Ferratt, Durham, & Pierce, 1981). Of primary interest from a psychological job design perspective is what this research has to say about two general questions. First, do such instruments measure what they are intended to measure? Second, do they predict differential job behaviors and attitudes? These two questions are considered next.

Perceived Versus Objective Task Characteristics

The answer to the question, "Do job enrichment instruments measure the actual richness of a job?'' is ''no.'' What questionnaires, such as JDS and JCI, measure is the extent to which a job is *perceived* to possess these characteristics by the person answering the questions.

Perceptual differences among those describing the same jobs were demonstrated dramatically by a recent study in which 76 public health nurses were the subjects (O'Reilly, Partletter, & Bloom, 1980). When the responses of various groupings of these nurses to the JDS were compared, a number of responses emerged.

- Nurses who expressed a strong preference for job autonomy saw the job as offering more autonomy than those who did not.
- Nurses whose fathers had less formal education described their jobs as more enriched than those whose fathers had more education.
- Older nurses described their jobs as having more skill variety and task significance than did younger nurses.
- Nurses who reported identifying strongly with their major professional organization saw their jobs as more enriched than those less committed to professionalism.

These findings suggest that individual preferences, background, age, and degree of professional commitment influence responses to questions about job characteristics. Similar effects have been reported with respect to other individual-difference variables, such as perceptual ability and general mental ability (O'Connor & Barrett, 1980). Even the sex of the job holder may be relevant. As shown in Exhibit 7–10, males and females have been found to differ significantly with respect to what they say they *want* in jobs, and such preferences are likely to affect perceptions of their current jobs.

Individual traits: See pages 28 to 33.

The data in Exhibit 7–10 provide a good illustration of the practical problems that arise when trying to implement a psychological approach to job redesign. To take only one example, females in the Brenner and Tomkiewicz (1979) sample ranked ''involves working with congenial colleagues'' significantly higher than did males. This suggests that redesigning jobs held mostly by females to allow them more interaction with coworkers would make their work more satisfying. But what if their jobs cannot be so designed? What if the next five new employees are male?

To some extent, the problem of job characteristic preferences can be gotten around at the hiring stage by means of the matching strategy discussed in Chapters 5 and 6. The problem of differences in *perception* of job characteristics is more difficult. In their review of this literature, O'Connor, Rudolf, and Peters (1980) make a number of suggestions to help researchers cope with this issue in future investigations. Among these suggestions is the use of job characteristic measures that are more objective than questionnaire measures. Unfortunately, no satisfactory alternative immediately presents itself, and this problem awaits the creativity of future I/O psychology researchers.

Job Enrichment and Worker Performance and Attitudes

The central thesis of the job enrichment approach to job design is that

	Rank	
Characteristic	Males	Females
Provides a feeling of accomplishment	1	1
Provides job security	2	3.5
Provides the opportunity to earn a high income	3	10.5*
Encourages continued development of knowledge and skills	4	2
	4	2*
Permits advancement to high administrative responsibility	5	10.5
Provides comfortable working conditions	6	3.5*
Provides change and variety in duties and activities	7	6
Is respected by other people	8	8
Rewards good performance with recognition	9	9
Involves working with congenial colleagues	10	5*
Provides ample leisure time off the job	11	15
Permits you to develop your own methods of doing the work	12	13
Is intellectually stimulating	13	7*
Requires originality, creativeness	14	17
Makes use of your specific educational background	15	14
Requires working on problems of central importance to the organization	16	19
Permits working independently	17	16
Requires meeting and speaking with many other people	18	18
Permits you to work for superiors you admire and respect	19	12*
Gives you the responsibility for taking risks	20	22*
Makes a social contribution by the work you do	21	21
Requires supervising others	22	23*
Satisfies your cultural and aesthetic interests	23	20
Permits a regular routine in time and place of work	24	24
Has clear-cut rules and procedures to follow	25	25

EXHIBIT 7–10

Male-Female Differences in Job Characteristic Preferences

Significance: See pages 58 to 59.

*Indicates that difference is statistically significant.

Note. From O. C. Brenner and J. Tomkiewicz. "Job Orientation of Males and Females: Are Sex Differences Declining?" *Personnel Psychology,* 1979, *32*(4), pp. 741–750. Table adapted by permission of the authors and the publisher.

more enriched jobs meet certain postulated human needs. Need fulfillment, in turn, leads to greater employee job satisfaction, which leads to better job performance. This line of thought has been modified because it is only when jobs are *perceived* to be enriched that these benefits follow. The matter of individual differences does not end here, however.

The assumption that people *respond* in the same way (with respect to attitudes and job performance) seems to be no more tenable than the assumption that they perceive the characteristics of the job in the same way. A number of recent studies have demonstrated that employee responses to job characteristics depend on certain characteristics of the employees themselves.

The most heavily-researched individual characteristic affecting worker responses to job characteristics is a psychological variable called *growth-need strength* (Hackman & Oldham, 1974). In general, research has tended to support the hypothesis that people who report weak needs for personal growth and development will respond less positively to enriched jobs (e.g., Pierce & Dunham, 1976).

Hypothesis: See page 47.

The moderating effects of individual differences with respect to (a) the *perception* of job characteristics and (b) the *response* to these perceptions is shown in Exhibit 7–11. Growth-need strength is located in the bottom right box—an individual-difference variable that affects worker responses to perceived job characteristics.

From a job design perspective, Exhibit 7–11 may be seen as a summary of the possible variables that can *moderate* the expected relationship between an enriched job and worker responses. Assume for the moment that the objective task characteristics (top left box) have been designed to be high on Hackman and Oldham's (1975) scale of motivating potential. According to job enrichment theory, worker responses to this task (upper right box) should include greater satisfaction with the work and better performance.

Moderator variable: See pages 97 to 99.

Whether or not the relationship described actually materializes depends on a number of things. First, it depends upon whether or not the individuals involved perceive the job to be enriched. This perception, as the study by O'Reilly, Partletter, and Bloom (1980) demonstrates, depends in turn upon a large number of personal worker characteristics (lower left box in Exhibit 7–11). Second, even if the job *is* perceived as enriched, the actual responses to it will depend upon other individual characteristics of workers (lower right box in Exhibit 7–11).

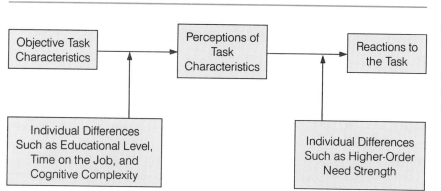

EXHIBIT 7–11

The Role of Individual Differences in Determining Worker Response to Task Characteristics

Note. From R. J. Aldag and A. P. Brief, *Task Design and Employee Motivation.* Glenview, IL: Scott, Foresman, 1979, p. 94. Copyright 1979 by Scott, Foresman and Company. Reprinted by permission.

In their recent review of 13 empirical studies of the relationship between job characteristics and employee responses to the job, Griffin, Welsh, and Moorhead (1981) found a mixture of results. Some studies show no correlation between task characteristics and employee performance and satisfaction; others provide partial or substantial confirmation of such a relationship. When viewed in the light of the number of variables that can moderate this relationship, there is nothing surprising in the authors' conclusion: Results from this line of research are at this time inconclusive and contradictory.

The Psychological Approach to Job Design in Perspective

The weight of existing evidence suggests that psychological approaches to job design are imprecise tools at best. Any organization planning to give prime consideration to psychological concerns in designing jobs should be aware that the expected motivational benefits may not materialize; on the other hand, they may. At the least, there is sufficient evidence to warrant including these issues in a balanced fashion with the human factors approach to job design discussed earlier.

With respect to the *redesign* of jobs to increase their motivating potential, the existing literature strongly suggests that consideration be given to the preferences of job incumbents. In practice, this must be done on an organization-by-organization basis, but a study by Giles and Holley (1978) sheds some interesting light on general employee preferences for enriched jobs.

Giles and Holley investigated the question of employee preferences for enriched jobs by asking unionized employees of two food-processing plants how much time they wished their union negotiators to spend bargaining for job enrichment. These employees were given a list of five bargaining issues—pay, fringe benefits, working conditions, job security, and job enrichment—and asked to state the percentage of bargaining time they would prefer be given to each in contract negotiations. As may be seen in Exhibit 7–12, job enrichment came last in both plants.

What does not show in Exhibit 7–12 is the result of other analyses of the Giles and Holley data. These analyses show that the time employees

EXHIBIT 7–12		

Issue	Plant A (N = 55)	Plant B (N = 76)
Fringe Benefits	28%	17%
Pay	24%	47%
Working Conditions	16%	13%
Job Security	18%	14%
Job Enrichment	13%	9%

Relative Percentage of Time Allocated by Union Members to Job Enrichment as a Labor Negotiation Issue

Note. From W. F. Giles and W. H. Holley, Jr. "Job Enrichment Versus Traditional Issues at the Bargaining Table: What Union Members Want." *Academy of Management Journal*, 1978, *21*(4), p. 728. Adapted by permission of the authors and the publisher.

in Plant B allocated to bargaining for job enrichment differed *significantly* only from pay. In Plant A it was significantly different only from pay and fringe benefits. In other words, this study does not show workers to be disinterested in job enrichment. It does show that things are relative; workers in this sample were *more* interested in tangible job rewards.

Concluding Remarks on Job Design

Two very different views of job design have been discussed in Chapter 7. Although they are conceptually complementary to one another, it is rare to find them applied in this fashion. When conscious thought and planning is given to job design (it must be noted that this is not always the case), emphasis usually is given to the physical aspects. Concern with psychological factors comes later when problems arise. As a result, the psychological approach to job design often is thought of exclusively as a job *redesign* approach.

Psychological principles are applicable to original job design as well as to redesign as long as appropriate selection procedures are followed. With respect to job design, the selection issue may be described simply: Jobs designed to be interesting and meaningful are best filled by people who want interesting and meaningful jobs.

SUMMARY

The human factors approach to job design focuses on the specification of work methods, tools and machines, and workspace arrangements that are compatible with human physical and perceptual/cognitive abilities. The goal of this approach is to allow work, whatever it may be, to be carried out more effectively and efficiently by reducing the strain incurred by the worker.

The psychological approach to job design is based on the assumption that people have a need for interesting and meaningful work. The number and kinds of tasks included in a job are believed to be an important determinant of whether or not this need is met. The psychological approach to job design rests on the assumption that meeting this need increases job satisfaction, which in turn leads to better worker performance.

AT ISSUE

Computer Phobia

The chief executive officer at a Florida financial institution demands that reports printed out by his firm's computers be retyped on nice, white, pre-computer revolution paper before he will even look at them. Without a hint of apology, he explains that he will not trust anything he reads on green-and-white printouts. At the headquarters of a large Atlanta company, the chairman of the board boasts that he has never touched a keyboard, and that neither he nor any of his right-hand men have a computer in their office (Taylor, 1982 p. 82).

It is predicted that some three-quarters of the work force will need to have computer skills to perform their jobs by the end of the 1980s. This prospect holds no terror for today's youth, most of whom seem to have been born wearing headsets and playing video games. But what about their elders?

Incredible as it may seem, the average adult who was 40 years old in 1980 got through childhood without benefit of television. More amazing still, this adult probably went all the way through high school without a transistor radio. As for computers—most had not even seen a computer printout by college graduation.

The employee who was 40 years old in 1980 will be 50 at the end of the current decade, still some 10 to 15 years away from retirement. Some of these individuals have adjusted happily to the computer revolution. Others are uncomfortable at best, and fearful at worst, at the prospect of "interfacing" with a computer. And some, like the executives described in the opening paragraph, reject the whole idea; if computers are necessary, let someone else talk to them.

Eventually, all of today's top executives probably will be replaced by the computer-wise and there will be no more resistance from the executive suite. In the meantime, those at the top have the power to avoid encounters with computers if they wish. Others are not so fortunate; well into their careers, they are faced suddenly with the prospect of functional illiteracy. The number of people in organizations who must be retrained and oriented to computers is large and growing. There is a more complex issue than either training or numbers involved, however.

Computer-based work methods sever human communication links to a far greater degree than any recent work method revolution. The information that used to be acquired after a nice chat with Pat about how the kids are doing in college is now available at the touch of a few keys. For many of today's workers, this is not an attractive prospect. Their computer phobia is based, not on a fear of computers, but on a fear of what their worlds will be like after their work has been redesigned around them.

Over 50 years ago, the Hawthorne Experiments brought the social aspects of the work place to the widespread attention of all concerned with organizational effectiveness. These experiments sparked a revolution in management practices and I/O theory and research built on the understanding that employees are people first and workers second. No one questions that tenet today, but those who design jobs involving computer components may be forgetting its most basic corollary: People need other people.

REFERENCES

ALDAG, R. J., & BRIEF, A. P. *Task Design and Employee Motivation*. Glenview, IL: Scott, Foresman, 1979.

AYRES, R., & MILLER, S. Industrial robots on the line. *Technology Review*, 1982, *85*(4), 35–48.

BABBAGE, C. *On the Economy of Machinery and Manufacturers* (4th ed.). London: Charles Knight, 1835.

BRENNER, O. C., & TOMKIEWICZ, J. Job orientation of males and females: Are sex differences declining? *Personnel Psychology*, 1979, *32*(4), 741–750.

BRIEF, A. P., & ALDAG, R. J. The Job Characteristic Inventory: An examination. *Academy of Management Journal*, 1978, *21*(4), 659–670.

BROUSSEAU, K. R. Toward effective work system management. In G. L. Cooper (Ed.), *Behavioral Problems in Organizations*. (pp. 29–58). Englewood Cliffs, NJ: Prentice-Hall, 1979.

CHAPANIS, A., & LINDENBAUM, L. E. A reaction-time study of four control-display linkages. *Human Factors*, 1959, *1*(4), 1–7.

CHASE, R. B., & AQUILANO, N. J. *Production and Operations Management* (3rd. ed.). Homewood IL: Richard D. Irwin, 1981.

CORDES, C. Human factors and nuclear safety: Grudging respect for a growing field. *APA Monitor*, 1983, *4*(5), 1; 13–14.

CUMMINGS, T. G., & MARKUS, M. L. A sociotechnical systems view of organizations. In G. L. Cooper (Ed.), *Behavioral Problems in Organizations* (pp. 59–77). Englewood Cliffs, NJ: Prentice-Hall, 1979.

FERRATT, T. W., DUNHAM, R. B., & PIERCE, J. L. Self-report measures of job characteristics and affective responses: An examination of discriminant validity. *Academy of Management Journal*, 1981, *24*(4), 780–794.

FORD, R. N. Job enrichment lessons from AT&T. *Harvard Business Review*, 1973, *51*(1), 96–106.

GILBRETH, F. B., & GILBRETH, L. M. First steps in finding the one best way to do work. Paper presented at the annual meeting of the American Society of Mechanical Engineers, New York, 1921.

GILES, W. F., & HOLLEY, W. H., JR. Job enrichment versus traditional issues at the bargaining table: What union members want. *Academy of Management Journal*, 1978, *21*(4), 725–730.

GRANDJEAN, E. *Fitting the Task to the Man: An Ergonomic Approach* (3rd ed.). New York: International Publications Service and London: Taylor & Francis, Ltd., 1982.

GRIFFIN, R. W., WELSH, A., & MOORHEAD, G. Perceived task characteristics and employee performance: A literature review. *Academy of Management Review*, 1981, *6*(4), 655–664.

HACKMAN, J. R., & OLDHAM, G. R. *The Job Diagnostic Survey: An instrument for the diagnosis of jobs and the evaluation of job redesign projects.* (Tech. Rep. No. 4). New Haven, CT: Yale University, Department of Administrative Sciences, 1974.

HACKMAN, J. P., & OLDHAM, G. R. Development of the Job Diagnostic Survey. *Journal of Applied Psychology*, 1975, *60*(1), 159–170.

HACKMAN, J. R., & OLDHAM, G. R. Motivation through the design of work: Test of a theory. *Organizational Behavior and Human Performance*, 1976, *16*, 250–279.

HOWELL, W. C., & GOLDSTEIN, I. C. *Engineering Psychology: Current Perspectives in Research.* New York: Appleton-Century-Crofts, 1971.

KATZ, D., & KAHN, R. L. *The Social Psychology of Organizations* (2nd ed.). New York: John Wiley and Sons, 1978.

KILBRIDGE, M. D. Reduced costs through job enrichment: A case. *The Journal of Business*, 1960, *33*, 357–362.

MASLOW, A. H. A theory of human motivation. *Psychological Review*, 1943, *50*, 370–396.

McCORMICK, E. J. *Human Factors Engineering* (2nd ed.). New York: McGraw-Hill, 1964.

O'CONNOR, E. J., & BARRETT, G. V. Informational cues and individual differences as determinants of subjective perceptions of task enrichment. *Academy of Management Journal*, 1980, *23*(4), 697–716.

O'CONNOR, E. J., & RUDOLF, C. J., & PETERS, L. H. Individual differences and job design reconsidered: Where do we go from here? *Academy of Management Review*, 1980, *5*(2), 249–254.

O'REILLY, C. A., III, PARTLETTER, G. N., & BLOOM J. R. Perceptual measures of task characteristics: The biasing effects of differing frames of references and job attitudes. *Academy of Management Journal*, 1980, 23(1), 118–131.

PIERCE, J. L., & DUNHAM, R. J.   Task design: A literature review. *Academy of Management Review*, 1976, 1(1), 83–97.

PLOUS, R. K. JR.   Flexiplace. *World of Work Report*, 1982, (May).

SIMS, H. P., SZILAGYI, A. D., & KELLER, R. T. (1976). The measurement of job characteristics. *Academy of Management Journal*, 19(1), 195–212.

TAYLOR, A. L., III.   Dealing with terminal phobia. *Time*, 1982, (July 19), p. 82.

TAYLOR, F. W.   *The Principles of Scientific Management*. New York: Harper, 1911.

TRIST, E., & BAMFORTH, K.   Some social and psychological consequences of the longwall method of coal getting. *Human Relations*, 1951, 4(1), 3–38.

CHAPTER 8

Working Conditions and Employee Health and Safety

I/O PSYCHOLOGY AT WORK

Shifting Work by the Bio-Clock

OGDEN, Utah—Shift workers here at the Great Salt Lake Minerals and Chemicals Corp. were complaining of insomnia at home and sleepiness on the job. Turnover was high. Frustrated company executives asked a team of Harvard and Stanford sleep researchers for help. After Charles Czisler and coworkers stepped in, productivity jumped about 20 percent and workers reported they felt healthier and happier. Management was delighted.

People's natural sleep-wake cycle runs about 25 hours—if left to our own devices we would go to sleep later and later each day. Large and abrupt time changes that force us to sleep earlier, such as eastbound air travel, throw the body into "jet-lag."

For the past 10 years, employees at the potash plant had changed every week to an earlier shift, working midnight to 8 A.M. one week, 4 P.M. to midnight the next, and 8 A.M. to 4 P.M. the next. That schedule was like making them fly every week to a time zone eight hours ahead, say the scientists.

A better schedule, they suggested, would not only take into account that it is easier to delay sleep, but also give the worker more time to adjust. The scientists rotated a group of 85 employees to later instead of earlier shifts. Thirty-three of the men changed shifts each week. The other 52 stayed on each new shift for three weeks. These 85 men and a group of 68 regular day and swing-shift workers were instructed about sleep-wake cycles and questioned about job satisfaction and health.

Three months later, 70 percent of the experimental group said they preferred rotating to later shifts. But only those who changed shifts every three weeks—who had initially complained that the new schedule would disrupt their family and social lives—said they felt better. Moreover, a nine-month follow-up showed that productivity was still improving and job turnover among workers who changed shifts dropped from about 55 percent to about 30 percent, comparable to that for regular day employees.

"I frankly didn't think it was going to work to start with," says Preston Richey, the company's manager of production. "Now we've gone to the three-week schedule every place we could."

From the American Association for the Advancement of Science, "Shifting Work by the Bio-Clock." *Science 82,* 1982, (October), p. 12. Copyright 1982 by the American Association for the Advancement of Science. Reprinted by permission of *Science 84 Magazine.*

A normal eight-to-five work day is only a dream to many American workers. Employees doing shift work in companies often are going to work when their families and friends are going to bed for the night, and many of them cannot even count on this schedule. Like the workers at the Great Salt Lake Minerals and Chemicals Corporation, many people change work schedules frequently.

Shift work is not new, but the number of employees in modern organizations affected is growing. Concern for the negative effects of such schedules is also growing, as evidenced by Great Salt Lake's decision to call in some experts. Their application of some basic human physiological research allowed the company to help both employees and itself. The change was not a large one, merely a change in direction and frequency of schedule change; but this alteration worked *with* the natural functioning of people, not *against it*.

The distribution of work hours is one of the aspects of general working conditions to be examined in Chapter 8. Temperature, lighting, noise, and physical layout and their effects on worker behavior are also discussed as well as the closely-related topic of employee health and safety.

PHYSICAL WORKING CONDITIONS

Industrial/organizational psychologists have always studied the physical work environment of employees. The famous Hawthorne Experiments originally were designed to investigate the effects of changes made in various aspects of this environment on employee work performance. Of the working condition variables that have been studied, temperature, lighting, and noise have received the most attention. More recently, some researchers have become interested in the physical architecture and arrangement of the work place itself. Finally, as suggested in the opening story, the distribution of work hours is an aspect of working conditions that is being examined from new perspectives.

Hawthorne experiments: See pages 4 to 5.

Temperature of the Work Place

In the United States, temperature is usually measured on a Fahrenheit scale (freezing at 32°), although there is a growing movement to convert to the more universal Celsius scale (freezing at 0°). Whatever type of scale is used, psychologists studying the effects of temperature on workers basically are trying to establish limits within which most people on a job can work comfortably and effectively.

Unfortunately, there is no simple one-to-one relationship between thermometer reading and perceived human comfort. Humidity, air flow, and the number, size, and temperature of objects in a work space all affect this relationship. So do clothing and the nature of the work being performed. Finally, individual differences in physiology can have large effects on perceptions of comfort. Some people do not feel cold until the

Perception: See page 36.

temperature gets into the 40° F to 50° F range; others start to shiver as soon as it dips below 65° F.

Because so many variables affect human perception of temperature, one line of research into this aspect of working conditions is directed toward ways of measuring what is called *effective temperature* (e.g., Vogt, Candas, & Libert, 1982). Effective temperature refers to the perceived temperature as distinct from a thermometer reading. For example, most people in a crowded movie theater would guess the temperature to be higher than an actual thermometer reading would show it to be, because effective temperature is affected by the number of people in the area.

Temperature and Work Behavior

Those who are investigating ways to measure effective temperature are doing basic research. In this particular area, most I/O psychologists are more interested in applied research. The specific focus is the relationship between effective temperature and work performance. Results from this line of research indicate that extremes of heat and cold can lead to physiological changes in people that can have dramatic effects on their work performance. The exact nature of these effects, however, varies considerably.

A wide range of studies carried out in both field and laboratory settings suggests that the two factors that have the greatest influence on the effects of extreme temperatures in the work environment are (a) the nature of the work performed—mental or physical—and (b) the length of exposure to the temperature extremes.

Most studies of mental, or *cognitive*, tasks indicate that subjects performing such work under prolonged exposure to high temperatures make far more errors than subjects working in lower temperatures (e.g., Fine & Kobrick, 1978). This point is illustrated by Exhibit 8–1.

Histogram: See page 161.
The histogram in Exhibit 8–1 shows the amount of time subjects in one laboratory study could continue to perform cognitive tasks to a particular accuracy standard at various room temperatures. Note that this time decreases sharply when the temperature rises above 80° F, a finding that is consistent with most research in this area (see Oborne, 1982).

Manual workers in general seem to be more adversely affected by extremes of cold than by heat (e.g. Lockhart, 1966). When very heavy manual labor is performed, however, most people seem to be both more efficient and more comfortable with temperatures below those in which cognitive tasks may be performed effectively. A review of this research may be found in Fox (1967).

Temperature Research and the Design of the Work Environment

The implications of the general findings discussed for the control of temperature in the work place are relatively straightforward. Office work and light manual labor probably will be performed most efficiently and comfortably with an effective temperature no higher than 80° F. Heavy manual work generally is performed better under somewhat cooler

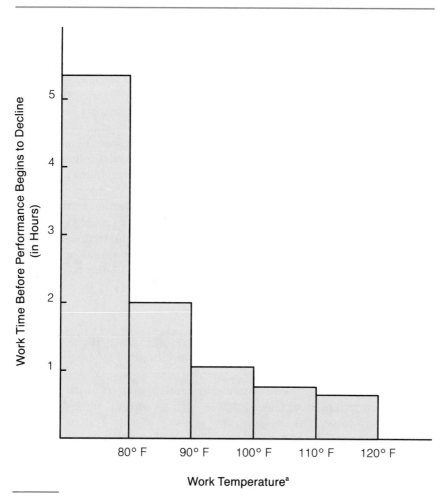

EXHIBIT 8–1

Temperature and
Performance of
Cognitive Tasks

Work Temperature[a]

[a]Conversion from Celsius to Fahrenheit scale is approximate.

Note. Data from J. F. Wing, "Upper Tolerance Limits for Unimpaired Mental Performance." *Aerospace Medicine*, 1965, *36*, pp. 960–964.

temperatures. The American Society of Heating, Refrigerating, and Air-Conditioning Engineers (ASHRAE) offers specific recommendations about temperature range for various work tasks in their *Fundamentals Handbook* (ASHRAE, 1977).

The general recommendations of ASHRAE are based on the assumption that work place temperature can be controlled, but this is not always the case. There are many people who work out-of-doors. Construction and telephone line crews, landscape gardeners, and firefighters, among others, work in whatever temperatures prevail. If they are extreme, both worker health and performance may be jeopardized unless the debilitating physiological effects are offset by job rotation or rest periods.

Illumination of the Work Place

Researchers interested in the effects of temperature on work performance and worker health have been concerned primarily with specifying the ideal temperature ranges for the work environment. In similar fashion, those who study the illumination of the work place want to prescribe the level of lighting required for workers to perform their tasks effectively. Related questions concern the number of light sources, or *luminaries*, their type, and their placement in the work area.

Although perceptions of illumination, like perceptions of temperature, can vary with individual visual ability and with room conditions, this variation is less on the whole. As a result, the measurement of illumination, at least in the physical sense, is less of a problem than the measurement of effective temperature. Lighting specifications almost always are given in a standard measure of illumination called *footcandles*.

To develop footcandle specifications for working environments is a complex process that requires an understanding of visual perceptual phenomena. It is possible, however, to note some of the factors that researchers have found to affect these specifications.

Illumination and Work Behavior

As with temperature, a primary factor in determining required work illumination is the basic *nature of the task*. Specifically, how large a visual component is involved? Reading, assembly, monitoring, and inspection have large visual components. Answering a telephone, conducting meetings, and certain manual tasks, such as shifting cartons, have relatively low visual requirements.

A second variable in determining illumination levels is the *visually-related attributes*, such as size and colors, of materials, tools, or other work aids used on the job. For example, although reading has a large visual component, all reading tasks do not require high illumination. More light is needed in order for people to read such material as the small print in a telephone book than for them to read the large letters on a packing carton. Similarly, certain colors, such as yellow, orange, and red, can be seen more easily under lower illumination than other colors, such as grey, brown, and many shades of blue and green.

A third variable of relevance in determining appropriate illumination is contrast. *Contrast* refers to the extent to which details stand out from a background. A long line of research suggests that the lower the level of illumination, the more contrast is required for accuracy in task performance (e.g., Gilbert & Hopkinson, 1949). Even when the parts are large, for example, more light is required to fit grey screws into grey metal than to fit orange screws into grey metal.

A recent demonstration of the effects of contrast on work performance is provided by the increased use of various electronic visual display units. Although the contrast between material on the screen and the screen itself is controlled, reading the material still can be difficult under the typical bright office illumination if there is insufficient contrast between the light on the screen and the light in the room. An ironic instance of this problem was discovered when employees of one electric power company were found to be turning the room lights off in order to read the newly installed screens.

Illumination Research and the Design of the Work Environment

The example of the lighting problem in the power company illustrates one reason that illumination levels are subjected to research as opposed to lights being put in and/or turned up until everyone can see. Another reason is that lighting costs money and uses energy; too much illumination wastes resources. In addition, bright lights, especially when accompanied by glare, give many people headaches or eye strain and affect their work performance negatively (McCormick, 1964).

Although there are a number of factors to be considered, lighting specifications that meet visual task requirements in various work environments have been described and reported extensively. A basic source-book is the *Lighting Handbook* of the Illuminating Engineering Society (IES; 1972).

A great deal of the research concerning work place illumination is directed toward lighting specifications for various jobs. Lighting specifications are not the only kind of research being conducted in this area, however. Some researchers have become interested in nonperformance-related aspects of lighting, such as the *impressions* created by the way a room is illuminated. For example, Flynn (1977) reports that feelings of spaciousness, privacy, and comfort are associated with lighting that is not too bright and that comes from a variety of sources in a room.

The lighting arrangements Flynn found to be associated with generally positive responses are rare in modern office buildings where overhead fluorescent lighting tends to be the rule. It may be expected, however, that more attention will be paid to this kind of research as concern for the quality of work life (see Chapter 15) of organizational employees grows.

Noise in the Work Place

Sound is created by vibrations that cause waves to travel out from the source of the vibration. Scientists measure these waves in terms of their *frequency* and *intensity.* Frequency and intensity, in turn, are perceived as *pitch* and *loudness* by the listener. Other sound variables of interest to researchers who study noise in the work place include the *duration* of noise and the number of different noise *sources.* This number can be surprising as illustrated by Exhibit 8–2, which lists 31 sources of noise identified in a study of noise control in electrical power plants (Teplitzky, Dubois, Hickman, Paladino, & Trykoski, 1981).

An electric power plant is a noisy work environment, but a careful study will reveal multiple sources of noise in almost any setting. For example, office workers must contend with (a) persistent clatter of typewriters and other standard office machines (b) insistent ringing of tel-

EXHIBIT 8–2

Sources of Noise in a
Power Plant Work
Environment

Main Plant Equipment
1. Boilers
2. Turbined-generator-exciters
3. Turbine condensors
4. Transformers

Auxilliary Plant Equipment
5. Electric motors
6. Boiler and reactor feeder pumps and other pumps
7. Deaerator vents
8. Auxilliary boilers
9. Auxilliary steam turbines
10. Air compressors
11. Outdoor PA system
12. Precipitator rappers and vibrators

Cooling Towers
13. Mechanical-draft cooling towers
14. Natural-draft cooling towers

Fan Noise Sources
15. Inlet of Forced-draft fans
16. Outlet of induced-draft fans
17. Axial-flow fans
18. Ventilating fans
19. Fan housing, casing
20. Fan breaching

Coal Handling Equipment
21. Coal-car shakers
22. Rotary car dumper
23. Conveyors and transfer towers
24. Coal crushers
25. Coal-yard mobile equipment
26. Stacker-reclaimers
27. Coal mills or pulverizers

Valves, Vents, Piping
28. High pressure vents
29. Steam leaks
30. Steam admission valves
31. Valves and piping

Note. Summarized from A. M. Teplitzky, T. J. Dubois, C. E. Hickman, R. C. Paladino, and M. A. Trykoski, ''Electrical Power Plant Environment Noise Guide.'' *Noise Control Engineering,* 1981, *16*(3), pp. 138–144.

phones, (c) conversations among people in the office, and (d) sometimes public address systems as well.

Work place noise, such as that found in electric power plants and offices, comes from tools, machinery, and people performing job tasks. Such noise always has been part of work in most organizations. Today, however, it is common to find sound, in the form of music, introduced into work settings that would be relatively quiet if left alone. For example, retail clerks in small boutique-type clothing shops often work their eight hours accompanied by popular music played at loud volume. Grocery store employees and those who work in medical or dental offices are also likely to work to music, though probably of a different kind.

Noise and Work Behavior

The fact that sound is being introduced deliberately into some work settings simultaneously with efforts to reduce noise in others reflects the complexity of this aspect of physical working conditions. Specifically, sound, or the lack of it, seems to have two distinct kinds of potential effects on job performance. One is physical, the other has to do with the effects of worker *preference* for noisy or quiet working conditions.

To some extent, the effects of noise in and of itself on work performance is still an open question. A number of studies indicate that long-term exposure to noise is detrimental to the cognitive performance of workers (e.g., Broadbent, 1954) and to their learning of psychomotor tasks (e.g., Key & Payne, 1981). Other research suggests that noise does not have any predictable negative effects unless the work being done requires listening to (or for) a particular sound (see McCormick, 1964). These mixed findings suggest that individual differences in noise tolerance may play a large part in such investigations.

Whatever its effects on work performance, there is no doubt that prolonged exposure to high levels of noise can lead to hearing loss. While some people have hearing receptors that are more sensitive to noise than others, the major determinants of hearing loss are (a) duration of exposure, and (b) intensity of noise. A classic study of hearing loss in one work environment is summarized in "Spotlight on Research."

As shown by the graph in "Spotlight on Research," long-tenure operators of earth-moving equipment can suffer substantial hearing loss. Research findings such as these have led the U.S. Department of Labor to establish ceilings on the amount of noise workers may be subjected to without wearing protective ear coverings. Such devices are now common in certain lines of work, even that done out-of-doors. The sight of a groundskeeper wearing protective "earmuffs" is a familiar one these days.

Noise Research and the Design of the Work Environment

The general trend of research with respect to the effects of noise on employees suggests the following strategy: *Take all possible steps to reduce noise in the work place.* Research does not support the hypothesis that noise is always detrimental to work performance. It does suggest, however, that reducing both the level and the duration of noise creates a more *healthful* work environment.

From a practical standpoint, the problem with a general strategy of work place sound reduction is that it ignores individual preferences. People do not always prefer what is good for them. For example, the manager of a teen-oriented clothing boutique reports that he was unable to hire and retain the younger clerks he preferred until he allowed them to work with a background of rock music from a local radio station.

Originally, music was introduced into work environments on the hypothesis that people would be more productive under these conditions. A review of early research (Fox, 1971) lends some support to this position, but situational differences are considerable and so are individual differences between workers. What is music to some is just irritating and distracting noise to others.

Hypothesis: See page 47.

To some extent, the problem of preference for sound or quiet at work can be solved by self-selection. People who find a work setting either too noisy or too quiet can quit or not take the job at all. This solution is partial at best. Many people like their jobs and would not want to leave them for a reason that seems so trivial. Others have no equally satisfying alternative employment.

As the world gets noisier, the issue of preference for working in noisy or quiet work environments may become more pressing. Undesired noise creates stress, but those who prefer noise find it soothing. The relative rights of these two groups in a work setting could become an issue as the relative rights of smokers and nonsmokers already has become.

Field observation: See page 55.

Independent / dependent variables: See page 52.

Operational definition: See page 48.

SPOTLIGHT ON RESEARCH

A Noise and Hearing Study of Earth-Moving Equipment Operators

Research question: What is the relationship between length of exposure to intense noise levels and hearing loss?

Type of study: Field observation.

Subjects: Sixty-three operators of earth-moving equipment.

Variables:
- Length of exposure to noise. Operational definition: Years on the job.
- Intensity of noise. Operational definition: Frequency level of equipment noise.
- Hearing loss of workers. Operational definition: Average hearing loss in number of decibels *over and above* normal loss at subjects' ages.

General procedure: Average hearing loss for workers was measured and analyzed by time on the job and noise level of equipment operated.

Results: The relationship between the noise level of machinery and the average hearing loss for three job tenure groups is shown in the graph below.

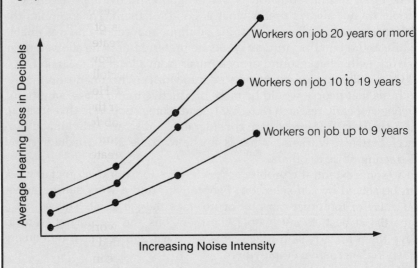

Conclusion: Hearing loss increases with time of exposure to the source of noise. This loss is greater at very intense levels of noise.

Summarized from P. LaBenz, A. Cohen, and B. Pearson, ''A Noise and Hearing Study of Earth-Moving Equipment Operators.'' *American Industrial Hygiene Association Journal,* 1067, *28,* pp. 117–128.

Architecture and Appearance of the Work Place

The interest of I/O psychologists in the relationships between worker behavior and various features of the layout and appearance of the physical work environment is comparatively new. While such studies do not form any substantial part of the relevant literature, they are appearing with greater frequency. The nature of some of the research being done in this area is summarized here. A detailed discussion of the relevant issues in this line of investigation may be found in the recent review by Davis (1984).

Work Place Size and Layout

One aspect of the architecture of a work place that has received attention is the *social density* associated with the design and layout; that is, the extent to which architectural features crowd workers together or spread them out. In one recent field study of this variable, the effects of a move to a new physical facility on 96 professional employees of a large petroleum-related company were investigated by means of questionnaires. The move resulted in more crowded conditions (greater social density) for approximately one-third of these employees, less crowded for another third, and no change for the remainder (Szilagyi & Holland, 1980).

In some ways, the results of the Szilagyi and Holland study are surprising. Employees who were more crowded after the move reported less job autonomy, but also less role stress, more job feedback, greater friendship opportunities, and more work satisfaction than employees who were not more crowded. The hypothesis that greater density would have negative effects was not supported.

Workspace Division

A second aspect of the architectural features of a work place that has been investigated is the way in which space is divided into work areas. At one extreme of this dimension, all employees have individual offices. At the other extreme, the space is an open-plan office such as that shown in Exhibit 8–3.

As seen in Exhibit 8–3, an open-plan workspace has no walls to divide individual work areas from one another. This plan has become quite

EXHIBIT 8–3

Open-Plan
Workspace
Arrangement

popular in the last decade. It is flexible, economical, and allows co-workers easy access to one another. Employee reactions to this arrangement have been consistently less favorable (e.g., Oldham & Brass, 1979). A major issue is the lack of privacy associated with such a layout.

In a recent series of three studies, Sundstrom, Burt, and Kamp (1980) concluded that all subjects, regardless of type of job, preferred the privacy of enclosed offices. Specifically, the investigators found that the physical and psychological privacy afforded by individual offices:

Correlation: See page 61.

- was positively correlated with satisfaction with the work environment;
- was positively correlated with job satisfaction;
- showed a limited positive correlation with job performance for certain jobs.

While conclusions based on correlational studies must be made with caution, the studies by Sundstrom and his colleagues do lend yet more weight to the growing evidence that the open office plan may have more drawbacks than advantages in the long run.

Office Arrangement

In general, the way in which a private office is arranged is left to the discretion of the occupant. There is ample evidence that decisions in this realm do send messages to others. In one study of student reactions to faculty offices, for example, an impression of friendliness was found to be associated with an open-desk (not placed against the wall) arrangement (Morrow & McElroy, 1981).

In many instances, the arrangement of a desk in an office is probably pure happenstance. The desk is against the wall because that is where the current job incumbent found it; or it is in the center of the room because the light is best there. However a particular arrangement comes about, it does seem to be true that visitors assume it expresses the incumbent's preference, and they draw conclusions accordingly. Morrow and McElroy suggest that people in certain kinds of authority positions in organizations may find it easier to promote open communication with subordinates by applying such research findings.

Wall Color

An exception to the statement that research into the appearance of the work environment is relatively new is the long-standing interest that psychologists have had in the influence of color on human behavior.

Office arrangement and general appearance send messages to others about the person who works there.

Certain colors, such as blues and greens, have been found to have a restful and soothing effect. Others, such as red, have a tendency to promote excitability. Yellows and oranges seem to increase attention and alertness. Grey tends to have a depressing effect.

The implications of the relationships between color and behavior found in early research were put to use in many applied settings at one time. High-risk work areas got yellow wall paint, for example, and the cafeteria was painted green. Modern buildings, by contrast, use little or no color in wall paint. White, off-white, or beige is the rule—these are unlikely to offend anyone and are easy to touch up or repaint. An exception to this increasing neutrality is the recent use of color coding; that is, the use of wall color to differentiate functional work areas, departments, or other groupings of employees, from one another.

Color coding has appeared in a variety of settings in recent years. The author has noted its use in the offices of a group of physicians, a large credit service company, several day-care centers, one insurance company, and a number of university buildings. In one university business school, for example, red, yellow, blue, and white paint set off areas of the building used by accounting, economics, finance, and management, respectively.

The general rationale for color coding in buildings is twofold. On the one hand, it may help foster some group identification among employees. On the other hand, color coding may make it easier for customers, clients, employees, or visitors to find their ways through the work space. Although there have been no studies to date on the relationship between color coding and increased work group closeness, there is some evidence that this use of wall color makes it easier for people to get around in the space.

In a study of color coding by Evans, Fellows, Zorn, and Doty (1980), one-half of the subjects were given a timed walk-through of a large institutional office building after the walls were color coded. The other half of the subjects went through it without the color coding. Relative to the other subjects, "color coded subjects":

- made significantly fewer errors when asked later to find the most direct route to three different locations within the building;
- showed higher recall and recognition memory for floor plans of the building.

This brief review of some of the research being conducted in the area of investigating relationships between work behavior and various architectural features of the work environment brings this section to a close. A different feature of employee working conditions—the arrangement of working hours—is addressed in the next section.

WORK HOUR DISTRIBUTION

Under a variety of influences, the standard work hour distribution pattern in this country has evolved into one of 8 hours a day for 5 consecutive days a week, or an *8/5 arrangement.* Organizations that must operate more than 8 hours a day usually have two or more 8-hour shifts. Lately, however, a number of variations on the standard 8/5 pattern have been suggested and implemented. Two of these variations—the compressed work week and flexible working hours—are discussed. In addition, some of the conclusions from research on more firmly-established shift-work patterns are reviewed.

The Compressed Work Week

The compressed work week (CWW) is a redistribution of the typical 40 hours of work. In its most common form, workers are on the job 10 hours a day for 4 days a week instead of 8 hours for 5 days. There are, however, variations. For certain kinds of duty and shifts, for example, some nurses are paid for 40 hours of work when they work 12 hours a day for 2 days in succession.

However it is actually set up, the CWW arrangement of working time gives employees a considerably greater block of leisure time than the standard 8/5 week. Among the benefits thought to be associated with this change are reduced anxiety and stress and an improved home life. It is expected that these will in turn be associated with less absenteeism from work, better attitudes toward the company, greater job satisfaction, and higher worker productivity.

Compressed Work Week Research

Research into the validity of the benefits thought to be associated with CWW has lagged behind adoption of various forms of this plan. A recent review of the literature (Ronen & Primps, 1981) found only 14 studies that clearly were relevant to the issues. A summary of changes that occurred after CWW was introduced into the companies studied in these investigations is shown in Exhibit 8–4.

Measure	Percent of Studies Reporting Positive Change After CWW
Attitudes toward:	
CWW	91%
Job	55%
Effect on:	
Home/Personal Life	66%
Leisure/Recreation	100%
Performance as measured by:	
Production/Service	57%
Fatigue	None
Absenteeism	60%

EXHIBIT 8–4

Changes Associated with the Implementation of CWW

Note. Data from S. Ronen and S. B. Primps, "The Compressed Work Week as Organizational Change: Behavioral and Attitudinal Outcomes." Academy of Management Review, 1981, 6(1), pp. 61–74.

The summary in Exhibit 8–4 is strongly supportive of the assumption that CWW schedules are associated with improvements in perceived quality of home life and leisure time. In slightly over half of the studies reviewed, there also was a positive change in attendance and reported job satisfaction. Worker fatigue, however, tended to increase under CWW.

Generalizability: See page 67.

The number of studies reviewed by Ronen and Primps (1981) is small and inadequate for researchers' purposes of drawing any conclusions about the effects on employees of working fewer, but longer, days. The review does lend sufficient support to the potential benefits of CWW to warrant more research, however. Ronen and Primps offer a number of recommendations for future investigations.

- Conduct longitudinal absenteeism studies that differentiate illness-related absenteeism from personal leave time.
- Research and clarify the influence of such individual-difference variables as sex and age, on worker reactions to CWW.
- Study the relationship between success or failure of CWW and supervisory styles.
- Compare various CWW schedules, such as a 10/4 distribution (10 hours a day, 4 days a week), 12/2, 12/3, and so on.
- Clarify the role of the increased worker fatigue associated with CWW with emphasis on a range of different kinds of tasks.

Flexible Working Hours

The term *flexible working hours*, or *flexitime*, refers to a range of variations in the distribution of work time. All flexitime plans are characterized by some number of core hours during which employees must be present, together with some flexibility of starting/stopping times on either side of this core. The basic concept is illustrated in the diagram in Exhibit 8–5.

In the illustration in Exhibit 8–5, all employees must be at work between the hours of 10 A.M. and 3 P.M. (the core). They have considerable flexibility, however, in when they arrive and leave. Assuming that the work day is the standard eight hours, an employee may come to work as early as 7 A.M. and leave as early as 3 P.M. At the other extreme, he or she may come in as late as 10 A.M. and stay until 6 P.M., with variations in between.

The advantages of the flexible schedule to employees are considerable. They can avoid rush-hour traffic, take care of personal business during normal business hours instead of trying to fit this in at lunch or on weekends, be home when children get out of school, or sleep late—whatever suits their particular situations. At this time, it is estimated that between 10% and 15% of the organizations in this country are experimenting with versions of flexitime.

Flexitime Research

The material on flexitime is somewhat more comprehensive than that on CWWs although much of it is anecdotal in nature. There have been,

EXHIBIT 8-5

The Concept
of Flexitime

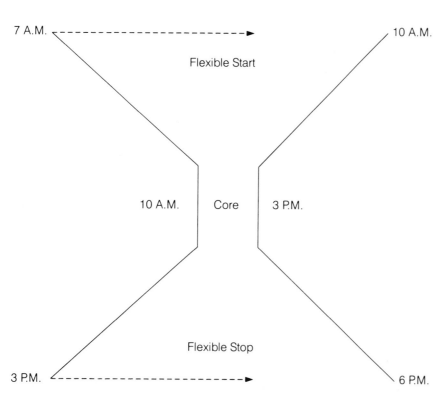

however, a number of field experiments, such as that conducted by
Narayanan and Nath (1982). Subjects in that study were employees of
a large multinational corporation. Experimental (flexitime) and control
(standard work hours) groups were matched on age, tenure, education,
salary, and absenteeism history.

*Field experiment: See page
52.*

Questionnaire and personnel department data in the Narayanan and
Nath study showed (a) employee work flexibility, work group relations,
and supervisor-subordinate relations improved and (b) absenteeism
declined. There was no difference between experimental and control
groups on production measures or reported job satisfaction.

The results of Narayanan and Nath's flexitime experiment described
are consistent with some of the earlier experiments and inconsistent with
others. For example, Orpen (1981) also found flexitime to be associated
with little change in performance, but in that study there was a significant change in reported job satisfaction. On the other hand, Kim and
Campagna (1961) report employee performance *higher* under flexitime.

As with CWW scheduling, more research is needed to help organizations make decisions about implementing flexitime plans. It seems
safe to conclude that most employees who have tried flexitime like it

(or at least are neutral toward it), but the conditions under which there are associated improvements in job satisfaction and job performance remain to be established.

Shift Work

The term **shift work** stands for work-hour scheduling strategies in which different groups of employees perform the same job duties in different blocks of time during a 24-hour period.

Shift work is the rule in such public-sector organizations as hospitals, fire departments, and police departments; it is common in the private sector. Surveys estimate that some 25% of the labor force in North America operates on shift-work schedules.

While shift work is an established method of work-hour distribution, the actual pattern of this scheduling can vary considerably. In addition to the basic variations shown in Exhibit 8–6, there are variations in shift starting/stopping times and in arrangements for individual assignments to shifts/days off.

Because there are so many variations possible on the basic arrangements shown in Exhibit 8–6, researchers of shift work have tended to use a simple definition of three shifts—*day, afternoon* (swing), and *night* (graveyard). The focus has been on reactions to and behaviors associated with (a) each of the three basic shifts and (b) work schedules that require employees to *change* shifts at intervals. Among the behaviors and reactions studied have been worker attitudes, performance, and health.

Shift Work and Attitudes

Many employees on shift work express a preference for permanent day work (e.g. Dunham, 1977). Disturbances of sleeping and eating habits and family and social life are the most common objections to deviations from this pattern. On the other hand, most studies in this area also report a fairly substantial percentage of employees (sometimes as high as one-third) who prefer a permanent night-shift arrangement. Among the advantages cited are:

- less work supervision
- lower performance expectations
- freedom to shop or take care of personal matters during normal business hours

	Number of		
Type	Hours Plant in Operation	Days Plant in Operation	Daily Shifts
Continuous	24	7	3
Semicontinuous	24	5–6	3
Consecutive	16	5–7	2
Split	8 +	5–7	2[a]

EXHIBIT 8–6

Typical Shift-work Schedules

[a]These 2 split shifts overlap.

More surprising, perhaps, than the fact that some workers prefer a permanent night-shift assignment is that a few express a preference for rotating shift work. Rotating shift work is characterized by changes in shift assignment following days off; for example, four days on night shift, three days off, and five on day shift. Wedderburn, whose 1975 studies of shift work in the steel industry are frequently cited, refers to the various preferences described above as "shift types."

Insofar as there are "shift types" and it is feasible to do so, it makes sense to give employees their choice of shift arrangements on a permanent basis. This strategy is backed by a substantial body of research showing that the most pronounced negative effects of nontraditional work hours are associated with rotating shifts (e.g., Smith, Colligan, & Tasto, 1982).

Shift Work and Performance

There are few reports of direct comparisons of worker performance on various shifts, but what is available suggests a tendency for worker output to be somewhat lower, and errors, scrap, and so on to be somewhat higher on night shifts (e.g., Jamal & Jamal, 1982). There may be several reasons for such a pattern.

- Employees who do not want to work nights but must to keep their jobs may indeed work less hard and/or make more mistakes.
- Many support services in an organization, such as data processing and personnel, shut down or go on skeletal crew at night even though other operations may be fully staffed. Thus some decisions and activities may of necessity be put off or made with less than complete or accurate information.
- There may be less direct supervision in some organizations on the night shift.
- Employees who work nights as part of a rotating shift schedule may be inadequately adapted to the change and unable to work up to par. In this regard, the experience of the Great Salt Lake Minerals and Chemicals Corporation reported in "I/O Psychology at Work" is instructive. In the study conducted there, a slight alternation in shift arrangements made physical adaption to shifts easier. As a result, workers felt better, and there were substantial productivity gains.

Shift Work and Employee Health

Both afternoon and night work shifts are deviations from long-established life patterns for most adults. As such, they are potential *stressors* and may therefore be expected to have adverse effects on employee health and well-being. Much of the evidence available supports this expectation; night-shift work frequently is found to be associated with more reported health disorders, including fatigue, than day-shift work.

A rotating shift schedule appears to be even more detrimental to health than night-shift work because (as it usually is implemented) it

Although some employees prefer working nights, research finds more health problems among night-shift than among day-shift employees.

does not allow for adaptation to unfamiliar patterns of working, sleeping, and eating. It should be kept in mind, however, that these conclusions are general.

Not all people are negatively affected by deviations from routine and the role of certain individual employee characteristics may be substantial. For example, Zedeck, Jackson, and Summer's (1983) recent study of shift work suggests that some of the health problems assumed to result from shift work actually may be the result of physical aging.

In summary, the literature on shift work supports the conclusion that there are fewer organizational and individual problems associated with day shifts than with other shift arrangements. Individual differences are important, however; some employees prefer nontraditional shifts, and many of these experience no negative physical symptoms as a result of such schedules. It is to this issue of employee health and safety that attention is given now.

WORKING CONDITIONS AND EMPLOYEE HEALTH AND SAFETY

Among other provisions, the Occupational Health and Safety Act (OSHA) passed in 1970, requires organizations to supply the U.S. Department of Labor with annual reports of certain work-related illnesses, accidents, and deaths. Decision guidelines from OSHA for recording any particular incident as summarized by Schuler (1984) are shown in Exhibit 8–7.

Information recorded and sent to OSHA through the process shown

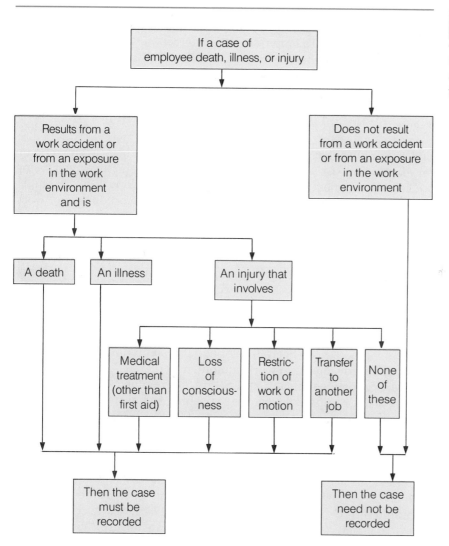

EXHIBIT 8–7

Occupational Health and Safety Act Guide to Records

in Exhibit 8–7 together with information from other sources, such as insurance companies, leads to an estimate of some 6 million occupational accidents per year in this country. Of these, some 10,000 to 14,000 result in death. In addition, there are somewhere in the region of a half million new cases of occupation-related diseases with 100,000 associated deaths per year. Together, work-related accidents, illnesses, and deaths are estimated to cost over $35 billion dollars a year. Staggering as these figures are, most people working to improve health and safety records believe that they are conservative estimates.

Behavior causation: See pages 27 to 28.

Accidents and illnesses, whatever the context in which they occur or originate, are the product of individual and situational factors. For example, a "careless" person working in a hazardous job is more likely to have an accident than is a careful person in the same job, or even a careless person in a *safe* job. To emphasize this interaction, some of the research into the *people* who have accidents or become ill on the job follows a discussion of situational factors found in general working conditions.

Environmental Factors and Accidents and Illness

Efforts to reduce hazards in the work environment have been going on for many years. As far as working conditions and employee well-being are concerned, most of these efforts have centered on (a) work equipment and materials and (b) general housekeeping procedures and work practices.

Work Equipment and Materials

The design of safe work equipment is largely an engineering problem, and one that is coming well under control. Electrical coils have replaced dangerous trailing cords; machines shut down automatically if a dangerous malfunction occurs or a foreign object (such as a finger) becomes immeshed; moving parts are shielded from worker hands and limbs; nonskid surfaces have been developed; and so on down a list of thousands of improvements in work equipment.

The Occupational Health and Safety Act reinforces the progress in making work equipment safer by publishing safety standards for most tools, machinery, and other work aids (OSHA, 1976). In many cases, safety equipment, such as helmets, goggles, earplugs, and special clothing, are required in addition to conformity with equipment standards.

There are no figures available to pinpoint the number of organization accidents actually caused by unsafe or defective equipment. When such accidents occur, they are often spectacular, such as the collapse of a scaffold or the explosion of a boiler. In the 1980s, however, it is likely that actual defects cause fewer accidents than misuse, abuse, faulty maintenance, or failure to use safety devices provided. A far more difficult problem (in terms of the extent to which its solution is known and under control) lies in work materials and substances that are *inherently* dangerous or toxic to humans.

The list of hazardous materials and substances in common use in organizations of the 1980s is a long one. Ten of the more deadly, together with associated diseases and workers who are most likely to be exposed to them, are given in Exhibit 8–8.

The list of substances and related diseases shown in Exhibit 8–8 is by no means complete. For example, skin diseases that result from contact with, or exposure to, various chemicals and irritants do not appear, although skin disease is the single largest category of occupation-related illnesses. Other hazards are being discovered all of the time. Among the dangers currently being investigated are exposure of workers to fluorescent lighting and to cathode ray tubes (CRT).

There are two basic approaches to reducing the hazards of dangerous substances in the work environment. One is to reduce the amount or level of the substance or to discontinue its use (or the use of the producing agent in the case of substances such as dust). The other is to restrict employee exposure to specified time limits or, in some cases, to forbid exposure entirely. As discussed in "At Issue," either strategy involves ethical dilemmas for which no one has any satisfactory solutions to date.

General Housekeeping and Work Practices

In addition to providing and maintaining safe work equipment and materials, both common sense and OSHA dictate that an organization is also responsible for seeing that the work environment is clean and free from obvious hazards. Among the more common of these hazards are trash piles, puddles of oil or water, and blocked safety exits. Some 5% to 10% of recorded OSHA violations each year fall into this category.

Housekeeping lapses are common, but those interested in worker health and safety frequently note the use of unsafe work practices as well. Some of these methods may in fact be the prescribed way the organization says to do things. Many more, however, are short-cuts or deliberate failures by workers to employ safety devices or to use safety equipment provided. Industrial/organizational psychologists concentrate their efforts to deal with such problems in two areas—safety education and training and safety incentive programs.

Safety education and training.   Safety education and training to reduce unsafe work methods are concentrated on worker *knowledge*. The means employed to educate workers range from posters and placards with safety slogans on them to job-specific training courses in safe work methods. Most organizations make some use of safety propaganda; specific training programs are less widespread, but they are gaining in popularity as the problem escalates.

Most safety training programs are focused on the transmission of information concerning specific safe work methods and housekeeping practices. In one such program, vehicle maintenance workers participated in a 45-minute discussion session in which slides depicting unsafe conditions and practices were contrasted with slides showing the corresponding safe conditions and practices (Komaki, Heinzmann, & Lawson, 1980).

EXHIBIT 8–8

Danger in the
Work Place

10 Suspected Hazards in the Workplace
As cited by federal agencies, here are some of the major agents linked to on-the-job diseases.

Potential Dangers	Diseases That May Result	Workers Exposed
Arsenic	Lung cancer, lymphona	Smelter, chemical, oil-refinery workers; insecticide makers and sprayers—estimated 660,000 exposed
Asbestos	White-lung disease (asbestosis); cancer of lungs and lining of lungs, cancer of other organs	Miners, millers, textile, insulation and shipyard workers—estimated 1.6 million exposed
Benzene	Leukemia; aplastic anemia	Petrochemical and oil-refinery workers; dye users; distillers; painters; shoemakers—estimated 600,000 exposed
Bischloromethylether (BCME)	Lung cancer	Industrial chemical workers
Coal dust	Black-lung disease	Coal miners—estimated 208,000 exposed
Coke-oven emissions	Cancer of lungs, kidneys	Coke-oven workers— estimated 30,000 esposed
Cotton dust	Brown-lung disease (byssinosis); chronic bronchitis; emphysema	Textile workers—estimated 600,000 exposed
Lead	Kidney disease; anemia; central nervous-system damage; sterility, birth defects	Metal grinders; lead-smelter workers; lead storage-battery workers—estimated 835,000 exposed
Radiation	Cancer of thyroid, lungs and bone; leukemia; reproductive effects (spontaneous abortion, genetic damage)	Medical technicians; uranium miners; nuclear-power and atomic workers
Vinyl chloride	Cancer of liver, brain	Plastic-Industry workers— estimated 10,000 directly exposed

Source: Occupational Safety and Health Administration, Nuclear Regulatory Commission, U.S. Depts. of Energy, Interior, plus other sources.

Note. From A. Trafford, "Is Your Job Dangerous to Your Health?" *U.S. News & World Report,* 1979, (February 5), p. 42. Copyright 1979 by U.S. News & World Report, Inc. Reprinted by permission from *U.S. News & World Report.*

Many organizations post safety information to remind employees to be safety conscious.

Consistent with the training principles discussed in Chapter 6, the presentation of safety information without employee practice, feedback, or reinforcement is unlikely to bring about a significant change in safety-related behaviors of employees. In the study by Komaki and her colleagues, for example, little improvement was recorded until feedback was incorporated into the program even though incentives were offered for safe behavior. People have to know how they are doing for incentives to be effective.

Feedback: See pages 148 to 150.

Safety incentive programs.   Although protecting oneself from injury, illness, or death would seem to be sufficient reinforcement for safe work practices, the observation that it is not is almost universal. Among the reasons advanced for this phenomenon are:

Positive reinforcement: See page 31.

- a desire on the part of some workers to be considered ''macho'' or ''tough'' through disregarding safety regulations;

- conflicting work demands, such as those created by simultaneous demands for a high rate of production and time-consuming safe work practices;
- a belief that accidents "only happen to other people."

The most effective way to deal with problems, such as those listed, is to provide incentives for worker compliance with safety rules and safe work practices. This approach, which concentrates on employee *motivation*, is not new; safety incentive programs have been around for years. In traditional form, the incentives were group ones—some form of recognition for a team, unit, department, or plant that had fewer accidents in a given period of time than others had, for example.

Evidence as to the effectiveness of traditional safety incentive programs was mixed. It also was confused considerably by the possibility (confirmed in some cases) that illness and accident data were being doctored to avoid making employees, supervisors, or plants look bad. Some believed the problem lay in the fact that group recognition was not a sufficiently powerful incentive. As J. Parsons, owner of a company whose incentive programs for promoting health and reducing accidents have been widely publicized, said *(Business Week, 1979)*:

> . . . *no matter what you do, it doesn't really make a dent until the people themselves see that they are going to lose a dollar by not being safe.*

Parsons' plan was simple. The company had an unusually high accident rate and paid correspondingly high premiums to the state's industrial accident fund. By distributing its retroactive refunds, based on reductions in accidents, to the firm's employees, Parsons cut its accident bill from $28,500 to $2,500 in one year; net gain to employees was $900 per individual.

The success of the safety incentive program at Parsons is dramatic, but it is not an isolated occurrence. Field experiments, utilizing the same principle, consistently confirm its effectiveness. The data in Exhibit 8–9, for example, are from a safety behavior modification study involving bus drivers in a large midwestern city (Haynes, Pine & Fitch, 1982).

The graph in Exhibit 8–9 shows average 6-week accident rates per bus driver over a 17-month period. Significant differences in accident rates between experimental and control groups appear only in the 18-week intervention (experimental) period.

During the intervention period, shown in Exhibit 8–9, experimental subjects were divided into teams. Every 2 weeks, members of the team with the lowest accident rate received monetary incentives ranging from cash to free gasoline. Members of teams that were accident free in any 2-week period received a double bonus. As a result of the intervention, the accident rate for the experimental group bus drivers fell 24.9% during the intervention period. Significant differences between experimental and control subjects disappeared when the incentive program was dropped (Baseline II).

Experiments such as that by Haynes, Pine, and Fitch strongly suggest that when it comes to employee health and safety, the bottom line is

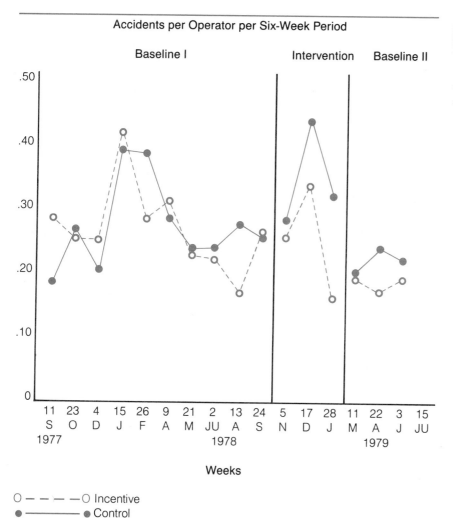

Accidents per Operator per Six-Week Period

Baseline I   Intervention   Baseline II

O – – – –O Incentive
●————● Control

Note. From R. S. Haynes, R. C. Pine, and H. G. Fitch. "Reducing Accident Rates With Organizational Behavior Modification." *Academy of Management Journal*, 1982, 25(2), p. 413.
Reprinted by permission of the authors and publisher.

EXHIBIT 8-9

*Employee Safety
Incentives and
Accident Rates*

the employee. Safe and healthful working conditions are a prerequisite
and an obligation of every employer, but no environment can protect
employees against themselves. For this reason, a look at health and
safety from the standpoint of the individual is warranted.

Individual Characteristics and Accidents and Illness

At this time, the federal government, state governments, and unions
are placing great emphasis on organizational responsibility for the health

and safety of employees. In the last decade, this emphasis has led to substantial progress by organizations in making working conditions safer and healthier for all employees. Characteristics and behavior of individuals play an equally important role in worker health and safety, however. Research suggests that worker abilities, skills, and experience are particularly important (e.g., Fell, 1976).

A useful way of looking at the interaction of work environment and individual abilities/skills/experience from the standpoint of work accidents is provided by Oborne (1982). Oborne argues that most accidents occur when the work environment (including the task, tools, machines, noise, coworkers, and so on) demands more of a worker than he or she is able to give at that time. This concept is illustrated graphically in Exhibit 8–10.

In Exhibit 8–10, the fluctuating demands of the work environment are shown by the lower wavy line. The upper line represents worker capacities relative to these demands. For example, if a worker is operating a commercial sewing machine, the environment demands a fairly high level of coordinating skill to operate controls and guide material through according to the pattern. Assuming the worker is experienced, he or she is capable of doing this although wandering attention (not using skills fully) brings demands and capabilities very close at Point A.

At Point B in Exhibit 8–10, an accident occurs. In the current example, perhaps the operator gets a finger under the machine needle. In the model, this happened because the demands of the environment exceeded

---

EXHIBIT 8–10

A Model of Accident Causation

Operator's Ability

Environmental Demands

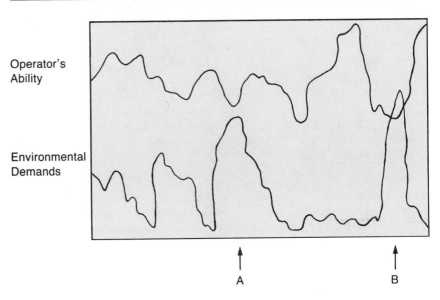

A   B

Note. From D. J. Oborne, *Ergonomics at Work.* Chichester, England: John Wiley & Sons, 1982, p. 248. Copyright 1982 by John Wiley & Sons, Ltd. Reprinted by permission of John Wiley & Sons, Ltd.

worker capabilities for a moment. There are any number of ways in which this might have happened, even with an experienced operator. For example, perhaps the worker continued to operate the machine while trying to explain to a coworker how to deal with a work problem. This added environmental demand (request for help from another worker) momentarily exceeded the capacities of the operator.

Oborne's model is a useful framework for understanding that accidents are the product of varying patterns of interactions between workers and their environments. Some 60 years of research leave no doubt that such accidents are not distributed evenly throughout the employee population; some people definitely have more accidents than others. The implied possibility of an "accident-prone" personality has excited the interest of many researchers.

Accident Proneness

Over the years, the possession of certain individual traits (as measured by particular tests) has been found to be correlated with number of work accidents in particular studies. Among these traits are pessimism, low level of trust in others, and a generally-depressed temperament (e.g., Davids & Mahoney, 1957).

Although individual findings have been interesting, the search for a stable "accident-prone personality" has not been successful on the whole. To some extent this is because chance factors alone will produce an uneven distribution of accidents regardless of the individuals involved (Mintz & Blum, 1949).

Failure of researchers to identify a stable pattern of personality characteristics associated with accident proneness also may be partially attributable to a certain ambiguity of definition. As Maier and Verser (1982) point out in their review of the research conducted on accident proneness, there is a difference between (a) accidents *precipitated* by individuals and (b) accidents caused by the failure of individuals to *avert* an accident when a hazardous situation arises. This distinction may be seen in the difference between (a) a traffic accident that occurs when a driver attempts to pass another car on a hill and meets an oncoming vehicle and (b) one that occurs because the driver did not know what to do when the automobile began to skid on an icy road.

If Maier and Verser's line of reasoning is accepted, it seems clear that no one set of characteristics is likely to define both (a) accident repeaters who cause accidents to themselves and others through unsafe acts and (b) people who lack the abilities, skills, and/or experience to avoid accidents. The characteristics that researchers have found to be associated most reliably with more accidents are more descriptive of the second group than the first. Among these characteristics, as discussed by McCormick and Ilgen (1980), are:

- youth
- inexperience on job
- basic perceptual skill deficiencies
- subnormal motor reaction times

These characteristics suggest that screening, selection, and job training play important roles in the promotion of worker safety that should not be overlooked in efforts to make the work place safer.

Stress, Accidents, and Illness at Work

Research into accidents at work leaves little doubt that both individual and environmental factors play their parts in causing accidents. The importance of this interaction is pointed out in studies of *stress* as a factor contributing, not only to accidents, but to work-related illnesses as well.

Sources of stress at work include the following:

- time pressures
- overtaxing work demands
- poor relationships with coworkers or bosses
- job insecurity
- job dissatisfaction
- a hostile physical environment (e.g., too hot or too noisy)

In terms of the accident causation model in Exhibit 8–10, sources of stress (sometimes called *stressors)* increase the environmental demands on an individual. If such demands exceed an individual's ability to cope with the situation, he or she may have accidents that would not otherwise have occurred. Some believe this situation also increases people's susceptibility to disease. The most stable evidence at this time for such an association is between stress and coronary heart disease. While no cause-effect relationship can be proven, there does seem to be sufficient evidence to warrant continued research (Sharit & Salvendy, 1982).

Possible connections between stress at work and accidents and illness have led some researchers to pursue the question of whether low tolerance for stress is a stable individual characteristic. This line of research, of course, is similar to the search for the "accident-prone personality."

Much of the work to investigate "stress types" centers around the Type A/Type B categories suggested some years ago by Rosenman et al. (1966). The qualities of a Type A person, as described by Cox (1978), are shown in Exhibit 8–11.

EXHIBIT 8–11	Personality and Behavioral Characteristics of Individuals with a High Sensitivity to Work Stressors

Type A Person

- An intense and sustained drive to achieve self-selected, but usually poorly defined, goals
- A profound inclination and eagerness to compete
- A persistent desire for recognition and advancement
- A continuous involvement in multiple and diverse functions constantly subject to time restrictions
- An habitual propensity to accelerate the rate of execution of many physical and mental functions
- An extraordinary mental and physical alertness

Note. Described in T. Cox, *Stress.* Baltimore: University Park Press, 1978.

The Type A employee, as described in Exhibit 8–11, is one who is more likely to perceive stress in the work environment and/or put himself or herself into a stressful situation. The behaviors, attitudes, career histories, and accident/illness records of these people and their Type B opposites currently are receiving considerable attention in I/O psychology literature. It is too early to draw any conclusions from this line of investigation, however.

Concluding Remarks on Employee Health and Safety

Efforts to identify stable patterns of individual personality, descriptive, and skill/experience variables that identify people more likely to have accidents or become ill at work are consistent with the focus of I/O psychology on the individual. If such patterns could be found and measured reliably, hiring, placement, and training activities could be modified so as to reduce potential problems. At this time, however, a practical approach to improvement of employee health and safety rests on three strategies.

1. Make the physical work environment as healthy and free from safety hazards as possible.
2. Be sure employees understand and have the ability to do their jobs in ways that promote health and safety.
3. Reinforce safety and health-oriented behaviors, such as wearing the safety equipment provided and taking advantage of company-paid medical checkups.

SUMMARY

General working conditions include such physical environmental variables as work-hour distribution, temperature, lighting, sound, and architectural features of the work place. The fact that such aspects of the environment affect work behavior is well established. The factors to be considered in applying the relevant research to any particular organization include (a) the nature of the work being performed in the organization, (b) the characteristics of the employees involved, and (c) the relevant external standards and regulations.

Employee health and safety is only partially a function of working conditions, but these conditions remain a basic focus for those concerned with this issue. Among the relevant aspects of working conditions regulated by OSHA are work equipment and materials, work methods, and general housekeeping.

Industrial/organizational psychologists emphasize the importance of safety education and training, coupled with positive reinforcement for safe work practices, as a way of encouraging workers to take an active part in their own health and safety. Research into the characteristics of those who have more accidents suggests that lack of knowledge, skill, and/or experience are important factors. Individual stress tolerance also may affect both accidents and work-related illnesses although research in these areas is still in the early stages.

AT ISSUE

Danger, Science, and Individual Freedom

There are some 13,000 known potentially dangerous substances that employees may encounter in the work place, and new ones are being identified with alarming frequency. In 1981, for example, DuPont Company reassigned 50 women in a West Virginia plant after Minnesota Mining and Manufacturing Company warned DuPont that one of 3-M's products (a compound used in making resins at DuPont) had been linked to birth defects in rats.

The DuPont Company acted swiftly to remove women employees of childbearing age from jobs with high exposure to a possibly toxic substance. Its action is commendable from many viewpoints, but it also raises two increasingly perplexing issues with respect to the problem of potentially dangerous substances in the work place.

The first problem raised by the DuPont action has to do with the definition of "exposure risk." Many of the substances whose use health experts say should be reduced or eliminated in work processes are critical to those processes. As in the DuPont case, the evidence for danger to humans is based on experiments with nonhumans. In many cases, these experimental animals have been subjected to exposure levels far beyond any proportional levels of exposure for humans in industry.

Many question the validity of extrapolating the results of research that subjects laboratory animals to extreme levels of dangerous substances to human beings in work organizations. The issue is: What should constitute proof that a given substance does present a real danger to humans? DuPont took action based on evidence that was suggestive at best. Other companies believe that the question deserves more rigorous attention.

The second issue raised by the DuPont action is more disturbing. While there is no indication that the women involved at DuPont objected to being reassigned to other jobs, the question of individual rights to seek employment and/or choose to remain in a potentially dangerous work environment is a real one. It is also an immediate one in certain industries.

The immediacy of the clash between employee safety in general and individual freedom in particular is clearly evident in organizations whose employees are exposed to radiation in the work place. The issue was raised by several participants in a recent hearing on revisions of the Environmental Protection Agency's guidelines for protecting such workers. A particularly sticky aspect also is addressed squarely in the guidelines themselves (Bukro, 1982).

"It is difficult to provide for protection of the unborn without affecting the rights of women to equal job opportunities" (p. 2A).

Where does an organization's responsibility to protect employees begin, and where does it end?

REFERENCES

AMERICAN ASSOCIATION FOR THE ADVANCE-MENT OF SCIENCE. Shifting work by the bio-clock. *Science 82*, 1982, (October), p. 12.

AMERICAN SOCIETY OF HEATING, REFRIGE-RATION, AND AIR CONDITIONING ENGI-NEERS. *1977 Fundamentals Handbook.* New York: Author, 1977.

BUKRO, C. Hiring women questioned in nuclear field. *The Atlanta Journal/Constitution*, 1982, (May 21), p. 2A.

BROADBENT, D. E. Some effects of noise on visual performance. *Quarterly Journal of Experimental Psychology*, 1954, *6*(1), 1–5.

BUSINESS WEEK. How to earn "well pay." 1978, (June 12), pp. 148–149.

COX, T. *Stress.* Baltimore: University Park Press, 1978.

DAVIDS, A., & MAHONEY, J. T. Personality dynamics and accident proneness in an industrial setting. *Journal of Applied Psychology*, 1957, *41*, 303–306.

DAVIS, T. R. V. The influence of the physical design in offices. *Academy of Management Review*, 1984, *9*(2), 271–283.

DUNHAM, R. B. Shift work: A review and theoretical analysis. *Academy of Management Review*, 1977, *2*, 624–634.

EVANS, G. W., FELLOWS, J., ZORN, M., & DOTY, K. Cognitive mapping and architecture. *Journal of Applied Psychology*, 1980, *65*(4), 474–478.

FELL, S. C. A motor vehicle accident causal system: The human element. *Human Factors*, 1976, *18*(1), 85–94.

FINE, B. J., & KOBRICK, J. L. Effects of altitude and heat on complex cognitive tasks. *Human Factors*, 1978, *20*(1), 115–122.

FLYNN, J. E. A study of subjective responses to low energy and nonuniform lighting systems. *Lighting and Design Application*, 1977, *7*(2), 6–15.

FOX, J. G. Background music and industrial productivity: A review. *Applied Ergonomics*, 1971, *2*, 70–73.

FOX, W. F. Human performance in the cold. *Human Factors*, 1967, *9*, 203–220.

GILBERT, M., & HOPKINSON, R. G. The illumination of the Snellen chart. *British Journal of Ophthalmology*, 1949, *33*, 305–310.

HAYNES, R. S., PINE, R. C., & FITCH, H. G. Reducing accident rates with organizational behavior modification. *Academy of Management Journal*, 1982, *25*(2), 407–416.

ILLUMINATING ENGINEERING SOCIETY. *Lighting Handbook* (5th ed.). New York: Author, 1972.

JAMAL, M., & JAMAL, S. M. Work and nonwork experiences on fixed and rotating shifts: An empirical assessment. *Journal of Vocational Behavior*, 1982, *20*(3), 282–293.

KEY, K. F., & PAYNE, M. C., JR. Effects of noise frequency on performance and annoyance for women and men. *Perceptual Motor Skills*, 1981, *52*(2), 435–441.

KIM, J. S., & CAMPAGNA, A. F. Effects of flexitime on employee attendance and performance: A field experiment. *Academy of Management Journal*, 1981, *24*(4), 729–741.

KOMAKI, J., HEINZMANN, A. T., & LAWSON, L. Effects of training and feedback: Component analysis of a behavioral safety program. *Journal of Applied Psychology*, 1980, *65*(3), 261–270.

LaBENZ, P., COHEN, A., & PEARSON, B. A noise and hearing survey of earth-moving equipment operators. *American Industrial Hygiene Association Journal*, 1967, *28*, 117–128.

LOCKHART, J. M. Effects of body and hand cooling on complex manual performance. *Journal of Applied Psychology*, 1966, *50*(1), 57–59.

MAIER, N. R. F., & VERSER, G. C. *Psychology in Industrial Organizations.* Boston: Houghton Mifflin, 1982.

McCORMICK, E. J. *Human Factors Engineering* (2nd ed.). New York: McGraw-Hill, 1964.

McCORMICK, E. J., & ILGEN, D. *Industrial Psychology* (7th ed.). Englewood Cliffs, NJ: Prentice-Hall, 1980.

MINTZ, A., & BLUM, M. L. A re-examination of the accident proneness concept. *Journal of Applied Psychology*, 1949, *33*, 195-211.

MORROW, P. C., & McELROY, J. C. Interior office

design and visitor response: A constructive replication. *Journal of Applied Psychology*, 1981, *66*(5), 646–650.

NARAYANAN, V. K., & NATH, R. A field test of some attitudinal and behavioral consequences of flexitime. *Journal of Applied Psychology*, 1982, *67*(2), 214–218.

OBORNE, D. J. *Ergonomics at Work*. Chichester, England: John Wiley & Sons, 1982.

OCCUPATIONAL HEALTH AND SAFETY ACT. *General Industry Standards* (rev. ed.). Washington, DC: U.S. Department of Labor, 1976.

OLDHAM, G. R., & BRASS, D. J. Employee reactions to an open-plan office: A naturally occurring quasi-experiment. *Administrative Science Quarterly*, 1979, *24*(2), 267–284.

ORPEN, C. Effects of flexible working hours on employee satisfaction and performance. *Journal of Applied Psychology*, 1981, *66*(1), 113–115.

RONEN, S., & PRIMPS, S. B. The compressed work week as organizational change: Behavioral and attitudinal outcomes. *Academy of Management Review*, 1981, *6*(1), 61–74.

ROSENMAN, R. H., HAHN, W., WERTHESSEU, N., JENKINS, C., MESSINGER, H., KOSITCHEK, R., WURM, M., FRIEDMAN, M., & STRAUS, R. Coronary heart disease in the western collaborative group study. *Journal of the American Medical Association*, 1966, *195*, 86–92.

SCHULER, R. S. *Personnel and Human Resource Management*. (2nd ed.). St. Paul, West, 1984.

SHARIT, J., & SALVENDY, G. Occupational stress: Review and reappraisal. *Human Factors*, 1982, *24*(2), 129–162.

SMITH, M. J., COLLIGAN, M. J., & TASTO, D. L. Health and safety consequences of shift work in the food processing industry. *Ergonomics*, 1982, *25*(2), 133–144.

SUNDSTROM, E., BURT, R. E., & KAMP, D. Privacy at work: Architectural correlates of job satisfaction and job performance. *Academy of Management Journal*, 1980, *23*(1), 101–117.

SZILAGYI, A. D., & HOLLAND, W. E. Changes in social density: Relationships with functional interaction and perceptions of job characteristics, role stress, and job satisfaction. *Journal of Applied Psychology*, 1980, *65*(1), 28–33.

TEPLITZKY, A. M., DUBOIS, T. J., HICKMAN, C. E., PALADINO, R. C., & TRYKOSKI, M. A. Electrical power plant environmental noise guide. *Noise Control Engineering*, 1981, *16*(3), 138–144.

TRAFFORD, A. Is your job dangerous to your health? *U.S. News and World Report*, 1979, (February 5), pp. 39–42.

VOGT, J. J., CANDAS, V., & LIBERT, J. P. Graphic determination of heat tolerance limits. *Ergonomics*, 1982, *25*(4) 285–294.

WEDDENBURN, A. A. I. *Studies of Shiftwork in the Steel Industry*. Edinburgh: Heriot-Watt University, 1975.

WING, J. F. Upper tolerance limits for unimpaired mental performance. *Aerospace Medicine*, 1965, *36*, 960–964.

ZEDECK, S., JACKSON, S. E., & SUMMERS, E. Shiftwork schedules and their relationship to health, adaption, satisfaction, and turnover intention. *Academy of Management Journal*, 1983, *26*(2), 297–310.

CHAPTER 9

Job Analysis and Job Evaluation

I/O PSYCHOLOGY AT WORK

Should Courts Write Your Job Descriptions?

A press release of the United States Labor Department's Employment Standards Division recently advised that nearly $21 million was found due 25,066 workers during the first nine months of fiscal year 1975 because of violations of the federal equal pay law. That was up from $14 million and 22,321 employees affected during the first nine months of fiscal year 1974.

The Equal Pay Act of 1963 has wider application among employers than any other piece of fair employment legislation because it has no statutory minimum on firm size based on number of employees in the firm. . . .

From the middle of 1974 to the middle of 1975 a continuing and increasing number of cases under the Equal Pay Act have arisen in U.S. district courts which involve banks, hospitals, school systems, universities, and retailers. . . . Courts have gotten into the business of writing job or position descriptions, as well as detailed examinations of job content and, in actuality, accomplished job evaluations. . . .

The courts have become involved in job evaluations because the Equal Pay Act describes equal jobs in the four component factors of modern job evaluation systems: skill, effort, responsibility, and working conditions. . . .

It should not be assumed that employers involved in the cases outlined [in the remainder of the article] did not have position descriptions or job evaluations. In most cases, they did. But, courts will rewrite descriptions and re-evaluate jobs when necessary. They will also write job descriptions if employers will not.

Excerpted from George R. Wendt, ''Should Courts Write Your Job Descriptions?'' *Personnel Journal*, 1976, *55*(9), pp. 442–450. Reprinted with permission of *Personnel Journal*, Costa Mesa, California. All rights reserved.

At the time the article from which the excerpt comes was written, the courts had begun to take a significant interest in job analysis—a formal process by which the duties, working conditions, and human requirements for a job are determined. Job analysis is the basis for job evaluation—the process by which the worth of a job is determined from its given requirements.

The central thesis of Wendt's (1976) article is that the courts have been finding existing job descriptions, which should have been written on the basis of job analysis, inadequate for job evaluations. And job evaluations are critical to determining the validity of "equal pay for equal work" claims under the Equal Pay Act of 1963.

Industrial/organizational psychologists understood the importance of job analysis long before the courts began to emphasize it, but certainly that emphasis has made it easier for them to convince organizations to undertake job analysis programs. In Chapter 9, the process of job analysis is examined together with research and recent developments in this area. Job evaluation also is reviewed.

INTRODUCTION TO JOB ANALYSIS

Organizations are social systems brought into being and designed to accomplish things that individuals acting alone can not accomplish. These things fit into two broad categories—the manufacture of a product, such as automobiles, or the delivery of a service, such as insurance. Many organizations market both products and services.

> **Job analysis** is a procedure by which information about job tasks and requirements is obtained through formal methods of data collection and analysis.

Products and/or services are the *output* of an organization. They are the end result of the thousands of *tasks* that are performed by members of the organization. Some of these tasks relate directly to the production of the product or the delivery of the service. Others relate to the management of the organization. Still other tasks, such as those performed in the personnel department or company health clinic, are support tasks for those who produce the organization's product or service and/or for those who manage the organization.

The tasks that are performed by any individual define his or her *position* in the organization; there is one position for each member of the organization. All of the identical or similar positions in an organization make up one *job* in that organization. Groups of jobs that are similar in terms of the demands they make on employees are called *job families*.

One example of the relationship between tasks, positions, jobs, and job families is shown in Exhibit 9–1. The top row of boxes in this exhibit indicates the various *tasks* that must be performed in the office of a group of physicians. Each employee occupies one *position* that is defined by primary responsibility for certain of these tasks. The positions defined by the same tasks make up one *job*. In the example, the three jobs (with seven positions) have duties similar enough to be considered as one *job family,* here called "front office, clerical."

Positions, jobs, and job families are the basic building blocks of an organization's structure. The tasks performed by the people who occupy these building blocks are the organization's fundamental activity.

Because job analysis is an activity that requires examining the work people do, it can be confused with other organizational activities that also focus on this work. Keep in mind that job analysis is a process for describing *what is done* on a job, not the best way to do it; how well it is currently being done; or what it is worth to have the job done.

EXHIBIT 9–1

Tasks, Positions, Jobs
and Job Families

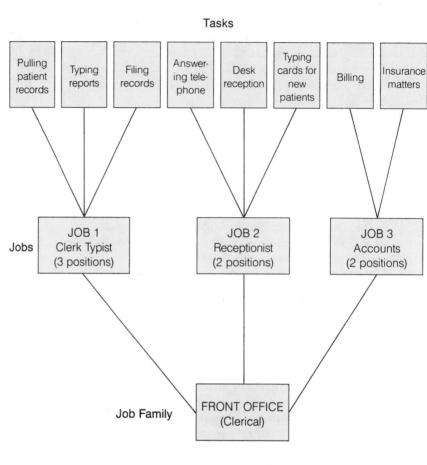

Job Analysis as a Source of Information

The end product of a job analysis is a *job description*, which is a factual statement of the tasks, responsibilities, and working conditions of a particular job. There also may be a *job specification*, which is a statement of the human characteristics needed in order for the job to be done. Although the specific information yielded by job analysis depends upon the method employed, job descriptions and job specifications may provide any or all of the details shown in Exhibit 9–2.

The information listed in Exhibit 9–2 can be used to help organizations carry out an impressive variety of individual-, organizational-, and research-oriented activities. Among these uses are:

I. Information about the job itself
   A. Work tasks
   B. Work procedures
   C. Machines, tools, equipment, materials used
   D. Responsibilities involved

II. Information about the outcome of worker activities
   A. Products made or services performed
   B. Work standards (time limits, quality, and so on)

III. Information about working conditions
   A. Place of job in organization structure
   B. Work schedule
   C. Physical working conditions
   D. Incentives (financial and other)

IV. Information about human requirements for job
   A. Physical requirements
   B. Work experience
   C. Education/training
   D. Personal characteristics, such as interests

EXHIBIT 9-2

Information Potential
of Job Analysis

- career counseling
- collective bargaining
- employee development
- fair employment practices
- human resources planning
- job classification
- job design/redesign
- performance appraisal
- personnel recruiting, selection, placement, and training
- safety training
- test validation
- wage and salary administration

The role job analysis plays in a number of the activities listed has been mentioned earlier. It is basic to the task analysis needed by organizations to set up employee training, for example. The decision to forego formal job analysis is a decision to get this information in some less systematic way.

The days in which organizations can continue to get the information provided by job analysis in informal ways appear to be numbered. More and more court decisions about fair employment practices are resting on this activity. In *Wade v. Mississippi Cooperative Extension Service* (1976), for example, the performance evaluations used by the Extension Service were ruled invalid because the appraisal instruments were not based on job analysis.

Job Analysis and Equal Employment Opportunity

The key phrase with respect to all fair employment practice guidelines is "job relatedness." To be legal, hiring and firing, performance appraisal, promotion practices, and eligibility requirements for special training and development opportunities all must be based on criteria relevant to job performance. For example, it would not be legal for an organization to refuse an employee promotion because he or she is thought by others to be unfriendly, unless it could be demonstrated that friendliness was essential to satisfactory performance on the new job.

To prove that the criteria by which personnel decisions are made are job related, it is necessary to know in some detail the specifics of the jobs involved. This is the purpose of job analysis. *Guidelines on Employment Testing Procedures* (EEOC, 1978) states explicitly that an organization is responsible for the performance of such analysis.

Title VII: See page 30.

The *Guidelines* are not laws; they are intended to assist organizations in complying with the laws and the court interpretations of the laws under Title VII of the 1964 Civil Rights Act. In the case of job analysis, the wisdom of following these guidelines is becoming increasingly clear. Time and money spent on this activity today may be time and money—and court appearances—saved tomorrow.

PREPARING FOR JOB ANALYSIS

Before job analysis is undertaken, there are three important decisions to be made.

1. Who is to do it?
2. What job or jobs are to be analyzed?
3. What method is to be used?

Who Performs a Job Analysis?

Job analyses most often are done by internal personnel staff trained in the process. They may be assisted by job incumbents, supervisors, managers, or technical experts. If no trained specialist is available, an outside consultant may do the analyses and/or train someone in the company to perform them in the future.

Job analysis is not for amateurs. It requires interpersonal skills as well as technical skills. Most methods of job analysis require that the analyst meet with one or more job incumbents at some point. This situation can be threatening to employees because many people still confuse job analysis with time and motion study. Time and motion study, in turn, often is associated with a desire on the part of management to get more work for the same money.

Time analysis and motion study: See pages 179 to 180.

The threat perceived by workers when someone comes to discuss what they do on the job can lead to deliberate distortion of information.

Even if workers do not feel threatened, some job incumbents may provide inaccurate information because they do not understand what is expected of them. In either case, knowing *how* to go about getting information, as well as *what* information to get, is vital in job analysis. Some tips for effective job analysis interviewing are presented later in Chapter 9.

What Jobs Are to be Analyzed?

Traditionally, job analysis has focused almost exclusively on employees who earn an hourly wage. This is changing, and may be expected to continue to change as the benefits of complying with external pressures for job analysis become clearer. Schuler (1984) lists the major position categories for which job analysis may be performed:

- nonsupervisory, nonoffice (e.g., machinist)
- nonsupervisory, office (e.g., clerk-typist)
- supervisory, technical and office (e.g., first-line supervisor)
- managerial, executive, and professional (e.g., salesmanager)

As one moves down the preceding list, job analysis gets more difficult because the work performed becomes increasingly nonroutine. For example, much managerial work is *responsive;* that is, it requires that a manager respond to deviations from normal procedure, such as problems or crises arising during a work day. A specific list of such possible situations is probably impossible to make. It would certainly be a long one if it were possible. In fact, what is probably the most thorough report of a managerial job analysis available is an entire book (Mintzberg, 1980).

Managerial and executive jobs are among the most difficult for job analysts to break down into component parts.

While a comprehensive, ongoing job analysis program of all jobs in an organization is desirable from many standpoints, this does not happen very often. Such a program requires a large commitment from an organization. Top management must support the employment of one or more full-time job analysts. Management also must back them in securing the cooperation of workers, managers, and line supervisors in (a) providing the necessary job analysis information and (b) tolerating a certain amount of work disruption during the process.

In practice, job analysis is more likely to be a response to some immediate need than an integrated part of the personnel program. Examples of such needs include:

- validating a selection test
- redesigning jobs to accommodate technology changes
- making changes in the compensation program

What Method Is to be Used?

There are many recognized techniques for performing job analysis. All can be categorized into one of three groups depending upon the primary source of information: (a) techniques based on obtaining information from one or more job incumbents, (b) from supervisors or outside experts, or (c) from records made by others.

Getting Information from the Job Incumbent

Job analysis methods that rely on information obtained from a job incumbent include:

- interview methods
- observational methods
- structured questionnaires and checklists
- worker logs and diaries

Hawthorne Effect: See page 5.

Of the methods listed, observation is probably the best way for those concerned to discover what actually is done on a job (Markowitz, 1981). It takes a considerable amount of time, however, and information can be biased as a result of the Hawthorne Effect; that is, the fact of being observed may affect the employee so that the observer does not see typical performance.

Interview methods of job analysis are the most frequently used of all procedures for collecting information about jobs. Two such methods are discussed later in Chapter 9. Worker logs and/or diaries have been used for job analysis, but this method is the least common of all procedures.

Getting Information from Supervisors or Outside Experts

Job analysis methods that rely upon getting information from someone other than the job incumbent include:

- interviews
- questionnaires/checklists
- critical incident technique (CIT)

In most instances, there is little difference between the way job analysts interview supervisors and outside experts and the way they interview job incumbents. Questionnaires and checklists also are used in a similar fashion. The critical incident technique (Flanagan, 1954) approach to job analysis requires supervisors or managers to record incidents of worker behavior that demonstrate especially good or especially poor performance for the job in question.

Getting Information from Records Made By Others

No one recommends that a job anlaysis be performed without talking to or observing someone who knows the job, but records can be valuable aids to the process. Among these sources of information are:

- company records (such as those relating to the initial design of the job);
- filmed records of the job being performed;
- blueprints of work layout, equipment, and so on;
- existing job descriptions or job specifications (from another source or organization).

A standard source of existing job analysis information available to anyone is the U.S. Department of Labor Employment and Training Administration's *Dictionary of Occupational Titles* (D.O.T.). The D.O.T. classifies some 40,000 jobs by means of a nine-digit numerical code. This was developed from the Functional Job Analysis (FJA) technique to be described below. The D.O.T. also offers narrative descriptions of many jobs, as for the sample entry shown in Exhibit 9–3.

The D.O.T. is a useful place to begin for analysts who are on unfamiliar ground. It also can help analysts in developing an overall picture of the job structure of an organization. For most purposes, however, information provided by the D.O.T. will not be an acceptable substitute for an in-house job analysis because organizations differ so widely.

Choosing a Method of Job Analysis

The many available methods for job analysis are not strictly comparable even though they are for the same purpose. They differ in several ways, including (a) type of information yielded, (b) time and expense involved, and (c) level of skill required of the job analyst. For practical purposes, the method chosen will depend to a considerable extent upon the resources available and the purpose for which the job analysis information is obtained. Two examples help to clarify this point.

First, suppose that the purpose of the proposed job analysis is to provide information to help develop *selection* procedures. For this purpose, it is necessary to know exactly what employees must be able to do, or to learn to do, in order for them to perform the job as well as those employees who currently are performing it satisfactorily. One of the

EXHIBIT 9–3

A Sample Entry
from the D.O.T.

JOB ANALYST: 166-267-018*

Collects, analyzes, and prepares occupational information to facilitate personnel, administration, and management functions of organization. Consults with management to determine type, scope, and purpose of study. Studies current organizational occupational data and compiles distribution reports, organization and flow charts, and other background information required for study. Observes jobs and interviews workers and supervisory personnel to determine job and worker requirements. Analyzes occupational data, such as physical, mental, and training requirements of jobs and workers and develops written summaries, such as job descriptions, job specifications, and lines of career movement. Utilizes developed occupational data to evaluate or improve methods and techniques for recruiting, selecting, promoting, evaluating, and training workers, and administration of related personnel programs. May specialize in classifying positions according to regulated guidelines to meet job classification requirements of civil service system and be known as POSITION CLASSIFIER (gov. ser.).

---

*166-267-018

166	1 indicates a Professional, Technical, or Managerial occupation
	16 indicates that the occupation is in Administration
	166 indicates that the occupation is in Personnel Administration
267	2 indicates that *data* are *analyzed*
	6 indicates that involvement with *people* is on a *speaking-signalling* level
	7 indicates that work with *things* is on a *feeding-offbearing* level
018	This code gives the job being described its unique classification number since other jobs may have the same first six digits. It is based on an alphabetical arrangement of the titles of those other jobs.

Note. From Employment and Training Administration, *Dictionary of Occupational Titles* (4th ed.). Washington, DC: U.S. Department of Labor, 1977, pp. 99–100. A complete explanation of codes and scales used in the D.O.T. may be found in the front of the volume.

---

worker sources of information is probably desirable, therefore.

By way of contrast with the above example, suppose that the purpose of the job analysis is to redesign the existing *performance appraisal* instrument for the job in question. In this case, the job analyst probably would prefer to get information from supervisors or managers, because they are the ones who usually carry out performance evaluations. If time permits, the critical incident technique (CIT) mentioned previously may be especially useful.

With the CIT, one or more supervisors or managers observe job incumbents and describe in specific behavioral terms some number of incidents (usually five or six) that demonstrate effective job performance and some that demonstrate poor job performance. An example of a positive critical incident might be as follows:

> *The operator of the machine shut it down immediately when the pressure gauge indicator started moving and probably saved the company the cost of a new machine.*

The CIT not only provides a job analyst with information about job tasks and duties, but it also provides information about the aspects of a job that tend to be noticed by supervisors and managers. Such information can be very useful in the development of performance appraisal instruments discussed in Chapter 13.

COLLECTING JOB ANALYSIS INFORMATION

Once decisions have been made as to what jobs are to be analyzed and what method is to be used, the heart of job analysis has been reached —collecting the information. One interview and one questionnaire method is used to illustrate this phase. In both methods, the source of job information is an individual who actually performs the work.

The most important criterion used in the selection of an employee(s) to provide this information is that his or her position be *representative* of the job being analyzed. For example, if "file clerk" is the title of the job to be studied, the file clerk(s) interviewed should perform typical file clerk duties. A single company librarian would be a poor choice even if that position happens to be classified as "file clerk" for payroll purposes.

An Open-Interview Method of Job Analysis

The most well-known interviewing job analysis technique is probably the *Functional Job Analysis* (FJA) procedure developed by the United States Training and Employment Service (USTES). The basis of the technique is a conversation between a job analyst and a worker about his or her job duties. This interview is combined with observation of job performance. Notes from both the observation and the interview are the basis for a narrative account of the job (see Fine, 1974), such as that in Exhibit 9-3.

The FJA technique is based on the premise that all jobs have three dimensions—interaction with *data, people,* and *things.* For example, among other duties, a movie projectionist in a theater keeps records pertaining to films shown (data), goes over the upcoming schedule with the theater manager (people), and operates projection equipment (things). This classification is the basis for the second three digits in the code number following each entry in the *D.O.T.* The code for "data" is shown in Exhibit 9-4.

In Exhibit 9-3, the code number for *data interaction* is 2. As seen in Exhibit 9-4, this means that a job analyst works with data at the *analysis* level. The FJA provides similar codes for worker interaction with *people* and *things.*

The FJA technique makes a basic distinction between work performed and its purpose or end result. For example, the movie projectionist does not "entertain people" or even "show movies." He or she takes film out of canisters, puts it on the projection equipment, turns knobs, and so on. This distinction is an important one because the results of a job

EXHIBIT 9–4

FJA Data Classification Code

DATA (4th digit)

0	Synthesizing
1	Coordinating
2	Analyzing
3	Compiling
4	Computing
5	Copying
6	Comparing
7 }	No significant
8 }	relationship

DATA

Information, knowledge, and conceptions, related to data, people, or things, obtained by observation, investigation, interpretation, visualization, mental creation; incapable of being touched; written data take the form of numbers, words, symbols; other data are ideas, concepts, oral verbalization.

0 *Synthesizing:* Integrating analyses of data to discover facts and/or develop knowledge concepts or interpretations.

1 *Coordinating:* Determining time, place, and sequence of operations or action to be taken on the basis of analysis of data; executing determinations and/or reporting on events.

2 *Analyzing:* Examining and evaluating data. Presenting alternative actions in relation to the evaluation is frequently involved.

3 *Compiling:* Gathering, collating, or classifying information about data, people, or things. Reporting and/or carrying out a prescribed action in relation to the information is frequently involved.

4 *Computing:* Performing arithmetic operations and reporting on and/or carrying out a prescribed action in relation to them. Does not include counting.

5 *Copying:* Transcribing, entering, or posting data.

6 *Comparing:* Judging the readily observable functional, structural, or compositional characteristics (whether similar to or divergent from obvious standards) of data, people, or things.

Note. Source: Employment and Training Administration. *Dictionary of Occupational Titles* (4th ed.). Washington, DC: U.S. Department of Labor, 1977.

analysis may be used by people who have never seen anyone performing the job in question.

Although the most comprehensive use of FJA has been in developing the D.O.T., anyone can use this system; it has been employed extensively in this country and abroad. Since the basis for this technique, as well as for many other job analysis methods, is a person-to-person interview, some basic *job analysis interview skills* will be considered briefly.

Interviewing skills, for job analysis or any other purpose, come only with practice, but there are some basic guidelines. The following four are summarized from Flippo (1971).

1. Always explain to the interviewee who you are and why you are there. The more the people being interviewed know about what is

going to happen, what is expected of them, and what will be done with the information, the more likely it is that the information they give will be candid.

2. Show a sincere interest in the interviewee and his or her job. Professional job analysts find it helps to remember that the job being discussed is a large and important part of the interviewee's life.

3. Do not try to tell the interviewee how to do the job. The rule here is simple: *The interviewee is the job expert.* The job analyst's expertise lies in studying and reporting on jobs in such a way that others can understand them.

4. Try to talk to interviewees in their own language. This is one of the more difficult interviewing skills because it requires analysts to walk what can be a thin line. Total ignorance of job-related terminology and in-group jargon suggests a lack of interest. On the other hand, an attempt to sound just like someone who actually does the job may fail and come across as insincere. Flippo suggests the following guideline for this problem: Do sufficient preparation to be familiar with as much of the language of a job as any member of the organization would acquire in day-to-day activities.

Once skill has been acquired, interview methods of job analysis have the advantage of a personal, job-specific approach. If a skilled interviewer is not available, however, or time is short, one of the structured methods for collecting job analysis information may be preferred.

A Structured Questionnaire Method of Job Analysis

A structured questionnaire is a detailed guide by which the same information normally sought in an open interview can be acquired. The difference between such an interview and the questionnaire approach may be seen in this example. If a census taker were to ask whomever answers the doorbell, ''Tell me about people in this house,'' he or she would be using an *open-interview* method of questioning. If, on the other hand, the interviewer asks a series of predetermined questions about the people in the house, ''How many are there? How many are female? How many are over the age of 21?'' the method is that of the *structured questionnaire.*

Structured interview: See pages 118 to 119.

Of the ready-made structured job analysis questionnaires that are available to job analysts, the one that is best known and has the most extensive research behind it is the Position Analysis Questionnaire (PAQ) developed at Purdue University (McCormick, Jeanneret, & Mecham, 1972). The current PAQ has 194 questions in six groups.

- information input
- mental processes
- work output
- relationships with other persons
- job context
- other job characteristics

EXHIBIT 9–5

A Structured
Questionnaire
Sample

Job Context

5.2 Physical Hazards (Con't.)

Code	Possibility of Occurrence (P)
N	Almost no possibility
1	Very limited
2	Limited
3	Moderate
4	Fairly high
5	High

144 P First-aid cases (minor injuries or illnesses which typically result in a day or less of "lost" time and are usually remedied with first-aid procedures)

145 P Temporary disability (temporary injuries or illnesses which prevent the worker from performing the job from one full day up to extended periods of time but which do not result in permanent disability or impairment)

146 P Permanent partial impairment (injuries or illnesses resulting in the amputation or permanent loss of use of any body member or part thereof, or permanent impairment of certain body functions)

147 P Permanent total disability/death (injuries or illnesses which totally disable the worker and permanently prevent further gainful employment, for example, loss of life, sight, limbs, hands, or radiation sickness, etc.)

Code	Importance to This Job (I)
N	Does not apply
1	Very minor
2	Low
3	Average
4	High
5	Extreme

5.3 Personal and Social Aspects

This section includes various personal and social aspects of jobs. Indicate by code the *importance* of these aspects as part of the job.

148 I Civic obligations (because of the job the worker assumes, or is expected to assume, certain civic obligations or responsibilities)

149 I Frustrating situations (job situations in which attempts to deal with problems or to achieve job objectives are obstructed or hindered, and may thus contribute to frustration on the part of the worker)

150 I Strained personal contacts (dealing with individuals or groups in "unpleasant" or "strained" situations, for example, certain aspects of police work, certain types of negotiations, handling certain mental patients, collecting past due bills, etc.)

151 I Personal sacrifice (being willing to make certain personal sacrifices while being of service to other people or the objectives of an organization, for example, in law enforcement, in the ministry, in social work, etc.: do not consider physical hazards here)

152 I Interpersonal conflict situations (job situations in which there are virtually inevitable differences in objectives, opinions, or viewpoints between the worker and other persons or groups of persons, and which may "set the stage" for conflict, for example, persons involved in labor negotiations, supervisors who must enforce an unpopular policy, etc.)

A sample page from the PAQ Job Context series of questions is shown in Exhibit 9-5.

Each question on the PAQ is rated on one of six scales, according to appropriateness. Two of these scales—*Possibility of Occurrence* and *Importance to this Job*—appear in Exhibit 9-5. The other four scales are: *Extent of Use, Degree of Detail, Amount of Time,* and *Applicability.*

The end result of rating a job on the 194 PAQ questions is considerable information about the pieces, or *elements,* of the job. Recent research, using a data analysis procedure called factor analysis, suggests that all of this information represents 12 relatively distinct basic job dimensions (e.g., Mecham, 1977).

- having decision-making/communicating/general responsibilities
- operating machines/equipment
- performing clerical/related activities
- performing technical/related activities
- performing service/related activities
- working regular day/versus other work schedules
- performing routine/repetitive activities
- being aware of work environment
- engaging in physical activity
- supervising/coordinating other personnel
- public/customer related contacts
- working in an unpleasant/hazardous/demanding environment

The PAQ manual provides the information required for those using the PAQ to match the questions with their appropriate dimensions. Questionnaire results then can be used to develop an overall profile of a job in terms of these 12 dimensions (rather than in terms of 194 elements). For example, a telephone operator's job might be described as high on dimensions 1, 2, 5, 7, and 11 and low on dimensions 3, 4, 6, 8, 9, 10, and 12 (although this simplifies the process somewhat).

The PAQ has been used successfully in this country and abroad by college students, job incumbents, and supervisors, as well as by professional job analysts. While it requires a relatively high reading level, it is not so dependent upon job analyst interpersonal skills as are open-interview techniques.

Along with other questionnaires for the same purpose, such as the Management Position Description Questionnaire (Tornow & Pinto, 1976), the PAQ offers the advantage of a final result that can be compared across different jobs (or different organizations). It also eliminates possible problems arising when different interviewers analyze different jobs. When the open-interview method is used, these analysts may ask different questions, focus on different job aspects, and produce final results that are difficult to compare with one another. Such comparisons are not always necessary, but in the case of activities such as job evaluation they are essential.

WRITING A JOB DESCRIPTION

A **job description** is an organized statement about the tasks performed and the responsibilities associated with a particular job.

Whatever method is chosen for obtaining information about what is done on a job, the purpose of collecting this information is to write a job description.

In scope, a job description can range from the D.O.T.'s nine-digit summary to Mintzberg's book *The Nature of Managerial Work* (1980). The more typical job description is a narrative of one to three pages in length, but not just any written information about a job is a job description. There are certain requirements as to both content and style.

The Content of a Job Description

There are two sections to a complete job description, (a) the identifying information and (b) the job summary. A third section, consisting of comments required to clarify any of the information in the first two sections, is optional:

Job description *identifying information* consists of (at least) the following items:

- name of company
- job or payroll title
- department and/or division where job is located
- name of job analyst and date of report

The sources of information, including the names of anyone interviewed, are optional.

The *job summary* includes:

- duties performed
- supervision given or received
- relation of job to others
- machines, tools, methods used
- working conditions

The Style of a Job Description

The purpose of a job description is to convey information. It is not intended to entertain, nor is it an appropriate vehicle for demonstrating an elegant writing style. A good job description is complete, direct, and succinct. There are several generally-accepted style guidelines.

- Start each sentence in the job summary with an action verb; "opens mail," not "the mail is opened."
- Use the present tense; "open," not "opened."
- Use "may" only if some people holding the job never perform the duty.

- Use "occasionally" only if every person holding this job performs the duty at one time or another.

Guidelines for writing job descriptions are not the brainstorm of some crank grammarian. They serve both to make communication clearer and to make it easier for people to compare job descriptions from different jobs (or different analysts).

One example of a job description written in the appropriate style can be seen in Exhibit 9–3. Another is shown in Exhibit 9–6.

Classification
Technical Assistant (Automotive)

EXHIBIT 9–6

A Sample Job
Description

Department
Operations

Under the general supervision of the Superintendent, Automotive Maintenance, conducts special technical studies, inspections, and investigations relative to the maintenance and operation of automotive and related equipment. Work is performed with independence guided by general policies and instructions of the superintendent. Work is subject to review through conferences and reports.

Regular Duties

Is assigned by the Superintendent, Automotive Maintenance, to conduct technical studies, inspections, investigations, or economic studies of various phases of the Automotive Program.

Compiles data and prepares analyses on economic aspects of purchasing, operating, and maintaining automotive and related equipment.

Conducts technical studies on new equipment, replacement of existing equipment, improvement, and vehicle and equipment specifications.

Analyzes maintenance and servicing methods, materials and equipment used, and schedules.

Makes recommendations as a result of studies to improve economic and technical aspects of the automotive program.

Prepares operating and technical manuals and instructions on automotive equipment including material for training programs.

Training
Graduation from a four-year college or university, with major work in automotive or mechanical engineering.

Experience
5 years' responsible and supervisory automotive or related maintenance experience.

WRITING A JOB SPECIFICATION

A **job specification** lists the human traits, knowledge, skills, and abilities required to do the job.

Examples of the qualities covered in a job specification (sometimes called *person* or *human specification*) include:

- education
- experience
- training
- eyesight
- strength
- intelligence
- manual dexterity
- personality traits

Training and experience specifications for the automotive technical assistant job described in Exhibit 9–6 are listed at the bottom of the description.

Compared with developing a job specification, writing a job description is a simple matter. One difficulty with job specifications is that there can be quite a range in the extent to which employees exhibit a particular quality and still perform the job satisfactorily. Complicating the matter is the fact that this range may be impossible to specify because organizational policy has limited the actual range in some way.

As an example of the problem described, consider Company R where all of the receptionists have high school diplomas. Does this mean that a high school education is required to perform the duties of a receptionist in this company? Probably it is not. If all of the employed receptionists have at least a high school education, however, lower educational limits for performing this job only can be estimated.

The Judgmental Versus the Statistical Approach to Writing Job Specifications

Inference: See page 58.

It probably is not possible to avoid altogether the kind of difficulty described when a job specification is developed on a *judgmental* basis, that is, when the characteristics required by the job are inferred from the job description. This is the approach used by the USTES in the D.O.T. and it may work well in practice. For example, as long as there are many applicants for the receptionist job who have high school diplomas, there is no immediate need to know if the educational requirements of the job can be lowered.

The alternative to a judgmental approach to job specifications is a *statistical* approach. Test scores on characteristics believed to be required for job success, biographical data, and interview ratings of current and/ or new employees are correlated with job performance criteria. Over time, test score ranges and characteristics of people (as determined by biographical data and interview ratings) associated with job success can be specified with some accuracy.

Correlation: See pages 61 to 63.

The statistical analysis upon which a job specification is based is the same analysis researchers use to validate selection tests. The role of the

Job specifications provide guidelines as to the skills, abilities, experience, and personal characteristics a person needs to do a particular job.

job description is to provide guidelines for the selection criteria to validate. The major drawback to this approach is that it can be a long, expensive process. Unless there are sufficient numbers of job positions to allow for a concurrent validity approach, the process can take years. Weighted against this disadvantage, however, are four long-term benefits.

Selection validation: See pages 86 to 88.

Concurrent validity: See page 88.

1. Possible sources of employees are less likely to be overlooked if the requirements for a job are known in detail.
2. Traditional selection criteria that turn out to be unimportant to job success can be eliminated, possibly conserving organizational resources.
3. The more effective screening and selection that eventually come from this process should lead to better job performance on the part of the labor force as a whole.
4. In the United States, this validation process is central to documentation of fair employment practices. To return to an earlier example, if challenged by an applicant turned down for not having a high school diploma, Company R must be able to prove that this requirement is relevant to acceptable job performance.

Job Specification Criteria

A job specification lists the qualities required for a person to perform a given job satisfactorily. The most important aspect of this specification is that it be as *specific* as possible. If experience is required, for example, the type and number of years should be stated as is done in Exhibit 9–6. If tests are involved, the upper and lower score limits should be specified. To the extent possible, job specifications also should be *behavioral*.

A behavioral emphasis for job specifications is easy to overlook if the judgmental approach to writing specifications is taken. This approach frequently produces statements such as: "must be dependable" and "must be able to communicate with others." Schneier (1976) suggests substituting appropriate behavioral statements for such vague specifications: "did not miss more than one day of work per month on last job" for dependability and "answers interview questions clearly," for communication ability, to take these two examples.

The superiority of the behavioral approach to a job specification is considerable when the specification is to be used for such purposes as employee screening, internal recruiting for promotion, and employee development. Many of the people involved in such activities know little or nothing about the specific jobs; the less left to interpretation or imagination, the better.

SOURCES OF ERROR IN JOB ANALYSIS

The number of uses to which job analysis information may be put suggests that it is important for this process to be carried out as carefully as possible. The specific kind of error to which job analysis is subject depends somewhat on the method used, but all such error stems from three sources—the data base, the interpretation of the information collected, and the environment in which the job analysis is carried out.

The Job Analysis Data Base

In the current discussion, the term *data base* refers to the number and representativeness of the positions examined in the performance of a job analysis. Any other information, such as technical specifications, is also part of this base. As a general rule, the smaller the data base, the more likely there is to be error in the final job description.

A major reason that a small data base can lead to error is that the information collected may be biased or incomplete. For example, if only one job incumbent is interviewed, he or she (a) may not perform the full range of duties actually encompassed by the job being analyzed and/or (b) may be unwilling or unable to report accurately on job duties (McGehee & Thayer, 1961). The best protection against such risks is multiple sources of information.

Interpretation of Job Information

Incomplete or distorted information, whether deliberate or not, is not the exclusive province of job incumbents or other interviewees involved in the process. A classic sample of a distorted *report* of information is shown in Exhibit 9–7. A more accurate description of the job in question may be found in the summary at the end of Chapter 9.

It is unlikely that much of the error in job descriptions comes from deliberate attempts to mislead as illustrated by Exhibit 9–7. Job analysts do make mistakes, however, or fail to notice things in the process of transforming job analysis information into job descriptions and job specifications.

In addition to making mistakes, there is some evidence that the biases and values of job analysts may creep unnoticed into their work. One study, for example, found a tendency for female job analysts using the PAQ to rate jobs somewhat lower than male analysts describing the same jobs with the same instrument (Arvey, Passino, & Lounsbury, 1977).

An Example of How Job Descriptions Can Mislead

Proposed Job Description

1 Job identification
   a Title: Director of Industrial and Agrarian Priorities
   b Dept.: Maintenance

2 Job duties
   a Directs, controls, and regulates the movement of interstate commerce, representing a cross section of the wealth of the American economy. Exercises a broad latitude for independent judgment and discretion without direct or intermediate supervision.
   b Integrates the variable factors in an evolving situation utilizing personal judgment, founded on past experience, conditioned by erudition, and disciplined by mental intransigence. Formulates a binding decision relative to the priority of flow of interstate and intrastate commerce, both animate and inanimate, such decisions being irreversible and not subject to appellate review by higher authority or being reversed by the legal determination of any echelon of our judicial complex. Influences the movement, with great finality, of agricultural products, forest products, minerals, manufactured goods, machine tools, construction equipment, military personnel, defense materials, raw materials, end products, finished goods, semifinished products, small business, large business, public utilities, and governmental agencies.
   c Deals with all types of personalities and all levels of education, from college president and industrial tycoon to truckdriver, requiring the exercise of initiative, ingenuity, imagination, intelligence, industry, and discerning versatility. Implements coordinated motivation on the part of the public, which is consistent with the decision of the incumbent, failure of which could create a complex objurgation of personnel and equipment generating a catastrophic loss of mental equilibrium by innumerable personnel of American industry, who are responsible for the formulation of day-to-day policy, and guidance implementation of the conveyances of transportation, both interstate and intrastate.
   d Appraises the nuances of an unfolding situational development and directs correction thereof commensurate with its seriousness and momentousness.

EXHIBIT 9–7

Can You Name
This Job?

The Environment of Job Analysis

Physical environment of behavior: See pages 33 to 34.

Social environment of behavior: See page 35.

The physical and social environments in which the process takes place are the sources of a number of possible errors in job analysis. Among these sources are:

- *time pressures* that restrict the data base or rush the analyst through information collecting and/or interpretation;
- *lack of interest and commitment* (or even obstruction of job analysis efforts) on the parts of managers and/or supervisors;
- *distracting physical environmental conditions,* such as extreme heat, cold, or noise;
- *rapidly-changing job technology* that can put a job description out of date in a very short time.

A general strategy for dealing with all of the potential sources of error in job analysis is (a) use multiple sources of information about the job, (b) use more than one analyst if possible, and (c) check and recheck information and results. This is a tall order and many organizations will lack the resources or the commitment to follow it. Industrial/organizational psychologists can help by continuing to research the development of methods less suspectible to errors stemming from the conditions under which they are used.

JOB ANALYSIS RESEARCH

Reliability/Validity: See page 67.

With the recent upsurge of interest in job analysis has come a more searching examination of the processes by which it is carried out. Some of this research is directed toward questions about the reliability and and validity of existing methods. Some is comparative in nature, such as the study summarized in ''Spotlight on Research.''

SPOTLIGHT ON RESEARCH

Evaluation of Job Analysis Methods by Experienced Job Analysts

Research question: How do experienced job analysts rate the effectiveness and practicality of available job analysis methods?

Type of Study: Survey research.

Survey research: See pages 57 to 58.

Subjects: Ninety-three experienced job analysts from industry, government, private consulting firms, colleges/universities, and the military. Median job analysis experience was 6.3 years.

Variables:
- Type of job analysis method (7)
- Effectiveness rating. Operational definition: Rating on a five-point scale as to effectiveness for each of eleven organizational purposes.
- Practicality rating. Operational definition: Rating on a five-point scale as to standardization, convenience, reliability, and time.

Operational definition: See page 48.

General Procedure: A questionnaire was mailed to subjects. In addition to the research questions, information about the respondents was collected. The seven job analysis procedures also were described on the questionnaire.

Analysis: Analysis of variance.

ANOVA: See pages 65 to 66.

Results:
- Effectiveness: At least one of the job analysis methods was rated as providing high-quality comprehensive information (being effective) for 8 of the 11 organizational purposes. Functional Job Analysis (FJA) and a task inventory approach received consistently high ratings.
- Practicality: The Position Analysis Questionnaire (PAQ) was ranked first (or tied for first place) on all four practicality scales.

Conclusion: "This study found that job analysis methods are perceived as differentially effective for various human resource purposes, and as differentially practical. . . . When multiple job analysis methods are used, a strategy that is endorsed overwhelmingly by the respondents, the increased costs of the job analysis are more likely to pay off in superior outcomes with the aid of these results" (p. 346).

Summarized from E. L. Levine, R. A. Ash, H. Hall, and F. Sistrunk, "Evaluation of Job Analysis Methods by Experienced Job Analysts." *Academy of Management Journal*, 1983, 26(2), pp. 339–348.

In "Spotlight on Research," Levine, Ash, Hall, and Sistrunk (1983) sought the opinions of experienced job analysts concerning the utility and practicality of seven popular job analysis methods. Of the two job analysis methods used in the study that are discussed in Chapter 9, the FJA fared very well on the effectiveness rating scales, while the PAQ got high marks for being easy to use. This finding is not surprising since the FJA is an observation/open-interview method that gives the analysts considerable leeway in getting whatever information will be useful. The PAQ, by contrast, is a structured questionnaire. It takes less time and requires less skill, but limits the information collected to the specific questions asked.

Toward Better Job Analysis

In addition to studying the characteristics of existing job analysis methods, researchers also are interested in developing new and better methods. For example, one critic of traditional job analysis points out that it does not specify the *conditions* under which job tasks are performed and the *standards* by which employees doing the job will be evaluated (Klinger, 1979).

Result-Oriented Job Descriptions

Klinger suggests an alternative to traditional job description, which he calls the Results-Oriented Description (ROD). Two examples of RODs are shown in Exhibit 9–8. The job duties (called "tasks") sections of these job descriptions are only illustrative and do not include the full range of tasks for the job described.

In Exhibit 9–8, the *tasks* sections correspond to the traditional job description. The two columns to the right, listing the *conditions* under which each task is performed and the *standards* by which the task will be evaluated, are new.

Domain: See page 90.

The major advantage of RODs seems to lie in the explicit link they make between the *task domain* (duties involved) and the *performance domain* (actual work) of the job. For example, it is one thing for a prospective employee to know that he or she must be able to type 40 words per minute, but another for the employee to know that this typing will be done on a particular machine in a particular style to an error-free standard in a given amount of time.

Results-Oriented Descriptions give employees clearer statements of expectations and explicitly set out the standards by which their performance will be evaluated. Their most obvious practical drawback seems to lie in this very specificity. Theoretically, an ROD must be written for every job position, because conditions (for the job of typist, for example) vary considerably from one office or supervisor to the next. In addition, RODs would be difficult or impossible to write in situations where groups of employees work cooperatively to accomplish some task.

Klinger notes the difficulties surrounding ROD and suggests some ways to circumvent them. To date, however, there has not been any empirical evidence either for or against this innovation. Both its effectiveness and its practicality await test.

Job Reward Analysis

A second inadequacy of traditional job analysis that many have noticed relates to the use of the resulting information for selection and placement. It has been recognized for some time that a successful individual/job/organization match is more than a matter of skills, knowledge and abilities. It also involves a fit between the needs of or rewards desired by the individual and those things which the organization and job can offer (Wanous, 1980).

Typist/Receptionist

EXHIBIT 9–8

Examples of Results-Oriented Job Descriptions

Tasks	Conditions	Standards
Type letters	When asked to by supervisor; using an IBM Selectric typewritter; according to the office style manual	All letters error-free; completed by 5 p.m. if assigned before 3 p.m.
Greet visitors	As they arrive, referring them to five executives with whom they have scheduled appointments	No complaints from visitors referred to the wrong office, or waiting before being referred

Skills, knowledge and abilities required:

- Ability to type 40 wpm
- Ability to use Selectric typewriter
- Knowledge of office-style manual
- Courtesy

Minimum qualifications:

- High school degree or equivalent
- Six months' experience as a typist, or an equivalent performance test

Salesperson

Tasks	Conditions	Standards
Sell plumbing fixtures	Over an 11-state area; to hardware retailers	$250,000 annually
Retain current customers	375 existing customers	95% of current customers reorder each year

Skills, knowledge and abilities required:

- Knowledge of plumbing fixtures
- Knowledge of contractors and purchasers
- Ability to sell
- Ability to work independently

Minimum qualifications:

- High school graduation or equivalent
- Two years' experience selling plumbing fixtures
- Proven sales record (equivalent territory and sales volume)

Note. From Donald E. Klinger, "When the Traditional Job Description is Not Enough." *Personnel Journal*, 1979, *58*(4), p. 246. Adapted with the permission of *Personnel Journal*, Costa Mesa, California. All rights reserved.

From a matching perspective, conventional job descriptions and specifications give those involved in selection and placement only half of the information they need. They know what an employee must be able to do for the job, but not what the job can do for the employee.

Matching Model: See page 133.

Job rewards are individually-valued outcomes of doing certain work and/or being in a particular work environment. The reward potential of work often has been examined from a motivational perspective. One example of this approach is discussed in the psychological approach to job design covered in Chapter 7. The relatively simpler systematic *description* of the rewards offered by a job and an organization as an addition to traditional job descriptions is a newer idea.

Psychological approach to job design: See pages 195 to 207.

One approach to identifying job rewards is offered by an instrument called the Minnesota Job Description Questionnaire (MJDQ, Dawis, Lofquist, & Weiss, 1968). This questionnaire asks job supervisors to rank the extent to which 21 potential job rewards are present in the jobs they supervise. These potential rewards include such job aspects as the ability to use skills, the opportunity to be creative on the job, and the security provided by the job.

The approach of the MJDQ to describing the rewards associated with a job is much like the approach of the PAQ to describing the duties required by a job. Results of this structured questionnaire approach can be used both for individual jobs and for making comparisons between jobs.

Perception: See page 36.

The MJDQ has been used in research and in applied job counseling and placement situations. Its primary weakness is that it is based upon the perceptions of those who make the rankings and the perceptions of a new employee may be different. Nevertheless, some variation of this approach that describes the rewards offered by a job seems worth investigating as a standard feature of job descriptions. As a way of rounding out the job picture, it offers another check against serious individual/job/organization mismatches.

JOB EVALUATION

Job evaluation is a formal process for determining the financial worth of a job to an organization.

The role job analysis plays as the source of information for a wide variety of personnel-related activities has been stressed repeatedly throughout Chapter 9. One of the functions with which job analysis is most often associated is job evaluation.

There is a variety of ways in which an individual may be compensated for his or her contribution to an organization. The core of this compensation usually is pay; a variety of bonuses and/or benefits may be added for total compensation. To be fair, this compensation should be based upon an analysis of what is required by the job, that is, upon job analysis. This analysis provides the information for someone to determine the value of a job relative to other jobs.

Compensable Job Factors

Job evaluation methods vary, but most are based on a point system, which involves assigning points to the relevant aspects of a job for which employees should be compensated. Among the more commonly used *compensable factors* are:

- physical demands of a job
- amount of responsibility the job carries
- experience and/or training the job requires
- working conditions under which the job is performed

In job evaluation, each compensable factor is broken down into degrees from lowest to highest, with points assigned accordingly. An example

First Degree: 15 points
Definition: A basic high school education is sufficient.

Second Degree: 30 points
Definition: High school plus one year of specialized training is required.

Third Degree: 45 points
Definition: High school plus extensive technical training is required.

Fourth Degree: 60 points
Definition: The job incumbent must have the equivalent of four years of college training.

EXHIBIT 9–9

Four Degrees of the Job Compensable Factor: "Training/Education Required by Job"

of a training/education compensable factor with four degrees is shown in Exhibit 9–9.

In the example in Exhibit 9–9, different levels, or degrees, of required training for a job are assigned different numbers of points. In the point system for job evaluation, the same procedure is followed for each compensable factor. The result is a yardstick that may be applied to any job. The total number of points from all the compensable factors is the worth of a job relative to other jobs in the organization.

Wage Trend Lines

If the same job evaluation yardstick is applied to all jobs in an organization, the number of points for each job may be compared directly. If these points are plotted graphically against the current compensation for each job, a picture of the organization's compensation program emerges. If compensation is generally consistent with job worth, most of the points in the graph will fall close to a straight line drawn through the graph. An example of such a *wage trend line,* is shown in Exhibit 9–10.

The graph in Exhibit 9–10 shows a compensation program that is well in line with the worth of jobs as determined by job evaluation. Two jobs, A and B, are somewhat underpaid relative to the number of points they have been assigned and job C is somewhat overpaid. In a formal wage adjustment program, such jobs are "red circled" (sometimes called "red lined"). Compensation for underpaid jobs is increased immediately. Cases of overcompensation are adjusted as the current incumbents vacate the positions.

The wage tend line shown in Exhibit 9–10 shows a considerably better fit between job worth and compensation than might be found in some organizations. Many factors, other than the nature of the work and human qualities required to do it, play a role in setting compensation. For example, some people are paid more for the position they hold than for the work they actually do; that is, *status* modifies the job worth/compensation relationship. Other factors affecting compensation and

Moderator variables: See pages 97 to 99.

EXHIBIT 9–10

A Wage Trend Line

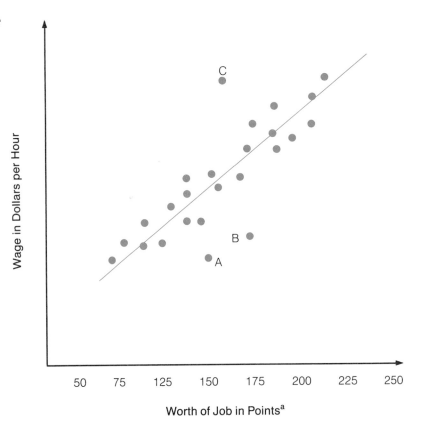

Worth of Job in Points[a]

_____
[a]Each point on graph is one job.

wage trend lines include:

- legal constraints (such as minimum wage laws)
- "going rate" of the job in industry or area
- cost of living in the company's location
- union agreements (that set pay rates for included jobs but not for others)
- what had to be paid to induce the current incumbent or a predecessor to take the job

The factors listed, along with a number of others, combine to produce wage trend lines that can deviate considerably from the relatively straight one in Exhibit 9–10. Such a situation can play a significant role in job dissatisfaction because what others are paid relative to what they do seems to be an important factor in the way people evaluate satisfaction with their own pay. This aspect of compensation is discussed further in Chapter 15.

SUMMARY

Job analysis is a formal process that yields information about job tasks, working conditions, and human characteristics required to do jobs. This information is basic to such personnel functions as selection, training, performance appraisal, and documentation of fair employment practices.

Before a job analysis is undertaken, it is necessary to decide who will perform it, what jobs will be analyzed, and what method will be used. Once it has been performed, job analysis provides the information used by psychologists or qualified persons to write job descriptions (which tell what is done on the job) and job specifications (which list the characteristics needed for the job to be done). A description of the job of regulating traffic flow on sites where highway construction makes one-way traffic temporarily necessary is used as an example of how *not* to write a job description.

Job descriptions and job specifications are the basis for job evaluation, a formal process for determining the worth of a job to an organization. A comprehensive job evaluation program provides the information necessary to adjust compensation to job requirements.

AT ISSUE

"It's Not My Job"

The important role of job analysis in organizational functioning is becoming more and more obvious. The job descriptions and job specifications that result from such analysis provide a logical and clear job-related base for selection, performance appraisal, and job evaluation. When these activities begin with job analysis, they are easier to carry out as well as being in compliance with fair employment practice standards.

In addition to the hard-line practical advantages of job analysis, there are other benefits in the building of related personnel functions on this activity. To put forth effort and do a good job, people need to know what is expected of them. A job description serves that purpose. People also need to know that if they do their jobs as expected, they will be rewarded. Thus, tying formal organizational rewards to performance appraisal based on job descriptions will have certain motivational benefits.

Despite its many advantages, some managers and executives resist formal job analysis for the jobs under their supervision. One reason lies in the specificity of job descriptions. To many, this specificity makes them double-edged swords. An employee who accepts a job described in the specific terms of a formal job description is agreeing to perform those duties in return for certain financial and other considerations. But it is also possible to interpret this job description as the sum total of *all* that is expected of an employee, an approach often characteristic of union agreements.

Unfortunately, the most carefully-developed set of job descriptions will leave some necessary organization tasks "uncovered." In addition, job descriptions make no provisions for creativity on the job. Every experienced supervisor or manager recognizes that employee creativity is valuable, and subordinate willingness to go beyond minimal job duties can be worth its weight in gold.

Because it makes their own jobs tougher, most managers and supervisors dread hearing the words "It's not my job." Some translate this dread into resisting job descriptions of the work for which they are responsible. As one executive put it: "The only job description I want to see in this company is that every employee will do whatever is necessary to get the job done."

From an overall perspective, there is no question that the advantages of job descriptions outweigh the disadvantages. But as more and more organizations do more and more job analysis, the question of what to do when job descriptions become a point of dissension will have to be given more attention.

REFERENCES

ARVEY, R. D., PASSINO, E. M., & LOUNSBURY, J. W. Job analysis results as influenced by sex of incumbent and sex of analyst. *Journal of Applied Psychology,* 1977, *62*(4), 411–416.

DAWIS, R. V., LOFQUIST, L. H., & WEISS, D. J. A theory of work adjustment (A revision). *Minnesota Studies in Vocational Rehabilitation: XXIII.* Minneapolis: University of Minnesota, 1968.

EMPLOYMENT AND TRAINING ADMINISTRATION. *Dictionary of Occupational Titles* (4th ed.). Washington, DC: U.S. Department of Labor, 1977.

EQUAL EMPLOYMENT OPPORTUNITY COMMISSION. *Guidelines on Employment Testing Procedures.* Washington, DC: U.S. Department of Labor, 1978.

FINE, S. A. Functional job analysis: An approach to a technology for manpower planning. *Personnel Journal,* 1974, *53*, 813–818.

FLANAGAN, J. C. The critical incident technique. *Psychological Bulletin,* 1954, *51*(4), 327–358.

FLIPPO, E. B. *Principles of Personnel Management* (3rd ed.). New York: McGraw-Hill, 1971.

KLINGER, D. E. When the traditional job description is not enough. *Personnel Journal,* 1979, *58*(4), 243–248.

LEVINE, E. L., ASH, R. A., HALL, H., & SISTRUNK, F. Evaluation of job analysis methods by experienced job analysts. *Academy of Management Journal,* 1983, *26*(2), 339–348.

MARKOWITZ, J. Four methods of job analysis. *Training and Development Journal,* 1981, *35*(9), 112–118.

MARTING, E. (Ed.). *AMA Book of Employment Forms.* New York: American Management Association, 1967.

McCORMICK, F. J., JEANNERET, P. R., & MECHAM, R. C. A study of job characteristics and job dimensions based on the Position Analysis Questionnaire (PAQ). *Journal of Applied Psychology,* 1972, *56*(4), 347–368.

McGEHEE, W., & THAYER, P. W. *Training in Business and Industry.* New York: John Wiley and Sons, 1961.

MECHAM, R. C. Unpublished manuscript, 1977. (Available from PAQ Services, Inc., P.O. Box 3337, Logan, UT 84321).

MINTZBERG, H. *The Nature of Managerial Work.* Englewood Cliffs, NJ: Prentice-Hall, 1980.

SCHNEIER, C. Content validity: The necessity of a behavioral job description. *The Personnel Administrator,* 1976, *21*(2), 38–44.

SCHULER, R. S. *Personnel and Human Resource Management* (2nd ed.) St. Paul: West, 1984.

TORNOW, W. W., & PINTO, P. R. The development of a managerial job taxonomy: A system for describing, classifying, and evaluating executive positions. *Journal of Applied Psychology,* 1976, *61*(4), 410–418.

WANOUS, J. P. *Organizational Entry: Recruitment, Selection, and Socialization of Newcomers.* Reading, MA: Addison-Wesley, 1980.

WENDT, G. Should courts write your job descriptions? *Personnel Journal,* 1976, *55*(9), 442–445; 450.

PART IV

The Organization

The jobs that most people do are carried out within an organizational context. Most organization employees are surrounded by other people—coworkers, friends, superiors, and subordinates—and the behavior of these others has a considerable impact on their responses to the work situation.

It is this organizational context that is examined in Part IV. Chapter 10 addresses organizations as social systems, their components, their relationships with the outside world, and the communication that maintains these systems. Group membership and leadership behavior are examined in Chapter 11. The focus of Chapter 12 is motivation. Theories of work motivation and impact of an organization's policies, actions, and decisions on the effort of its employees are discussed.

CHAPTER 10

The Organizational Social System and Communication

I/O PSYCHOLOGY AT WORK

"Cultured" Corporate Winners

Japanese management techniques will not reverse America's economic decline. Neither will obsessive number crunching or strategic planning. O.K., so what will? Strong corporate cultures . . . [say] Terrence E. Deal of the Harvard Graduate School of Education and Allan A. Kennedy, a Boston-based consultant [in their book entitled *Corporate Cultures*, Addision-Wesley Publishing Company]. Executives, say Deal and Kennedy, must recognize that "a strong culture has almost always been the driving force behind continuing success in American business."

In defining what constitutes corporate cultures, the authors include not only a company's overall goals but also the subtle yet compelling little signals, like styles of dress or who gets promoted that tell employees how to behave. Industrial powerhouses often sum up their cultural values in slogans like General Electric's "Progress is our most important product," or DuPont's "Better things for better living through chemistry." Those mottoes not only help sell light bulbs, refrigerators and synthetic fibers, but tell the employees what their companies stand for. . . .

As often as not, a firm's in-house culture is reflected in the face that the company presents to the world at large. The "work hard/play hard" cultures of companies like McDonald's, IBM, Xerox, Pittney Bowes, and R. H. Macy carry well beyond the office, showing up in a dedication to sales and customer service. A spirit of entrepreneurial risk-taking helps "bet-your-company" firms like Exxon and Boeing to make huge investments in high-risk ventures that take years to develop.

Skills that create success in one company's culture can cause failure in another. Deal and Kennedy would urge a rising GE executive to think hard, for example, before accepting a bigger job at Xerox. Reason: GE moves slowly and cautiously, while Xerox runs at "a near frenetic pace."

Excerpted from "Cultured" Corporate Winners: How Clear Goals—and Some Office Heroes—Can Bring Success." *Time*, 1982, (July 5), p. 46. Copyright 1982 by Time, Inc. All rights reserved. Reprinted by permission from *Time*.

Corporate culture, a concept encompassing the sum total of the traditions, values, and priorities that characterize a company, is a term appearing more and more often in the analysis of business operations. It provides a shorthand definition for how both employees and outsiders (including competitors) view a company. In addition, analyses from this perspective provide those who study organizations with some interesting insights into such matters as the origin of corporate policies and decisions, the ability of new employees to be successful in an organization, and why certain company mergers are successful and others have been relatively disastrous.

Although I/O psychologists speak more often of an organization's *climate* than its culture, the two are closely related aspects of the same thing—the *social environment* of an organization. It is that environment and the communication maintaining it that is examined in Chapter 10.

THE NATURE OF THE SOCIAL ENVIRONMENT IN ORGANIZATIONS

As discussed in Chapter 2, the social environment of an individual is created by other people and the individual's relationship with them— with other individuals, groups, organizations, and society as a whole. The nature of this environment in organizations is complex; among other factors, it includes:

Social environment: See page 35.

- relationships with coworkers, superiors, and subordinates
- rules and policies of the organization
- norms (unwritten rules) of work groups and the organization
- the leadership of the organization

All of the factors listed influence the behavior of people in organizations. Three that have particular significance for employee performance and satisfaction—membership in groups, leadership, and the organization's reward policies—are examined later in the text. The purpose of Chapter 10 is to provide an overview of an organization's social environment. This view is built on the concept of an organization as an open system.

General Systems Theory

In every field of study, there are events that stand out because they dramatically change the thinking of people in the field. Of the events that have influenced the development of I/O psychology in this way, two in particular stand out. One is the Hawthorne Experiments described briefly in Chapter 1. It is these experiments and the subsequent theorizing and research brought about by their unexpected results that often are credited with focusing psychologists' attention on the social environments of organizations.

Hawthorne experiments: See pages 4 to 5.

A second event that has had far-reaching influence on the study of organizations and the people in them was the publication of a paper by biologist Ludwig von Bertalanffy (1950) on the subject of *general systems theory*. In his paper, von Bertalanffy proposed that the biological concept of a system is a useful framework for studying the phenomena of all sciences.

As far as the study of organizations was concerned, von Bertalanffy's idea was not a new one. What came out of his statement that was new was a general shift of an entire field toward this view. Today, both the theory and the application of I/O psychology, organizational behavior, and organization theory are grounded firmly upon a conceptualization of organizations as systems. More specifically, the conceptualization is that of *open systems*, that is, systems that interact with their external environments.

Organizations as Open Systems

A **system** is a whole, made up of parts (sub-systems) that function together in an interdependent fashion to meet the goals of the system.

The essentials of conceptualizing an organization as an open system include (a) stressing the *interrelatedness* of the various components and functions of the organization and (b) recognizing the reciprocal dependency of the organization with its external environment. This environment is the source of labor and raw materials and the recipient of the organization's product and/or service. It also places *constraints* on organizational functioning in the form of laws, regulations, competition, and the general state of the economy.

From a systems viewpoint, an organization will survive and prosper to the extent that its various internal components function in harmony with one another and the system as a whole maintains a viable relationship with its environment. A pictorial representation of these interdependencies is shown in Exhibit 10-1.

In Exhibit 10-1, the heavy line that approximates a circle is the boundary of the organization. Outside this boundary, the external environment (the *suprasystem*) is shown as a dotted area completely surrounding it. In that environment are all of the outside factors that affect an organization's functioning. Among these are:

- customers/clients
- stockholders
- local/state/federal government regulations
- suppliers
- environmentalists
- trade associations
- community groups impacted by organization activities

Kast and Rosenzweig (1973) describe five subsystems within the boundary of the organizational system in Exhibit 10-1. Each has some independent functioning and some that overlaps with each of the other subsystems (as represented by the dashed lines).

These five subsystems are described briefly as follows:

1. *Technical*—Techniques, equipment, processes and facilities used in transforming inputs to the organization to outputs;
2. *Goals and Values*—Purpose, strategies, philosophy, and assumptions of the organization;
3. *Psychosocial*—Individual behavior, role and status hierarchies, group dynamics, and influence patterns within the organization;
4. *Structural*—Formal job descriptions, rules and procedures, formal authority and communication relationships, and defined work flows of the organization;

EXHIBIT 10–1

An Organizational
System

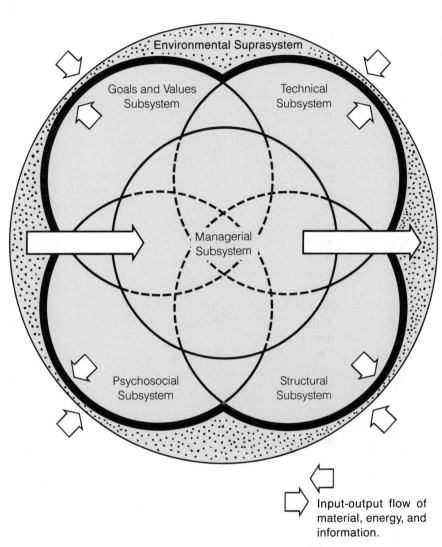

Input-output flow of
material, energy, and
information.

5. *Managerial*—Management objectives, planning, organizing, control-
    ling, and relating the organization to the environment.

The large arrows in Exhibit 10–1 represent (a) what the organization
takes in (labor, materials, information, and so on) from the environment
and (b) what it puts back (products, services, information, and so on)
into that environment. The smaller arrows depict this same passing back

and forth across organizational boundaries of inputs and outputs relevant to the specific subsystems. For example, the technical subsystem takes in relevant technical information and uses technical products and services from the environment to make its own contribution to the organization. It also makes contributions to the external technical environment in the form of shared information and trained personnel who leave the company.

The picture of an organizational system in Exhibit 10-1 is useful in a number of ways. In particular, it provides a more concrete reference for the basic premise that behavior is the result of a large number of *interacting* factors (see Chapter 2). In terms of Exhibit 10-1, the behavior of any particular individual at work may be seen to be a function of

Behavior causation: See pages 27 to 28.

Within these walls is a complex social system made up of individuals and groups working to accomplish personal and organizational goals.

(among other variables) the following:

- the tools and equipment worked with (in the Technical subsystem)
- the nature of the "corporate culture" (in the Goals and Values subsystem)
- relationships with coworkers (in the Psychosocial subsystem)
- organizational rules (in the Structural subsystem)
- the reward policies of management (in the Managerial subsystem)

A term for describing the sum total of all of these interacting factors, that is, for describing the particular social system of an organization, is *organizational climate.*

ORGANIZATIONAL CLIMATE

Reviews of the organizational climate literature (e.g., Schneider & Reichers, 1983) reveal that many definitions of this concept have been proposed. The one offered here is paraphrased from Hellriegel and Slocum (1974) and is preferred for its consistency with a systems view of organizations.

Another way of looking at the concept of organizational climate is to liken it to an organization's "personality" as Landy and Trumbo (1980) have suggested. Both descriptions convey the meaning of organizational climate, but neither is precise. This problem is so common when researchers attempt to define *organizational climate* that some doubt that it is a useful concept (e.g., Guion, 1973). Certainly the measurement difficulties associated with the various definitions have created research problems.

> Organizational climate refers to the consensus of member perceptions about how a particular organization and/or its subsystems deals with its members and its external environment.

The Measurement of Organizational Climate

Most measures of organizational climate are based on questionnaires. These ask employees of an organization to give their perceptions of such aspects of the organizational system as its goals and values and leadership policies and behavior. Among the questionnaires developed specifically for use in business organizations are the Organizational Climate Questionnaire (Litwin & Stringer, 1968) and the Business Organization Climate Index (BOCI, Payne & Pheysey, 1971). Some items from the BOCI's 24 scales are shown in Exhibit 10-2.

Respondents to BOCI items, such as those shown in Exhibit 10-2, reply "true" or "false" to each question. Answers for all respondents are combined to get a measure of climate on each scale. A statistical analysis procedure called factor analysis has found the 24 scales to be measuring two basic aspects, or *dimensions,* of an organization's climate.

Payne and Pheysey call the two BOCI factors *organizational progressiveness* (progressive attitude toward employees and problems concerned with the central task of the company) and *normative control* (extent of rules and formality in the company). These factors are consistent with

Perception: See page 36.

EXHIBIT 10-2

Some Questions from
the Business
Organization
Climate Index

Personal Relations Scales

T F   Most people here seem to be especially considerate of others.

Sociability

T F   There is a lot of group spirit.
T F   Social events get a lot of enthusiasm and support.

Interpersonal Aggression

T F   There always seem to be a lot of little quarrels going on here.

Homogeneity

T F   There are many differences in nationality, religion, and social status here.

Routine Scales

Rules Orientation

T F   Formal rules and regulations have a very important place here.
T F   People ask permission before deviating from common policies or practices.

Administrative Efficiency

T F   Work is well organized and progresses systematically from week to week.
T F   The flow of information downwards is smooth and efficient.

Note. From R. L. Payne and D. C. Pheysey, "G. G. Stern's Organizational Climate Index: A Reconceptualization and Application to Business Organizations." *Organizational Behavior and Human Performance*, 1971, 6(1), pp. 77–98. Reprinted by permission of the authors and the publisher.

those reported by Field and Abelson (1982) as characteristic of this research:

- autonomy/control
- degree of structure
- rewards
- consideration/warmth/support for employees

Although considerable research has gone into the development of organizational climate questionnaires, such as the BOCI, some believe the concept too subtle to be measured in this way (e.g., Katz & Kahn, 1978). Others raise the issue of whether such perceptual questionnaire measures of climate are measuring characteristics of the organization or characteristics of those who answer the questions (e.g., Campbell, Dunnette, Lawler, & Weick, 1970).

It may be that the complexity of the concept of organizational climate eludes the tools available for measuring it, at least at the present. Such a situation is not uncommon in the study of human behavior. Theoretical and measurement problems, however, do not alter the fact that members of organizations are aware of and respond to organizational climate. Furthermore, there is reasonable evidence of substantial employee agreement as to the nature of any particular organization's climate (e.g., Drexler, 1977; Offenberg & Cernius, 1978).

Behavioral and Attitudinal Correlates of Organizational Climate

The difficulties I/O psychologists have in reaching agreement about the measurement of organizational climate have created corresponding difficulties in their efforts to investigate the effects of this variable on the behavior of those at work. Nevertheless, some I/O psychologists and others have made a start by developing models of some possible relationships. One such model is shown in Exhibit 10-3.

Correlate: See pages 63 to 64.

Variable: See page 47.

The model in Exhibit 10-3 is a traditional organizational climate model based on Field and Abelson's (1982) extensive review of the relevant literature. Three aspects of this model are of particular importance. First, there is the multiplicity of influences on individuals' perceptions of climate. Managerial behavior may be the most significant means by which these influences are communicated to individual employees, but it is still only one determinant of climate perceptions.

The second aspect of the model in Exhibit 10-3 that merits attention is the moderating effects of the workgroup, the task, and the personality of the individual employee on perceptions of climate. Finally, individual characteristics modify responses to perceived climate in similar fashion.

Moderator variable: See pages 97 to 99.

Individual characteristics: See pages 28 to 33.

As shown at the bottom of the model in Exhibit 10-3, the three responses to a work situation generally believed to be influenced by organizational climate are motivation, performance, and reported job satisfaction. Of these three, the relationship between climate and job satisfaction has received the most attention.

Organizational Climate and Job Satisfaction

A substantial amount of research into the relationships between organizational climate and other variables has been focused on the attitude of job satisfaction. Research evidence as to a correlation between the two may be described as mixed. An alternative hypothesis was put forth by Johannesson (1973) who suggested that *organizational climate* and *job satisfaction* are only two different terms for the same phenomenon.

Correlation: See pages 61 to 63.

Hypothesis: See page 47.

Johannesson's hypothesis generated a substantial amount of research, but most findings failed to support it. For example, LaFollette and Sims (1977) found quite dissimilar correlations between (a) measures of organizational climate and performance and (b) measures of job satisfaction and performance. If organizational climate and job satisfaction were the same, the correlations should have been similar.

Schneider and Snyder (1975) have proposed a conceptual distinction between the terms *organizational climate* and *job satisfaction* that seems well on its way to general acceptance. These authors take the position that organizational climate is a *descriptive* concept based on perceptions of the organization's environment. Job satisfaction, by contrast, is an *affective* (feeling) concept based on evaluations of those perceptions. From this perspective, the two concepts clearly are related, but they are not redundant.

EXHIBIT 10–3

A Model of
Organizational
Climate Causes
and Effects

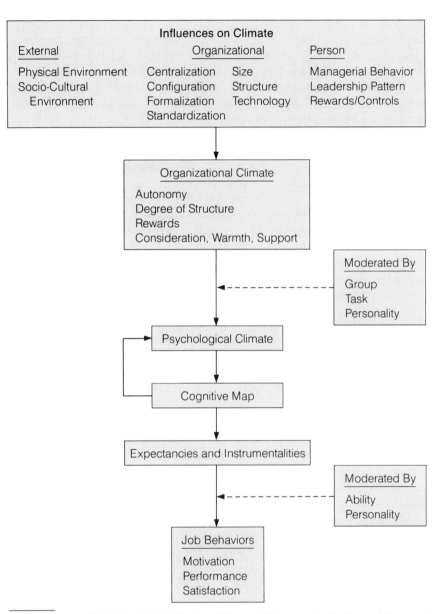

Note. From R. H. G. Field and M. A. Abelson, "Climate: A Reconceptualization and Proposed
Model." *Human Relations*, 1982, *35*(3), p. 183. Reprinted by permission of the authors and
the publisher.

   Schneider and Snyder's distinction is attractive in that it allows for
the range of correlational relationships that have been found between
organizational climate and job satisfaction. It also allows for the varying
relationships found between the two measures and behavior. For some
people in some situations, perceptions of climate may be an important

component of job satisfaction. In this case, a positive correlation would be observed between these two variables.

For other people in other situations, climate may not be important to job satisfaction, so no correlation between the two would be observed. Similarly, in some cases, the factors that affect climate may be relevant to job performance, absenteeism, and turnover, but in others, these factors may not be relevant. Again, the result would be a range of reported correlational relationships between organizational climate measures and job behaviors.

Organizational Climate and Other Employee Responses

Research into the relationships between measures of organizational climate and other employee responses to work lags behind that of research into its relationship with job satisfaction. In their review of this literature, Field and Abelson (1982) cite only five such studies that describe relationships of significance. For example, a relationship between climate and work performance was reported by Kaczka & Kirk (1968).

To date, one of the most systematic attempts to address the relationship of organizational climate to job behavior is that of Bonoma and Zaltman (1981). These authors draw on the organizational climate research, especially that of Franklin (1975), to propose the model shown in Exhibit 10–4.

Bonoma and Zaltman's model shows that organizational climate has a strong and direct effect on managerial behavior as managers interact with subordinates. This interaction, in turn, has a direct effect on peer leadership within work groups, and peer leadership affects such group processes as cooperation, enthusiasm for doing a good job, and sharing information (Bonoma & Zaltman, 1981). These relationships are shown

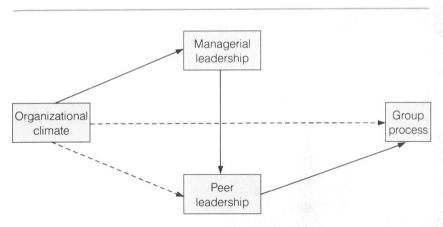

EXHIBIT 10–4

A Model of Some Effects of Organizational Climate on Work Behavior

Note. From Thomas V. Bonoma and Gerald Zaltman, *Psychology for Management*. Boston: Kent Publishing Company, 1981, p. 289. Copyright 1981 by Wadsworth, Inc. Reprinted by permission of Kent Publishing Company, a division of Wadsworth, Inc.

by the solid lines in Exhibit 10-4. The dotted lines represent the direct effects of organizational climate on peer leadership and group processes, that is, effects that do not operate through managerial behavior.

Having developed their model, Bonoma and Zaltman discuss its implications for investigating organizational problem solving. This discussion is not empirically based, but it does help to strengthen the case for further research into the influence of an organization's climate on work behavior as well as on job satisfaction.

In summary, organizational climate is a descriptive concept based on individual perceptions of the social environment of an organization. The nature of this concept creates measurement difficulties, but there seems sufficient evidence for its influence on employee behavior for researchers to pursue this line of investigation. The remainder of Chapter 10 is concerned, not with describing the organizational system, but with the energy that maintains it—communication.

COMMUNICATION

Communication is the exchange of information, ideas, or concepts between two or more individuals or groups.

The interaction of the subsystems of an organizational system creates the social environment, or organizational climate, of that organization. The means by which these interactions take place and the means by which individuals are affected by them is communication.

To quote Katz and Kahn (1978), who have done much to develop formal understanding of organizations as social systems:

> *Communication is . . . a social process of the broadest relevance in the functioning of any group, organization, or society. It is possible to subsume under it such forms of social interaction as the exertion of influence, cooperation . . . imitation, and leadership (p. 478).*

Given the importance of influence, cooperation, imitation, and leadership in organizations, is it clear that communication is the means through which things get done. In this chapter, however, it is not the uses to which specific communications are put (e.g., to influence) nor the skills required to make these communications effective that are the focus.

Communication goals and individual communication skills are important topics that have been met before (e.g., interviewing) and will be met again (e.g., performance appraisal) in this book. Here the focus is broader; specifically, interest is centered around the patterns and processes of the communication system of an organization.

The Communication Process in Organizations

Communication is a process involving at least two individuals and/or groups. One individual or group is initially in the role of *sender* of the communication. The other is in the role of *receiver*. Communication is initiated when the sender forms *symbols* (words, numbers, expressions, voice tone, and so on) into a *message* that is sent through a *channel* to the receiver. Communication is effective if the intended meaning is received and understood. This process, which is summarized in Exhibit 10-5, continues via the *feedback* loop until one party or the other breaks it off.

All members of organizations are senders and receivers in the process shown in Exhibit 10-5 many times a day. Sometimes they are senders and receivers at the same time. For example, an executive may be speaking on the telephone (message sender) and reading a letter (message receiver) at the same time. He or she may interrupt both activities to answer a secretary's question (receiver, then sender, of a message).

The communications of the executive are work-related communications, but much communication in organizations is of a nonwork nature. In addition, the executive's communications are *formal* in nature—he or she is the designated person to make that call, read that letter, and answer the secretary's question.

Informal communication in organizations is communication that goes outside or around the formal organizational information exchange policies or authority lines. Such communication is often gossip, but this does not mean that all informal communication is social or nonwork related. Asking the boss's assistant to "break the bad news that we lost the Arnold account when it looks like he's in a good mood" is both work-related and informal; a channel other than the prescribed one is being utilized.

Flow of Organizational Communication

Because so much communication goes on in organizations, those who study the process have found it useful to examine the flow of this communication in terms of the various routes or directions it takes. The characteristics of the three basic directions—*upward, downward,* and *horizontal*—are described in Exhibit 10-6.

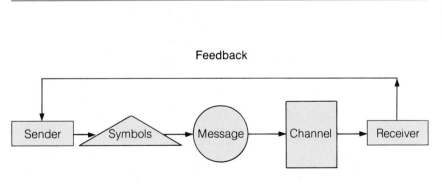

Feedback

EXHIBIT 10–5

The Communication Process

In Exhibit 10–6, the flow of communication within an organization is superimposed on a simple organization chart in order to convey that the terms *upward*, *downward*, and *horizontal* refer to the formal authority/responsibility hierarchy. Upward communication flows from subordinate to superior; downward communication is the opposite. Horizontal communication goes between people at the same level in the organizational hierarchy. The prescribed flow of communication in these three directions makes up the organization's formal communication network.

The overall patterning of the formal upward, downward, and horizontal communication flow in an organization is called a **communication network.**

Informal communication can be a considerably more complex matter than formal communication in an organization because it is bound by no policies. In a study that has become a classic in this area, Davis (1953) investigated the informal communication among the managers in a medium-sized leather goods factory. The four basic types of informal

---

EXHIBIT 10–6

The Flow of Communication in Organizations

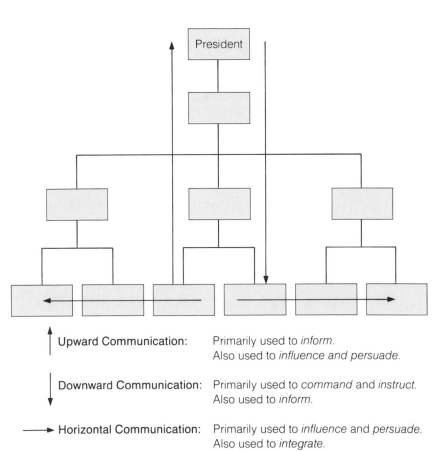

Upward Communication:	Primarily used to *inform.* Also used to *influence and persuade.*
Downward Communication:	Primarily used to *command* and *instruct.* Also used to *inform.*
Horizontal Communication:	Primarily used to *influence* and *persuade.* Also used to *integrate.*

communication patterns or *grapevine patterns* described by Davis are shown in Exhibit 10–7.

The four grapevine patterns shown in Exhibit 10–7 are described as follows:

1. *Single strand*—Message passes from A to B to C and so on to the ultimate receiver.
2. *Gossip*—A seeks out and passes message on to a number of selected receivers—B, C, and so on.
3. *Probability*—Both A and A's first receiver (B or F in Exhibit 10–7) transmit message to others in a random fashion.
4. *Cluster*—A communicates to selected receivers (B and E in Exhibit 10–7) who, in turn do the same (B to C and D; E to F and G).

EXHIBIT 10–7

Informal Communication in Organizations: "The Grapevine"

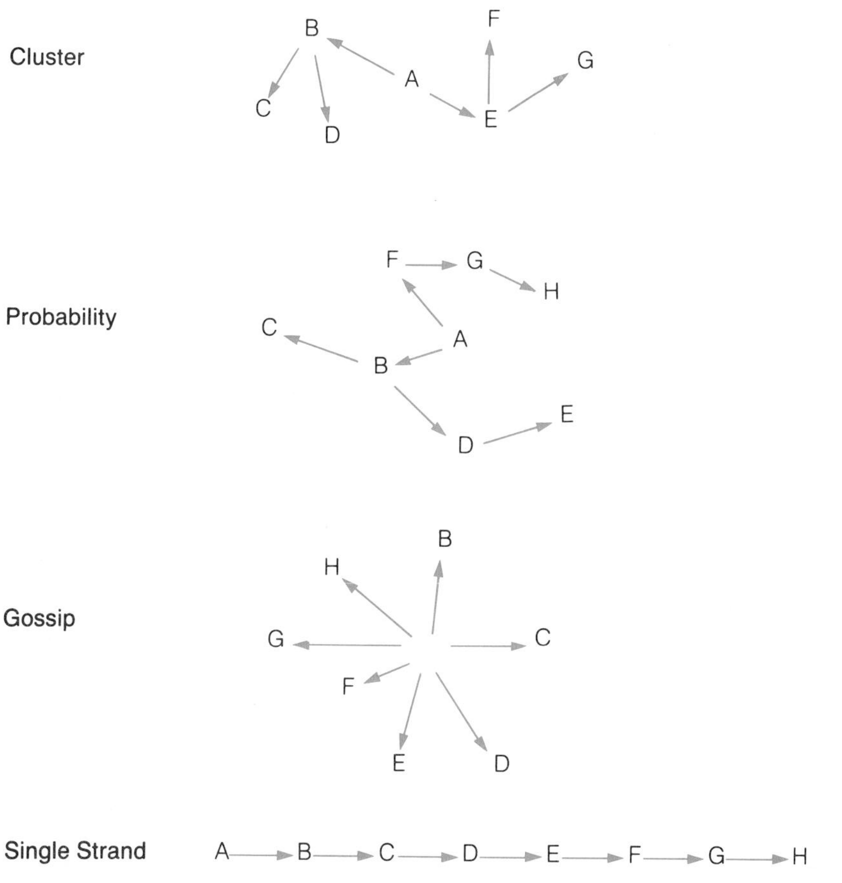

Note. Letters refer to people in an organization, A being the person who originally disseminates the message. Arrows indicate the direction in which the message flows.

Replication: See page 48.

Davis describes a number of interesting characteristics of grapevines as informal communication patterns. Two of these characteristics were later confirmed by Sutton and Porter (1968) in a well-known replication of Davis' study. The study by Sutton and Porter, in which all employees in the organization and not just the managers were used, is summarized in "Spotlight on Research."

Even when the scope of the study was expanded considerably over that of Davis (1953), Sutton and Porter found confirmation for two of Davis' especially interesting findings. First, the informal communication network appears to have a relatively small number of disseminators, or "A's" (called "Liasons" by Sutton and Porter). Second, the higher an individual's level in the organizational hierarchy, the greater his or her knowledge of what is going on. Note that the managers in the Sutton and Porter study received virtually all of the grapevine information.

SPOTLIGHT ON RESEARCH

A Study of the Grapevine in a Governmental Organization

Research question: Do grapevine patterns found among managers in a small manufacturing organization hold among all employees of a larger government organization? Are these patterns related to personality characteristics?

Survey research: See pages 57 to 58.

Type of Study: Field survey research.

Subjects: All 79 employees of a state regional tax office, 8 of whom were managers.

Variables:
- Grapevine items (9 selected pieces of information).
- Classification of subjects. Operational definition:

Operational definition: See page 48.

  —"Isolates" had not heard information more than 50% of the time.
  —"Liasons" were nonisolates who had passed on information more than one-third of the time.
  —"Dead-enders" were nonisolates who had passed on information less than one-third of the time.
- Scores on a personality measure.

General procedure: The progress of nine particular pieces of information ("grapevine items") through the organization was studied over seven months by means of questionnaires asking employees when, where, and how they learned (or did not learn) the information.

Results:

- Managers received slightly over 97% of all grapevine information, and all passed it on at least 50% of the time (were "Liasons").
- Rank-and-file employees received about 56% of the grapevine information, but only about 10% were "Liasons." Fifty-seven percent were classified as "Dead-enders" and 33% as "Isolates."
- The predominate flow of information for all subjects was within, rather than between, their own functional groups (auditors, clerical, executive, and enforcement).

Conclusion:

"The purposes of this investigation were to replicate a classic study of the grapevine reported by Davis in 1953 and to extend the results by obtaining personality data . . . on the subjects. . . . Two of Davis' findings . . . were confirmed. Two other findings of Davis . . . were not confirmed. [The personality data were not significant and are not reported here.] . . ." (p. 230).

Summarized from H. Sutton and L. W. Porter, "A Study of the Grapevine in a Governmental Organization." *Personnel Psychology*, 1968, *211*(2), pp. 223–230.

Sutton and Porter caution against over-generalization of their results, but most research evidence supports their finding that a relatively small number of organizational members spread most of the information around. In another well-known study, for example, Allen (1967) found that a very few individuals in a research and development organization were named consistently as important sources of information within the laboratory.

Generalization: See page 67.

Communication and Behavior in Organizations: Traditional Research

Although the informal communication patterns, or grapevines, in organizations have interested many I/O psychologists, more of the traditional communication research is relevant to formal communication networks. Of particular interest has been the relationship between various aspects of formal communication patterns and the way people in organizations use and react to them. Four lines of this research are discussed here:

- the use of communication channels
- the relationship between direction of communication and type of message
- the relationship between direction of communication and accuracy of message
- the relationship between an organization's formal communication patterns and individual performance and satisfaction

Use of Communication Channels

For each of the three directions in which communication in an organization may flow, there are various mechanisms, or channels, for sending messages. The once-popular suggestion box is an upward communication channel as are "open-door" policies on the parts of managers and various monthly reports sent from subordinate to superior.

Plant tours, written newsletters "from your president," and superior-instigated meetings with subordinates for various purposes are examples of downward communication channels. Staff meetings and written memoranda may serve as channels for communication in any direction.

Communication research indicates that upward communication channels in organizations are the least used on a voluntary basis (e.g., Dubin & Spray, 1964). There seem to be certain inhibiting psychological factors when employees communicate with someone who has greater status and/or formal authority. As a result, much communication that usefully might be sent upward is diverted horizontally to peers.

It often has been noted that failure to make use of upward communication channels in organizations is particularly likely when there is bad news—an unexpected problem with a project, expenditures over budget, or customer dissatisfaction (e.g., Rosen & Tesser, 1970). Instead of communicating this information to superiors so that it may be incorporated into planning and decision making, those involved may discuss it among themselves. They also may attempt to correct or cover up the situation before it becomes general knowledge.

Direction of Communication and Type of Message

The types of messages most likely to go through the various channels in the three main directions of organizational communication are described in Exhibit 10–6. Researchers find, however, that characteristics of certain channels tend to encourage people to send other kinds of messages as well. The most important of these characteristics is the status and/or authority differences between the communicating parties.

As seen in Exhibit 10–6, upward communication channels most often are used to inform or to attempt to influence or persuade. Such channels, however, are also useful ways to manage impressions having to do with the prestige of the sender or the relationship between the sender (lower in the organization hierarchy) and the receiver (higher in the organization).

One experiment that is cited frequently in the communication literature serves to illustrate the use of subordinate to superior communication to manage impressions. Cohen (1958) found that subordinates with little hope of actual upward career advancement sent more and longer non-work-related messages upward than their more mobile peers. This behavior served to create an impression of a personal relationship between the parties that somewhat offset the lack of actual upward movement.

Downward communication channels also offer an opportunity for uses other than the usual ones. For example, an executive may communicate certain information only to particular subordinates. This selective communication conveys messages to others about the executive's perception of subordinate importance. Such communication also can be used as a reward. For some people, being the boss's confidant can be a powerful incentive for them to support the superior's plans and goals.

Direction of Communication and Accuracy of Message

One of the more active lines of traditional research in the area of organizational communication concerns the relationship between direction of communication and the accuracy of the information flowing through the channel. Message inaccuracy occurs in all three directions, but the mechanisms often differ. Much of the inaccuracy in downward communication seems to stem from transmission loss, or *filtering*. Each time information moves from one receiver to another, it tends to lose something.

One well-known study of filtering was carried out by Nichols (1962). Nichols tracked the *content* of messages in much the same way that Davis (1953) and Sutton and Porter (1968) tracked the *progress* of messages. He found that some 80% of the information in the content of messages had been lost by the time the messages were passed from the top of the organizational hierarchy down to the level of the individual worker.

By contrast with the typical information loss associated with downward communication channels, inaccuracies in horizontal channels often appear to stem from addition to or embroidering on the orginal message. Thus, Sam's hangnail becomes a broken leg, and a minor production flaw becomes the likelihood of a massive recall.

The extent to which distortion is deliberate in messages sent horizontally is not known. Deliberate distortion of messages sent through upward communication channels appears to be relatively frequent, however. Gaines (1980) found the most common form of this distortion to be the sending of incomplete messages.

Communication Patterns and Employee Performance and Satisfaction

Most of the employees in any particular organization are part of the informal communication system known as the grapevine. Each employee is also one link in one or more formal upward, downward, and horizontal channels; that is, he or she is part of the organization's communication network. For example, a head nurse (a) gives any unusual information about patients to doctors making their rounds (upward communication), (b) gives special instructions to floor nurses for the day (downward communication) and (c) meets with other head nurses to plan for an administrative board tour of inspection (horizontal communication).

Most of the information available about the relationships between place in a communication network and job performance and satisfaction comes from laboratory studies of small groups. These groups are set up to perform experimental tasks of controlled difficulty within the context of communication networks manipulated by the experimenter. Three of the more common networks studied are shown in Exhibit 10–8.

Laboratory experiment: See pages 52 to 54.

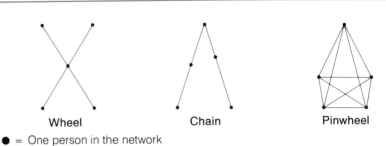

Wheel   Chain   Pinwheel

● = One person in the network

The communication networks diagrammed in Exhibit 10–8 bear a resemblance to the grapevine patterns in Exhibit 10–7, but there is a fundamental difference. The grapevine is an *informal* communication network; it develops over time. The *formal* patterns shown in Exhibit 10–8 are part of an organization's structure. In the wheel network, for example, the person at the center is *designated* by organizational policy to deal directly with the other four members of the network. These members, in turn, communicate with one another (at least formally) through the central position.

Communication is the means through which the activities of the members of an organizational social system are coordinated.

The *wheel* network of the laboratory may be found approximated in decentralized organizations with geographically dispersed units. The head of each unit reports to a common executive at corporate headquarters. A pattern more typical of many organizations is the *chain* with formal communication roughly following the organization's chain of command. The *pinwheel* network, where every member communicates directly with every other member, usually is found only in very small companies or in departments of larger ones.

Laboratory research with small groups is most clearly relevant to departmental (or workgroup) communication in organizations. The extent to which results of these studies may be generalized to organizations as a whole is speculative and the following summary of these findings should be considered accordingly.

1. Relatively *centralized* communication networks (such as the wheel in Exhibit 10–8) are associated with better job performance when job tasks are relatively simple.
2. *Decentralized* communication networks (such as the pinwheel in Exhibit 10–8) are associated with better job performance when the job tasks require more communication of ideas, information, and problem-solving strategies.
3. General member satisfaction is greatest in communication networks that are *less centralized*, that is, where members of the network have formal communication links with many other network members.
4. The greatest individual satisfaction is associated with centrality of individual position in the network. Most members of a wheel network report less satisfaction with the communication process than members of a pinwheel network, for example. The *single most satisfied* member of either network, however, is likely to be the one in the center of the wheel, the person who has access to (and control over) the maximum amount of information.

The findings just summarized have been taken from the detailed presentation of small group communication research by Shaw (1976). Further discussion of work groups and communication may be found in Jewell & Reitz (1981). Groups themselves are examined in more detail in Chapter 11.

Communication and Behavior in Organizations: Trends in Contemporary Research

Traditional communication research is concentrated to a considerable degree on particular aspects of the communication process, such as the channel or the direction of communication. While no sharp line can be drawn between this research and newer approaches, current researchers seem to place more emphasis on the communication *process* in organizations. By way of illustrating this shift, three current lines of research and theory are described briefly: (a) interpersonal communication dynamics, (b) relationships between power and communication, and (c) contingency approaches to setting up communication networks.

Interpersonal Communication Dynamics

Much of the literature that relates to communication in organizations focuses on communication between superior and subordinate and is characterized by a strong emphasis on the superior's skills as communication sender. Contemporary research in this area is giving more attention to the interactive process, recognizing that subordinate responses to superior communication can have an important effect on further communication between the two. A field study by Hatfield and Huseman (1982) illustrates this line of research.

In their study, Hatfield and Huseman asked over 1,200 hourly employees questions covering three topics: (a) superior-subordinate communication, (b) satisfaction with work and supervision, and (c) general satisfaction. A number of relationships emerged. One of the more interesting of these was that subordinate satisfaction was positively related to the extent to which they and their superiors were in *agreement* about the nature of their communication.

Agreement in the Hatfield and Huseman study refers to the extent to which subordinates and superiors perceived their communication interactions in a similar fashion. For example, when there was substantial agreement that this communication encouraged subordinate participation in job-related decisions, white male subordinates reported higher satisfaction with the work situation. Hatfield and Huseman note that the implications of this *perceptual congruence* research need more investigation, but as research it illustrates a focus on interaction in communication that is appearing in other areas as well. One of these areas, leadership, is examined in Chapter 11.

Communication and Power

A connection between power and the possession of information long has been recognized at the individual level of analysis. For example, in their classic typology of power, French and Raven (1959) describe *expert power* as the ability of a person to influence others by being able to communicate to them information that is perceived to be both useful and valid.

Within organizations, the balance of power between various groups and/or individuals also has been recognized as an important factor in organizational functioning. More recently, there has been considerable research interest in the effects of computerized management information systems on communication patterns in organizations. A model that brings these three concepts—communication, power, and management information systems—together has been proposed by Saunders (1981). This model is shown in Exhibit 10–9.

Brief descriptions of the three determinants of power shown in Saunders' model in Exhibit 10–9 are:

1. *Coping with uncertainty*—Reduction of the unpredictability stemming from lack of information about the future. Up to a point, ability to decrease uncertainty increases power.

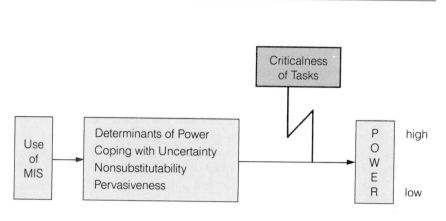

Note. From C. S. Saunders', "Management Information Systems, Communications, and Departmental Power: An Integrative Model." *Academy of Management Review*, 1981, 6(3), p. 440. Reprinted by permission of the author and the publisher.

EXHIBIT 10–9

Power, Communication, and Management Information Systems

2. *Non-substitutability*—The extent to which the activities of a department cannot easily be performed by some other department. Greater power is associated with greater nonsubstitutability.
3. *Pervasiveness*—The number of communication or work-flow links with other departments. The greater the pervasiveness, the greater the power.

Drawing on a wide base of relevant research, Saunders proposes that the use of management information systems can increase the ability of people to cope with uncertainty, nonsubstitutability, and pervasiveness in a department whose tasks the system was designed to facilitate. *Provided* these tasks are critical to the primary activities of the organization, the power of this department, relative to other departments, will be higher.

Saunders' model is presented as a theoretical link between communication, power, and management information system usage. As such, it is consistent with this chapter's focus on communication as the basic linking mechanism of organizational subsystems. To date, no tests of the model have appeared although Saunders has suggested a number of operational definitions for the various components.

Contingency Approaches to Organizational Communication

Several years ago, Tushman and Nadler (1978) proposed that organizations will be more effective to the extent that their *information-processing capacities* match their *information-processing requirements*. In other words, the best way to structure an organization's communication network depends upon the nature of the work being performed (Tushman, 1979).

Since different parts of organizations do different work, Tushman's

(1979) hypothesis suggests that organizations require different communication networks to be effective. This "it depends" approach to organizational communication policy is called a *contingency approach*. This approach, which will be met again, is characterized by a rejection of the idea that there is one best way to set up or carry out every organizational function.

A variety of hypotheses may be generated from a contingency approach to organizational communication. For example, it might be spectulated that more complex work requires more communication among those performing it. Tushman (1978) investigated this and other hypotheses in a research and development laboratory. A summary of the findings with respect to the average amount of technical communication over a 15-week period is shown in Exhibit 10–10.

The research and development laboratory in which Tushman carried out his observations had employees who performed relatively routine service projects as well as employees who performed complex research projects. As may be seen in Exhibit 10–10, those performing the complex tasks (dotted lines) engaged in significantly more communication within the laboratory and within the project than did those performing more routine work (solid lines). There was no significant difference between the two groups in amount of communication outside of the organization.

O'Reilly (1980) has taken an individual-level approach to the matching of work requirements and the communication of information. He notes a tendency for organizations and their decision makers to seek more information than is required by the task at hand. His hypothesis is that the resulting information *overload* leads to poorer employee performance than information *underload* does. Information underloaded employees believe that they have less information than they need to do their jobs.

Field study: See pages 55 to 56.

O'Reilly tested his hypothesis in two field studies and confirmed that employees who believed they were working with insufficient information received higher performance evaluations. These employees, however, also reported *lower* job satisfaction than employees working with an information overload. O'Reilly believes this finding suggests that greater care should be given to the dissemination of information within organizations, an idea that is explored further in "At Issue."

Concluding Remarks

The lines of communication research presented are still in their formative stages. Nevertheless, it is possible to see some relationships emerging, both within this newer research, and between it and more traditional approaches. For example, O'Reilly's finding that perceived information underload (being the recipient of too little work-related communication) is associated with less job satisfaction seems consistent with the information-power connection made by Saunders. It is also consistent with traditional laboratory communication research findings that people with access to (and control over) more information are more satisfied than other members of communication networks.

EXHIBIT 10–10

Differences in
Amount of
Communication for
Employees Performing
Complex and
Routine Work

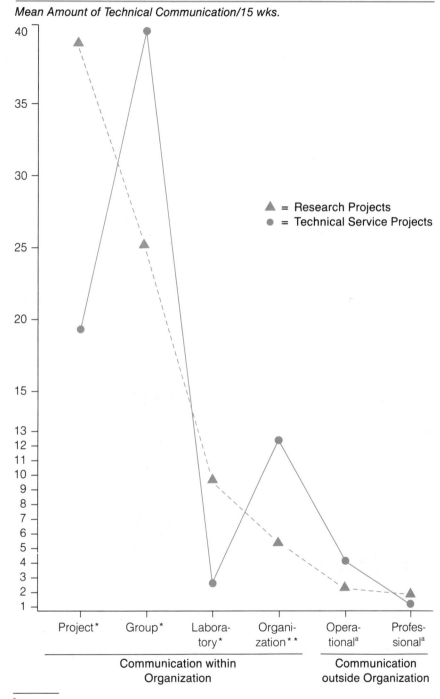

Mean Amount of Technical Communication/15 wks.

▲ = Research Projects
● = Technical Service Projects

Project*   Group*   Labora-   Organi-   Opera-   Profes-
                      tory*   zation**   tional[a] sional[a]

Communication within   Communication
Organization   outside Organization

[a]*n.s.*
*p < .05
**p < .01

Note. From M. L. Tushman, "Technical Communication in R & D Laboratories: The Impact of
Project Work Characteristics." *Academy of Management Journal,* 1978 *21*(4), p. 637. Reprinted
by permission of the author and the publisher.

SUMMARY

If an organization is viewed as a system, its social environment may be seen as created by a complex interaction of the various components of this system. Although it is somewhat controversial, the concept of organizational climate appears to be the most useful way to describe this environment that is currently available.

Organizational climate is measured in terms of individual perceptions of organization policies and practices. These perceptions appear to affect employee attitudes and behavior although the exact nature of these relationships is still speculative.

Communication is the means by which the people in an organization interact, so it may be described as the energy of the organization's social system. Communications run in formal and informal channels up, down, and across the organizational hierarchy on a continual basis. Much of the research into this process has been focused on various aspects of the nature and the use of these channels and on increased personal communication effectiveness. More recently, researchers are shifting toward investigations of the process as a whole and the relationship of this process to organizational functioning.

AT ISSUE

Is More Communication the Answer?

In 1971, Kursh wrote: "An ailment called 'lack of communication' has taken the place of original sin as an explanation for the ills of the world, while 'better communication' is trotted out on every occasion as a universal panacea. It is guaranteed to appear at least once, and usually several times, on any TV panel discussion. Usually it is offered with the mock modest air of one who is making a substantial contribution which is bound to be well received, while the correct response is solemn nods all around" (p. 189).

Six years after Kursh, Katz and Kahn (1978) noted: "The discovery of the crucial role of communication led to an enthusiastic advocacy of increased information as the solution to many organization problems. More and better communication (and especially more) was the slogan. . . . Although there were and are good outcomes of this simplistic approach, there are also weak, neglible, and negative outcomes" (pp. 429–430).

If a portion of the vast literature relating to organizations that is available in the 1980s is examined, it is clear that not much has changed. A substantial number of employees in today's organizations spend most of their working hours sending and receiving oral and written messages. Nevertheless, the cry for "more and better communication" has never been louder.

The arguments of Kursh, Katz, and Kahn, and others who have addressed the same issue vary, but all question the blanket assumption that more communication is the answer to all organizational problems. Even if *more* is changed to *better,* the question remains. As Kursh points out, most people's definition of "better communication" is communication that ends up with the other party accepting their views. And even if *better communication* is defined as *clearer communication,* the effects are not always desir-able. Some conflicts, for example, would never arise unless "clearer communication" forced them out into the open.

Katz and Kahn's basic argument for reining in the full-tilt rush toward more communication in organizations is based on their analysis of organizations as systems. For an organization to function as a system, it must be *organized,* and this means that there must be some restriction of communication. Unrestrained communication raises problems as well as solves them (as Kursh points out), obscures issues, and generally creates noise in the system.

Others who question the assumption that more communication is a cure-all for organizational problems take a decision-making perspective. They point out that a common result of the increasing number of formalized communication channels through which people collect and disseminate information in today's organization is information overload —a glut of information that interferes with rather than helps decision making. In this regard, a belief in more information as the key to better decision making in modern organizations is similar to a belief in more water as a remedy for drowning.

Those who persist in the search for simple answers to complex organizational problems are impressive in their tenacity; but the time appears to have come to face the fact that more communication is not always the answer. In fact, it may be creating as many problems as it can solve at this stage of the game. In addition, there seems to be a danger that communication in organizations is becoming an end, rather than a means to an end, (Katz & Kahn, 1978), ". . . an unattractive preoccupation with communication as a means of changing the perception of things without the expense and inconvenience of changing the things themselves" (p. 429).

REFERENCES

ALLEN, T. J. Communications in the research and development laboratory. *Technology Review,* 1967, *70,* 2–8.

BONOMA, T. V., & ZALTMAN, G. *Psychology for Management.* Boston: Kent, 1981.

CAMPBELL, J., DUNNETTE, M. D., LAWLER, E. E., & WEICK, K. E. *Managerial Behavior, Performance, and Effectiveness.* New York: McGraw-Hill, 1970.

COHEN, A. R. Upward communication in experimentally created hierarchies. *Human Relations,* 1958, *11,* 41–53.

DAVIS, K. Management communication and the grapevine. *Harvard Business Review,* 1953, *31*(5), 43–49.

DREXLER, J. A. Organizational climate: Its homogeneity within organizations. *Journal of Applied Psychology,* 1977, *62,* 38–42.

DUBIN, R. S., & SPRAY, S. Executive behavior and interaction. *Industrial Relations,* 1964, *3,* 99–108.

FIELD, R. H. G., & ABELSON, M. A. Climate: A reconceptualization and proposed model. *Human Relations,* 1982, *35*(3), 181–201.

FRANKLIN, J. L. Relations among four social-psychological aspects of organizations. *Administrative Science Quarterly,* 1975, *20*(3), 422–433.

FRENCH, J. R. P., & RAVEN, B. The bases of social power. In D. Cartwright (Ed.), *Studies in Social Power.* Ann Arbor, MI: Institute for Social Research, 1959, 118–149.

GAINES, J. H. Upward communication in industry: An experiment. *Human Relations,* 1980, *33*(12), 929–942.

GUION, R. M. A note on organizational climate. *Organizational Behavior and Human Performance,* 1973, *9,* 120–125.

HATFIELD, J. D., & HUSEMAN, R. C. Perceptual congruence about communication as related to satisfaction: Moderating effects of individual characteristics. *Academy of Management Journal,* 1982, *25*(2), 349–358.

HELLRIEGEL, D., & SLOCUM, J. W. Organizational climate: Measures, research, and contingencies. *Academy of Management Journal,* 1974, *17,* 255–280.

JEWELL, L. N., & REITZ, H. J. *Group Effectiveness in Organizations.* Glenview, IL: Scott, Foresman, 1981.

JOHANNESSON, R. E. Some problems in the measurement of organizational climate. *Organizational Behavior and Human Performance,* 1973, *10*(1), 118–144.

KACZKA, E., & KIRK, R. Managerial climate, work groups, and organizational performance. *Administrative Science Quarterly,* 1968, *12,* 253–272.

KAST, F. E., & ROSENZWEIG, J. E. Evolution of organization and management theory. In F. E. Kast and J. E. Rosenzweig (Eds.), *Contingency Views of Organization and Management.* Palo Alto, CA: Science Research Associates, 1973, 1–19.

KATZ, D., & KAHN, R. L. *The Social Psychology of Organizations* (2nd ed.). New York: John Wiley and Sons, 1978.

KURSH, C. O. The benefits of poor communication. *The Psychoanalytic Review,* 1971, *58*(2), 189–208.

LaFOLLETTE, W. R., & SIMS, H. P. Is satisfaction redundant with organizational climate? *Organizational Behavior and Human Performance,* 1975, *13*(2), 257–278.

LANDY, F. J., & TRUMBO, D. A. *Psychology of Work Behavior* (2nd ed.). Homewood, IL: Dorsey Press, 1980.

LITWIN, G. H., & STRINGER, R. A. *Motivation and Organizational Climate.* Boston: Harvard University Press, 1968.

NICHOLS, R. G. Listening is good business. *Management of Personnel Quarterly,* 1962, *4,* 4.

OFFENBERG, R. M., & CERNIUS, V. Assessment of idiographic organizational climate. *Journal of Applied Psychology,* 1978, *14*(1), 79–86.

O'REILLY, C. A., III. Individuals and information overload in organizations: Is more necessarily better? *Academy of Management Journal,* 1980, *23*(4), 684–696.

PAYNE, R. L., & PHEYSEY, D. C. G. G. Stern's Organizational Climate Index: A reconceptualization and application to business organizations. *Organizational Behavior and Human Performance,* 1971, *6*(1), 77–98.

ROSEN, S., & TESSER, A. On reluctance to communicate undesirable information: The mum effect. *Sociometry,* 1970, *33,* 253–263.

SAUNDERS, C. S. Management information systems, communications, and departmental power: An integrative model. *Academy of Management Review,* 1981, *6*(3), 431–442.

SCHNEIDER, B., & REICHERS, A. E. On the etiology of climates. *Personnel Psychology,* 1983, *36*(1), 19–39.

SCHNEIDER, B., & SNYDER, R. A. Some relationships between job satisfaction and organizational climate. *Journal of Applied Psychology,* 1975, *60*(3), 318–328.

SHAW, M. E. *Group Dynamics: The Psychology of Small Group Behavior* (2nd ed.). New York: McGraw-Hill, 1976.

SUTTON, H., & PORTER, L. W. A study of the grapevine in a governmental organization. *Personnel Psychology,* 1968, *21*(2), 223–230.

TIME. "Cultured" corporate winners: How clear goals—and some office heroes—can bring success. *Time,* 1982, (July 5), p. 46.

TUSHMAN, M. L. Technical communication in R & D laboratories: The impact of project work characteristics. *Academy of Management Journal,* 1978, *21*(4), 624–645.

TUSHMAN, M. L. Work characteristics and subunit communication structure: A contingency analysis. *Administrative Science Quarterly,* 1979, *24*(1), 82–98.

TUSHMAN, M. L., & NADLER, D. A. Information processing as an integrating concept in organizational design. *Academy of Management Review,* 1978, *3*(3), 613–624.

VON BERTALANFFY, L. The theory of open systems in physics and biology. *Science,* 1950, *111,* 23–28.

CHAPTER 11

Groups and Leadership in Organizations

I/O PSYCHOLOGY AT WORK

Motorola's Participative Management

Motorola is a multinational corporation that employs 80,000 people worldwide, with about $3.8 billion in annual sales in commercial, industrial and government electronics. The company's structure is decentralized, with many profit-and-loss centers—a key factor in the design of the participative management program. . . .

Motorola's participative management program consists of two levels. At the employee level, teams are established. Essentially, these teams consist of the employees and managers of each department.

These first-level teams meet regularly on at least a weekly basis. They review ideas for productivity and quality improvements, reduction of scrap or material consumption, or rework costs—any of the variable costs over which they have control. They develop their own priorities, and proceed to solve those problems over which they have control and for which they have the necessary resources.

Those ideas which have a wider scope or which involve higher-level control of resources are referred to the second-level team steering committee, which contains a cross-section of members from the organizational structure.

Excerpted from E. L. Simpson, "Motorola's Participative Management." *Management World,* 1983, (July), pp. 19–29. Copyright 1983 by the Administrative Management Society. Reprinted with permission from the Administrative Management Society, Willow Grove, PA 19090.

Quality circle: See page 158.

The first-level teams at Motorola are similar to quality circles—groups of employees and managers who meet to brainstorm problems and problem solutions at the production level. At Motorola, these groups not only influence what goes on in the company, they also earn bonuses when their ideas allow them to meet or exceed specific cost-reducing goals.

The teams at Motorola are formal task groups. Because each group cuts across the organizational hierarchy to some extent and is linked to *Communication channel: See page 296.* other groups as well, these teams also constitute a new communication channel within the organization. After some initial resistance on the parts of some managers, the plan is working smoothly, and Motorola expected to have it in operation in all of its facilities by the end of 1983.

Being part of the participative management program at Motorola adds a new dimension to the social work environment of these employees. In addition to their friendships with coworkers and their membership in informal groups within the organization, employees are also part of formal groups with coworkers. These groups have a specific purpose that goes beyond employees' normal job duties. The groups also open up new lines of communication with the leadership of the company.

Social environment: See pages 282 to 283.

Being part of a new kind of task group and having increased access to the "ear" of the organization's leadership influences the work behaviors of Motorola's rank-and-file employees. The arrangement also affects those who are in positions of leadership in the company. Leadership and the influence of groups on behavior form the subject matter of Chapter 11.

GROUPS IN ORGANIZATIONS

Although organizations are made up of individuals, few of these individuals work alone. Most are members of some smaller group within the organizational social system. Thus, while a manager may have a private office, he or she is still part of the company's management team. In addition, the manager identifies with (and is seen by others as part of) the particular group of employees for whose work he or she is responsible. In other words, organizations are perceived by most people as sets of groups rather than as collections of individuals.

Perception: See page 36.

Formal and Informal Work Groups

Every member of an organization is perceived by others as a member of some group within the organization. That group may be as large and as loosely defined as "management," or it may be as specific as "Project Team A." These groups are defined on the basis of the work that is done by the group members and are called *formal groups;* like the teams at Motorola, they have been created deliberately for some purpose. Other examples of formal groups in organizations include committees, crews of various kinds, and boards of directors. These groups often are called *task* groups.

Informal groups, as the name implies, are groups that are defined in terms of individual liking and/or similarity of interests, background, or characteristics. In organizations, such groups may be subsets of a formal work group, or they may have no basis in work assignments. For example, four of eight automobile salespeople may become friends, have lunch together, and share customer leads. A fifth may get along well with the others but not join in these activities. Instead, he or she is part of another informal group whose members—a mechanic, a bookkeeper, and a lot boy—share his or her interest in basketball.

Reference Groups

A **reference group** is any group that an individual uses as (a) a source of personal values, beliefs, or attitudes, and/or (b) a standard for evaluating his or her own behavior.

Most people are members of several groups, both formal and informal. Some of these groups are more important to them than others. A group that is personally important to an individual in a particular way is called a reference group. (Reitz, 1981). For example, the local union may be a reference group for an electrician. He or she measures career success partly by comparison with other members of the same local. In addition, opinions, attitudes, and beliefs with respect to work-related issues (such as the proper relationship between employees and management) are partially formed by the opinions of others in the local.

The concept of a reference group is an individual psychological concept. A work group that is a reference group for one employee may not be for another, and any employee may have several reference groups at work. The significance of such groups is that their importance to their members gives them a substantial degree of influence over those members.

THE FOUNDATIONS OF GROUP INFLUENCE ON INDIVIDUAL BEHAVIOR

The fact that group membership can alter the behavior of its members is a long-established phenomenon in psychology (Tedeschi & Lindskold, 1976). This group influence can act to make members do things in the company of other group members they would not do alone. Group membership also can influence the behavior of a member when the group is not present. This influence on behavior is particularly strong in groups with a high degree of group cohesiveness.

Group Cohesiveness

A **highly cohesive group** is one whose members are attracted to one another and to being in the group; every member has a strong commitment to keeping the group together.

Group cohesiveness develops over time, and some groups never reach the stage of mutual attraction and commitment that characterizes strong cohesiveness. A number of psychologists have described the process of *group development* and the factors that play a part in its progress (e.g. Bennis & Shepard, 1965; Tuckman, 1965). One of these factors is the degree of similarity of attitudes, opinions, values, and behaviors among group members (Cartwright, 1968).

Initially, some degree of group member similarity serves to reduce the possibility of interpersonal conflict that could split the group into factions or break it up entirely. As the group develops, it may be able to tolerate considerable difference of personal opinions among members on certain issues. Group consensus as to the characteristics of the group and how these set it apart from other groups, however, will increase.

Differences in perceptions about one's own group and other groups are illustrated by a recent study of intergroup relations in a large corporation (Alderfer & Smith, 1982). Opinions about the goals and values of

Item: The White Foremen's Club works to improve working conditions for its members.
   % WFC[a] Agreeing: 86   % BMA[b] Agreeing: 75

EXHIBIT 11–1

Item: The Black Managers' Association works with top management to solve racial problems in XYZ.
   % WFC Agreeing: 84   % BMA Agreeing: 81

Group Membership and Perception of Self and Others

Item: The Foremen's Club is essentially a social organization.
   % WFC Agreeing: 85   % BMA Agreeing: 57

Item: The Black Managers' Association is essentially a social organization.
   % WFC Agreeing: 43   % BMA Agreeing: 34

Item: The Foremen's Club is essentially a racist organization.
   % WFC Agreeing: 23   % BMA Agreeing: 53

Item: The Black Managers' Association is essentially a racist organization.
   % WFC Agreeing: 64   % BMA Agreeing: 16

---

[a]WFC = White Foremen's Club
[b]BMA = Black Managers' Association

Note. From C. P. Alderfer and K. K. Smith, "Studying Intergroup Relations Embedded in Organizations." *Administrative Science Quarterly*, 1982, *27*(1), pp. 35–65. Adapted by permission of the publisher.

---

two organizational groups from (a) each group's own members and (b) members of the other group are summarized in Exhibit 11–1.

The relative uniformity of member perceptions within each group and the difference between these perceptions and those of members of the other group show up clearly for most questions in Exhibit 11–1. For example, 64% of the members of the White Foremen's Club (WFC) agreed that the Black Managers' Association (BMA) was essentially a racist organization; only 16% of the BMA agreed with this statement.

While the different racial composition of the two groups may have intensified differences, it should be noted that these groups also had much in common. All members of both groups were employees of the same organization, and all were at a similar level in the management hierarchy of that organization. Although the Black Managers' Association did not limit its membership to first-level management (as did the White Foremen's Club), most of the black managers in this organization were in fact at this level.

The similarity of opinions about one's own group and another group illustrated by Exhibit 11–1 is one aspect of group member adherence to group norms. *Norms* are unwritten standards for behavior, values, and attitudes that grow out of the interaction of a group. The more cohesive the group becomes, the stronger the norms become and the more able the group is to enforce individual conformity to them (Kiesler & Kiesler, 1969).

Norms in Organizational Groups

Corporate culture: See page 280.

From one perspective, an organization is a group, so it has norms that affect the behavior of its members. These norms are a strong component of the "corporate culture" described in Chapter 10. Most organizations are too large to become highly cohesive groups, however, and many of the more powerful norms that affect individual employees originate in their smaller work or friendship groups. Some of the norms described to the author by various members of one organization are listed in Exhibit 11–2.

EXHIBIT 11–2	

Some Work Group Norms for Employee Behavior

- Speak up for the boss if anyone outside of the group is criticizing him or her.
- Begin closing up shop 15 minutes before formal quitting time.
- Leave the work area spotlessly clean each night.
- Help yourself to paper, pens, scissors, or whatever you need for home use.
- Do not wear your earplugs; they are for sissies.
- If you need help, ask a coworker, not the boss.
- Never wear a dirty uniform to work.

Notice that the norms listed in Exhibit 11–2 relate to a variety of different behaviors and that they vary considerably in specificity. "Close up 15 minutes before quitting time" is very specific. On the other hand, "Help yourself" leaves substantial room for individual interpretations. For this norm as for most, there is usually a *range* of behaviors that constitute acceptable conformity to the group. Taking home the self-correcting typewriter, for example, probably lies outside of that range. At the other extreme, the group may be expected to take exception to a "holier-than-thou" reaction from one member when another takes home some typing paper.

The Return Potential Curve for Norms

Not only is there variation in the behaviors that are considered appropriate conformity to group norms, there is also variation in the strength of group approval or disapproval that goes along with conformity or non-conformity. A model that incorporates both (a) range and (b) strength of approval associated with behaviors relevant to group norms was developed by Jackson (1966). An example of this *Return Potential Curve* is shown in Exhibit 11–3. The norm used to illustrate this concept centers on unexcused absences from work.

The diagram in Exhibit 11–3 shows that maximum approval (return) from the group is associated with a member's having several unexcused absences per year (point a). Group approval changes to disapproval if too few absences are taken (point b) and to extreme disapproval if too many are taken (point c). The logic of this from the group's viewpoint is clear enough: If too few days off are taken by some people, those who

EXHIBIT 11–3

The Return Potential
Curve for an
Unexcused Absence
Norm

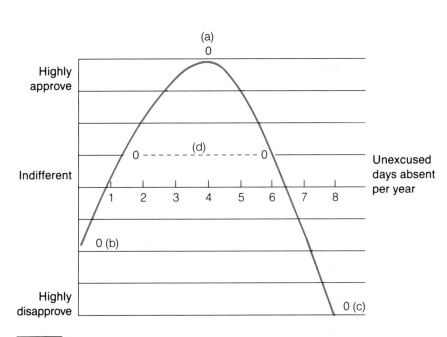

Note. From Thomas V. Bonoma and Gerald Zaltman, *Psychology for Management*. Boston: Kent Publishing Company, 1981, p. 236. Copyright 1981 by Wadsworth, Inc. Reprinted by permission of Kent Publishing Company, a division of Wadsworth, Inc.

take more will look bad. If too many are taken, other group members will have to take up the work slack.

In the example in Exhibit 11–3, the *range* of acceptable behavior with respect to the norm governing unexcused absences is between two and six days per year (dotted line labeled d). In a highly cohesive work group, this standard may be as powerful as any organizational rule about attendance, because conforming to this norm is a price to be paid for acceptance by the group. While it seldom is feasible to draw such a specific picture of group norms in operation, the model in Exhibit 11–3 is a useful representation of the influence such norms have on individual behavior.

GROUP INFLUENCES ON BEHAVIORS AND ATTITUDES AT WORK

The discussion of group norms considerably simplifies a complex set of group processes. It also neglects some interesting issues, such as how norms develop, change, and sometimes become institutionalized into formal rules. The discussion, however, is sufficient to make the basic point that norms are the primary mechanism through which groups influence the behavior of their members. Penalties, called *sanctions,* for violating norms can include teasing, ignoring, scapegoating, physical punishment, or expulsion from the group.

The reader interested in more details of the development and enforcement of work group norms may refer to the recent discussion by Feldman (1984). In this section, some of the work behaviors and attitudes found to be influenced by group membership are examined.

Group Influences on Performance

Hawthorne experiments: See pages 4 to 5.

The ability of a work group to affect the performance of its individual members first gained wide-spread attention in the Hawthorne Experiments (Roethlisberger & Dickson, 1939). The Bank Wiring Room studies from that series of experiments clearly demonstrated the existence of two sets of production standards—one set by the company and a lower one representing a norm of the employees who wired the terminals in this phase of production.

The Hawthorne researchers collected a great deal of interesting data about the social processes among the Bank Wiring Room employees. Among other things, they found two distinct small groups with two different sets of norms about appropriate behavior at work. They also found that a few individuals belonged to neither group; however, all employees conformed to some degree to a general (Wiring Room) norm of not doing as much work as engineering standards specified.

Work restriction refers specifically to limits on production output set by workgroup norms.

The phenomenon observed in the Hawthorne Bank Wiring Room almost 50 years ago is so common that is has its own name—work restriction. *Work restriction* is such a well-known phenomenon that many may think this to be the only direction in which group influences on individual performance operate. As suggested by the examples of organizational norms listed previously, however, norms can have positive effects as well as negative ones.

The Hawthorne Bank Wiring Room studies initiated considerable research interest in the nature and effects of group norms on the performance of those in the group. On the whole, these studies found that highly cohesive groups have positive work norms in some cases and negative ones in others. As a result, such work groups tend to be among *either* the most *or* the least productive groups in an organization (Seashore, 1954). Consistent with the discussion of uniformity, performance

Variance: See page 60.

norms serve to reduce the *variance* of individual performance in a group.

Many experiments and case studies of the influence of groups on worker performance focus on volume of productivity. Groups also influence other performance-related behaviors, however. There are norms about the *way* things are done as well as about *how much* is done. A common example is the chronic problem many companies have with work norms that encourage dangerous work practices and can jeopardize individual worker safety. Other work-method norms include:

- Norms about the use of resources: "Don't worry about waste—the company can afford it."

- Norms about task priorities: "We always do M. Clark's work first."
- Norms about customer treatment: "The young ones never buy anything—ignore them."

Learning such work norms is part of the process by which a newcomer to a work group becomes an accepted insider (socialization), as the conversation in Exhibit 11–4 illustrates.

Socialization: See pages 166 to 170.

Group Influences on Satisfaction

The classic study of the influence a work group can have on the job satisfaction of members is a participant observation study conducted by Roy (1960). In a famous report he called "Banana Time," Roy discusses his experiences and observations as part of an actual four-man work group. The task of the employees in this group was to stamp plastic into various shapes by means of a machine designed for this purpose. The job was repetitive, boring, and incorporated very little opportunity for task variety into its 12-hour day.

"Banana time" refers to a patterned social interaction in which one member of the group regularly seized and ate the banana another member had brought for his own lunch. Each day this "time" went the same way. One group member craftily extracted the banana from the other's lunch and devoured it against the protestations of its owner and the chiding of the third member for "all the fuss." By contrast, "peach time," while equally structured in terms of the social interaction pattern, led to the entire group sharing the peaches brought by one member.

The influence of a work group on individual production output can be substantial.

EXHIBIT 11-4

Learning the Ropes:
Peer Influences
on Performance

For eighteen years Ginny had been doing about the same thing—packing expandrium fittings for shipment. So well practiced was she that she could do the job perfectly without paying the slightest attention. This, of course, left her free to "socialize" and observe the life of The Company as it took place about her.

Today, however, she was breaking in a new packer. It was instructive.

"No, not that way. Look, honey, if you hold it that way, well, then you have to twist your arm when you pack this corner, see. This way it's easier."

"But that's the way Mr. Wolf (methods engineer) said we had to do it."

"Sure he did, honey. But he's never had to do it eight hours a day like me. You just pay attention to what I say."

"But what if he comes around and says I should pack the other way?"

"Oh, that's easy. When he's here you do it his way. Anyway, after a couple weeks you won't see him again."

"Slow down, you'll wear yourself out. No one's going to expect you to do eighty pieces for a week anyway."

"But Mr. Wolf said ninety."

"Sure he did. Let *him* do it. Look, here's how to pace yourself. It's the way I was taught, and it works. You know the *Battle Hymn of the Republic* (Ginny hummed a few bars). Well, you just work to that, hum it to yourself, use the way I showed you, and you'll be doing eighty next week."

"But what if they make me do ninety?"

"They can't. Y'know, you start making mistakes when you go that fast. No, eighty is right. I always say, a fair day's work for a fair day's pay."

Note. From R. Richard Ritti and G. Ray Funkhouser. *The Ropes to Skip and the Ropes to Know.* Columbus, OH: GRID, Inc., 1977. Reprinted by permission of John Wiley and Sons, Inc.

In addition to "banana time" and "peach time," the group had "fish time," "coke time," "window time," and "pickup time." There were also a number of conversational themes that followed an almost unvarying pattern. Roy describes a number of themes, both comical and serious, such as "getting Dannelly a better job" and "George's daughter's marriage."

Roy discusses the meaning of times, themes, and various work games (such as cutting off one member's machine every time he left the work area) in terms of their effects on the job satisfaction of the members of the entire group. In this group, social interaction was being used to combat the "beast of monotony" and to inject some satisfaction into a particularly sterile job situation. Roy discovered for himself that the patterned social interactions of the group (which had initially seemed meaningless, silly, and even irritating) provided the psychological support to make the long days relatively easy to endure. In his words: "The 'beast of boredom' was gentled to the harmlessness of a kitten" (p. 168).

The method Roy used to collect his data about social interaction and job satisfaction in a work group is called a *participant observation study.* Such studies make fascinating reading, and they are almost always rich sources of experimental hypotheses. The active involvement of the researcher in the behavior he or she is studying, however, can make it difficult to draw objective conclusions about that particular data.

Group Influences on Other Responses to Work

While job performance and job satisfaction have been the focus of much of the research on the influence of group membership on employee responses to work, there have been other kinds of investigations. For example, it has been suggested that the kind of satisfaction described by Roy (1960) that can be found in the social aspects of a work situation may offset absenteeism, turnover, and job stress. A recent study by Mossholder, Bedeian, and Armenakis (1982) illustrates this line of research.

Mossholder, Bedeian, and Armenakis investigated relationships between (a) group member interaction and (b) individual differences in self-esteem and the following:

- experienced job tension
- tendency to leave the job
- job performance

Questionnaires were used to measure members' self-esteem, peer group interaction (PGI), experienced job tension, and likelihood of leaving the job. Supervisory ratings were used as a measure of job performance. Subjects were nursing employees at a large hospital.

A summary of the findings by Mossholder, Bedeian, and Armenakis is shown in Exhibit 11-5. As hypothesized, all subjects who reported *high* interaction among members of their peer groups reported *less* job strain and a *lower* propensity to leave the job (Graph a and b). As shown by the steeper lines for this group, however, this relationship was stronger for employees with low self-esteem than for those with high self-esteem.

Graph (c) of Exhibit 11-5 depicts the relationship between group interaction and performance in the study by Mossholder and his colleagues. It was only the performance of *low* self-esteem individuals that was related to amount of peer group interaction. The performance of high self-esteem individuals was high regardless of what happened in work groups.

The findings of the study in Exhibit 11-5 suggest that group membership may indeed affect job adjustment for certain employees. Should these findings be replicated, they suggest that low self-esteem employees *Replication: See page 48.* will function better in work situations requiring interpersonal interaction and teamwork. By contrast, jobs requiring independent performance might better be filled by high self-esteem employees.

Unions: A Special Case of Group Membership

Much research on groups in organizations is centered on small groups that have their origins within a particular company. Employees also have membership in larger groups and groupings that originate outside of organizational boundaries and crosscut formal organizational groups. Foremost among such *identity groups* (Alderfer & Smith, 1982) are unions.

The number of union members in any particular organization may be large or small, but "being in a union" is a characteristic shared by

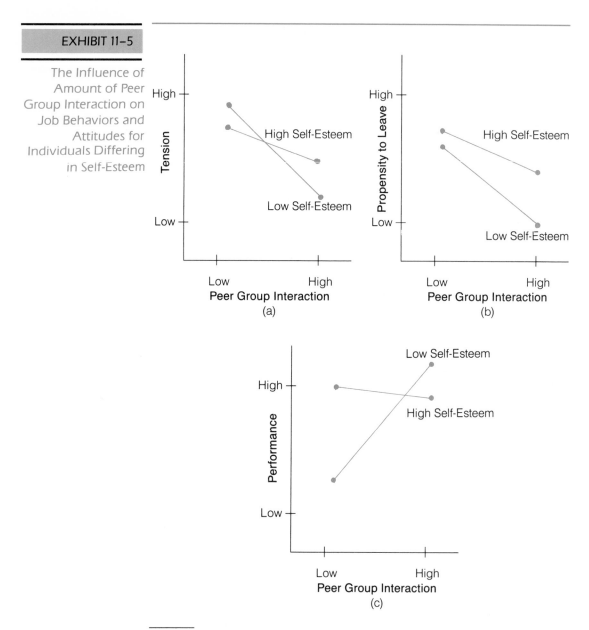

EXHIBIT 11–5

The Influence of
Amount of Peer
Group Interaction on
Job Behaviors and
Attitudes for
Individuals Differing
in Self-Esteem

Note. From K. W. Mossholder, A. G. Bedeian, and A. A. Armenakis, "Group Process-Work Out-come Relationships: A Note on the Moderating Impact of Self Esteem." *Academy of Management Journal,* 1982, *25*(3), p. 581. Reprinted by permission of the authors and the publisher.

approximately 25% of all American workers. For union members, some important norms originate outside the immediate work group or employing organization.

The study of why people join unions, union-management relations, and union constraints on organizational functioning is not new. In much of this work, however, "the union" is treated as a homogeneous entity. As a result, there is a considerable body of knowledge about "union behavior" and about differences in characteristics between union and nonunion workers. There is little about the effects of various characteristics of unions on individual member behavior and attitudes, however.

One exception to this generalization is a study done by Hammer (1978) in which the relationship between the strength of a union and certain worker perceptions, attitudes, and performance were investigated. Hammer's subjects were over 200 members of a building construction union. They were located on 25 different building sites in 17 cities (in the East, Midwest, and South), but all worked for the same company.

Union strength in the Hammer study was assessed in two ways: (a) the relative wage per hour reached in the last bargaining session in each area and (b) the percentage of construction workers in the same trade in each area who belonged to the union. Worker perceptions and attitudes were measured by means of questionnaires, and worker performance was measured by supervisory ratings made on a scale developed for the study. Hammer's analysis of these data revealed a number of interesting relationships.

- Union strength (wage rate) was positively correlated with workers' perceptions of job security, earning good money, and a belief that attaining desirable work rewards was tied to work performance. *Correlation: See pages 61 to 63.*
- Union strength (wage rate) was positively correlated with workers' perceptions of supervisory authority and negatively correlated with their perceptions of supervisor reward and punishment power.
- Union strength was unrelated to workers' job satisfaction, except for satisfaction with pay.
- Union strength was unrelated to ratings of worker job performance. Workers in the stronger locals, however, received significantly lower ratings for being friendly and cooperative, showing up on time for work, and supporting company goals.

A construction union, like all unions, is composed of people with certain things in common; it would be difficult to guess to what extent Hammer's findings might be generalized to other unions. Nevertheless, his results challenge the assumption that "a union is a union and a union member is a union member." On the basis of these findings, it would seem that more research into the differential effects of union characteristics on member behavior and attitudes is warranted. *Generalization: See page 67.*

Group Influences on Behavior in Perspective

It should be clear that group membership is an extremely important aspect of any individual's social environment at work. It should not be assumed, however, that all people conform all the time to the norms of the groups of which they are members. As noted by Jewell and Reitz (1981):

The psychological force causing one to conform is a complex of individual motives and group expectations. Certain individual characteristics, combined with certain situational factors, produce independence or even occasional anticonformity responses to group influence attempts (p. 67).

Among the individual characteristics that have been found to be associated with resistance to group influences on behavior are:

- high self-esteem
- strong values that run counter to group norms
- strong confidence in one's own knowledge and abilities

The reaction of a group to individual deviance from group norms has been studied extensively. The classic study by Schachter (1951) and the work of those who followed this line revealed a pattern; for a time the deviant will be the center of attention as the group members attempt to bring him or her into conformity. Eventually, the members will give up trying and the deviant will be ignored or even expelled from the group.

The pattern first described by Schachter was modified and refined by later work in the area. Dentler and Erikson (1959), for example, suggest that some deviance usually will be tolerated in a group because it helps keep group norms clear and defined. Hollander (1964) presents a detailed analysis of the relationship between member status in the group and the extent to which deviance is tolerated.

Hollander's idea is that individual group members accumulate what he calls *idiosyncratic credits*; that is, a credit account against which individual acts of nonconformity may be balanced. The higher the individual's status, the greater the credit. Since the greatest status is usually accorded to a group's leader, a group often will accept considerable deviance from norms from this individual(s). It is to the topic of leadership that the discussion now turns.

LEADERSHIP IN ORGANIZATIONS

In this chapter, leadership is viewed as a process opposite to the process previously presented, which focused on the influence that a group has on individual behavior. Here, focus is on the influence that an individual has on group behavior. In organizations, this individual may be in a *formal leadership position*, such as the foreman of a construction crew, the supervisor of a typing pool, the chairwoman of a committee, the manager of a sales force, or the executive vice-president of the company.

Not all individuals who influence groups in organizations are in formal leadership positions. Most groups have *emergent leaders*—members who influence others in the group more than they are influenced by others (Gibb, 1969). Such an individual may be said to occupy an *informal leadership position*.

Formal and Informal Leadership

In organizations, it is not uncommon to hear remarks such as: "Our problem is that the president of this company (or the supervisor of production, or whomever) is not a real leader." Such comments are symptomatic of a degree of confusion about what the words *leader* and *leadership* mean. This confusion arises from a failure to distinguish between leadership as a position and leadership as the outcome of group interaction processes, that is, between formal and informal leadership. This distinction may be described as follows:

> *Formal leaders are expected to influence groups because they are in leadership positions. Emergent leaders are in informal leadership positions because they can influence groups.*

From the standpoint of the distinction between formal and emergent leadership, an ideal situation in an organization would seem to be one in which the company was managed by emergent leaders committed to company goals. Unfortunately, this is not a practical suggestion, but a bridge between emergent and formal leadership exists in a concept called *endorsement* (Tedeschi & Lindskold, 1976).

The power of an individual in a formal leadership position is based on the authority that an organization gives to that particular position in its hierarchy. The ability to use that power to influence subordinates depends to a considerable degree upon the willingness of others to have that individual in that position with that authority, that is, upon the *endorsement of the leader* by his or her group.

Among the factors identified by Jewell and Reitz (1981) as influences on extent of leadership endorsement are:

- whether the individual is appointed or elected to the position
- the extent to which he or she upholds group norms
- the way in which he or she goes about attempting to influence the group
- the success or failure that the group experiences with that particular person in the leadership position

With respect to achieving organizational goals, a formal leader with high endorsement from his or her subordinates is in a position that closely resembles the influence of an emergent leader. Since the I/O psychology leadership literature is addressed almost exclusively to formal leadership, emergent leadership will not be discussed further.

A Short History of Leadership Theory

Most of the literature on leadership, both academic and popular, is directed toward answering the question: What makes for an effective leader? Effectiveness is defined in various ways, but most definitions incorporate the twin goals of (a) getting the job done and (b) promoting subordinate (or group) satisfaction in the process. Historically, the two most influential approaches to the question of leadership effectiveness have been the trait theory approach and the leader behavior approach.

The Trait Theory of Leadership

As far as popular ideas about leadership are concerned, emphasis always has been on personal traits, or leadership qualities. The underlying corollary is that people either have these qualities or they do not. Acquiring effective leadership from this perspective is a matter of finding people who do have these qualities. Some advocates of this approach even specified the physical attributes, such as height and eye color, by which leaders could be identified.

The formal study of leadership also passed through a trait theory phase, but the search for a "shopping list" of personal traits by which leaders could be picked out of a crowd did not work very well (Gibb, 1969). Although organizations still use screening and evaluation procedures for purposes of identifying individuals with leadership *potential* (e.g., assessment centers), there are no longer any formal trait theories of leadership as such. A recent discussion of this approach may be found in Kenny and Zaccaro (1983).

Assessment center: See page 125.

Leader Behavior Theories of Leadership

Individual characteristics: See pages 28 to 33.

Although the personal characteristics approach was abandoned by those who formally studied leadership, the idea that the person is the major determinant of effectiveness did not disappear. Attention turned instead to the *behavior* of people in leadership positions. At first, emphasis was placed on what were believed to be basic differences in patterns of leader behavior that stemmed from leader personalities and philosophies. The most well-known typology of such patterns is the *authoritarian, democratic,* and *laissez-faire* distinction of Lewin, Lippitt, and White (1939). Behavioral differences among these three patterns are summarized in Exhibit 11–6.

Operational definition: See page 48.

The behavioral descriptions shown in Exhibit 11–6 are the operational definitions used in two classic studies of the influence of leadership style on behavior. The second of these two studies is summarized in "Spotlight on Research."

"Spotlight on Research" gives a simplified summary of a complex study lasting approximately five months. The authors' interest was in the relationships between (a) the social climates associated with their manipulations of leader behavior and (b) the social interaction patterns of the subjects. Nevertheless, the obvious parallel to organizational leadership excited many researchers, and the study is so often cited in the leadership literature that it may be considered a classic in this line of research.

Subsequent researchers of authoritarian, democratic, and *laissez-faire* leadership styles have investigated the influence of these behavior patterns on the traditional leadership criteria of task accomplishment and subordinate satisfaction. Some of these studies have supported the findings of Lewin, Lippit, and White that people *like* democratic leadership

Authoritarian	Democratic	Laissez-faire
1. All determination of policy by the leader.	1. All policies a matter of group discussion and decision, encouraged and assisted by the leader.	1. Complete freedom for group or individual decision, without any leader participation.
2. Techniques and activity steps dictated by the authority, one at a time, so the future steps were always uncertain to a large degree.	2. Activity perspective gained during first discussion period. General steps to group goal sketched, and where technical advice was needed the leader suggested two or three alternative procedures from which choice could be made.	2. Various materials supplied by the leader, who made it clear that he would supply information when asked. He took no other part in work discussions.
3. The leader usually dictated the particular work task and work companions of each member.	3. The members were free to work with whomever they chose, and the division of tasks was left up to the group.	3. Complete nonparticipation by leader.
4. The dominator was "personal" in his praise and criticism of the work of each member, but remained aloof from active group participation except when demonstrating. He was friendly or impersonal rather than openly hostile.	4. The leader was "objective" or "fact-minded" in his praise and criticism, and tried to be a regular group member in spirit without doing too much of the work.	4. Very infrequent comments on member activities unless questioned, and no attempt to participate or interfere with the course of events.

EXHIBIT 11–6

Authoritarian, Democratic, and *Laissez-faire* Leadership

Note. From K. Lewin, R. Lippitt, and R. K. White, "Patterns of Aggressive Behavior in Experimentally Created 'Social Climates'." *Journal of Social Psychology,* 1939, *10*(2), 170. Reprinted by permission of the authors and the publisher.

better. Others (e.g., Vroom & Mann, 1960) have found that it depends on the situation. With respect to task accomplishment, most investigations have found situational variables to be critical. In particular, authoritarian leadership appears to be associated with greater productivity when the situation is highly stressful to workers in some way (e.g., Rosenbaum & Rosenbaum, 1971).

The authoritarian-democratic-*laissez-faire* typology of leadership is a one-dimensional view having to do primarily with the degree of control the leader keeps over decision making. The general assumption was that people have a preference for and tend to use one such style consistently. Researchers, as described, were oriented toward trying to find which style worked best.

SPOTLIGHT ON RESEARCH

Patterns of Aggressive Behavior in Experimentally Created "Social Climates"

Research question: What are the effects of different climates created by different leadership styles on various aspects of the behavior of group members?

Simulation experiment: See page 54.

Type of study: Field simulation experiment.

Subjects: Ten-year-old male volunteers.

Independent variable: Leadership style. Operational definition: (a) "Authoritarian," (b) "Democratic," (c) *"Laissez-faire."* (See Exhibit 11–6.)

Independent / dependent variables: See page 52.

Dependent variable: Aggressive behavior of subjects. Operational definition: Several based on a variety of social analysis techniques.

General procedure: Four new clubs of 10-year-old boys were organized on a volunteer basis. The clubs engaged in a variety of social activities. Every six weeks each club had a new leader with a different style of leadership. A large amount of observational data were collected according to predetermined methods.

Results:
- Under authoritarian leadership most boys showed extremely non-aggressive, apathetic behavior and notable outbursts of aggression on the days of transition to a new leader.
- Nineteen out of 20 boys liked their democratic leader better than their authoritarian leader, and 7 out of 10 liked their *laissez-faire* leader better.
- There were two "wars" between clubs and two striking instances of aggression against inanimate objects.

Conclusion: "A general interpretation of the . . . data on aggression can be made in terms of four underlying factors: tension, restricted space of free movement, rigidity of group structure, and style of living (culture)" (p. 299).

Summarized from K. Lewin, R. Lippitt, and R. K. White, "Patterns of Aggressive Behavior in Experimentally Created 'Social Climates'." *Journal of Social Psychology,* 1939, *10*(2), pp. 271–299.

The Vroom-Yetton Model

A newer model of leadership that also focuses on leader decision making has been proposed by Vroom and Yetton (1975). This model is not based on the assumption that leaders have relatively inflexible styles. Rather, it is assumed that more effective leaders vary their decision-making strategies according to the particular demands of the situation. Although the basic determinant of strategy remains control over decision making, Vroom and Yetton describe five, rather than three, approaches.

1. Leader makes decision using all information available to him or her at the time.
2. Leader makes decision after getting information from subordinates.
3. Leader asks subordinates individually for ideas and suggestions, then makes his or her own decision.
4. Leader makes decision after discussing it with subordinates as a group.
5. Leader and group together discuss issues and make decision.

Vroom and Yetton offer a series of rules to guide leaders in choosing one of the decision-making strategies to fit a particular situation. To date, research on this approach is limited. There is some evidence, however, for the basic premise that more effective decisions are made by matching strategy to the goals and constraints of the situation at the time (e.g., Vroom & Jago, 1978).

Although Vroom and Yetton (1975) call their model a *normative* one (it prescribes what a leader *should* do), its basic premise is consistent with a *contingency* approach to leadership. More formal contingency theories of leadership have grown out of a series of studies carried out independently by research teams at the University of Michigan and The Ohio State University. These two groups of researchers conducted an exhaustive study of the question: What do leaders actually *do?* They came up with similar answers although they used different terms to describe them.

Contingency theories: See page 302.

According to the research, leader behaviors fall into two basic categories. One category consists of behaviors centered around the task, such as deciding what will be done, assigning work, and maintaining standards of performance. This class of behaviors was called *production-centered* by the Michigan team (Katz, Maccoby, & Morse, 1950) and *initiating structure* by the Ohio State team (Hemphill, 1950).

The other category of leader behaviors centers around employees, such as looking out for the personal welfare of subordinates, trying to make working conditions pleasant, and seeking subordinate ideas about work. This class of behaviors was labeled *employee-centered* in the Michigan studies and *showing consideration* in the Ohio State studies.

Contingency Theories of Leadership

The Ohio State and Michigan studies of leadership led to a long line of research, and these findings have left little room for doubt that the task-versus-people-centered behavior dimension is a stable one (Landy & Trumbo, 1980). This raised the question: Which kind of behavior is more effective? The answer was always the same: It depends on the situation. From that rather unsatisfactory conclusion grew contemporary contingency theories of leadership.

Unlike older approaches to leadership, contingency theories do not try to identify the one best way for leaders to behave at all times. Rather, they concentrate on identifying *matches* between leader behaviors and elements of the situation that increase performance and/or subordinate satisfaction. One recently-proposed contingency model is shown in Exhibit 11–7 (Griffin, 1979).

EXHIBIT 11–7

A Contingency Model of Leadership Effectiveness

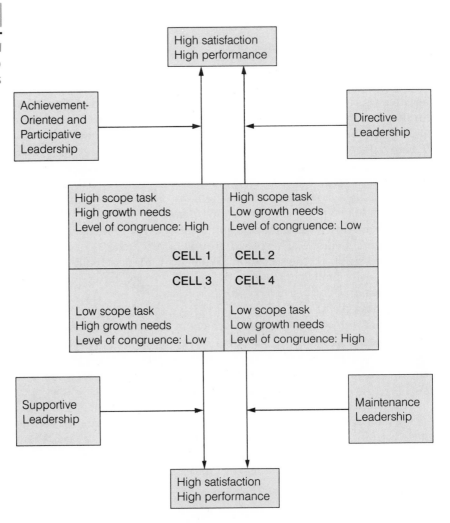

Note. From R. W. Griffin, "Task-Design Determinants of Effective Leader Behavior." *Academy of Management Review,* 1979, 4(2), p. 221. Reprinted with permission of the author and publisher.

The four boxes in the center of Exhibit 11–7 (Cells 1–4) describe four possible situations a leader might be in when "the situation" is examined from the standpoint of the fit, or *congruence*, between subordinate needs and the work they do. Cell 2, for example, is a situation where this fit is poor; a complex (high scope) job is being done by people with low needs for challenging work (low growth needs).

Griffin suggests that the most effective leader behavior for the Cell 2 situation is *directive*, or task-centered, leadership. Since subordinates do not find the challenge of the job rewarding, they will not be motivated to master it and perform well without direction. Accordingly, such subordinates should both perform better and be more satisfied when the leader provides a high degree of task-oriented structure. Similar predictions are made for matches between the three other situations and leadership styles described.

Growth need: See page 205.

Griffin's model is new and still largely untested. It is a good illustration of the concept of a contingency theory of leadership, however. As such, it is a useful point of reference for a brief description of the two leading contingency theories in this area.

A Contingency Model of Leadership Effectiveness

Fiedler's (1965) Contingency Model of Leadership Effectiveness also is based on a match between leader behavior and the situation. It differs from Griffin's model, however, in two important respects. First, it is assumed in this model that people have basic and stable styles of leadership that lean either toward people-centered behaviors or toward task-centered behaviors. Griffin, on the other hand, describes four styles and

Some directive task-centered behaviors are required of most people in formal leadership positions.

assumes that leaders can vary the style to fit the situation.

The second important way in which Fiedler's model differs from Griffin's is in the perspective on the situation. Fiedler defines the three important aspects of the situation as follows:

- the extent of formal authority the organization gives the leader
- the quality of the relations between the leader and subordinates
- the degree to which the work task is structured

From Fiedler's perspective, leaders who are primarily people-oriented are more effective in situations where (a) formal authority is weak, (b) relations with subordinates are good, and (c) the task is unstructured (Fiedler, 1971). Since Fiedler believes that leadership style is a relatively stable personal characteristic, a mismatch requires changing the situation or transferring the leader to a more compatible environment.

Fiedler's theory has attracted a lot a research attention since it first appeared, but results remain mixed. A major difficulty with testing the theory is that it is almost impossible for investigators to duplicate the conditions Fiedler specifies (Landy & Trumbo, 1980). A review of the various issues surrounding the investigations of Fiedler's model may be found in Strube and Garcia (1981).

The Path-Goal Theory of Leader Effectiveness

House's (1971) Path-Goal Theory of Leader Effectiveness is similar to Fiedler's in that it proposes only two main styles of leader behavior, but it is similar to Griffin's in that it does not suppose these styles to be stable personal traits. (More accurately, Griffin's model is similar to House's because Path-Goal Theory is the major theoretical underpinning of Griffin's approach.)

The Path-Goal Theory is different from the models of both Griffin and Fiedler in the way it defines the important aspects of the situation to which leader behavior should be adapted. House defines these characteristics as:

- the extent to which work tasks are clear
- the extent to which work is intrinsically satisfying
- the extent to which the work environment is stressful

House proposes that people-centered leadership (called *supportive behavior* in his model) will be more effective when (a) the task is clear, (b) the work is not especially satisfying, and (c) the environment is somewhat stressful. Task-centered behaviors (called *instrumental behaviors* by House) will lead to greater satisfaction and better performance when the work is more interesting and the environment less hostile.

At this time, empirical support for House's Path-Goal Theory is somewhat weak; in fact, Griffin's model was stimulated by an attempt to strengthen the Path-Goal Theory's potential. A recent review of the Path-Goal Theory, some of the problems identified by relevant research, and some suggestions for future testing may be found in Schriesheim and Schriesheim (1980).

Leadership Theory in Applied Situations

Despite what some believe to be serious flaws in current approaches to the study of leadership (see "At Issue"), the basic idea that leader behavior is critical to subordinate satisfaction and productivity is central to many applied organization change programs. The most well-known of these approaches is the Managerial Grid© (Blake & Mouton, 1978), a management theory based on concern for people and concern for production. A copy of the Managerial Grid appears in Exhibit 11–8.

The Managerial Grid has nine degrees each of leader behaviors that encompass concern for the task at hand (horizontal axis) and concern

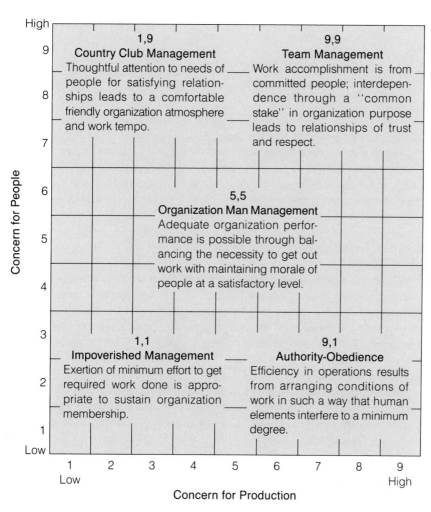

Note. The Managerial Grid figure from *The New Managerial Grid,* by Robert R. Blake and Jane Srygley Mouton. Houston: Gulf Publishing Company, Copyright 1978, page 11. Reproduced by permission.

EXHIBIT 11–8

The Managerial Grid©

for people (vertical axis). Various combinations of these behaviors produce leadership styles described in sometimes colorful terms. Exclusive concern with employees, for example, is termed *Country Club Management* (task or production, Level 1; people, Level 9). In all, there are 81 possible variations of the two dimensions (i.e., different leadership styles).

The Managerial Grid is the basis of an extensive organization development program that has been used successfully by many organizations. As usually implemented, it is not a contingency approach to leadership because the ideal manager is considered to be a 9/9 *(Team Management)* one. Specific tactics for change in any particular organization are based on the situation, however.

A summary of Grid Development and a review of relevant research may be found in Huse (1980). At this point, the influence of leadership variables on employee behavior and attitudes is examined.

LEADERSHIP INFLUENCES ON BEHAVIORS AND ATTITUDES AT WORK

An overview of the findings of leadership research with respect to behavior and attitudes at work is presented here. Much, but not all, of this research was carried out within the theoretical framework of Fiedler's Contingency Model or House's Path-Goal Theory. The focus in this discussion is not on evidence for or against any particular theory, however, and this research is treated as one line.

Leader Behavior and Job Performance

Much of the available research on the effects of leader behavior on work performance is based on questionnaires. These measure subordinates' perceptions of the extent to which those in formal leadership positions demonstrate a basic task or people orientation. These responses then are correlated with some measure or measures of job behavior or attitudes. A study by Sheridan and Vredenburgh (1979) illustrates this general approach.

Sheridan and Vredenburgh administered a series of questionnaires to measure both personal and job characteristics to over 200 nursing employees in a large hospital. One of these questionnaires, the Leader Behavior Description Questionnaire (Stogdill, 1963), provided measures of the extent to which nurses perceived their particular supervisors to exhibit task-centered and employee-centered behavior. Sheridan and Vredenburgh also collected a variety of data about subject behavior, including job performance. This performance was measured in terms of ratings made by the head nurses.

On the basis of their analytical procedures, Sheridan and Vredenburgh conclude that in their study, initiating structure (task-centered) behavior had no direct effect on nursing performance. By contrast, there appeared to be a *negative* relationship between extent of showing consideration (employee-centered behavior) and job performance; subordinates of head nurses who were perceived to be higher on consideration received lower performance ratings.

Although Sheridan and Vredenburgh's basic approach to the question of the relationship between leader style and job performance is consistent with most such research, their findings are not. In general, such investigations are more likely to show relationships between task-centered behaviors and job performance (Reitz, 1981).

Although reported employee-centered leadership style/job performance relationships are in the minority, those of Sheridan and Vredenburgh do not stand alone. Taken as a whole, this entire line of research may be said to support the contingency approach to leadership. Other things being equal, task-centered behaviors may have the greatest effect on employee performance, but other things seldom are equal. In their review of research stemming from the Ohio State studies, Kerr, Schriesheim, Murphy, and Stodgill (1974) identified 18 situational variables that may moderate this relationship. These variables are listed in Exhibit 11–9.

Moderator variable: See pages 97 to 99.

I. Characteristics of subordinates
   A. Competence
   B. Expectations about leader behavior
   C. Experience
   D. Expertise
   E. Job knowledge
   F. Job level

II. Characteristics of the leader
   A. The extent of his or her upward influence
   B. The extent to which his or her behavior and attitudes are similar to those at higher levels in the organization

III. Characteristics of the task
   A. Ambiguity of task
   B. Autonomy of worker
   C. External stress of work situation
   D. Importance of work
   E. Meaningfulness of work
   F. Permissible error rate
   G. Physical danger in job
   H. Scope of job
   I. Time pressures in work

EXHIBIT 11–9

Aspects of the Situation That Modify Relationships between Leader Style and Employee Behaviors and Attitudes

---

Note. Summarized from S. Kerr, C. A. Schriesheim, C. J. Murphy, and R. M. Stodgill, "Toward a Contingency Theory of Leadership Based upon the Consideration and Initiating Structure Literature." *Organizational Behavior and Human Performance*, 1974, *12*, pp. 62–82.

Leader Behavior and Subordinate Satisfaction

Research into the relationship between leader style and subordinate job satisfaction is similar to investigations of job performance. Results show a similar pattern in that the influence of moderator variables, such as those listed in Exhibit 11-9, appears to be strong. A major difference, however, lies in the fact that the nature and effects of such variables on the relationship between leader style and employee satisfaction appear to be more stable, allowing for more specific conclusions.

- In general, people-oriented behaviors on the parts of those in leadership positions are positively related to job satisfaction when tasks are relatively simple, structured, and/or unambiguous (e.g., Valenzi & Dessler, 1978; Greene, 1979).
- In general, task-oriented behaviors are positively related to satisfaction when tasks are perceived as complex, unstructured and/or ambiguous (e.g., Szilagyi & Sims, 1974; Schriesheim & DeNisi, 1981).

Significance: See pages 58 to 59.

An interesting refinement of the findings just summarized is suggested by Griffin's (1980) investigation carried out in one manufacturing unit of a large corporation. In a test of his model (which is shown in Exhibit 11-7), Griffin found confirmation for the prediction that leader behavior effects on satisfaction would be significant only when there was low congruence between individual growth needs and the demands of the task (Cells 2 and 3 in Exhibit 11-7).

Griffin's findings suggest that it is not specifically the nature of the task that moderates the leader style/job satisfaction relationship, but the extent to which the task suits or does not suit those who are performing it. This is entirely consistent with earlier discussions of selection, placement, and job design. Employee satisfaction with work is likely to be greater when there is a good job/individual match. The present discussion leads to the interesting possibility that what those in leadership positions do is more important when the match is poor than when it is good.

Leader Behavior and Absenteeism/Turnover

A 1978 study by Johns investigated the relationship between (a) absenteeism and expressed intentions to leave the company and (b) the people-versus-task leader styles House calls *showing consideration* and *initiating structure*. The study also examined job characteristics as possible moderators of these relationships. The characteristics included were:

- task variety
- job identity
- job significance
- job feedback from task
- job feedback from others
- job motivating potential

Subjects in the Johns study were all 700 operatives of a Canadian paper products plant. Results with respect to absenteeism did not support job characteristics as moderators of the leader style/employee behavior relationship. These results were clear on their own, however. Employee-centered leader behaviors were significantly and negatively correlated with absenteeism. In other words, subordinates of those in leadership positions who were perceived to be high on *showing consideration* were absent less than subordinates of other supervisors.

With respect to expressed turnover intentions, Johns' results confirmed expectations.

1. *Initiating structure* (task-oriented) leader style was significantly and negatively correlated with turnover intentions for employees whose jobs were *high* on the task characteristics named above.
2. *Showing consideration* (people-oriented) leader style was significantly and negatively correlated with turnover intentions for employees whose jobs were *low* on these characteristics.

These findings suggest that task-oriented behaviors offset turnover when jobs are "rich," and people-oriented behaviors have a similar effect on more routine jobs. This pattern is identical with the trend of research findings into the leader style/job satisfaction relationship, suggesting a connection between job satisfaction and turnover. This relationship is explored in Chapter 14.

Job enrichment: See pages 200 to 206.

Other evidence for a relationship between leader style and turnover generally is supportive of that reported by Johns. For example, Krackhardt, McKenna, Porter, and Steers (1981) found a significant relationship between turnover and supervisor-initiated communication, a behavior most perceive as employee-centered. Bank employees whose supervisors initiated regular communication sessions with individuals and groups had a lower turnover rate than those whose supervisors did not initiate such communication.

Leader Behavior and Group Decision Making

Although group behavior as such is not the subject of Chapter 11, the present discussion of leadership would be incomplete without some consideration of the effects of leader behavior on group decision making. The leader being discussed is an individual in a formal position of leadership. He or she may be the actual designated leader of the group or a group member who holds a leadership position in the organization that is higher than that of other group members.

The use of groups to make decisions and/or solve problems has become common practice in American organizations. Committees wrestle with where to build the new plant facility. Research and development teams try to come up with viable new products. Labor and management representatives form groups to brainstorm ways to improve labor relations. Groups of employees, such as those at Motorola, meet regularly to identify and solve efficiency-reducing problems.

The use of groups, such as those described, to make decisions or solve problems is predicated on two assumptions. The first is that group members will be more satisfied with the decisions or solutions than if these tasks were left to individuals and simply "handed down." The second is that groups will make better decisions or solve problems more effectively than individuals (Shaw, 1976).

The group decision-making literature in general supports the first of the assumptions listed above (e.g. Bragg & Andrews, 1973). The second one, however, rests on a number of further conditions. As mentioned earlier, one condition is that the nature of the task is suitable for a group (Kelley & Thibaut, 1969). The second is that the leadership of the group facilitates the free exchange of ideas, information, and perspectives required to take advantage of the greater potential resources of a group.

The influence of leader behavior on group decision making is discussed at some length in a classic article by Maier (1967). As Maier points out, a leader's position in such a group is both different and critical, whether or not he or she wishes it to be so. Among the leader behaviors noted by Maier that serve to facilitate better group decisions are:

- keeping the group discussion moving
- summarizing for the group at various points in time
- being sensitive to unexpressed feelings
- protecting minority points of view

Maier's analysis of the role of leader behavior in group decision making has been confirmed many times. Unless the person in the leader position combines the behavioral steps that Maier points out with a firm resolution to avoid pushing his or her own preferred decision, the group decision will most likely be more a reflection of the leader than of effective use of group resources. Of interest in this regard is the work of Janis (1972).

Janis describes a phenomenon he calls *groupthink*. Groupthink is characterized by ". . . a deterioration of mental efficiency, reality testing, and moral judgement that results from in-group pressures" (p. 9). Such a group is more concerned with presenting a united front than with arriving at a good solution to a problem or with making a good decision. This type of group is particularly vulnerable to the behavior of a strong leader. Janis illustrates the concept of groupthink with a number of examples from political and military history. In Exhibit 11–10, a brief discussion of one of these examples by two social psychologists (Tedeschi & Lindskold, 1976) is presented.

Janis believes the disastrous Bay of Pigs decision to have been a classic example of groupthink. President John F. Kennedy, a strong leader, exploited group needs for consensus as a means to discourage the discussion of dissenting opinions and to push for his personal perferred solution. Alternatively, Kennedy could have *countered* the groupthink syndrome by means of the steps outlined by Maier.

The work of Janis and of Maier is consistent with the general group decision-making literature in emphasizing the important role that a leader

President Kennedy's highly intellectual set of advisors were basking in the euphoria of invulnerability; everything had gone right since the opening of the Kennedy drive in 1956 to capture the 1960 Presidential election. It seemed that nothing could stop them from succeeding in implementing their plans, so they tended to ignore glaring defects in their thinking. The group had an assumed air of consensus. Several of the President's senior advisors had strong doubts about the Bay of Pigs planning, but the group atmosphere inhibited them from voicing criticism. Thinking became simplified into black-and-white, either-or terms. . . .

The way the meetings were conducted served to suppress dissent. When a point of criticism was raised, the President encouraged the CIA planners of the invasion to respond immediately to it. In a specific instance recounted by Janis [1972], Senator Fulbright raised strong objections to the plan and correctly predicted some of the adverse effects the invasion would have on American foreign relations. Rather than discuss Fulbright's criticism, the President returned to taking a straw vote of his advisors on the plan. The group maintained its consensus to support the plan, and Arthur Schlesinger, Jr., one advisor who was known to be in agreement with Fulbright, was not even called upon for his vote because time had run out.

EXHIBIT 11-10

Groupthink, Leadership, and the Bay of Pigs

Note. Excerpted from J. T. Tedeschi and S. Lindskold, *Social Psychology: Interdependence, Interaction and Influence.* New York: John Wiley & Sons, 1976. Copyright 1976 by John Wiley & Sons, Inc. Reprinted by permission of John Wiley & Sons, Inc.

has in a group. Yet, it must not be forgotten that leadership is a social influence process involving two parties. Just as leader characteristics and behaviors influence groups, so do the personal characteristics and behaviors of group members influence the leader; that is, there is reciprocal causation between leader and subordinate behavior.

RECIPROCAL CAUSATION: BRINGING LEADERSHIP FULL CIRCLE

In the present discussion, the term *reciprocal causation* refers to the influence that subordinates have on the way those in leadership positions attempt to influence them. As a simple example of this process, consider a boss who expresses as a hint what is intended as an order to subordinates to work late: "Well, if everyone would stay late tonight, we could get this mess cleared away." The subordinates, who may or may not understand the intent of the boss's communication, ignore the hint and go home at the usual time. The next night the boss leaves no room for doubt: "We're all staying here tonight as late as we have to to catch up on this work." The boss's original approach to influencing subordinates has been altered by their response.

Take the example further and suppose that the subordinates, now under order to stay late, grumble, and do not work very efficiently. In addition, several are late to work the next morning. This behavior also will influence the boss's future behavior. He or she may get even more "hard line," demanding still more overtime. Alternatively, the boss's whole idea of asking subordinates to work late may be given up as a poor one.

Someone interested in trying to help the boss figure out what went wrong might point out that the trouble started with the original communication from boss to subordinates. There is, in fact, a good deal of evidence, both anecdotal and other, to suggest that it is not so much what people in leadership positions say that causes them difficulty, but the way they say it. A laboratory study of communication patterns between subjects in leader roles and subjects in subordinate roles illustrates the reciprocal causation between initial communication and subsequent response (Watson, 1982).

The five types of communications studied by Watson are shown in Exhibit 11-11. Examination of the patterning of these responses revealed some interesting relationships. For example, it was found that when a subordinate initiated a *dominance* communication, the leader was most likely to reply with a *structuring* communication. When a subordinate initiated a *structuring* communication, however, the leader was equally likely to reply with a *deference* or *equivalence* communication.

Laboratory experiment: See pages 52 to 54.

The Watson study was done in a laboratory with only one "subordinate" per "leader," and a real-life leadership situation is usually far more complicated. The study illustrates an important point, however, with respect to leadership and reciprocal causation: In human interactions, one party has many responses to the behaviors and actions of another, and choice of response depends partly on what the first party does. This

EXHIBIT 11-11 Categories of Leader-Subordinate Communications	
1. Dominance (+1)	—attempt to severely restrict the behavioral options of others (e.g., abrupt topic change, disconfirmation of previous comment, ideational or personal challenge, personal nonsupport).
2. Structuring (1)	—attempt to restrict the behavioral options of others but leaving a variety of options open, such as the option to disagree (e.g., asserted opinion in response to a request for an opinion, asserted ideational extension, asserted procedural direction, disagreement, justification).
3. Equivalence (−)	—attempt at mutual identification, an interactional mode that does not seek to control the flow of interaction (e.g., repetition, restatement, expression of understanding, conditional agreement, incomplete utterance).
4. Deference (1)	—willingness to relinquish some behavioral options to others while retaining some choice of options (e.g., simple agreement, seeking information or opinions).
5. Submissiveness (+1)	—willingness to relinquish behavioral options to others while retaining little choice (e.g., personal support, nonextended idea).

Note. From K. M. Watson, "An Analysis of Communication Patterns: A Method for Discriminating Leader and Subordinate Roles." *Academy of Management Journal*, 1982, *25*(1), p. 111. Reprinted by permission of the author and the publisher.

process is continued indefinitely—the first party's choice of the next response depends partially on what the second party did and so on.

Reciprocal causation between leader and subordinate behavior is a complex phenomenon that is difficult to investigate scientifically in actual situations. This may be one reason that so much leadership research has the flavor of treating leadership as an independent variable; that is, as a pattern of behavior that differs between people, but remains consistent for one person regardless of subordinate characteristics or responses. An exception to this tendency is the Vertical Dyad Linkage Model.

The Vertical Dyad Linkage Model of Leadership

One formal approach to a leadership theory that emphasizes differences in the way a leader interacts with different subordinates is the Vertical Dyad Linkage Model (VDLM) proposed by Dansereau, Graen, and Haga (1974). In this model, an individual in a position of leadership forms a two-person group, or *dyad*, with each member of the group. Because the relationship is one of superior-subordinate, this dyad is a *vertical* one that *links* two levels of the organizational hierarchy together.

The VDLM makes a distinction between *leadership* and *supervision*. Leadership, or influence, is not exerted in a group-wide fashion, but grows out of each interpersonal dyad. By contrast, supervision is based primarily on the leader's formal position and power, and supervisory behavior is similar in concept to the dimension of task-directive behavior.

To date, most of the research with the VDLM has been carried out by Graen and colleagues (e.g., Graen & Schiemann, 1978; Liden & Graen, 1980). Results support the hypothesis that leaders do not treat all subordinates alike, nor do all subordinates have the same perceptions of, and reactions to, a leader.

Hypothesis: See page 47.

Mainstream leadership research long has been based on average perceptions of leadership behavior by subordinates. Early research with the VDLM suggests that this approach may be inadequate to the task of understanding the impact of leader behavior on individual employee responses to work. Certainly, more research based on the concept of reciprocal causation is warranted.

SUMMARY

Organizations are made up of groups, both formal and informal. Membership in these groups is an aspect of an employee's work social environment. This membership has particular relevance to his or her behavior if the group serves a personal reference function.

The basis for group influence on individual behavior is group norms, which serve to maintain the behavior of group members within limits that protect the cohesiveness of the group. In turn, group cohesiveness allows a group greater ability to influence its members' conformity to norms. Among the more important of these norms for the study of behavior in organizations are those relating to the means and quantity of work production.

Membership in groups also affects the satisfaction employees find with their work situation. Group interaction processes have been found to be related to absenteeism and turnover. Unions, as a special case of group membership with important norms that originate outside the organization, deserve more formal attention in the investigation of such relationships.

The study of leadership is focused on the influence of individuals on groups as opposed to the influence of groups on individuals. Whether they occupy formal leadership positions or emerge as leaders from interaction within the group, leaders occupy special positions.

Most contemporary leadership research focuses on the effects of different behavior patterns, or styles, of formal leaders on subordinate behavior and attitudes. The intent is to identify the situations under which certain kinds of leader behavior facilitate job performance and subordinate satisfaction. A different approach is based on the concept of leadership as a process, the outcome of which is affected by both leader and follower.

AT ISSUE

Can "Leadership" be Saved?

Over the past few years, the number of I/O psychologists and others interested in organizations who are questioning the direction of contemporary leadership research has been growing (e.g., Karmel, 1978; Davis & Luthans, 1979; McElroy, 1982). Some even question the utility of the whole concept of leadership for understanding the complexities of behavior in a social situation (Pfeffer, 1977). "If the interest [of the researcher] is in understanding the causality of social phenomena as reliably and accurately as possible, then the concept of leadership may be a poor place to begin" (p. 111).

One of the more organized challenges to traditional leadership research lies in a concept referred to in the literature as *substitutes for leadership* (Kerr, 1976). Substitutes for leadership are conditions that make specific kinds of leader behaviors unnecessary. Among the conditions that will substitute for *task-centered* leader behaviors are:

- subordinate knowledge of the work to be done (from experience, training, and so on)
- a professional orientation on the parts of subordinates
- organizational formalization of objectives, work schedules, and policies
- situations in which the actual work is routine, unvarying, and clear to all

Substitutes for *employee-centered* leader behaviors include intrinsically satisfying work tasks and a cohesive, supportive work group (Kerr, 1977).

Implicit in the lists of possible substitutes for leadership in organizations is the idea of *self-management.* Theoretically, if all of the above conditions held true, there would be no need for leaders in the sense suggested by most leadership research.

Self-management as a substitute for leadership is discussed from a social learning theory point of view by Manz and Sims (1980). From this perspective, the role of the individual in a leadership position becomes one of developing self-management in subordinates. A different slant on this same approach is to be found in the literature on autonomous work groups and socio-technical job design.

Research on substitutes for leadership is still somewhat limited, and results to date are mixed (e.g., Howell & Dorfman, 1981; Mills & Posner, 1982). Nevertheless, the handwriting appears to be on the wall; if "leadership" is indeed a viable concept in helping researchers to understand the behavior of people in organizations, those who study leadership must break free of the current narrow approach. It is time for new conceptualizations and methodologies that focus, not on leadership as something done to subordinates, but on leadership as ". . . a social influence process, operating within constraints" (Pfeffer, 1977, p. 111).

REFERENCES

ALDERFER, C. P., & SMITH, K. K. Studying intergroup relations embedded in organizations. *Administrative Science Quarterly,* 1982, 27(1), 35–65.

BENNIS, W. G., & SHEPARD, H. S. A theory of group development. *Human Relations,* 1965, 9, 415–457.

BLAKE, R. R., & MOUTON, J. S. *The New Managerial Grid.* Houston: Gulf, 1978.

BONOMA, T. V., & ZALTMAN, G. *Psychology for Management.* Boston: Kent, 1981.

BRAGG, J., & ANDREWS, I. Participative decision making: An experimental study in a hospital. *Journal of Applied Behavioral Science,* 1973, 9, 727–735.

CARTWRIGHT, D. The nature of group cohesiveness. In D. Cartwright and A. Zander (Eds.), *Group Dynamics: Research and Theory* (3rd ed.). New York: Harper & Row, 1968.

DANSEREAU, F., GRAEN, G., & HAGA, W. J. A vertical dyad linkage approach to leadership in formal organizations. *Organizational Behavior and Human Performance,* 1975, 13(1), 46–78.

DAVIS, T. R. V., & LUTHANS, F. Leadership reexamined: A behavioral approach. *Academy of Management Review,* 1979, 4(2), 237–248.

DENTLER, R. A., & ERIKSON, K. T. The functions of deviance in groups. *Social Problems,* 1959, 7(2), 98–107.

FELDMAN, D. C. The development and enforcement of group norms. *Academy of Management Review,* 1984, 9(1), 47–53.

FIEDLER, F. E. Engineer the job to fit the manager. *Harvard Business Review,* 1965, 43(5), 115–122.

FIEDLER, F. E. Validation and extension of the Contingency Model of Leadership Effectiveness: A review of empirical findings. *Psychological Bulletin,* 1971, 76(2), 128–148.

GIBB, C. A. Leadership. In G. Lindzey and E. Aronson (Eds.), *Handbook of Social Psychology* (Vol. IV). Reading, MA: Addison-Wesley, 1969. 205–282.

GRAEN, G., & SCHIEMANN, W. Leader member agreement: A vertical dyad linkage approach. *Journal of Applied Psychology,* 1978, 63, 206–212.

GREENE, C. N. Questions of causation in the Path-Goal Theory of Leadership. *Academy of Management Journal,* 1979, 22(1), 22–41.

GRIFFIN, R. W. Task-design determinants of effective leader behavior. *Academy of Management Review,* 1979, 4(2), 215–224.

GRIFFIN, R. W. Relationships among individual, task design, and leader behavior variables. *Academy of Management Journal,* 1980, 23(4), 665–683.

HAMMER, T. H. Relationships between local union characteristics and worker behavior and attitudes. *Academy of Management Journal,* 1978, 21(4), 560–577.

HEMPHILL, J. K. *Leader Behavior Description.* Columbus, OH: Ohio State University Press, 1950.

HOLLANDER, E. P. *Leaders, Groups, and Influence.* New York: Oxford University Press, 1964.

HOUSE, R. J. A Path-Goal Theory of Leader Effectiveness. *Administrative Science Quarterly,* 1971, 16(1), 19–30.

HOWELL, J. P., & DORFMAN, R. W. Substitutes for leadership: Test of a construct. *Academy of Management Journal,* 1981, 24(4), 714–728.

HUSE, E. F. *Organization Development and Change* (2nd ed.). St. Paul: West, 1983.

JACKSON, J. A conceptual and measurement model for norms and roles. *Pacific Sociological Review,* 1966, 9(1), 35–47.

JANIS, I. L. *Victims of Groupthink.* Atlanta: Houghton Mifflin, 1972.

JEWELL, L. N., & REITZ, H. J. *Group Effectiveness in Organizations.* Glenview, IL: Scott, Foresman, 1981.

JOHNS, G. Task moderators of the relationship between leader style and subordinate reponses. *Academy of Management Journal,* 1978, 21(2), 319–325.

KARMEL, B. Leadership: A challenge to traditional research methods and assumptions. *Academy of Management Review,* 1978, 3(3), 475–482.

KATZ, D., MACCOBY, N., & MORSE, N. C. *Productivity, Supervision, and Morale in an Office Situation.* Ann Arbor, MI: University of Michigan, 1950.

KELLEY, H. H., & THIBAUT, J. W. Group problem solving. In G. Lindzey and E. Aronson (Eds.), *The Handbook of Social Psychology.* (Vol. IV). Reading, MA: Addison-Wesley, 1969.

KENNY, D. A., & ZACCARO, S. J. An estimate of variance due to traits in leadership. *Journal of Applied Psychology,* 1983, *68*(4), 678–685.

KERR, S. Substitutes for leadership. *Proceedings of the American Institute for Decision Sciences,* 1976.

KERR, S. Substitutes for leadership: Some implications for organizational design. *Organization and Administrative Sciences,* 1977, *8*(1), 135–146.

KERR, S., SCHRIESHEIM, C. A., MURPHY, C. J., & STOGDILL, R. M. Toward a contingency theory of leadership based upon the consideration and initiating structure literature. *Organizational Behavior and Human Performance,* 1974, *12,* 62–82.

KIESLER, C. A., & KIESLER, S. B. *Conformity.* Reading, MA: Addison-Wesley, 1969.

KRACKHARDT, D., McKENNA, J., PORTER, L. W., & STEERS, R. M. Supervisory behavior and employee turnover: A field experiment. *Academy of Management Journal,* 1981, 24(2), 249–259.

LANDY, F. J., & TRUMBO, D. A. *Psychology of Work Behavior* (rev. ed.). Homewood, IL: Dorsey Press, 1980.

LEWIN, K., LIPPITT, R., & WHITE, R. K. Patterns of aggressive behavior in experimentally created "social climates." *Journal of Social Psychology,* 1939, *10*(2), 271–299.

LIDEN, R. C., & GRAEN, G. Generalizability of the Vertical Dyad Linkage Model of Leadership. *Academy of Management Journal,* 1980, 23(3), 451–465.

MAIER, N. R. F. Assets and liabilities in group problem solving: The need for an integrative function. *Psychological Review,* 1967, 74(4), 239–249.

MANZ, C. C., & SIMS, H. P., JR. Self-management as a substitute for leadership: A social learning theory perspective. *Academy of Management Review,* 1982, 7(3), 413–417.

McELROY, J. C. A typology of attribution leadership research. *Academy of Management Review,* 1982, 7(3), 413–417.

MILLS, P. K., & POSNER, B. Z. The relationships among self-supervision, structure, and technology in professional service organizations. *Academy of Management Journal,* 1982, 25(2), 437–443.

MOSSHOLDER, K. W., BEDEIAN, A. G., & ARMENAKIS, A. A. Group process-work outcome relationships: A note on the moderating impact of self-esteem. *Academy of Management Journal,* 1982, 25(3), 575–585.

PFEFFER, J. The ambiguity of leadership. *Academy of Management Review,* 1977, 2(1), 104–111.

REITZ, H. J. *Behavior in Organizations* (rev. ed.). Homewood, IL: Richard D. Irwin, 1981.

RITTI, R. R., & FUNKHOUSER, G. R. *The Ropes to Skip and the Ropes to Know.* Columbus, OH: GRID, Inc., 1977.

ROETHLISBERGER, F. J., & DICKSON, W. J. *Management and the Worker.* Cambridge, MA: Harvard University Press, 1939.

ROSENBAUM, L. L., & ROSENBAUM, W. B. Morale and productivity consequences of group leadership style, stress, and type of task. *Journal of Applied Psychology,* 1971, *55,* 343–348.

ROY, D. F. "Banana Time"—Job satisfaction and informal interaction. *Human Organization,* 1959–60, *18*(4), 158–168.

SCHACHTER, S. Deviation, rejection, and communication. *Journal of Abnormal and Social Psychology,* 1951, 46(2), 190–207.

SCHRIESHEIM, C. A., & DeNISI, A. S. Task dimensions as moderators of the effects of instrumental leadership: A two-sample replicated test of Path-Goal leadership theory. *Journal of Applied Psychology,* 1981, *66*(5), 589–597.

SCHRIESHEIM, J. F., & SCHRIESHEIM, C. A. A test of the Path-Goal Theory of Leadership and some suggested directions for future research. *Personnel Psychology,* 1980, *33*(2), 349–370.

SEASHORE, S. *Group Cohesiveness in the Industrial Work Group.* Ann Arbor, MI: Institute for Social Research, 1954.

SHAW, M. E. *Group Dynamics: The Psychology of Small Group Behavior.* New York: McGraw-Hill, 1976.

SHERIDAN, J. E., & VREDENBURGH, D. J. Structural model of leadership influence in a hospital organization. *Academy of Management Journal,* 1979, *22*(1), 6–21.

SIMPSON, E. L. Motorola's participative management. *Management World,* 1983, (July), 19–29.

STOGDILL, R. M. *Manual for the Leader Behavior Description Questionnaire—Form XII.* Columbus, OH: Ohio State University, 1963.

STRUBE, M. J., & GARCIA, J. E. A meta-analytic investigation of Fiedler's Contingency Model of Leadership Effectiveness. *Psychological Bulletin,* 1981, *90*(2), 307–321.

SZILAGYI, A. D., & SIMS, H. P., JR. An exploration of the Path-Goal Theory of Leadership in a health care environment. *Academy of Management Journal,* 1974, *17*(4), 622–634.

TEDESCHI, J. T., & LINDSKOLD, S. *Social Psychology: Interdependence, Interaction, and Influence.* New York: John Wiley & Sons, 1976.

TUCKMAN, B. W. Developmental sequence in small groups. *Psychological Bulletin,* 1965, *63,* 384–399.

VALENZI, E., & DESSLER, G. Relationships of leader behavior, subordinate role ambiguity, and subordinate job satisfaction. *Academy of Management Journal,* 1978, *21*(4), 671–678.

VROOM, V. H., & JAGO, A. G. On the validity of the Vroom-Yetton model. *Journal of Applied Psychology,* 1978, *63*(1), 151–162.

VROOM, V. H., & MANN, F. C. Leader authoritarianism and employee attitudes. *Personnel Psychology,* 1960, *13,* 125–140.

VROOM, V., & YETTON, P. W. *Leader Decision Making.* Pittsburgh: University of Pittsburgh Press, 1975.

WATSON, K. M. An analysis of communication patterns: A method for discriminating leader and subordinate roles. *Academy of Management Journal,* 1982, *25*(1), 107–120.

CHAPTER 12

Motivation

CHAPTER CONTENTS

I/O PSYCHOLOGY AT WORK

Thinking Bureaucrat Awarded $13,942

TALLAHASSEE (AP)—Clifford "Sonny" Hay will end his career in the massive state Department of Transportation with proof that he was a thinking bureaucrat.

Hay has won the fattest check yet in a state program aimed at spurring bright ideas among government employees.

Hay, 65, who devised a new method to compensate property owners forced to sell because of roadway construction, received a state bonus of $13,942 last week.

The award was based on 10 percent of the statewide savings during the first year Hay's idea was used. Part of the prize money will help retire his 1968 Plymouth, he said.

In a week, Hay himself will retire after 14 years at the giant transportation agency.

"You know, up until this happened, I was just a bit apprehensive about retiring," he told the *Tallahassee Democrat.* "You just start wondering if you'll have enough."

Excerpted from "Thinking Bureaucrat Awarded $13,942." Jacksonville *Times-Union and Journal,* 1982, (January 24).

Sonny Hay is the happy beneficiary of a state program that encourages employees to think creatively about new ways of doing things in their jobs. Hay was *rewarded* for a specific *desired behavior*—coming up with an idea that will save the Florida Department of Transportation money.

Incentives often are used to increase employee effort, or work motivation. Incentives work best when they are of a nature that is valued by the employees concerned. For Hay, who was about to retire, a substantial monetary incentive was effective in helping him develop an idea that the state of Florida expects will save it almost $140 thousand dollars the first year. In turn, Hay expects his bonus to make retirement considerably easier.

The principle of rewarding desired behavior is central to the issue of work motivation, but it raises many questions. What is a reward? How can it be connected to the desired behavior in such a way as to make it an effective motivator? What other conditions are necessary to increase employee work motivation? How does the process work conceptually? These and other questions are addressed in Chapter 12.

THE ROLE OF MOTIVATION IN WORK PERFORMANCE

The term *motivation* is one that is encountered frequently in the management and I/O psychology literature. It is given a variety of definitions (see, for example, Steers & Porter, 1979), but all incorporate the idea that motivation explains what people do and how much effort they put into it.

Although *motivation* can be defined, it cannot be *seen*. It is a *construct* —a term that is used to explain observed patterns in behavior. For example, when someone takes a job in sales and works very hard at selling, it might be said that he or she is "motivated to become a successful salesperson." In other words, motivation is *inferred* on the basis of observed behavior.

When people work hard and perform their jobs well, whatever they may be, it is inferred that their work motivation is high. When people do not seem to try hard or perform well, it often is assumed that their work motivation is low. Such inferences are only partially correct, however, because motivation is only one of the factors that determine work behavior.

For some time, work performance has been conceptualized as the result of an interaction between ability and motivation. This conceptualization usually is referred to as the *performance equation:* $P = f(A \times M)$. The problem with this equation is that it ignores the environment of the employee. In terms discussed in Chapter 2, ability and motivation are both individual variables. All behavior, including work performance, results from an interaction of these variables with the environment of the individual.

A more complete model of the determinants of work performance is presented in Chapter 13, which is devoted to work performance and its measurement. Motivation is an important variable in that model and warrants separate discussion, but it should be kept in perspective. There are a number of conditions under which motivation is one of the least important determinants of work performance.

One of the more obvious situations in which motivation is relatively unimportant as a determinant of performance occurs when the individual involved lacks the basic ability required to do the job. A high level of motivation may compensate somewhat for limited ability, but cannot make up for it entirely. As Dunnette (1973) points out, the available empirical data make it clear that ability is still the most important factor explaining differences in job performance. In terms discussed in Chapter 3, ability accounts for more of the *variance* in job performance than does motivation.

Motivation also can be less important than environmental factors in determining job performance. Some jobs, such as work on an assembly line, are designed in order to minimize the role of employee effort. Some is required, but more effort can improve performance only up to the limit set by the job. In other cases, employee effort may be of little importance as a determinant of performance because work objectives are not clear or because there are obstacles to performance, such as

Motivation refers to the sum of the forces that produce, direct, and maintain effort expended in particular behaviors.

Construct: See page 80.

Inference: See page 58.

Behavior causation: See pages 27 to 28.

Variance explained: See page 64.

insufficient information or outdated work aids (Peters & O'Connor, 1980).

Even if motivation is not the single most important determinant of work performance, it is important enough to be of great concern to those who manage organizations; interest in how to "motivate people" is always high. Actions and decisions taken for this purpose may be referred to collectively as the *reward system* of an organization. This reward system is part of the *social environment* of the organization's employees, and perceptions of its appropriateness and fairness are an important part of perceptions of organizational climate.

Social environment: See page 35.

Organizational climate: See pages 285 to 290.

The practical problems of motivation are of interest to I/O psychologists as well as to managers; but to understand how to cope with them, those concerned must understand the forces that produce, direct, and maintain effort. Some psychologists have approached the question of observed differences in how much work effort people expend and where they expend it from the viewpoint of internal states that drive behavior. As a group, the resulting statements may be called *need theories of work motivation*.

Other I/O psychologists have examined work motivation from a decision-making perspective. They have attempted to identify and describe the variables that affect employees' decisions to put forth various levels of effort in certain situations. These may be called *cognitive theories*. Finally, some psychologists have taken an empirical *reinforcement approach* to motivation. From this perspective, effort in a work setting is determined by whether or not employees have been rewarded for their efforts in the past.

NEED THEORIES OF WORK MOTIVATION

Need theories of motivation are based on the premise that people exert effort in behaviors that allow them to fill deficiencies in their lives; that is, people exert effort to meet their needs. The best-known of these theories, as far as work behavior is concerned, is that put forth by Maslow (1943).

Maslow's Need Hierarchy

Maslow, a clinical psychologist, postulated that people have a common set of five needs and these may be arranged in a hierarchy of importance, or *prepotence*. This concept is shown in Exhibit 12–1.

The most basic needs, the ones that people must satisfy first, are physiological needs, as shown in Exhibit 12–1. Such needs are followed in importance by safety, social, and esteem needs. At the top of the hierarchy is a postulated need for self-fulfillment. According to Maslow's

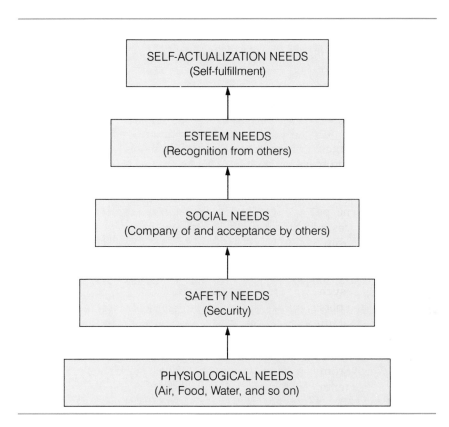

EXHIBIT 12–1

Maslow's Hierarchy of Needs

theory, each need in the hierarchy must be satisfied in turn. Once satisfied, that need ceases to motivate behavior, and the next one up the hierarchy becomes prepotent.

Applied to a work setting, Maslow's theory means that people at work will exert effort to fill the *lowest* unsatisfied needs. For example, someone just starting out may be working primarily for money to pay off educational debts and to provide food and shelter, that is, to meet physiological and safety needs. This individual would be expected to work hard for a raise in pay because this would help to meet those needs. Someone else may have prepotent social needs and be working primarily to meet needs for friendship and a sense of belonging.

Practical applications of Maslow's theory have focused on upper-level need fulfillment through the psychological approach to job design. As discussed in Chapter 7, the basic principle behind this approach is that interesting and challenging work, which incorporates substantial worker control, allows people an opportunity to meet their needs for esteem and self-acutalization. From a need-theory approach to motivation, if people can meet such needs through work they will expend more effort in the work situation. The idealized model of a job that incorporates these features is the individual craftsperson. A portion of one such individual's description of his work is excerpted in Exhibit 12–2.

Psychological approach to job design: See pages 195 to 207.

EXHIBIT 12–2

Work with the "Motivators Built In"

As my hands press the plane forward, a smooth shaving curls up from the keen edge, filling the air with the tangy scent of fresh-cut pine.

There is a soothing rhythm to the strokes of the plane and a delightful uniqueness in each spiraled shaving.

My chisel and mallet seek some more-organic form hidden within a block of Hawaiian koa wood. The power saw that cut the block is no respector of the flowing lines of light and dark that mark the pattern of growth. Sometimes, when my efforts at seeking the life-lines in the wood succeed, the form seems to take on a liveliness reminiscent of the forces that shaped the once tall and supple tree.

Now, as I seek to shape my life in more flexible, natural ways, the schools and offices that claimed so many of my years seem like a buzz saw that cut me into blocks irrespective of the life forms hidden within.

There are so many joys in my new vocation I wonder that I did not find it sooner. Perhaps, my life had to be cut into blocks in order for me to know that was not the form I sought. Yet, there are connections, too. The enjoyment I once got from organizing ideas and programs and peace marches I now find in planning the sequence of tasks and gathering materials to build a table. It is satisfying to see my hands transforming boards and glue into functional and even beautiful objects.

Working for myself I have a flexibility and a discipline that is rarely found in offices that structure work into eight-hour days and fifty-week years. I find freedom within my work, not just during my "time off." Even when I choose to discipline myself to eight-hour days, I feel more free knowing that I am choosing that schedule, either as self-discipline or so I can conveniently work with others. I struggle, when working for myself, to find a balance between demanding regular eight-hour days of myself in order to earn money, learn new skills, and do quality work, on the one hand, and taking time to play with my family, on the other.

I have time between jobs for other activities. I can take a day off each week to build projects for my own pleasure. In fact, the line between work and play blurs because I have such fun at my work. Tools become toys when I go to play in the shop.

As a free-lance woodworker I work for myself or for a client with whom I have some personal contact. The client knows that it is I and not some impersonal factory or machine creating the product. Both praise and criticism come directly to me. Expectations for the form and quality of the job are set by me, alone or in dialogue with the client. In either case I participate directly in setting expectations for my work, and thereby find myself committed to them. This brings pleasure when the product meets the standard and anguish when I sometimes fall short. As in any demanding personal endeavor, part of myself becomes invested in my work, so that I am happy when it is going well and sometimes depressed when I do poorly.

Note. From C. Mosher. "Woodworker." This article first appeared in *The Humanist* issue of January/February, 1975. Reprinted by permission.

Herzberg's Two-Factor Theory

Herzberg's Two-Factor Theory of Motivation (1966) is based on a division of Maslow's five-category list of needs into upper and lower needs. It is postulated that only conditions allowing people to fill upper-level needs for esteem and self-actualization increase work motivation. An organization must allow employees to meet lower-level needs through work, but this is primarily a way to keep them with the company, not to influence their work motivation.

In the Two-Factor Theory of Motivation, working conditions that allow people to meet upper-level needs are called *motivators* and those that are relevant to lower-level needs are called *hygiene factors*. Among the motivator factors identified by the theory are achievement, recognition, responsibility, opportunity to advance, and interesting work.

Hygiene factors, according to the Two-Factor Theory, include working conditions, type of supervision, relations with coworkers, company policies, and pay. As might be expected, this dichotomy, based on an extensive study of some 200 accountants and engineers, is controversial. Although it has not stood up well to empirical tests, this theory was a significant stimulus to work motivation research in the years following its appearance.

Alderfer's ERG Theory

Yet another theory of work motivation based on Maslow's need hierarchy was proposed by Alderfer (1972). Alderfer, in his ERG Theory, hypothesizes three sets of needs ranging from most basic, or *concrete*, to least concrete. These needs, existence (E), relatedness (R), and growth (G) are essentially only another rearrangement of Maslow's hierarchy. The rigid ordering of that hierarchy, however, is not part of ERG theory.

In Maslow's conception, an individual's primary effort is expended in behaviors that will satisfy the lowest level of unsatisfied needs. Once these have been fulfilled, they no longer motivate the individual. Until then, these needs remain the major driving force behind behavior. According to Alderfer, if an individual's efforts to satisfy needs at one level are continually frustrated, he or she may fall back, or *regress*, to behavior that meets more concrete needs. For example, an employee who is unable to find a way to meet personal growth needs on the job may settle for performing it in order to meet lower social (relatedness) needs.

McClelland's Need for Achievement Theory

A need theory approach to work motivation that is not based on Maslow was proposed by McClelland (1961). *Need for Achievement* (usually abbreviated to *N'Ach*) is hypothesized to be a learned need, developed in childhood. Other things being equal, people who have a high level of this need are more motivated to put effort into work than people who do not. This motivating desire for achievement, however, is balanced against a desire to avoid failure (Atkinson & Feather, 1966) so behavior may be directed at goals of intermediate, rather than high, difficulty.

A unique feature of the need for achievement approach to work motivation is the hypothesis that people who have a low level of this need can be trained to develop it (McClelland & Winter, 1969). This aspect removes much of the deterministic flavor of other need theories of work motivation from this approach.

Need Theories of Work Motivation and Research

Maslow's theory was published some 40 years ago, and both it and its derived theories subsequently excited considerable research interest. This research has died out almost entirely due to persistent nonsupport for this approach. A review of this research may be found in Wahba and Bridwell (1973).

The need for the achievement approach to work motivation has fared somewhat better from an empirical standpoint. There does seem to be a relationship between measures of this need and certain work behaviors, such as an employee staying with a job longer (e.g., Rhode, Sorenson, and Lawler, 1976). Despite its label, however, this approach is not truly representative of the need theory approach to work motivation. Both the idea that there is some selectivity of activity based on probability of success and the idea that people can be *trained* in this need tend to set it apart.

A high need for achievement often is found in successful people.

COGNITIVE THEORIES OF WORK MOTIVATION

Need theories of motivation postulate that the forces that initiate, direct, and maintain behavior are inner states of deprivation; people have needs and they behave in ways at work (and elsewhere, it should be noted) to meet these needs. Cognitive theories of motivation do not deny that people have needs, but the *drive* concept implicit in need theory is replaced by a *cognitive* element.

From a cognitive perspective, complex decision-making processes of weighing alternatives, costs, and benefits, and likelihood of achieving desired outcomes underlie motivation. This approach predates need theory by at least a decade (e.g., Tolman, 1932). Cognitive theories of work motivation, however, did not achieve a place of significance in the I/O literature until the 1960s. Three such theoretical approaches are discussed here—expectancy theories, balance theories, and goal-setting approaches to work motivation.

General Expectancy Theory

Of the cognitive approaches to work motivation that have been proposed, a group variously called *perceptual theories, VIE theories,* and *expectancy theories* have been the most influential. The first such model was proposed by Vroom (1964) and subsequently was modified by a number of researchers (e.g., Porter & Lawler, 1968; Campbell, Dunnette, Lawler, & Weick, 1970). The term *general expectancy theory* is used here to reflect these multiple influences on this approach to work motivation.

The general expectancy theory of work motivation is based on the premise that it is the *expectation* that effort exerted in a particular direction will lead to desired outcomes that determines motivation. A model of this approach is shown in Exhibit 12–3.

The model in Exhibit 12–3 shows four determinants of motivation that interact in a multiplicative fashion to produce an observed level of effort. *The Effort-Performance Expectancy* is a belief (expressed in formal statements as a probability ranging from zero to 1.00) that effort will pay off in performance. This belief is heavily influenced by a person's perceptions of his or her job-related skills and knowledge and by the support provided by working conditions, coworkers, and so on.

Probability: See pages 58 to 59.

The *Performance-Outcome Expectancy* is a similar probability concept, but it relates to the belief that performance will be followed by certain outcomes. These first-level outcomes include everything from raises, promotions, and a sense of accomplishment to recognition, more work, and longer hours. Expectancies as to which of these sorts of outcomes are likely to follow particular levels of employees' performance depend to a considerable degree on what happens to others and on employees' personal experiences in the past.

Instrumentality is a concept reflecting the extent to which the first-level outcomes that result from performance are useful, or *instrumental,*

EXHIBIT 12–3

A Generalized
Expectancy Model
of Motivation

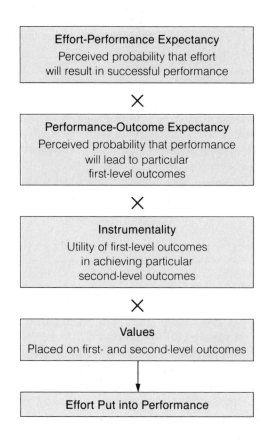

Note. Based on the discussion by D. A. Nadler and E. E. Lawler, III, ''Motivation: A Diagnostic Approach,'' in R. M. Steers and L. W. Porter (Eds.), *Motivation and Work Behavior* (2nd ed.). New York: McGraw-Hill, 1979.

in attaining certain second-level outcomes. For example, a bonus (first-level outcome) may be the means by which an employee can raise his or her status in the home community (a second-level outcome) by joining a prestigious country club.

Both first- and second-level outcomes of effort have values (sometimes called *valences)* associated with them. *Value* refers to the personal attractiveness of an outcome. For example, the raise (first-level outcome) that goes with a promotion may have a high value because it is instrumental in achieving valued second-level outcomes for the employee, such as a better standard of living. The promotion has other outcomes for the employee, however, such as longer working hours, that he or she may value negatively.

Together, the Effort-Performance Expectancy, the Performance-Outcome Expectancy, and the values placed on first- and second-level outcomes for which they are instrumental, determine motivation to exert effort in a particular direction. Motivation will be highest when two conditions are met.

- The Effort-Performance Expectancy is high.
- The Performance-Outcome Expectancy of receiving one or more valued first- and second-level outcomes is high.

When expectancies are lower and/or outcomes have low or negative value, motivation will be reduced accordingly. Consider two middle managers in a large corporation as an illustration of this concept. Both managers are bright and well educated. Both place a high value on promotion up the company ladder (a first-level outcome of effort) and the esteem they believe this advancement will bring them (a second-level outcome).

Both of these hypothetical managers believe they can perform well if they put forth the effort (have high Effort-Performance Expectancies). The difference between the two is in their Performance-Outcome Expectancies. Manager A believes that doing well will lead to promotion (high expectancy). Manager B believes that promotions in this company depend more on "getting in good with the boss" than on performance (low expectancy). The general expectancy model, therefore, would predict substantially greater job effort from Manager A than from Manager B.

Expectancy Theory and Research

Expectancy theories have generated considerable research, and a number of hypotheses derived from this approach have been supported. In one frequently-cited study, for example, Georgopoulos, Mahoney, and Jones (1957) confirmed the hypothesis that workers who reported higher Performance-Outcome Expectancies would perform at a higher level than those with lower expectancies. These authors found a positive correlation between level of production and perceived instrumentality of work performance for achieving (a) more pay, (b) promotion, and (c) acceptance into the work group. Subjects were employees in a factory making household appliances.

Hypothesis: See page 47.

Research also has offered some support for the hypothesis that the Effort-Performance Expectancy is associated with level of production. In one experimental study, for example, Arvey (1972) manipulated this expectancy by means of what subjects were told about the likelihood of being among the top performers in a group. As hypothesized, subjects in the high expectancy condition (likelihood of 75%) performed better on the experimental task than subjects in the low expectancy condition (likelihood of 20%).

Despite successful results, such as those reported, there is no empirical evidence for general expectancy models of motivation in their entirety. In the words of Campbell and Pritchard (1979), this model is ". . . a simple appearing formulation that encompasses a highly complex and poorly understood set of variables and variable dynamics" (p. 243). Among the associated research difficulties are:

- the large number of outcomes and associated values that may be perceived by an individual as associated with performance;
- the difficulties in putting numbers on the probabilities of these outcomes and their values;
- the many factors that can affect the Effort-Performance and Performance-Outcome Expectancies;
- the complex "mental arithmetic" process implied by the model.

The problems that surround efforts to test general expectancy approaches to motivation make this the most difficult of the various approaches to evaluate empirically. Many believe, however, that expectancy theory is theoretically sound, and work directed toward overcoming methodological difficulties in order to make it more amenable to testing is in progress (e.g., Shiflett & Cohen, 1980).

Balance Theory: Adams' Equity Theory

The basic premise behind balance theories of work motivation is that people attempt to keep a balance between the effort they put into work and what they get out of it. The most widely-researched version of this approach to motivation is Adams' Equity Theory (1965). According to Adams' formulation, people make a cognitive comparison of their contribution to a work situation (their inputs) and the things they get out of it (their outcomes) with those of other people. Among the important inputs are skills and knowledge, experience, time on the job, and education/training; outcomes include pay, status, and job level.

The basic comparison process of Equity Theory looks as follows:

$$\frac{\text{Self-outcomes}}{\text{Self-inputs}} \quad \text{Versus} \quad \frac{\text{Other Outcomes}}{\text{Other Inputs}}$$

If the term connecting the two sides of the equation above is "equal to," there is equity and the individual will continue the current level of effort and performance. Inequity occurs whenever the two ratios are unequal. Inequality that favors the individual making the comparison is seen as affecting his or her effort as well as inequality that favors the relevant other or others.

The "relevant others" used as a standard in balance theory is a concept similar to that of *reference group* discussed in Chapter 11. That is, it is an individual, psychological concept. For many people, the relevant others are coworkers in the same organization known (or believed) to have about the same qualifications and experience. Other people may compare themselves with members of a professional group, with what they believe is an industry standard, or even with members of their own families.

Reference group: See page 312.

According to Equity Theory, a perceived imbalance of self–outcomes/inputs relative to others leads an individual to make attempts to restore the balance. One way to do this to make a change in the amount of

	Underpayment	Overpayment
Hourly payment	Subjects underpaid by the hour produce less or poorer-quality output than equitably paid subjects	Subjects overpaid by the hour produce more or higher-quality output than equitably paid subjects
Piece-rate payment	Subjects underpaid by piece rate will produce a large number of low-quality units in comparison with equitably paid subjects	Subjects overpaid by piece rate will produce fewer units of higher quality than equitably paid subjects

EXHIBIT 12-4

Equity Theory Predictions of Employee Reactions to Inequitable Payment

Note. From R. T. Mowday, "Equity Theory Predictions of Behavior in Organizations." In R. M. Steers and L. W. Porter (Eds.), *Motivation and Work Behavior* (2nd ed.). New York: McGraw-Hill, 1979, p. 129. Copyright 1979 by McGraw-Hill. Reprinted with permission.

work effort (input) expended. Exhibit 12–4 shows the effort adjustments predicted by Equity Theory under inequitable conditions defined in terms of amount of payment for work.

Two unbalanced conditions are given in Exhibit 12–4. *Underpayment* is a situation in which outcomes are perceived to be less than contributions, and Equity Theory predicts that work quantity and/or quality will go down in this case, depending upon the basis for payment. By contrast, *overpayment* is an unbalanced situation in which outcomes are perceived to outweigh contributions. In this case, it is predicted that quality and/or quantity of work will be increased.

A review of the relevant research indicates considerable support for Equity Theory predictions about changes in work motivation under perceived conditions of imbalance between inputs and outcomes (e.g., Adams & Freedman, 1976). It should be noted, however, that Equity Theory also allows for other ways to correct imbalance. Instead of adjusting effort, the individual may adjust his or her evaluation of the balance.

Adjusting the evaluation of input/output equity may be accomplished in a number of ways. Self-inputs may be revised downward or self-outcomes revised upward. Alternatively, other inputs and outputs may be reevaluated. For example, an individual getting paid less than a coworker perceived to have the same skills may give more weight to that worker's seniority; in this way, the coworker gets credit for more inputs and so is entitled to more money (higher outcome) for doing the same work. Extreme imbalances that cannot be handled by such *cognitive restructuring* or by adjustments in effort may lead the individual to quit the job (Adams, 1965).

Locke's Goal-Setting Approach to Work Motivation

The idea that human behavior has purpose is the central tenet of goal-setting approaches to motivation. People set goals for themselves and are motivated to work toward these goals because achieving them is rewarding. The best-known application of this idea to work motivation is that of Locke (1968). The basic proposition of this approach is that people who set themselves higher work goals (or accept such goals as set by others) perform at a higher level.

There are many laboratory experiments to support the hypothesis that harder goals are associated with better performance than easier goals. Field research also has been supportive, especially of the proposition that goals themselves are critical to motivation. Whatever the nature of the research, it seems clear that specific goals are more effective than vague "do-your-best" instructions. The study summarized in "Spotlight on Research" illustrates this line of research.

SPOTLIGHT ON RESEARCH

Effects of Goal Specificity and Performance Feedback to Work Groups on Leadership, Performance, and Attitudes

Research hypothesis: The introduction of specific work goals and performance feedback will be associated with increases in the production of first-quality goods.

Field experiment: See page 52.

Type of study: Field experiment.

Subjects: One hundred fifty female sewing machine operators performing the 34 operations involved in assembling and inspecting pairs of pants. The average age of the subjects was 26 to 30 years; most had been with the company between six months and one year, and most had a high school education.

Independent / dependent variable: See page 52.

Independent variable: Performance goals. Operational definition: (a) *Poor,* (b) *Good,* and (c) *Excellent* quality goals as set by actual performance in another plant.

Dependent variable: Quality data. Operational definition: The percent of substandard ("seconds") production.

General procedure: At the time of intervention, feedback as to the achievement of goals was provided daily on large plexiglass boards. Quality data were collected for 12 months before and 12 months after this intervention.

Results: As seen in the following graph, the hypothesis was supported. There was a 66% improvement in "seconds" rate after the experimental intervention.

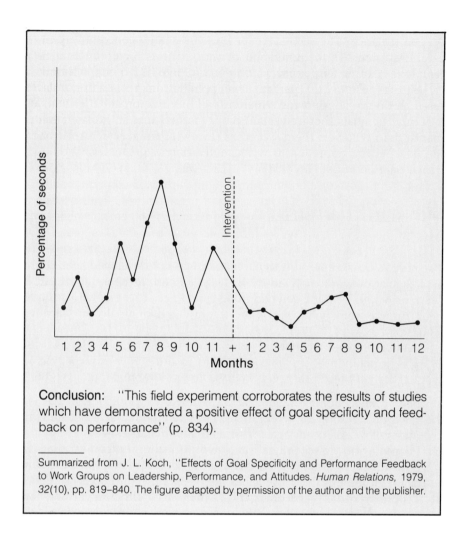

Conclusion: "This field experiment corroborates the results of studies which have demonstrated a positive effect of goal specificity and feedback on performance" (p. 834).

Summarized from J. L. Koch, "Effects of Goal Specificity and Performance Feedback to Work Groups on Leadership, Performance, and Attitudes. *Human Relations*, 1979, 32(10), pp. 819–840. The figure adapted by permission of the author and the publisher.

The plant used in the study from which "Spotlight on Research" is taken afforded an ideal opportunity to investigate the effect of goals and feedback on performance. Prior to the experiment, the plant employees had operated on the basis of sporadic, unfocused feedback and "do-your-best" performance goals. As shown in the graph, the introduction of specific goals and specific feedback (the intervention) produced a dramatic drop in finished items of inferior quality ("seconds").

As a check on a possible Hawthorne Effect, Koch (1979) gave employees at a sister plant (to the one used in the experiment) attention in the form of attitude questionnaires and expressed interest in quality data. There was no experimental intervention and no production improvement at that plant. Koch also noted that the dependent variable was free of contamination from the effects of having attention focused on inspection since "quality cannot be inspected into a garment."

The study in "Spotlight on Research" illustrates one main line of goal-setting research—the effect of specific goals and their difficulty level

Hawthorne Effect: See page 5.

on performance. The second major line of research generated by goal-setting approaches to motivation concerns the relative effects of self (employee), other (supervisor), and participative (joint) goal setting.

With respect to work performance, results from goal-setting process research do not support the superiority of any one process. In general, it seems the goals themselves are more important to improved performance than who sets them. A recent review of the research relative to the goal-setting approach to work motivation is presented by Locke, Shaw, Saari, and Latham (1981).

THE REINFORCEMENT MODEL OF WORK MOTIVATION

The reinforcement approach to motivation was not developed specifically as a theory of work motivation. In fact, it is not a theory at all but a set of principles relating behavior to its outcomes. These principles have been drawn from behavioral data accumulated originally in learning laboratory settings.

As an approach to work motivation, the reinforcement model consists of an extrapolation of learning principles to the behavior of people at work. Three of these principles are basic to work motivation.

Behavior outcome: See pages 30 to 32.

1. People keep doing things that have rewarding outcomes; that is, rewards *reinforce*, or strengthen, the likelihood that the behavior they follow will occur again in similar circumstances.
2. People avoid doing things that have punishing outcomes; that is, punishment *reduces* the likeliness that the behavior it follows will occur again, at least in the presence of the punishing conditions or agent.
3. People eventually stop doing things that have neither rewarding nor punishing outcomes; that is, behavior that has neutral outcomes will be *extinguished* sooner or later.

As a theory of work motivation, the reinforcement model is quite simple. Since people continue to behave in ways that have been reinforced, effort at work is a direct function of the extent to which connections between work behaviors and rewards have been built up and strengthened.

From a reinforcement perspective, work motivation depends upon the extent to which work behaviors have been *reinforced* in the past. If working hard and doing what was expected was rewarded, the individual will continue these behaviors. If, on the other hand, the outcomes of work effort were perceived to be punishing, effort will be reduced. Effort also will be reduced, but more gradually, when work effort seems to be neither rewarded nor punished. A simple model of this process is shown in Exhibit 12–5.

The reinforcement model shown in Exhibit 12–5 is a backward-looking model. With respect to work performance, it is not incentives as such that produce effort, but the fact that these incentives have been delivered in the past when a certain level of performance was achieved. Although

EXHIBIT 12-5

A Reinforcement
Model of Motivation

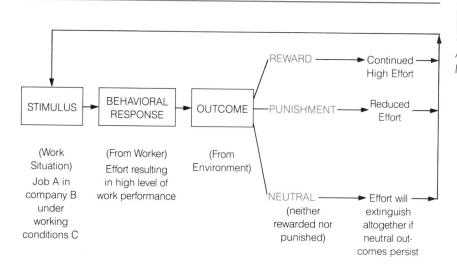

expectancy theory also recognizes the importance of what has happened in the past, this is only one of the factors affecting beliefs about what will happen in the future, and the expectancy model is a forward-looking model.

A pure reinforcement model approach to work motivation, such as that shown in Exhibit 12-5, is based on the effects on work effort of reinforcement from the environment, that is, on *extrinsic reinforcement* that comes from others. Such reinforcement is provided by informal rewards, such as praise or recognition, as well as from formal organizational rewards, such as bonuses or promotions.

Most I/O psychologists believe that *intrinsic reinforcement* is also important to work motivation; some believe it is more important (Deci, 1972). This type of reward, however, which includes feelings of pride, accomplishment, and satisfaction that result from a person's work, does not play any formal role in the reinforcement model. Research on this model is focused on external reinforcement; increasing work motivation is a matter of observing and rewarding desired behavior in order to build up a *positive reinforcement history.*

It is not practical to reward every show of effort and every desired behavior on the part of every employee in a company every time it occurs; nor is it necessary. Studies of the timing of rewards, or *reinforcement schedules,* show that much behavior will persist for quite a long time if it is *occasionally* reinforced. The effects of occasional rewards, or *intermittent reinforcement,* on worker performance are shown in Exhibit 12-6.

As shown in the fourth graph of Exhibit 12-6, very high levels of performance can be maintained by rewarding at uneven intervals that average out to be after every 10 units of work. For example, a manager might take time to compliment a secretary's good work after 5 days, again after another 15, and again after another 10—every 10 days on the

EXHIBIT 12–6

Performance under
Various Schedules
of Reinforcement

1. Fixed interval schedule of reinforcement

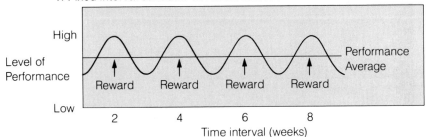

Note: Performance average lower than for a variable schedule and fluctuation in performance higher than under variable interval schedule.

2. Variable interval schedule of reinforcement

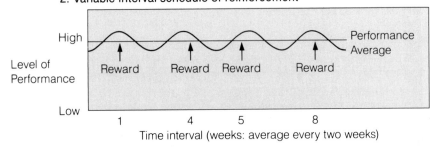

3. Fixed ratio schedule of reinforcement

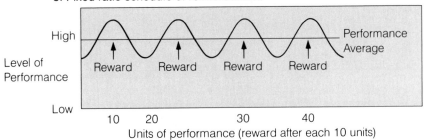

Note: Performance average lower and fluctuation greater than variable ratio schedule but superior to interval schedule.

4. Variable ratio schedule of reinforcement

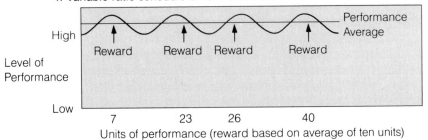

Note. From D. W. Organ and W. C. Hamner, *Organizational Behavior: An Applied Psychological Approach* (rev. ed.). Plano, TX: Business Publications, Inc., 1982, p. 55. Copyright 1982 by Business Publications, Inc. Reprinted by permission.

Being able to see successful results of their efforts is powerful positive reinforcement for many workers.

average. Although such an automated approach to reinforcement is not advocated, the point is critical. There should be *some* reinforcement for desired work behavior.

The Reinforcement Model and Research

In testing the reinforcement model of work motivation, researchers must determine whether or not principles of behavior derived from quite different settings generalize to behavior in organizations. Generally the answer has been in the affirmative. For example, Luthans, Paul, and Baker (1981) found a significant improvement in three aspects of the sales performance of retail clerk subjects when paid time off and other rewards depended upon their work performance. There was also a significant drop in absenteeism among these subjects.

The most famous example of the reinforcement model at work is probably the Emery Air Freight case (see *Organizational Dynamics*, 1973). Among other applications of these principles, a positive reinforcement program to encourage employees to make full use of containers on each shipment saved the company well over a half million dollars a year—indeed a significant savings a decade ago. A review of other relevant studies may be found in Babb and Kopp (1978). A guide to implementing this approach is described by Hamner and Hamner (1976).

Comment on Theories of Work Motivation

The approaches to the study of work motivation reviewed in the preceding sections may be considered the leading theoretical statements of the forces that initiate, direct, and maintain people's behavior at work. As far as empirical evidence is concerned, there is no basis for the clear superiority of any of these approaches. Each has strengths and weaknesses as a theory, and each has both successes and failures in application.

Conceptually, the theories of motivation reviewed are not mutually exclusive although they are different. Each focuses on different variables, and the likelihood that all are relevant to work motivation is leading an increasing number of I/O psychologists to push for an integrated approach (e.g., Fedor & Ferris, 1981). Consistent with this view, the remainder of Chapter 12 presents a nonpartisan discussion of some practical implications of the various motivation theories for organizational application.

THE APPLIED IMPLICATIONS OF MOTIVATION THEORIES

Some of the more important applied implications of the various theories of work motivation are discussed here. These are presented, not as motivation techniques, but as a set of hypotheses about raising the overall motivation level of organizational employees through coordinated personnel and management policies. No technique-based approach for solving motivation problems will be successful in the long run unless the system as a whole is directed toward and supportive of increased employee effort.

Hypotheses Based on Need Theories of Motivation

Although need theories of motivation fare poorly as theories, they do have implications for increasing employee effort, primarily through selection policies and job design.

> ONE. *Selection, placement, and promotion practices that include the self-diagnosed needs of applicants/employees in the decision-making process will have a positive effect on the overall level of employee effort in an organization.*

Whatever their specific premises, as a group, need theories offer clues about what people will find rewarding enough to direct effort toward. To the extent that people can appreciate *in advance* the likelihood that a particular job will give them an opportunity to meet what they see as their own needs, some individual/job/organization mismatches may be avoided. The overall level of effort in the organization may be expected to rise as the number of such mismatches falls.

The basic mechanisms for attempting to improve the match of individuals to jobs with respect to needs already have been mentioned. As discussed in Chapter 9, I/O psychologists are becoming more aware that a thorough job analysis will include the opportunities and rewards offered by a job as well as the tasks and responsibilities it entails.

The Realistic Job Preview (RJP), discussed in Chapter 5, may be another way to help job applicants evaluate the likelihood of a job meeting what they see as their needs. The effectiveness of RJPs appears to be subject to many constraints, but they do have potential for reducing honest mistakes made on the basis of incomplete information about what a job can offer.

RJP: See pages 133 to 134.

> TWO.   *Job design and job redesign strategies guided by psychological as well as physical and efficiency-oriented concerns will have a positive effect on the overall level of employee effort in an organization.*

Trying to design jobs to meet postulated upper-level needs is the most common application of need theory in organizations. As discussed in Chapter 7, *job enlargement* and *job enrichment* programs have had both successes and failures. Success seems to be moderated by individual differences with respect to (a) preference for interesting, challenging work, and (b) perceptions of the kind of work that *is* interesting, challenging, and satisfying (e.g., O'Connor, Rudolf, & Peters, 1980).

Job enlargement: See pages 196 to 199.

Job enrichment: See pages 200 to 206.

The role played by individual differences in determining the effectiveness of job enlargement and job enrichment limits their potential as solutions to effort *problems,* even if the jobs involved can be changed. A policy of designing and/or redesigning jobs to be more interesting and challenging as the opportunity to do so arises, however, will offer more scope for employees who want such jobs.

Hypotheses Based on Expectancy Theories of Motivation

The research difficulties presented by expectancy theories of work motivation do not alter the fact that this approach is rich in practical implications for influencing employee effort. Four hypotheses relative to these implications are discussed here.

> THREE.   *Selection, placement, and promotion practices that match ability (in the form of basic ability to be trained) or experience/knowledge/skills to job requirements will have a positive effect on the overall level of employee effort in an organization.*

Since job-related abilities are the traditional basis for screening, Hypothesis 3 is not a new idea. The possible effects of this matching on motivation (as well as on capabilty) often have been overlooked, however. This clarification of the role that ability plays in motivation is one of the more important contributions made by expectancy theories to date.

In expectancy theories, the key to the role of ability in motivation lies in the Effort-Performance Expectancy. A low expectancy means in effect, "Even if I exert substantial effort, it is unlikely that I can perform well enough to get the incentives I am being offered." In many cases, then, "lack of motivation" may reflect a belief that effort will not compensate for a person's perceived inadequacies in his or her job-related ability. This possibility leads directly to the next implication of expectancy theory for motivation.

FOUR. A formal job training program for all jobs will have a positive effect on the overall level of employee effort in an organization.

The role that such concrete activities as selection and training may play in affecting employee effort is often overlooked. In fact, training is related to motivation in several ways. Trainee motivation is often high at first, and the quality of the training program may either reinforce or reduce this motivation. More specifically, the Effort-Performance Expectancy concept in expectancy theory suggests that confidence acquired during training may be an important influence on the effort that people put into job tasks (if the training is seen as relevant).

A person's lack of confidence in being able to do a job well may affect his or her effort directly in a "what's the use?" fashion described earlier. It also may affect effort through the influence of the social environment. No one likes to look incompetent to others, and lack of effort is one way people can defend themselves against this possibility. This idea may be summed up as: "I could do it if I tried, but who cares?"

FIVE. Comfortable and appropriate physical working conditions and the provision of adequate tools, work aids, information, and other resources will have a positive effect on the overall level of employee effort in an organization.

The physical work environment is discussed extensively in Chapters 7 and 8. The issue here, again an issue raised by the concept of an Effort-Performance Expectancy, is whether or not this environment *supports* employee effort. A "what's the use?" attitude can be fostered by the realization that conditions make the desired performance impossible, as well as by the lack of ability or training. Among these conditions are time pressures, lack of space or privacy, inadequate or outdated work aids, and insufficient information, human resources, raw materials, or other resources (Peters & O'Connor, 1980).

SIX. A good performance appraisal system will have a positive effect on the overall level of employee effort in an organization.

It is difficult to overestimate the importance of a good performance appraisal system to organizational functioning. By *good* is meant a method that:

- is job, rather than personality, related
- is used by people who have been trained to do so
- is understood and perceived as fair by those being evaluated

Performance appraisal, like training, has a number of links with motivation. The most obvious is that the possibility of getting a good evaluation can serve as an *incentive* to a worker to perform well, and the receipt of this favorable appraisal can serve as *reinforcement* for the effort by which the worker achieved it. Expectancy theory also suggests that performance appraisal is a source of *information* relative to the Effort-Performance Expectancy component of motivation.

Performance appraisal tells an employee how the results of his or her effort are perceived by others. If all-out effort is continually followed by average evaluations, the employee's Effort-Performance Expectancy and level of motivation may be lowered. (Alternatively, the unsatisfactory evaluations may be attributed to supervisor bias, a poor appraisal method, or other nonperformance factors.)

In addition to providing information about the Effort-Performance Expectancy, performance appraisal also provides information about the *instrumentality* of job performance for attaining valued outcomes. Performance appraisal results are often the basis upon which companies allocate such organizational rewards as raises, promotions, and desirable career opportunities. If, for any reason, these appraisals do not make meaningful distinctions between individual job performance levels, an important link is broken. For the good performance of an employee to be instrumental in helping that employee to achieve rewards, it must be noticed and recognized as good performance. If it is not, employee effort will be reduced accordingly.

Hypotheses Based on Goal-Setting Approaches to Motivation

One implication of goal-setting approaches to work motivation already has been discussed.

SEVEN.   Clear goals that can be measured are more effective than vague do-your-best instructions in raising the overall level of employee effort in an organization.

This hypothesis is the basis for one very popular application of goal-setting theory to organizations—Management by Objectives (MBO; Drucker, 1954).

MBO is a complex, multistep goal-setting and performance appraisal process used primarily at the management level in organizations. The core of this process, as explained by Drucker in Exhibit 17-7, is an up-and-down the line mutual understanding of specific goals and performance expectations. A review of the theory, research, and application of MBO may be found in Albrecht (1978).

EXHIBIT 12–7

Drucker on
Management by
Objectives

In this letter to his superior, each manager first defines the objectives of his superior's job and of his own job as he sees them. He then sets down the performance standards which he believes are being applied to him. Next, he lists the things he must do himself to attain these goals—and the things within his own unit he considers the major obstacles. He lists the things his superior and the company do that help him and the things that hamper him. Finally, he outlines what he proposes to do during the next year to reach his goals. . . .

The "manager's letter". . . brings out whatever inconsistencies there are in the demands made on a man by his superior and by the company. Does the superior demand both speed and high quality when he can get only one or the other? And what compromise is needed in the interest of the company? Does he demand initiative and judgment of his men but also that they check back with him before they do anything? Does he ask for their ideas and suggestions but never uses them or discusses them? . . . Does it expect a manager to maintain high standards of performance but forbid him to remove poor performers? Does it create the conditions under which people say: "I can get the work done as long as I can keep the boss from knowing what I am doing."?

Note. Abridged and adapted from Peter F. Drucker, *The Practice of Management.* New York: Harper & Row, 1954, pp. 129–130. Copyright 1954 by Peter F. Drucker. Reprinted by permission of Harper & Row Publishers, Inc.

EIGHT.   Work objectives that are sufficiently difficult to be challenging will have a positive effect on the overall level of employee effort in an organization.

Hypothesis 8 is not precise because there is at least one basic theoretical disagreement about the relationship between goal difficulty and motivation. Locke (1968), it can be recalled, presents evidence that difficult goals are more effective. On the other hand, Atkinson and Feather's (1966) work with people's need for achievement suggests that greater effort will be put into goals that are neither too easy nor so hard as to be perceived as unattainable (see also, Forward & Zander, 1971). Both theories and relevant research, however, are in agreement that very easy goals do not stimulate increased effort.

Hypotheses Based on the Reinforcement Model of Motivation

Since the basic tenet of the reinforcement model is that people exert effort in behaviors that have been rewarded, the implications of this model have to do exclusively with rewards.

NINE.   Rewards for desired behavior will have a positive effect on the overall level of employee effort in an organization.

One of the more striking aspects of general organizational functioning to those who are trying to help solve organizational problems is the extent to which behaviors desired by management are ignored. This is true of job performance and extends to other important behaviors as well. Among these are:

- reliable attendance
- punctuality
- helping others
- creative behavior
- compliance with rules, regulations, and standard operating procedures

It must be assumed that managers' rationale for ignoring desired employee behaviors at work is a belief that employees *should* do these things; that is, that these behaviors are part of the obligation that goes with employment. From this perspective, it might be argued that employees who (a) are kept on by the company, (b) receive whatever rewards are attached to formal performance evaluations, and (c) experience the satisfaction of doing their jobs well are sufficiently reinforced in these desired behaviors. Although this may be true for some people, the lateness, absenteeism, turnover, and mediocre performance records in many companies suggest strongly that it is not true for everyone.

Ignoring desired work behaviors is not the only way in which organizations fail to take advantage of the basic principles of the reinforcement model of motivation. It also is not uncommon to find employees being rewarded for *undesired* behaviors. In Exhibit 12–8, the excerpt from a well-known article on the misunderstanding and misuse of rewards in organizations illustrates this point.

In the policies of the insurance firm as described by Kerr (1975), three examples of rewarding undesired behavior and discouraging desired behavior may be seen. In Section I of Exhibit 12–8, the desired behavior is accuracy in making insurance claim payments, but the measure of accuracy is the number of complaint letters received. Since overpaid clients seldom complain, a claims clerk is rewarded for inaccuracy in such cases.

In Section II of Exhibit 12–8, the desired behavior is "outstanding performance." The odds of receiving such an evaluation, however, are very slim, and the difference between the merit increase for this category and the next lowest is only 1%. Effectively, the rewarded behavior is average performance. (It is called "above average," but note that almost all employees are put into this category).

In Section III of Exhibit 12–8, the desired behavior is good performance, but since about the only way an employee can fail to receive a 4% "merit increase" is by absenteeism and/or lateness, the rewarded behavior is "coming to work on time every day."

Concluding Remarks on Applied Implications of Motivation Theories

The hypotheses about increasing employee effort, or motivation, set forth in Chapter 12 are drawn in a straightforward fashion from the theoretical and research literature on work motivation. At the applied level, they may be seen as strategies for taking a long-term proactive

EXHIBIT 12–8

Backfiring
Reward Systems

Whether dealing with monkeys, rats, or human beings, it is hardly controversial to state that most organisms seek information concerning what activities are rewarded, and then seek to do . . . those things, often to the virtual exclusion of activities not rewarded. The extent to which this occurs of course will depend on the perceived attractiveness of the rewards offered, but neither operant nor expectancy theorists would quarrel with the essence of this notion.

Nevertheless, numerous examples exist of reward systems that are fouled up in that behaviors which are rewarded are those which the rewarder is trying to *discourage,* while the behavior he desires is not being rewarded at all. . . .

BUSINESS RELATED EXAMPLES

An Insurance Firm

I.   Attempting to measure and reward accuracy in paying surgical claims [a large eastern insurance company] . . . systematically keeps track of the number of returned checks and letters of complaint received from policyholders. However, underpayments are likely to provoke cries of outrage from the insured, while overpayments often are accepted in courteous silence. . . . the new hire in more than one claims section is soon acquainted with the informal norm: "When in doubt, pay it out!"

II.   Annual "merit" increases are given to all employees in one of the following three amounts:

1. If the worker is "outstanding" (a select category, into which no more than two employees per section may be placed): 5 percent.

2. If the worker is "above average" (normally all workers not "outstanding" are so rated): 4 percent.

3. If the worker commits gross acts of negligence and irresponsibility for which he might be discharged in many other companies: 3 percent.

III.   [There is a] rule which states that, should absences or latenesses total three or more in any six-month period, the entire 4 or 5 percent due at the next "merit" review must be forfeited.

Note. Excerpted from S. Kerr, "On the Folly of Rewarding A, While Hoping for B." *Academy of Management Journal,* 1975, *18*(4), pp. 769–783. Reprinted by permission of the author and the publisher.

view of motivation by incorporating what is known about the subject into the ongoing functions of an organization.

The motivational impact of the strategies outlined will be gradual. This impact also should be cumulative because the greater the coordination and integration of the relevant activities with respect to their motivational implications, the greater the impact should be. The various links in this chain are diagramed in Exhibit 12–9, which also serves as a summary of the hypotheses about work motivation presented in this section.

EXHIBIT 12-9

An Integrated
Approach to
Influencing
Employee Effort

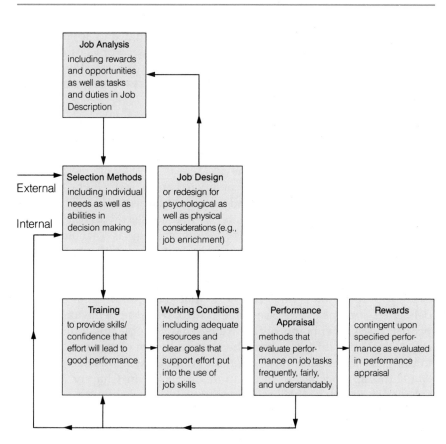

SUMMARY

The term *motivation* is a construct use to explain observed differences in what people do and in how much effort they put into these behaviors. Work motivation is of great interest to organizations because generally the more effort put into the behaviors associated with a job, the better the performance.

There are currently three mainstream approaches to understanding work motivation. Need theories take the position that behavior is determined by a drive to fill certain postulated human needs. Cognitive theories emphasize the decision to exert effort in certain ways. Expectancy theories see this decision as determined by the expectation that the effort will result in performance instrumental to achieving certain desired outcomes. Other cognitive approaches emphasize the role of goals and reward equity. The third approach, the reinforcement model, considers motivation to be a function of past outcomes of effort.

The various approaches to understanding work motivation all have contributions to make to theory and practice, but none is adequate alone. An integrated approach is needed if both knowledge and application of that knowledge is to advance beyond the current state. A practical approach to this integration in applied settings would incorporate the relevant aspects of each theory into a coordinated human resource program.

Note on a Special "At Issue"

The following "At Issue" consists entirely of excerpts from one of the most famous debates in the history of psychology. The protagonists are psychotherapist Carl Rogers and learning theorist B. F. Skinner. The issue is the control of human behavior.

Behavior control: See page 26.

As discussed in Chapter 2, the ability to control is the highest level at which human behavior can be understood, and this is the level at which applied psychologists must operate. In that sense, the debate that follows is applicable to the science of I/O psychology as a whole. *Control* is an emotionally-loaded word, however, and its possible negative connotations seem to arise most frequently in discussions of motivation.

There is no doubt that making decisions and taking actions for the express purpose of getting people to put more effort into work is a deliberate attempt to exercise some control over the behavior of those people. As Skinner points out, however, many people find it uncomfortable to look at it this way; thus the closer a theory of motivation comes to being explicit about control, the more controversy it seems to generate.

Of the approaches to motivation discussed in Chapter 12, need theories appear to be the least controlling, and the reinforcement model appears to make the least effort to disguise the control element. Thus, these two approaches tend to draw the lines in debates about the ethics of efforts to motivate people in a work situation. B. F. Skinner, the most famous and outspoken proponent of the reinforcement model, and Carl Rogers, the leading proponent of the human need and right to self-actualization, are uniquely qualified to speak to the control issues that lie behind these lines.

AT ISSUE

The Control of Human Behavior

I (SKINNER)

Science is steadily increasing our power to influence, change, mold—in a word, control —human behavior. It has extended our "understanding". . . so that we deal more successfully with people in nonscientific ways, but it has also identified conditions or variables which can be used to predict and control behavior in a new, and increasingly rigorous, technology. . . .

Now, the control of human behavior has always been unpopular. Any undisguised effort to control usually arouses emotional reactions. We hesitate to admit, even to ourselves, that we are engaged in control, and we may refuse to control, even when this would be helpful, for fear of criticism. . . .

The dangers inherent in the control of human behavior are very real. The possibility of the misuse of scientific knowledge must always be faced. We cannot escape by denying the power of a science of behavior or by arresting its development. It is no help to cling to familiar philosophies of human behavior simply because they are more reassuring. . . .

If the advent of a powerful science of behavior causes trouble, it will not be because science itself is inimical to human welfare but because older conceptions have not yielded easily or gracefully. We expect resistance to new techniques of control from those who have heavy investments in the old, but we have no reason to help them preserve a series of principles that are not ends in themselves but rather outmoded means to an end. What is needed is a new conception of human behavior which is compatible with the implications of a scientific analysis. All men control and are controlled. The question of government in the broadest possible sense is not how freedom is to be preserved but what kinds of control are to be used and to what ends. Control must be analyzed and considered in its proper proportions.

II (ROGERS)

I believe that in Skinner's presentation . . . there is a serious underestimation of the problem of power. To hope that the power which is being made available by the behavioral sciences will be exercised by the scientists, or by a benevolent group, seems to me like a hope little supported by either recent or distant history. . . . If behavioral scientists are concerned solely with advancing their science, it seems most probable that they will serve the purposes of whatever individual or group has the power.

But the major flaw I see in this review of what is involved in the scientific control of human behavior is the denial, misunderstanding, or gross underestimation of the place of ends, goals, or values in their relationship to science. . . .

I would point out . . . that to choose to experiment is a value choice. Even to move in the direction of perfectly random experimentation is a value choice. To test the consequences of an experiment is possible only if we have first made a subjective choice of a criterion value. . . . So even when trying to avoid such choice, it seems inescapable that a prior subjective value choice is necessary for any scientific endeavor, or for any application of scientific knowledge. . . .

It is my contention that science cannot come into being without a personal choice of the values we wish to achieve. And these values we choose to implement will forever lie outside of the science which implements them; the goals we select, the purposes we wish to follow, must always be outside of the science which achieves them. To me this has the encouraging meaning that the human person, with his capacity of subjective choice, can and will always exist, separate from and prior to any of his scientific undertakings. Unless as individuals and groups we choose to relinquish our capacity of subjective choice, we will always remain persons, not simply pawns of a self-created science.

III (SKINNER)

If we are worthy of our democratic heritage we shall, of course, be ready to resist any tyrannical use of science for immediate or selfish purposes. But if we value the achievements and goals of democracy, we must not refuse to apply science . . . even though we may then find ourselves in the position of controllers. Fear of control, generalized beyond any warrant, has led to a misinterpretation of valid practices and the blind rejection of intelligent planning for a better way of life. In terms which I trust Rogers will approve, in conquering this fear we shall become more mature and better organized and shall, thus, more fully actualize ourselves as human beings.

REFERENCES

ADAMS, J. S. Inequity in social exchange. In L. Berkowitz (Ed.), *Advances in Experimental Social Psychology* (Vol. II). New York: Academic Press, 1965.

ADAMS, J. S., & FREEDMAN, S. Equity theory revisited: Comments and annotated bibliography. In L. Berkowitz and E. Walster (Eds.), *Advances in Experimental Social Psychology* (Vol. IX). New York: Academic Press, 1976.

ALBRECHT, K. *Successful Management by Objectives.* Englewood Cliffs, NJ: Prentice-Hall, 1978.

ALDERFER, C. P. *Existance, Relatedness, and Growth Needs in Organizational Settings.* New York: Free Press, 1972.

ARVEY, R. D. Task performance as a function of perceived effort-performance and performance-reward contingencies. *Organizational Behavior and Human Performance,* 1972, 8(4) 423-433.

ATKINSON, J. W., & FEATHER, N. T. *A Theory of Achievement Motivation.* New York: John Wiley & Sons, 1966.

BABB, H. W., & KOPP, D. G. Application of behavior modification in organizations: A review and critique. *Academy of Management Review,* 1978, 3(2), 281-293.

CAMPBELL, J. P., DUNNETTE, M. D., LAWLER, E. E., III, & WEICK, K. E., JR. *Managerial Behavior, Performance, and Effectiveness.* New York: McGraw-Hill, 1970.

CAMPBELL, J. P., & PRITCHARD, R. D. Research evidence pertaining to expectancy-instrumentality-valence theory. In R. M. Steers and L. W. Porter (Eds.), *Motivation and Work Behavior* (2nd ed.). New York, McGraw-Hill, 1979, 229-245.

DECI, E. L. The effects of contingent and non-contingent rewards and controls on intrinsic motivation. *Organizational Behavior and Human Performance,* 1972, 8(2), 217-229.

DUNNETTE, M. D. *Performance equals ability and what?* (Tech. Rep. No. 4009). Minneapolis: University of Minnesota, Center for the Study of Organizational Performance and Human Effectiveness, 1973.

DRUCKER, P. F. *The Practice of Management.* New York: Harper & Row, 1954.

FEDOR, D. R., & FERRIS, G. R. Integrating OB Mod with cognitive approaches to motivation. *Academy of Management Review,* 1981, 6(1), 115-125.

FORWARD, J., & ZANDER, A. Choice of unattainable group goals and effects on performance. *Organizational Behavior and Human Performance,* 1971, 6(2), 184-199.

GEORGOPOULOS, B. S., MAHONEY, G. M., & JONES, N. W. A path-goal approach to productivity. *Journal of Applied Psychology,* 1957, 41, 345-353.

HAMNER, W. C., & HAMNER, E. P. Behavior modification on the bottom line. *Organizational Dynamics,* 1976, 4(1), 2-21.

HERZBERG, F. *Work and the Nature of Man.* Cleveland: World, 1966.

JACKSONVILLE *TIMES-UNION AND JOURNAL.* Thinking bureaucrat awarded $13,942. January 24, 1982.

KERR, S. On the folly of rewarding A, while hoping for B. *Academy of Management Journal,* 1975, 18(4), 769-783.

KOCH, J. L. Effects of goal specificity and performance feedback to work groups on peer leadership, performance, and attitudes. *Human Relations,* 1979, 32(10), 819-840.

LOCKE, E. A. Toward a theory of task motivation and incentives. *Organizational Behavior and Human Performance,* 1968, 3(2), 157-189.

LOCKE, E. A., SHAW, K. N., SAARI, L. M., & LATHAM, G. P. Goal setting and task performance: 1969-1980. *Psychological Bulletin,* 1981, 90(1), 125-152.

LUTHANS, F., PAUL, R., & BAKER, D. An experimental analysis of the impact of contingent reinforcement on salespersons' performance behavior. *Journal of Applied Psychology,* 1981, 66(3), 314-323.

MASLOW, A. H. A theory of motivation. *Psychological Review,* 1943, 50(4), 370-396.

McCLELLAND, D. C. *The Achieving Society.* Princeton, NJ: D. Van Nostrand, 1961.

McCLELLAND, D. C., & WINTER, D. C. *Motivating Economic Achievement.* New York: Free Press, 1969.

MOSHER, C. Woodworker. *The Humanist*, 1975, *1*, 36–37.

MOWDAY, R. T. Equity theory predictions of behavior in organizations. In R. M. Steers and L. W. Porter (Eds.), *Motivation and Work Behavior* (2nd ed.). New York: McGraw-Hill, 1979, 124–146.

NADLER, D. A., & LAWLER, E. E., III. Motivation: A diagnostic approach. In R. M. Steers and L. W. Porter (Eds.), *Motivation and Work Behavior* (2nd. ed.). New York: McGraw-Hill, 1979.

O'CONNOR, E. J., RUDOLF, C. J., & PETERS, L. H. Individual differences and job design reconsidered: Where do we go from here? *Academy of Management Review*, 1980, *5*(2), 249–254.

ORGAN, D. W., & HAMNER, W. C. *Organizational Behavior: An Applied Psychological Approach* (rev. ed.). Plano, TX: Business Publications, 1982.

ORGANIZATIONAL DYNAMICS. At Emery Air Freight: Positive reinforcement boosts performance. 1973, *1*(3), 41–50.

PETERS, L. H., & O'CONNOR, E. J. Situational constraints and work outcomes: The influences of a frequently overlooked construct. *Academy of Management Review*, 1980, *5*(3), 391–397.

PORTER, L. W., & LAWLER, E. E. *Managerial Attitudes and Performance.* Homewood, IL: Dorsey Press, 1968.

RHODE, J. G., SORENSON, J. E., & LAWLER, E. E., III. An analysis of personal characteristics related to professional staff turnover in public accounting firms. *Decision Sciences*, 1976, *7*, 771–800.

ROGERS, C. R., & SKINNER, B. F. Some issues concerning control of human behavior: A symposium. *Science*, 1956, *124*(3231), 1057–1066.

SHIFLETT, S., & COHEN, S. L. Number and specificity of performance outcomes in the prediction of attitudes and behavioral intentions. *Personnel Psychology*, 1980, *33*(1), 137–150.

STEERS, R. M., & PORTER, L. W. (Eds.). *Motivation and Work Behavior* (2nd ed.). New York: McGraw-Hill, 1979.

TOLMAN, E. C. *Purposive Behavior in Animals and Men.* New York: Century, 1932.

VROOM, V. H. *Work and Motivation.* New York: John Wiley & Sons, 1964.

WAHBA, M. A., & BRIDWELL, L. G. Maslow reconsidered: A review of research on the need hierarchy theory. *Proceedings of the 33rd Annual Meeting of the Academy of Management*, Academy of Management, 1973, 514–520.

PART V

Outcomes of Individual/ Organization Interactions

Some of the more important individual and organizational variables that affect the behavior and attitudes of people at work have been examined previously in this book. In Part V, the focus shifts specifically to those behaviors and attitudes, that is, to the various *outcomes* of individual/organization interactions.

The outcome of individual/organization interactions that tends to command the greatest attention is performance. The determinants and measurement of work performance are examined in Chapter 13. Chapter 14 is focused on absenteeism and turnover, the second two most frequently-used criteria by which the success of individual/ organization interactions is assessed. The related attitude of job commitment also is examined.

In Chapter 15, the tables are turned on the usual view of individual/organization interactions—outcomes are examined from the viewpoint of the employee. Topics for discussion in Chapter 15 are job satisfaction, employee development, and the quality of work life.

CHAPTER 13

Work Performance and Its Measurement

I/O PSYCHOLOGY AT WORK

The Best on the Shelf

GREENVILLE, S.C.   Between 3,000 and 4,000 J. P. Stevens managers—from the chief executive officer to most plant shift supervisors—have signed this pledge of quality: "I freely pledge myself to make a constant conscious effort to do my job right the first time, recognizing that my individual contribution is a vital part of the overall effort."

The oath is symbolic of a comprehensive quality-management system begun 18 months ago involving every division of this mammoth textile firm that employs 35,000 at 74 plants, in its headquarters and other offices.

As an important part of the program, Stevens executives from division president down to plant managers attend 2½-day training sessions on quality and job requirements. Shift supervisors attend a 5-hour session. These people, in turn, make sure that those under them perform well. Defect rate charts, which measure such problems as loom stops—a costly occurrence in textile plants—also are being placed in every department.

So far, the quality campaign has saved the company about 9 million dollars. The percentage of defective goods or "seconds" is going down, and maintenance costs are less because equipment is better maintained.

Excerpted from G. White, W. D. Hartley, S. Peterson, and L. K. Lanier, "A Drive to Put Quality Back into U.S. Goods." *U.S. News & World Report,* 1982, (September 20), pp. 49–50. Copyright 1982 U.S. News & World Report, Inc. Reprinted by permission.

The two basic criteria for evaluating employee performance in organizations are quantity and quality. In past years, concern for declining worker productivity in the United States has tended to keep the spotlight on quantity. But things are changing. As one J. P. Stevens's official put it: "Today's consumer is not a 'throwaway society' person any more." The Stevens campaign to "do it right the first time" is part of a growing national movement to convince consumers that they are getting value for their money when they "buy American."

Stevens combines employee written commitment to quality with managerial training as to how managers can bring quality about. It also provides employees with daily feedback about the quality of their performance. These issues—what aspects of performance to emphasize, how to evaluate them, and how to communicate the results to employees —are the subjects discussed in Chapter 13. As a preface to this general examination of performance appraisal, the factors that determine work performance are reviewed.

THE DETERMINANTS OF WORK PERFORMANCE

Those who study organizations and the behavior of people in them are concerned with a host of issues, but work performance always has been the bottom line. Unless members of an organization do their jobs, the organization ultimately will fail. In Chapter 12, it is noted that a host of variables play a part in determining this work performance and the traditional performance equation—Performance = f(Ability × Motivation) —is deficient as a framework for incorporating all of these variables.

Performance equation: See page 347.

Recently, Blumberg and Pringle (1982) have proposed a model of work performance that attempts to incorporate the full range of individual and environmental variables that interact to produce level and quality of work performance. This model, shown in Exhibit 13-1, consists of three components that the authors call *Opportunity, Capacity,* and *Willingness* to perform.

Environmental variables in the Blumberg-Pringle model are included in the *Opportunity* component. Among the topics discussed earlier that relate to opportunity to perform are job design, working conditions, communication, group membership, and leadership.

Capacity to perform includes relevant physical, physiological, and knowledge/skill variables, such as age, education, energy, health, and ability. The extent to which a work force has the characteristics that make it capable of performing depends to a considerable extent on the recruiting, selection, placement, and training methods of the organization.

Motivation, as discussed in Chapter 12, is a *Willingness* variable in the Blumberg-Pringle model. These variables are individual psychological characteristics and include values, attitudes, and perceptions as well as motivation. Together, Opportunity (O), Capacity (C), and Willingness (W) combine to produce observed work performance: Performance = f(O × C × W).

The Blumberg-Pringle model of work performance assumes that the variables within the Opportunity, Capacity, and Willingness components are additive. For example, of two people with equal *ability,* the one with the greater *energy* would have the greater capacity to perform. As indicated by the multiplication sign in the equation, however, the components themselves operate multiplicatively.

Because Opportunity, Capacity, and Willingness interact, some level of each must be present for work performance to occur; a change in any of the component variables will produce a change in the observed performance of the employee. In addition, the components themselves interact, as indicated by the two-way arrows in Exhibit 13-1. For example, a favorable environment (Opportunity) may increase employee Willingness that, in turn, gives him or her performance experience. Over time, performance experience is likely to increase the employee's job-related skills and knowledge (Capacity).

The Blumberg-Pringle model is an attempt to organize and integrate what is already known about the simple relationships between work

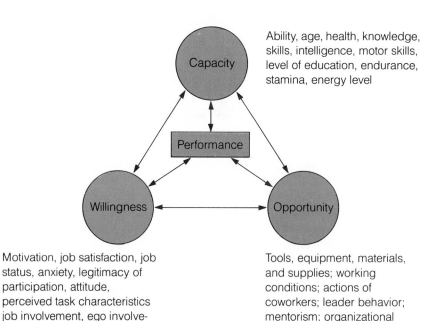

Ability, age, health, knowledge, skills, intelligence, motor skills, level of education, endurance, stamina, energy level

Motivation, job satisfaction, job status, anxiety, legitimacy of participation, attitude, perceived task characteristics job involvement, ego involvement, self-image, personality, norms, values, perceived role expectations, feelings of equity

Tools, equipment, materials, and supplies; working conditions; actions of coworkers; leader behavior; mentorism; organizational policies, rules, and procedures; information; time; pay

Note. From M. Blumberg and C. D. Pringle, ''The Missing Opportunity in Organizational Research: Some Implications for a Theory of Work Performance.'' *Academy of Management Review,* 1982, 7(4), pp. 562 and 565. Adapted by permission of the authors and the publisher.

Correlate: See pages 63 to 64.

Behavior causation: See pages 27 to 28.

Operational definition: See page 48.

performance and its correlates. The result is consistent with the basic theme of this book—behavior is determined by individual characteristics (both inherited and learned) interacting with the environment (both physical and social).

Blumberg and Pringle recognize the research difficulties created by their model, but suggest a number of possibilities for operationalizing the variables. They also point out that important variables not being investigated in a particular study of performance should be controlled. Of particular concern are those environmental variables they believe often are dismissed too lightly. Peters and O'Connor (1980) give examples of such variables found to be relevant to performance differences; they include:

- tools and equipment
- job-related information
- budgetary support
- required services and help from others
- materials and supplies
- task preparation
- time availability

On the practical side, the Blumberg-Pringle model of work performance points again to the multiple avenues for attempting to influence employee behavior. This theme is expanded in Chapter 12 where nine hypotheses that relate to how employee motivation may be influenced are discussed. The current framework, however, is considerably broader, making explicit the large number of ways in which employee performance might be influenced with or without an intention to increase motivation.

Hypothesis: See page 47.

THE EVALUATION OF WORK PERFORMANCE

An understanding of the large number of variables that interact to produce work performance makes it easier to appreciate the difficulty psychologists or others concerned have in evaluating that performance. For example, a manager whose performance is partially evaluated by his or her ability to stay within a defined budget will receive a low rating if he or she goes 20% over the budget figure in a given period. Yet, a careful examination of the situation might reveal that it was only this manager's superior knowledge and skill that kept expenditures even *that* low under the conditions prevailing in the company at the time.

Depending upon perspective, the performance of the manager reasonably might be evaluated as either "unsatisfactory" or as "outstanding." Which is fair? Which is accurate? The answer is very important to the individual concerned, but it also has a broader significance. From the standpoint of effective human resource utilization, performance appraisal is one of the most important activities performed in organizations.

The Importance of Effective Job Performance Appraisal

The information generated by the performance evaluation process serves a major coordinating function for personnel-related activities; it is a control system with both feedback and feedforward aspects. As a *feedback* mechanism, performance appraisal sends information back to those who were involved in recruiting, screening and selecting, and training employees. Although many factors affect job performance, a pattern of poor evaluations among new employees suggests that the processes by which these individuals are brought to the job may need reexamining.

Performance appraisal is the process utilized by an organization to evaluate the extent to which its members are doing their work satisfactorily.

As a *feedforward* mechanism, performance appraisal provides information for the future distribution of individual employee incentives, for individual employee development needs, and for general human resource planning. For example, if there are several outstanding performers at a particular level in the organization, the company may want to take steps to develop these people for promotion rather than to look for outsiders to fill upcoming vacancies.

The various relationships between the information provided by performance appraisal and other personnel-related organizational activities are depicted in Exhibit 13–2. These relationships may be summarized

The Feedback and
Feedforward
Information Functions
of Performance
Appraisal

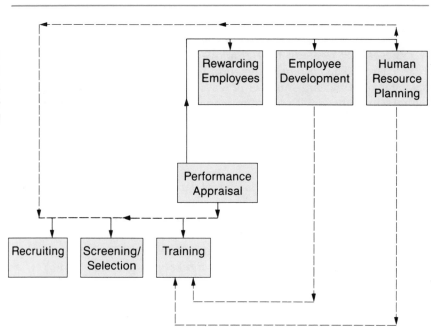

in terms of the specific purposes to which performance appraisal information may be put. There are three broad categories of these uses—administrative, developmental, and internal personnel process uses.

Administrative Uses of Performance Appraisal Information

Organizations traditionally use performance appraisal information to make administrative decisions about the distribution of formal work-related rewards, such as raises, bonuses, and promotions (or in some instances, just retention of the job). When this information is used as a basis for such decisions, performance appraisal is serving an administrative function, and this remains its most common usage.

Developmental Uses of Performance Appraisal Information

The information provided by performance appraisal is used developmentally at the individual level to help organizations and individuals assess individual strengths and weaknesses and make decisions for improving employee performance. At the organizational level, performance appraisal information gives a picture of overall personnel strengths and weaknesses. Both kinds of information can be used to help organizations determine training and recruiting needs.

Internal Personnel Process Uses of Performance Appraisal Information

The administrative and developmental uses of performance appraisal information are directly relevant to a company's current personnel. This information, however, also is useful for a variety of purposes that have little or nothing to do with specific individuals. These purposes include:

- selection test validation
- training method revision
- job design and redesign
- documentation of fair employment practices

Effective performance appraisal gives good value for the resources put into it. The key word, however, is *effective*. A poor program does little for anyone and actually can be counterproductive. For example, if performance appraisal methods do not accurately distinguish between good and poor employee work performance, then using the results of these appraisals to validate a selection test will make the results of the validation study highly questionable.

Criterion-related validity: See pages 86 to 88.

Decisions in Setting Up a Performance Appraisal Program

Wherry and Bartlett, (1982) have stated that effective performance appraisal is a function of three variables: (a) the performance of the ratee, (b) the observation of that performance by the rater, and (c) the recall of those observations by the rater. Expanding upon this framework, they present a comprehensive and highly technical model of the appraisal process, including a large number of theorems and corrolaries that generate testable hypotheses.

Variables: See page 47.

Wherry and Bartlett's model is mathematical in nature, but from its conceptual base may be drawn the conclusion that effective performance appraisal depends upon four decisions: what aspects of the ratee are appraised, who does the appraisal, how often is the appraisal done, and what method is used.

What to Appraise?

Those concerned have basically three choices when considering what aspect of ratees should be evaluated. The oldest approach is to appraise personal characteristics, or traits, of the individual ratee. This approach, often called the *trait approach* to performance appraisal, puts an emphasis on an employee's "worth" as a person because the traits most often appraised are those such as personality characteristics, intelligence, and loyalty. An example of such a performance appraisal form is shown in Exhibit 13–3.

The trait approach to performance evaluation leads to a method that is very dependent on individual rater interpretation, or perception, of the traits. This interpretation is affected substantially by individual opinions, biases, and experiences. As a result, trait instruments often have poor interrater reliability; one rater's idea of a "likeable personality" may differ significantly from another's, to use one example from Exhibit 13–3.

Perception: See pages 36 to 37.

Reliability: See page 67.

The validity of the trait approach to performance appraisal is also highly

EXHIBIT 13-3		EXCELLENT	GOOD	AVERAGE	FAIR	POOR
The Trait Approach to Performance Appraisal	**Personality** The external mannerisms consciously adopted in meeting situations	Radiant, confident, poised, courteous	Pleasant, forceful	Likeable	Ill at ease, not too forceful	Negative colorless person
	Appearance Outward impressions made by a person	Superior style, grooming, taste and a sense of the fitness of things	Well dressed and neat	Neat, but not particularly striking	Intermittently careless	Slovenly and untidy
	Character Integrity of an individual	Has the courage of his convictions and unquestioned habits	Morally sound, tolerant	An average human being possessing average personal weaknesses	A person whose behavior harms no one but himself	A person who is a bad influence on the behavior of the group
	Mentality Quality of mind, mental power, and creative intellectual ability of a person	Superior ability to think clearly and arrive at sound conclusions	Worthwhile ideas of his own, and ability to make useful decisions	Well informed on certain subjects useful in his daily work	Little ability to comprehend, interpret or grasp new ideas	Unable to reason logically
	Sociability Sense of mutual relationship, companionship, and friendliness with others	A genuine interest in people and extremely well liked by others	A friendly, pleasant person, happy in a group	Willing to be a part of a group but makes little contribution	Poorly adjusted to the group	Unwilling to be a part of any group activities

problamatical. A close examination of the trait instrument in Exhibit 13–3 reveals an interesting fact. It would be quite possible for an employee being evaluated on such a scale to get a rating of "excellent" on every item and still be a *poor* worker because many of the rating dimensions are irrelevant to performance on most jobs.

Aside from the fact that items to be evaluated are usually familiar to raters (and so often "make sense" to the unsophisticated), about the only advantage of the trait approach to performance appraisal is economic. Such an instrument can be used to evaluate any individual on any job. The reliability and validity problems inherent in this approach more than offset this advantage, however.

An alternative to the trait approach to performance appraisal is to appraise ratees on their *behaviors*. For example, instead of appraising a salesperson on his or her "sales personality," the individual would be appraised on sales-related behaviors, such as number of calls, submission of required paperwork, follow-up activities, and so on. This approach is generally more reliable and more valid than the trait approach (Cummings & Schwab, 1973); however, it has the opposite disadvantage: the job specificity of such an approach gives it limited applicability.

The third choice of what should be evaluated in performance appraisal is not the job behaviors themselves, but the *results* of those behaviors. For example, the salesperson described would be evaluated in terms of dollar volume of sales (or perhaps, profit made on the sales). This approach sometimes is called a *direct index measure* of performance. Other direct index measures include profit, amount of waste, worker-hour productivity, machine "up time" relative to "down time" (mechanics), and number of customers served.

While measuring performance by measuring its results sounds like an attractive solution to the problem of what to evaluate in performance appraisal, it raises a number of problems that affect both its reliability and its validity (e.g., Landy & Trumbo, 1980). First, this approach depends on accurate records, and records may be neither accurate nor complete or even available.

A second problem with direct index measures of performance is that results in organizations are seldom solely dependent on the performance of the individual being evaluated. The low volume of sales for one salesperson, for example, may be due primarily to quality control problems

Quantity of output is a direct index measure often used in the appraisal of work performance.

with the product or to the fact that a competitor has introduced a dramatic price cut in that person's territory.

Finally, direct index measures of work often bypass a number of aspects of work performance that may be important. For example, a given supervisor may get only average productivity from his or her subordinates, but have such a good relationship with them that turnover in that department is almost zero.

This last example raises a final issue with respect to what to evaluate in performance appraisal: How many aspects, or dimensions, of work performance should be appraised? Although quantity and quality are the primary criteria, these may be broken down into a number of dimensions including:

- timeliness
- amount of waste/scrap
- self-inspection of work
- cooperation with coworkers
- ability to plan ahead

There also may be many specific aspects of quantity and quality of work performance for particular jobs. For example, a supervisor's good relationship with subordinates (mentioned above) is one dimension of quality for this job, and number of repeat customers is one measure of quality for salesperson performance.

Although arguments have been made for appraising performance on the basis of a single measure of "job success" (e.g., Brogden & Taylor, 1950), most evaluation is based on multiple dimensions. There is no set *Job analysis: See pages 247* number of such criteria, and no one to date has offered a rule of thumb *to 270.* that all can agree upon. There is agreement, however, that the basis for determining the relevant dimensions is job analysis as discussed in Chapter 9.

When to Appraise?

If performance appraisal is to be used for developmental purposes, it is a form of feedback. Consistent with the principles discussed in connec-*Feedback: See pages 148 to* tion with job training, this feedback should come at relatively frequent *150.* intervals so that the individual involved does not get too far down the wrong path if his or her performance is unsatisfactory. Surveys indicate, however, that formal appraisal is done relatively infrequently in most companies, once a year being the norm (e.g., Lazer & Wikstrom, 1977). In addition, most appraisal systems are fixed-date, such as 6 months after an employee joins the company and every 12 months after that.

Infrequent, fixed-date appraisal policies have the effect of separating evaluation from the natural flow of work performance (Cummings & Schwab, 1973). This limits its utility as feedback and makes an already difficult task more difficult for those who must do the appraisal. A long time span between evaluations taxes the memory of the rater and can *Laboratory experiment: See* introduce error into appraisal. In one recent laboratory experiment, for *pages 52 to 54.* example, a delay of only three weeks between observation and evaluation of performance led to a significant decrease in rater accuracy (Heneman & Wexley, 1983).

One form of error resulting from a long time span between performance appraisals is a tendency on the part of a rater to recall only job behaviors that are characteristic of the way that rater generally thinks of an employee (e.g., Wyer & Srull, 1980). For example, if a new employee makes an early impression as an especially industrious worker, it will be behaviors consistent with this impression that tend to come to the rater's mind at evaluation time.

Attempts by evaluators to overcome their tendency to recall only "typical behaviors" by seeking more information about employees as appraisal time draws near can create a different kind of problem. *Recent behavior bias* refers to a rater's tendency to bias performance appraisal by giving greatest weight to work observed immediately prior to the formal evaluation. This performance may be typical of usual performance, but not necessarily.

Suggestions for coping with evaluation problems stemming from organizational policies that call for infrequent formal performance evaluations are discussed at the end of Chapter 13. It should be noted here that such policies do not prohibit supervisors supplementing formal evaluation with more frequent informal feedback for purposes of employee development.

Who Will Appraise?

There are many choices as to who will carry out performance appraisal, but as Exhibit 13–4 shows, the most common practice is for appraisal to be done by the *immediate supervisor* of the employee. The primary rationale for this practice is that the supervisor both understands the job and has the opportunity to observe its performance by subordinates. This same factor, however, often gives rise to considerable resistance toward this task. Because they do work closely with those they are asked to evaluate, many supervisors feel unable to perform appraisals objectively. In addition, many believe that this task interferes with superior-subordinate relationships.

There is ample evidence that superiors and subordinates often disagree in their evaluations of subordinate performance (e.g., Baird, 1977). There is also evidence that they do not understand one another's perspectives on this evaluation. A study of performance feedback interviews by Ilgen, Peterson, Martin, and Boeschen (1981) suggests that superiors and subordinates do not always even *hear* the same thing when evaluations are being discussed. Even though feedback was given in a straightforward manner and based on an instrument with which they were very familiar, subordinates still overestimated the evaluations of their performance in subsequent questioning.

As may be seen in Exhibit 13–4, there are a number of alternatives to an immediate supervisor doing performance appraisals. Of these alternatives, only *self-evaluation* achieves any significant use relative to immediate supervisors. And since this particular survey is based on the appraisal

	EXHIBIT 13–4

A Survey of
Practices: Who
Does Appraisal?

Appraiser[a]	Lower Management (217 Companies)		Middle Management (208 Companies)		Top Management (160 Companies)	
	Number of Companies	Percent of Companies	Number of Companies	Percent of Companies	Number of Companies	Percent of Companies
Immediate supervisor	106	95%	198	95%	138	85%
Self	25	12	27	13	23	14
Peers or coworkers	0	—	0	—	1	*
Subordinates	0	—	0	—	0	—
Group or committee	11	5	9	4	14	9
Representative from the divisional personnel department	6	3	4	2	3	2
Representative from the corporate personnel department	7	3	10	5	7	4
Internal staff consultant	0	—	0	—	0	—
External management consultant	1	*	1	*	1	*
Other	7	3	7	3	5	3

[a]Some companies report that more than one person has the responsibility for doing the appraisal; therefore, the percentages do not add to 100.

*Less than one percent.

Note. From R. I. Lazer and W. S. Wikstrom, *Appraising Managerial Performance: Current Practices and Future Directions.* New York: The Conference Board, 1977, p. 81. Reprinted by permission.

MBO: See pages 267 to 268.

of manager performance, this finding probably is not typical. At this organizational level, appraisal techniques (such as Management by Objectives) that require self-evaluation are more common.

While not used extensively in industry, self-appraisals have been subject to considerable research. In general, results of these investigations find self-appraisals to show more leniency and less variability than other methods. They also tend to be lower on discriminant validity, that is, on the extent to which they differentiate between good and poor performance (Thornton, 1980). Self-appraisals, however, have been found useful in predicting nonwork behaviors, such as intellectual achievement and improvement in psychotherapy (Shrauger & Osberg, 1981).

Although the numbers are not representative for all performance evaluation, the choices of who should appraise shown in Exhibit 13–4 cover the basic possibilities. Most of these methods receive more use than that shown in Exhibit 13–4, but this use tends to be concentrated in certain kinds of organizations. *Committees, specialists,* and *outsiders,* for example, often are used in public-sector organizations, such as public school systems.

Rating by *subordinates* is common in the evaluation of college and university professors, but relatively rare in other organizations. Such appraisals probably are most useful as information to help a third party evaluate the performance of individuals whose *primary* task is considered to be leadership (such as team leaders or officers in the military).

Of the remaining choices as to who is to do performance appraisal shown in Exhibit 13–4, peer appraisals have received the most attention in the literature. *Peer nominations,* as the name implies, call for peers to nominate, or vote, for outstanding coworkers. *Peer rankings* require each member of a group to rank all members on some dimension, while *peer ratings* use an individual's peers to do the performance appraisals more often done by the immediate superior.

Most of the research done with peer appraisal methods has been with peer nominations, and these generally have been found to be acceptably reliable and valid (e.g., Kane & Lawler, 1978). A recent study comparing peer nominations with other peer evaluation methods found both nominations and rankings to be more reliable and valid than peer ratings (Love, 1981).

Despite promising research findings, peer appraisal is not generally liked by either raters or ratees (e.g., DeNisi, Randolph & Blencoe, 1983), and its use tends to be confined to professional occupations. Peer appraisal also has been used extensively in the Peace Corps. This organization, however, is not typical of most that make formal performance evaluations. It is distinguished both by a noncompetitive reward system

Although formalized peer appraisal is not found in many organizations, informal evaluation of an individual's work by his or her peers takes place frequently.

and by training that gives members unusual opportunity to observe and get to know one another. It seems likely that for the foreseeable future, most organizations will continue to rely on evaluations by ratees' immediate superiors.

How to Appraise?

How to evaluate is a question of method. There are two broad classifications of performance appraisal methods—*comparative methods* and *individual methods*. Within each classification are a variety of approaches. The physical means by which the method is implemented is called the performance appraisal *instrument*.

Correlation: See pages 59 to 63.

As are all measuring instruments, those measuring performance are subject to two basic criteria. They should be *reliable*; that is they should give highly correlated results when used by two different raters (interrater reliability) or the same rater twice (intrarater reliability). They should also be valid; that is, they should measure what they are intended to measure—work performance.

Performance appraisal is plagued by both reliability and validity problems. To some extent these problems stem from difficulty in the assessment of whether or not a method meets these criteria. For example, the concept of reliability presumes that what is being measured remains constant or "holds still" for measurement. The work performance of a given individual, however, can vary randomly or systematically over relatively short time periods.

The validity of performance appraisal methods is even more difficult to establish. Basically, the problem is: If there were some standard of true performance good enough to use in assessing the validity of a performance appraisal method, the standard and not the appraisal instrument would be used. This criterion problem is considered by many to be one of the most difficult problems in I/O psychology.

The more common comparative and individual performance appraisal instruments are discussed briefly in this chapter. Discussions of their reliability and validity are general; there are many variations of these methods, and situational differences can be substantial.

Comparative methods of performance appraisal.   Performance appraisal methods that require a comparison of all those to be appraised (ratees) at a given time usually are called comparative methods. Most of these are variations of *straight ranking* by means of which ratees are ordered from best to poorest on some dimension, such as "overall quality of work." This method has several advantages.

- It costs nothing to develop.
- It is easy for raters to understand.
- It forces raters to make distinctions between ratees.

Along with its advantages, straight ranking also has several disadvantages. One problem is that the evaluations of *different groups of ratees cannot be compared* because rankings give no information about the absolute level of ratee performance. It would not be a good idea, for example, to use supervisor rankings from 10 different departments to identify a company's 10 most promising employees. The top-ranked individual in one department might be performing at a level that would rank him or her only in the middle in another department.

Another difficulty with straight ranking is that it can be a very *difficult task for the rater,* especially in the center of the ranks when the number of ratees is fairly large. Most people find it relatively easy to distinguish among the top few performers in a group and the bottom few; however, a rationale for ranking an employee 9th out of 20 instead of 8th or 10th is more difficult.

Yet another problem with straight ranking procedures is that they have *little utility for developmental purposes.* Rankings are not descriptive; that is, they are not based on defined aspects of job performance. This, combined with the problem of justifying precise rankings in the center of the distribution, makes it difficult for a rater to give ratees the kind of information they need to improve their performance.

Variations of straight ranking solve some of the problems of using this method. A *forced-distribution ranking scale* format requires raters to assign a certain percentage of all ratees to each of a set number of categories in order to approximate a normal distribution. This method, illustrated in Exhibit 13–5, is easier than straight ranking because it requires distinctions that are less fine. This format presents no real improvement over straight ranking for employee development, however.

Normal curve: See page 5.

Yet another variation of straight ranking is the *paired-comparison* method, which requires the rater to compare each ratee with every other ratee. Final ranking depends on the number of times each ratee is ranked number one. This method makes rankings easier for raters because it breaks the task into components—each ratee is ranked only first or second in each pair.

Because it eliminates the necessity for a rater to evaluate a ratee's performance against the performance of all other ratees at once, the paired-comparison method tends to be more reliable than either straight ranking or forced distribution. It also tends to encounter rater resistance, however, unless the number of people to be evaluated is very small. For example, if there are as many as 18 ratees, the rater must make over 150 separate comparisons.

Directions: Distribute the twenty-six ratees as shown by the numbers below on the basis of your appraisal of their overall job performance.

Job Dimension		Lowest 10%	Next 20%	Middle 40%	Next 20%	Highest 10%
Overall Quality of Work	# of Ratees 26	2	6	10	6	2

EXHIBIT 13–5

The Forced-Distribution Approach to Performance Appraisal

Individual methods of performance appraisal. Psychologically, comparative methods of performance appraisal are probably closest to a natural approach to such a task. In general, people tend to compare the work of subordinates when evaluating performance. Nevertheless, such methods create problems, and as a group, these methods have little utility for employee development. An alternative approach to performance appraisal is the use of individual methods. Such methods evaluate work performance against defined standards and are referred to also as *evaluation by absolute standards*.

The most popular individual performance appraisal method is the *graphic rating scale*, such as the one shown in Exhibit 13–6. This method calls for a rater to appraise the degree to which a ratee exhibits the behaviors and/or traits shown on the scale. Degree usually is indicated by a number, adjective, or descriptive phrase.

The graphic rating scale in Exhibit 13–6 has two adjectives and three descriptive phrases to describe the degree to which ratees plan, organize, control costs, and possess technical knowledge. This is a relatively common mixing of standards that can be confusing. For example, it is not at all clear what *outstanding* means because *exceeds requirements* is used to define a lower degree of performance.

The graphic rating scale is somewhat of an improvement over comparative assessment methods. It allows both for comparing different

EXHIBIT 13–6 A Graphic Rating Scale Example		Outstanding	Exceeds Requirements	Meets Requirements	Meets Minimum Requirements	Poor
Planning and Organizing Consider how this employee plans work and organizes job activity. Comments: _____						
Technical, Scientific, Professional Knowledge and Ability Consider how this employee applies technical, scientific, or professional knowledge and ability on the job. Comments: _____						
Control of Costs Consider how this employee utilizes materials, equipment, processes, work time, and services. Comments: _____						

groups of ratees and for more specific feedback to ratees. The improvement may be slight, however. As in the example, definitions of the various degrees of the trait or behavior being rated often are vague, and different raters may use quite different standards in defining such terms as *outstanding*.

A form of graphic rating scale widely believed to be a significant improvement on the traditional form shown in Exhibit 13-6 is the *behaviorally anchored rating scale*, or BARS (Smith & Kendall, 1963). Behaviorally anchored rating scales, as the name implies, *anchor* graphic rating scale points with *specific behaviors* to help raters make their appraisals.

The sample behavior anchors provided by BARS are not used in a checklist fashion; that is, it is not necessary that an employee be observed performing the specific behavior listed. Rather, the anchors are examples of the kind of behaviors that might be *expected* of an employee at a particular level of job performance. For this reason, BARS also are called *behavioral expectation scales* (BES). One item from such a scale is shown in Exhibit 13-7.

Cooperative Behavior: Willingness to help others to get a job done.

Highest Performance

5 ┼   This employee can be expected to seek out opportunities to help others with their work to get a job done even if it means working overtime.

4 ┼   This employee can be expected to help others if asked for assistance even if it means working overtime.

3 ┼   This employee can be expected to help others if asked by supervisor, and it does not mean working overtime.

2 ┼   This employee can be expected to refuse to assist others if asked for such help by pleading too much of own work to do.

1 ┼   This employee can be expected to criticize the ability of others to do their jobs if asked to render assistance.

Poorest Performance

EXHIBIT 13-7

A Behaviorally Anchored Rating Scale (BARS)

Critical incident technique:
See pages 254 to 255.

Developing a behaviorally anchored rating scale starts with a version of Flanagan's (1954) Critical Incident Technique; the behavioral statements are actual examples of good and poor job behaviors observed at one time or another by those who will do performance appraisal with the new scale. The process then proceeds through a number of categorizing and scaling steps (see Latham & Wexley, 1981, for a detailed description) to produce an item of the general form shown in Exhibit 13–7.

Given that cooperative behavior, referred to in Exhibit 13–7, is only one item for evaluation of one aspect of an employee's performance, it is clear that developing behaviorally anchored rating scales for all (or even most) jobs in a company is going to be a time-consuming and expensive process. Many have argued that the result is not worth this resource expenditure. For example, in their review of studies comparing BARS with other appraisal instruments, Kingstrom and Bass (1981) conclude that there is little difference with respect to reliability, validity, or rater preference.

Bernardin and Smith (1981) disagree with the conclusions of Kingstrom and Bass. Among other points discussed in support of BARS, Bernardin and Smith raise an interesting issue. Pointing out that this approach helps to standardize the *observation* of performance as well as the appraisal itself, they argue that BARS is a valuable tool for documenting fair performance appraisal practices. In these days of increasing pressures on organizations to justify the numbers by which they make their personnel decisions, the point seems to strengthen the case for BARS considerably.

Behaviorally anchored rating scales were developed some years ago, and a number of variations on the basic technique have since been put forward. Latham, Fay, and Saari (1979) have proposed what they call a *behavioral observation scale* (BOS). Like BARS, AND BOS method is based on descriptions of actual job behaviors.

A major difference between BARS and BOS is that with the BOS, raters evaluate the extent to which ratees have been observed performing *each* listed behavior. This approach is too new to permit any conclusions about the improvement it affords over BARS. At least one review identifies some basic problems and concludes that if these were corrected, BOS would be little better than BARS (Kane & Bernardin, 1982).

Yet another variation of BARS is the *mixed standard scale* of Blanz and Ghiselli (1972). The mixed standard scale uses behavioral descriptions to anchor performance evaluations, but limits the number of anchors for each item to three. This *triad* of anchors includes one behavior that defines "excellent" performance, one that defines "average" performance, and one that defines "poor" performance for the item in question. Triads for each of three highway patrol task items are shown in Exhibit 13–8.

Each of the three statements for each of the three highway patrol job tasks shown in Exhibit 13–8 is an example of either excellent, average, or poor performance. To do the actual evaluation, the rater marks a plus (+) if the ratee's performance is *better* than the statement, an equal sign (=) if it is about the *same*, and a minus (−) if it is *poorer*. Numerical

Stop Vehicles for a Variety of Violations

- Stops vehicles for a variety of traffic and other violations
- Concentrates on speed violations, but stops vehicles for other violations also
- Concentrates on one or two kinds of violations and spends too little time on the others

Detect OMVI (Intoxicated Drivers)

- At all times of the day, watches for driving patterns and driver behavior which may indicate OMVI
- Is alert to OMVI mostly at prime times and in prime locations
- Responds only to obvious signs of OMVI. Sometimes avoids high OMVI areas

Secure Accident Scenes

- Utilizes available equipment and solicits any available assistance to secure scene of accident quickly and effectively
- Generally secures scene adequately before beginning accident investigation
- May fail to adequately secure the scene before beginning accident investigation

Note. From G. Rosinger, L. B. Myers, G. W. Levy, M. Loar, S. A. Mohrman, and J. R. Stock, "Development of a Behaviorally Based Performance Appraisal System." *Personnel Psychology,* 1982, *35*(1), pp. 75–88. Pp. 81, 82 reprinted by permission of the authors and the publisher.

> **EXHIBIT 13–8**
>
> *Three Triads from a Mixed Standard Performance Evaluation Scale*

values may be attached to each. A single evaluation may be obtained by summation of the pluses, equals, and minuses across all items.

To date, use of the mixed standard scale has been limited, but at least one study suggests it may present reliability problems (Saal & Landy, 1977). A number of researchers, however, have suggested that this approach may be useful in identifying raters whose appraisal behavior is inconsistent, even if its utility for actual appraisal is limited. An example of such inconsistent behavior would be a rater who marks the "excellent" anchor "plus" (employee performs better than excellent) and the "poor" anchor for the same item "equal" (employee performs about the same as poor performance).

The potential of a mixed standard scale to identify raters who are rating inconsistently (whether through carelessness or misunderstanding of the task) illustrates what some believe to be one of the greatest strengths of a behavior-based approach to performance appraisal—forcing attention to specifics and away from vague value judgments about employee job performance (Landy & Trumbo, 1980). This advantage is particularly strong when those who will be using a performance evaluation instrument are involved in its construction (as with the original BARS).

The major disadvantages to behavior-based performance appraisal remain development cost and lack of generalizability. A standard old-style graphic rating scale, such as that in Exhibit 13–6, may be used to evaluate performance on a wide variety of jobs. A behavior-based scale is generally considered to be job specific. However, Goodale and Burke (1975) suggest that it is possible for psychologists to develop a more general instrument by working with basic dimensions of job behavior.

Graphic rating scales, whether standard or behaviorally anchored, do not exhaust the possibilities for individual performance appraisal methods. Although they are the most commonly used, at least two other methods should be mentioned—the forced-choice scale and the behavior checklist.

A forced-choice approach to performance appraisal requires raters to pick one of two (or two of four) statements as most descriptive of the ratee. The statements have been equated ahead of time as to apparant favorableness or unfavorableness (called degree of *social desirability*). Despite this apparent equality, only one has been established as differentiating between good and poor job performance. Two items from one such scale are shown in Exhibit 13–9.

Forced-choice performance evaluation items, such as those shown in Exhibit 13–9, are difficult and time consuming to develop because each pair of statements must *look* equally favorable or unfavorable. In addition, it is necessary to keep the key (the list of which item in each pair is the ''real'' one) confidential if the instrument is to serve its purpose of making biased evaluations difficult. This makes forced-choice instruments worthless for developmental purposes. It also gives rise to considerable rater resistance. The logic of raters having to choose one of two quite dissimilar statements as a way of evaluating employee job performance is by no means obvious, and many are not prepared to take it on faith.

The last major individual performance appraisal method is the *behavior checklist*. The checklist method merely requires the rater to record, not to appraise, behavior. The question is: Did the behavior described occur or did it not? The checklist, then, is at the opposite extreme from straight ranking, which is pure evaluation. It also has the opposite advantage. Ranking is of little use for developmental purposes, which is the primary strength of the checklist provided that raters have the opportunity to observe the behaviors on the list.

To recapitulate, available methods for performance appraisal may be classified as comparative methods and individual methods. Within each group is a number of alternatives, each with strengths and weaknesses that make them more or less appropriate for certain purposes. (Porter, Lawler, & Hackman, 1975). For example, straight ranking has little utility

---

EXHIBIT 13–9	Directions: For each item, place a check by the *one* statement that best describes the ratee. You must choose one statement from each pair.

Two Items from a
Forced-Choice
Performance
Appraisal Instrument

Item One

_____ Is generally at work on time in the mornings.
_____ Gets along well with almost everyone.

Item Two

_____ Usually takes a little longer than the specified deadline to finish work.
_____ Does not make a very good first impression with strangers.

for employee development and creates reliability problems if the number of ratees is large. If there are few employees to be rated or if the purpose of the evaluation is merely to identify the top few performers, however, the ease, speed, and economy of this method do much to recommend it.

Concluding Remarks

The decisions to be made by those setting up a performance appraisal program and the relative strengths and weaknesses of the alternative choices have been outlined as clearly as possible. There is no one ideal performance appraisal program, only ones that serve an organization's purposes better than others. Building a program suited to the goals and consistent with the resources of a particular organization begins with understanding the issues.

By way of clarifying these issues, the foregoing discussion has treated the various questions as if they were independent. Of course, they are not. Decisions concerning what to appraise, for example, tend to play a large part in determination of the method to be used. The basic criteria of reliability and validity underlie every decision. Some of the ways these basic criteria are affected by alternative solutions to the various decisions required by performance appraisal already have been mentioned. Errors in performance appraisal now are examined more closely.

ERROR IN EVALUATING WORK PERFORMANCE

Performance appraisal is basically a measurement problem, and a complex one. Specifically, the problem is to find some combination of what, who, when, and how to appraise work performance that will yield a reliable and valid measurement. The errors that will act to reduce the accuracy of this measurement stem from three main sources: (a) the performance appraisal instrument, (b) the environment in which the appraisal takes place, and (c) the individual doing the appraisal.

Instrument Sources of Error in Performance Appraisal

A performance appraisal instrument is like a test in that it consists of some scale by which an estimate can be made about certain aspects of an individual's job performance—the items. As is true for any test, the items on a performance appraisal instrument are only a sample of all of the possible items that might be on it, that is, of the *domain* of items that describe job performance.

Domain of test: See page 90.

To the extent that a performance appraisal instrument does *not* include items that represent the important aspects of job performance, it is *deficient*. Deficiency is a major issue with respect to performance being appraised on the basis of a single item of overall work satisfactoriness. It also can be a problem with direct index measures of performance, which include only items having to do with work output.

To the extent that a performance appraisal instrument contains items that are *irrelevant* to work performance, it is *contaminated*. Contamination often is a problem with traditional trait approaches to performance appraisal, which tend to include such job-irrelevant items as "cheerfulness" and "sincerity." Items whose evaluation is heavily dependent on nonperformance factors (such as type of job or length of time on the job) are also sources of contamination in performance appraisal.

Deficiency and contamination are two major sources of constant, or built-in, error in performance appraisal. In the language of Chapter 4, instruments with these problems (and the same instrument may have both) have reduced *content validity*. The most direct route to improving this situation is job analysis. This strategy is considered further when improvement of performance appraisal is discussed.

Content validity: See pages 90 to 92.

In addition to contamination and/or deficiency, performance appraisal instruments also may suffer from *ambiguity* in the instructions, format, or terms by which the evaluation is to be made. For example, the word *good* by itself probably has as many definitions as there are people defining it. Reducing this source of ambiguity is one of the main goals behind behavior-based approaches to performance appraisal.

Environmental Sources of Error in Performance Appraisal

Although a performance appraisal instrument has aspects in common with any test, the situation for the rater who must use such an instrument is far more complicated than for the job applicant taking a clerical knowledge test or the student taking an exam. The knowledge the performance appraisal rater must draw on is knowledge of work performance observed over some time period and within a particular social environment.

Social environment: See page 35.

Because the work performance that a rater must evaluate is not observed in isolation, appraisal can be affected by a number of social factors that introduce error into the appraisal because they are not relevant to job performance. One such factor is a ratee's apparent social standing in his or her work group.

Field experiment: See page 52.

In a pair of studies, one done in the laboratory and one in the field, Mitchell and Liden (1982) found that coworker perceptions of a ratee affected performance appraisal. Although the effect was stronger in the laboratory, results of both studies supported the hypothesis that ratees who were more popular with their peers received more favorable work performance evaluations.

A second example of a social environmental factor that has been found to affect performance appraisal is the *value* that the particular environment places on results of work behavior. A study by Mitchell and Kalb (1981) using nurses and their supervisors as subjects illustrates this effect.

Mitchell and Kalb found that nursing supervisors tended to give different appraisals to the same nursing behavior when they had knowledge of some outcome of that behavior and when they did not. Furthermore, the effect of knowledge on performance appraisal varied systematically with whether the outcome was seen as positive or negative. For example, a nurse who forgot to change a dressing would be thought less

competent if the patient's wound became infected (a negative consequence) than if it did not.

The studies described suggest that the social environment of an
organization affects rater perceptions of the work performance that he
or she observes. There is also evidence that the social context of performance appraisal affects evaluations in other ways, especially through
the relationships of the rater with individual ratees.

As mentioned earlier in Chapter 13, many supervisors dislike the
performance evaluation task because they believe it is not good for superior-
subordinate relations. Certainly, as Porter, Lawler, and Hackman (1975)
have pointed out, the situation holds considerable potential for conflict.
Exhibit 13–10 illustrates some of these possibilities.

Exhibit 13–10 shows some of the potential conflicts for each of the
three major participants in a performance appraisal situation—the organization, the rater, and the ratee. At the *company* level, this conflict is
primarily a matter of resource expenditure. It costs more time and money
to develop and use performance appraisal methods that are useful for
employee development as well as for administrative purposes.

Some evidence of the effects of the potential conflicts in performance
appraisal on *those being rated* is provided in the study by Ilgen, Peterson,
Martin, and Boeschen (1981) mentioned earlier. These authors found
that subordinates overestimated their own work performance even after
receiving contrary appraisal feedback. One explanation for this result is
that the employees' desire to maintain a good self-image won out over
the desire for objective feedback; these ratees heard only what they
wanted to hear in the interview.

Ilgen and his colleagues offer an alternative explanation for some of
the disagreement they found between the actual performance ratings
and the subordinates' reports of this feedback. They suggest that some
raters may have attempted to deal with their own conflicts about giving
negative feedback by verbally explaining it away to certain subordinates.
The extent to which this occurred is not known, but there is evidence

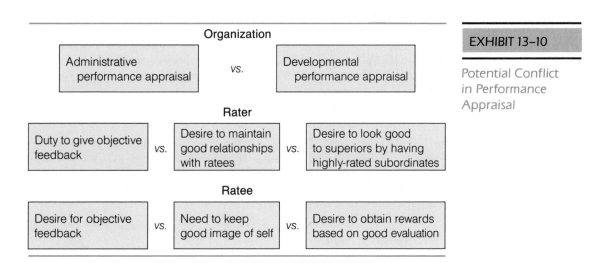

EXHIBIT 13–10

Potential Conflict
in Performance
Appraisal

that the upcoming rater-ratee conference affects ratings themselves. Fisher (1979) reports greater leniency in ratings when raters knew that they would have to meet with ratees face-to-face about the results than when they would not have to have such a meeting.

The amount of error introduced into performance appraisal by the kinds of problems discussed above is not known, but it seems likely that it can be substantial. Support for this possibility is offered by Gandz and Murray (1980) who found performance appraisal to be one of the two activities managers cited most frequently as an example of workplace politics in action. In a broader statement, Zammuto, London, and Rowland (1982) believe that the social environment of an organization is a sufficiently important independent source of error in performance appraisal results to warrant vigorous research efforts.

Rater Sources of Error in Performance Appraisal

The effect that the performance appraisal ratings of one individual has on the lives of others may be substantial. For example, one subordinate may be denied a promotion and another may get a large increase in salary as a result of this evaluation. Given such possibilities, it is unfortunate that raters often are the weakest link in a performance appraisal program. As will be seen, they are the source of a variety of measurement errors.

Unpredictable Errors

Measurement error: See pages 78 to 79.

In the evaluation of others' work performance, measurement error that originates with the rater may be divided roughly into the two general measurement error categories listed in Chapter 4. One type is unpredictable error, the other is constant error.

Unpredictable errors stemming from the individual doing performance appraisal arise from unexpected events or circumstances that may never recur simultaneously with the performance appraisal task. For example, Rater A got into a traffic jam on the way to work and arrived in a foul temper 45 minutes late to be faced with the semiannual performance evaluation forms. Rater B, on the other hand, just got word that a long-awaited promotion has come through and everything looks rosy. Rater C is in the early stages of a bad head cold and finds concentration difficult.

The error that Raters A, B, and C may introduce into their ratings as the result of their unusual physical and/or psychological states may be considerable, but there is no systematic way to control such errors. The only remedy is for raters to monitor themselves and to avoid doing appraisals when they are out of usual form—either way. This remedy assumes, however, that the rater recognizes the state and the effect it might have on the performance appraisal task. It also assumes that it is possible for this task to be put off until things are back to normal, and neither assumption may be correct.

Constant Errors

As the name implies, *constant errors* in performance appraisal are regular and characteristic of the rater even though he or she may not be aware of making them. Constant errors *bias* performance appraisal results in a particular direction. Thus, such errors often are called *rater bias*. This bias may affect all ratees evaluated by a particular individual or only certain ones, depending upon whether it is task based or ratee based.

Task-based rater bias.   Task-based bias in performance appraisal is characterized by an oversimplification of the appraisal task; it tends to be consistent across evaluation situations. In other words, task-based bias is a response to the appraisal task itself and not to the particular individuals being appraised. The most common form of this bias is called evaluative set.

The term **evaluative set** refers to a characteristic tendency on the part of a rater to use only a narrow range of a performance evaluation scale.

Broadly defined, there are three classes of evaluative sets.

1. *Strictness set*—A rater's tendency is to confine appraisals to the lower end of the evaluation scale.
2. *Leniency set*—A rater's tendency is to confine evaluations to the upper end of the evaluation scale.
3. *Central tendency set*—A rater's tendency is to confine appraisals to the center of the scale.

The central tendency set probably is more common in performance appraisal than strictness or leniency sets. Going down the middle and calling everybody "average" is an easy out for raters unable or unwilling to identify differences among ratee levels of performance. Using a scale with no midpoint forces the issue somewhat, but the central tendency set is strong, and those who take this approach to rating will continue to stick as close to the center as possible.

While evaluative sets are very common, they can be circumvented by the rating method used. Ranking methods do not allow for the use of such sets, nor do forced-choice or behavior checklist instruments. The common graphic rating scale is the most susceptible. Behaviorally anchored forms of such scales, if understood and used correctly, may reduce the problem, but empirical evidence is lacking.

Ratee-based rater bias.   Evaluative sets bias performance appraisal results in a general fashion; that is, all of those being evaluated tend to get high, low, or average evaluations regardless of their actual performance. Ratee-based rater bias is not a response to the evaluation task, but a response to the individuals being evaluated. As a result, the actual performance of some ratees may be overestimated, that of some underestimated, and that of others not affected at all by this source of error. The most common form of this bias is called *halo error* (Thorndike, 1920).

The basis for the impression that casts a "halo" over an individual's work behavior can vary. It may stem from a particular piece of information, such as the knowledge that a new employee made the highest score ever recorded on a certain screening test. It may come from some dramatic work performance incident or from a simple personal liking or disliking for the ratee.

Halo error is the tendency of a rater to evaluate all of the behaviors or traits of a ratee in a direction consistent with a global impression or evaluation of that person.

Halo error may introduce bias into performance appraisal in either a positive or a negative direction. Either way, the result is a general similarity of evaluations across all of the traits or behaviors on a rating instrument for a given employee. An example of this is seen in the behavior of Rater 1 in Exhibit 13–11. Such consistency may be justified, of course, but this is unlikely to be the case for more than a very few ratees (Cummings & Schwab, 1973).

Unlike evaluative sets, halo error cannot be circumvented by comparative methods of evaluation, such as ranking. In fact, there is some doubt that halo error can be controlled at all. Even highly specific behaviorally anchored rating scales seem to be vulnerable. In a comprehensive review of the literature on halo error, Cooper (1981) concludes that the most effective approach to reducing this source of error in performance appraisal is to observe a large sample of ratee behavior over time. He goes on to note, however, that it is unlikely that halo error ever can be eliminated entirely.

Halo error is interesting in that the tendency to make this error is predictable, but the direction it will take is not; that is, it seldom is possible to predict in advance which ratees will have a positive bias introduced into their appraisals in this way and which will have a negative bias. A different case is presented by error stemming from *rater prejudice* or *stereotypes*.

A variety of ratee attributes that tend to attract prejudice or stereotypes in a work situation have been investigated as possible sources of rater bias in performance appraisal. Among those more frequently researched are sex (e.g., Nieva & Gutek, 1980), race (e.g., Cascio & Valenzi, 1978), and physical attractiveness (e.g., Ross & Ferris, 1980). Results of these studies vary considerably; systematic performance appraisal bias against females, nonwhites, and less physically attractive people has been found in some cases and not in others.

To an extent, it is likely that the inconsistent findings in personal bias performance appraisal research are a reflection of actual differences in different situations. As Dunnette and Borman (1979) point out, obtained differences in the appraisals of males/females, whites/nonwhites, and other groups may be due to (a) real differences in performance, (b) rater bias, or (c) a combination of these factors, and most researchers do not separate out these effects.

| EXHIBIT 13–11 | Who Is Most Likely Making A Halo Error, Rater 1 or 2? |

Halo Error in Performance Appraisal

	Dimension Ratings on One Ratee						
RATER	A	B	C	D	E	F	G
1	9	9	8	9	8	9	8
2	9	6	4	5	6	4	8

Note: From H. J. Bernardin and E. C. Pence, "Effects of Rater Training: Creating New Response Sets and Decreasing Accuracy." *Journal of Applied Psychology*, 1980, 65(1), p. 60–66. Copyright 1980 by the American Psychological Association. P. 62 reprinted by permission of the authors and the publisher.

Wendelken and Inn (1981) go a step further than Dunnette and Borman and suggest that systematic prejudice and stereotype bias in performance appraisal may be largely a product of laboratory experiments. They postulate that the day-by-day and face-to-face interactions with ratees of different races, ages, and sexes would tend to reduce any such tendencies. This view seems more hopeful than actual. It cannot be evaluated, however, without more carefully controlled research to separate out the different sources of variance in performance appraisal identified by Dunnette and Borman.

IMPROVING PERFORMANCE APPRAISAL

Performance appraisal is vulnerable to many sources of error that act to reduce the reliability and validity of work performance evaluation. Certain decisions about what, when, and how to evaluate will reduce some error, but there almost always are trade-offs. For example, straight ranking offsets bias from a central tendency set, but introduces reliability problems. (A central tendency set produces very reliable ratings—the error it introduces has to do with the *validity* of the evaluations.)

Despite the complexity of the situation, the performance appraisal literature does offer a number of suggestions for improving performance appraisal. Most of these suggestions have to do with the raters who perform the evaluations because no method will ever be any better than those who use it. Two of these suggestions, rater training and use of multiple raters, are discussed here. There is also a brief discussion of the role that job analysis can play in improving performance appraisal.

Rater Training

The most frequently-made recommendation for improving performance appraisal is to give those who will do the evaluations practice in using the actual instrument and training in avoiding common evaluation errors. Investigators report that such training reduces a number of errors in appraisal, including sex and race bias (Schmidt & Johnson, 1973). One recent study in rater training is summarized in "Spotlight on Research."

The rater training method employed in the study from which "Spotlight on Research" is taken was elaborate and may not be practical for many organizations. Fortunately, simpler lecture and practice training is also effective. For example, the Sybron Corporation in Rochester, New York, reports favorable increases in rater skills and confidence with a four-week, one-day-a-week program of this nature.

Improving performance evaluation by improving rater skills and confidence can have results that go far beyond the immediate evaluation situation. For example, Pursell, Dossett, and Latham (1980) report that rater training was followed by a significant improvement in the correlation between performance ratings and four of five predictor tests used

SPOTLIGHT ON RESEARCH

Effects of Training and Rating Scales on Rating Errors

Research question: Is rater training effective in reducing certain types of rating errors, and does effectiveness depend on the type of scale?

Type of study: Laboratory experiment.

Subjects: Ninety upper-level business students.

Independent / dependent variables: See page 52.

Independent variables:
- Rater training. Operational definition: Training versus No training.
- Type of rating instrument. Operational definition: One trait, One BARS, One BOS.

Dependent variable: "Correctness" of ratings with respect to the following errors: first impression, halo, contrast effect.

General procedure: All of the subjects were shown videotapes designed to illustrate the various errors. For example, the tape to illustrate the effect of first impressions showed a person upsetting a cup of coffee and talking about the problems of a recent divorce before settling down to a job interview.

Half of the subjects received training in avoiding target errors during the process of recording and evaluating relevant performance behavior. The other half (the control group) did not. One week later, all subjects were shown new tapes, provided with relevant job descriptions, and reminded again of the importance of accuracy in evaluating the behaviors of relevance.

ANOVA: See pages 65 to 66.

Analysis: Analysis of Variance.

Results: The four-hour training program was effective in reducing the target rating errors, regardless of scale. Improvement was smallest on the trait instrument, however.

Conclusions: "On the basis of this study and previous research . . . it would appear that training programs will increase rater accuracy. . . . Rater training programs, if they are to be effective, should concentrate on enhancing the accuracy of rating through discussion of the multidimensionality of work performance, the importance of recording objectively what is seen, and the development of specific examples of effective and ineffective employee behavior" (p. 112).

Summarized from C. H. Fay and G. P. Latham, "Effects of Training and Rating Scales on Rating Errros." *Personnel Psychology,* 1982, *35*(1), pp. 105–116.

for selection. What had appeared initially to be a problem with selection tests turned out to be a problem with the criterion by which the tests were being evaluated—performance appraisal results.

The I/O psychology literature leaves little doubt that various rater training programs have been successful in producing performance evaluation results that are free of certain constant errors, such as evaluative sets. Two points must be added to this conclusion, however. The first is that the extent to which these benefits persist without periodic refresher training has been questioned by a number of studies (e.g., Ivancevich, 1979).

The second point about the effectiveness of rater training is that not all I/O psychologists agree that this form of training helps raters produce *more accurate* appraisals. In their review of the rater training literature, Bernardin and Buckley (1981) point out that the typical rater training experiment may result in substitution of the approach recommended by the training (such as the use of all points of the rating scale) for the previous approach used (such as a leniency set). They call such training programs Rater Error Training (RET; Bernardin & Pence, 1980).

Bernardin and Buckley believe that real improvements in performance appraisal require a different emphasis in training. They see three critical areas to be:

- helping raters to overcome the threat in the rating situation in order to reduce "defensive rating" (see the discussion on social environmental influences on rating);
- establishing a frame of reference for observing and appraising performance that is common to all raters involved;
- standardizing the *observation* of performance that is the basis for appraisals.

The rather different emphasis of the training program described is called Rater Accuracy Training (RAT). With respect to training for standard observation of performance, Bernardin and Buckley suggest that those who do appraisals should keep ongoing notes (diaries) about day-to-day job performance of ratees. They also suggest that the rater's superior monitor this diary to reinforce the commitment of the organization to good performance appraisal. This idea of making good evaluation matter to those who do it is explored further in "At Issue."

Use of Multiple Raters

Although the suggestion is infrequently implemented, the performance appraisal literature has been consistent in recommending the use of more than one rater for each individual being evaluated (e.g., Kane & Lawler, 1979). This practice serves, first of all, as a check on rater sources of error.

Although the evidence suggests that all raters introduce some error into performance evaluations, the use of multiple raters provides an opportunity for some of these errors to cancel out one another. For example, one rater's strictness set would be offset by another's leniency set. In addition, one rater's lack of information about a particular facet of work behavior could be offset by another rater's observations.

Using two raters in performance evaluation can serve yet another purpose if one is the individual being evaluated. As discussed earlier, differences between rater and ratee perceptions of performance are common, and they can be substantial. Formalizing ratee perceptions into self-appraisals (on the same instrument used by the rater) is one way to force rater and ratee to confront, rather than to dismiss, one another's evaluations.

Although empirical studies are limited, Bassett and Meyer (1968) found evidence that subordinates who bring their own appraisals to the performance feedback session behave less defensively during this session. These authors also report that employees who participated in this experimental type of interview received subsequently higher performance ratings than those who did not. This finding seems to merit further research. If the improved performance was partly a result of the more effective discussions made possible by reduced defensiveness, this approach deserves more attention.

Job Analysis

Job description: See pages 260 to 261.

Despite some differences of opinion as to the details of performance appraisal methods, I/O psychologists are in agreement that performance appraisal should be based on the behaviors relevant to performing a job. And an increasing number are beginning to stress job descriptions, based on job analysis, as the logical basis for specifying these behaviors (e.g., Latham & Wexley, 1981).

Job analysis is the process by which a job is examined in order for its component duties and responsibilities to be determined. These are written into a formal statement called a job description, which *describes* the job an employee is to perform. The logic of basing performance appraisal on this description seems self-evident. Certainly from an employee's point of view, being evaluated on the 10 specific tasks on the job description makes more sense than being evaluated on "character" (see Exhibit 13–3).

There is ample evidence that employees are more receptive to job-relevant performance appraisals (e.g., Murray, 1981), but a job description-based approach offers other advantages as well. Most performance appraisal is done by immediate supervisors and managers whose basic day-to-day responsibility is to see that their employees are carrying out defined job duties. Thus, these are the behaviors they have opportunity and reason to observe. Other things being equal, these should be the behaviors they can evaluate most accurately.

Basing performance appraisal on job analysis offers a number of avenues for the improvement of this important function, and external forces are beginning to push in this same direction. Both unions and the Equal Employment Opportunity Commission are becoming increasingly firm about job-related performance appraisal, and job analysis is the means by which this job-relatedness is documented. In a recent review of unfair discrimination cases related to performance appraisal, Feild and Holley (1982) found that defendants (organizations) lost 11 of 14 cases where no job analysis had been used to develop the performance appraisal instrument.

EEOC: See page 112.

Concluding Remarks on Improving Performance Appraisal

There seems little doubt that beginning with job analysis can help build a better performance appraisal program, but it is not a guarantee. A job description is a guide to *what* to appraise. An instrument developed from this base does not eliminate the need for rater training although its specificity may facilitate such training. Nor does it invalidate the suggestion that more than one rater may be useful, especially when it comes time to discuss evaluations with employees.

It also should be noted that the suggestions discussed here are the most frequently-encountered ones for the improvement of performance appraisal in general. Improving any particular program depends upon an analysis of existing procedures. A useful first step in such an analysis is to gather information as to how those who use the current program perceive its utility and effectiveness. One questionnaire for this purpose is shown in Exhibit 13–12.

The questionnaire in Exhibit 13–12 asks for user opinions as to the specificity and availability of performance appraisal information and its perceived utility for employee development. This questionnaire is a particularly interesting one in that it asks those who do performance appraisal to look at the program from the viewpoint of ratee as well as rater. This "in-the-middle" position of many of those who do performance appraisal in organizations and its possible effects on rating behavior often is overlooked in discussions of program effectiveness.

THE PERFORMANCE APPRAISAL INTERVIEW

Throughout the entire discussion of performance evaluation in Chapter 13 the assumption has been that there will be a face-to-face interview between rater and ratee at which results of performance appraisal are discussed. This is not always the case. Some organizations have no such policy; many managers and supervisors are pressed for time, and some believe that such interviews do little good anyway.

While it may be true that feedback sessions are not a sufficient condition for employee performance improvement, they are a necessary condition if performance appraisal is to have any developmental utility. It also appears that the Equal Employment Opportunity Commission is beginning to see such interviews as necessary if performance appraisal

EXHIBIT 13–12

An Organizational
Performance
Appraisal
Questionnaire
Evaluation

Instructions

Respond to the following six statements by indicating the extent to which you agree (or disagree) that the statements accurately describe performance appraisal in your organization. Some statements refer to your experiences in appraising your subordinates' performance; others refer to your experiences in being appraised yourself. Try to reflect as accurately as you can the current conditions in your organization based on your experiences.

SA = Strongly Agree   A = Agree   ? = Neither Agree nor Disagree
D = Disagree   SD = Strongly Disagree

1. I have found my boss's appraisals to be very helpful in guiding my own career development progress.　SA　A　?　D　SD

2. The appraisal system we have here is of no use to me in my efforts toward developing my subordinates to the fullest extent of their capabilities.　SA　A　?　D　SD

3. Our performance appraisal system generally leaves me even more uncertain about where I stand after my appraisal than beforehand.　SA　A　?　D　SD

4. The appraisal system we use is very useful in helping me to clearly communicate to my subordinates exactly where they stand.　SA　A　?　D　SD

5. When higher levels of management around here are making major decisions about management positions and promotions, they have access to and make use of performance appraisal records.　SA　A　?　D　SD

6. In making pay, promotion, transfer, and other administrative personnel decisions, I am not able to obtain past performance appraisal records that could help me to make good decisions.　SA　A　?　D　SD

Note. From M. Sashkin, "Appraising Appraisal: Ten Lessons From Research for Practice." *Organizational Dynamics,* 1981 (Winter), p. 38. Copyright 1981 by Marshall Sashkin. Reprinted by permission of the publisher. Published by AMACOM, a division of American Management Associations, New York. All rights reserved.

information is to be used for administrative purposes. In the Feild and Holley (1982) analysis mentioned earlier, it was discovered that organizations won seven out of nine cases in which performance appraisal results had been reviewed formally with employees. All cases in which there had been no such review were lost.

In general, I/O psychologists have recognized the importance of the performance appraisal interview, and a fair-sized body of literature on this topic has accumulated. The relevant research encompasses a number of issues centering around the question of how such interviews can be made both effective and satisfactory to the participants.

Performance Appraisal Interview Research

A review of the performance appraisal interview literature suggests that a major stumbling block to the effectiveness of this interaction is the very different perspectives of the participants. As discussed earlier, this difference holds the potential for conflict that can have a variety of negative effects on both the interview and the effectiveness of the feedback.

The potential for conflict in a performance appraisal interview is least likely to surface when the performance of the ratee is evaluated as good. Things are different when the rater must give negative feedback. In general, the performance appraisal literature is agreed that most ratees do not react well to interviews when such feedback is given (e.g., Kay, Meyer, and French, 1965).

In one recent study of ratee reactions to negative performance feedback, Dipboye and dePontbriad (1981) found a strong positive correlation between (a) favorability of the feedback received in the interview and (b) ratee satisfaction with the interview and the appraisal method. In further analysis, the authors found that there was greater acceptance of negative feedback if:

* ratees were allowed to participate in the feedback session;
* plans and objectives for the future were discussed in addition to evaluations of past performance;
* ratees were evaluated on factors they perceived as relevant to their work.

The findings of Dipboye and dePontbriad are consistent with other findings in related literature (see Cederblom, 1982). The trend of these findings indicates that fairly frequent, mutual problem-solving and goal-setting discussions based on job-relevant factors are likely to make for more effective and satisfactory performance appraisal feedback.

A Contingency Approach to Performance Feedback

Like the suggestions for improving performance appraisal, the implications of the feedback interview research are general. Cederblom (1982) suggests that such general findings be applied, not in a routine fashion, but in a manner tailored to the particular employees and job situation. He offers several specific suggestions for such tailoring.

* Interviews with high performers in jobs that are not routine should be scheduled at flexible intervals and focused on development.
* Interviews with satisfactory employees in routine jobs should be held at relatively infrequent set intervals and focus on evaluation.
* New or poorly performing employees should have frequent performance feedback interviews with a dual focus on evaluation and development.
* Interviews should be structured for high ratee participation only when

the interview message is not likely to be threatening and the ratee is highly knowledgeable and personally independent or is accustomed to interview participation.

Cederblom's suggestions are somewhat unique in that they integrate a large body of research into a specific set of guidelines for action. There may be certain practical difficulties for organizations in implementing such an approach, but the fundamental message that performance appraisal interviews should not be conducted according to cut-and-dried formulas could be an important stimulus to research in this area.

SUMMARY

The evaluation of work performance involves finding a combination of what, who, when, and how to measure this performance in order to produce a measurement that is sufficiently reliable and valid to be used for a wide variety of organizational and employee-centered purposes. The potential for error in this measurement is substantial because it can come from the instrument used, the environment in which appraisal takes place, and/or the individual doing the rating.

The performance appraisal interview is the usual vehicle for providing feedback to ratees about the results of appraisals. This process can be considerably hampered by the different perspectives of the participants and by the necessity for giving negative feedback to some ratees. A joint problem-solving approach consistent with the limits of the situation can often improve the effectiveness of, and satisfaction with, such interviews. Other suggestions for improving performance appraisal include (a) basing it on job analysis, (b) using multiple raters, and (c) rater training.

AT ISSUE

Appraising the Appraisers

Anyone given the opportunity to observe the performance appraisal process over a period of time in a number of organizations must come away impressed with the amount of indifference, resistance, or downright hostility exhibited toward this task by those charged with performing it. A natural reluctance of people to set themselves up as judges of others may account for some of these reactions. A belief that "nothing is ever done with them anyway" may account for others. Still, these seem inadequate explanations for the frequency with which such reactions are encountered.

A closer look at the administration of performance appraisal programs often reveals a curious phenomenon that may go some way in explaining common negative rater attitudes toward this task. Despite sophisticated instruments, elaborate feedback interview arrangements, and numerous written and verbal statements from top management as to the importance of performance appraisal, there are seldom any rewards for doing it well or any consequences for doing it poorly. Raters understand they must do it and do it by the date specified, but past that it often simply does not matter.

Some years ago, Mager and Pipe (1970) wrote a book on the subject of analyzing the causes of discrepancies between actual behavior and desired behavior in organizations. Along with many other factors, they discuss the frequency with which such disprepancies occur because doing "it" the way someone wants doesn't matter to an individual one way or the other. All too frequently this seems to be the case when "it" is performance appraisal.

To make any work behavior matter it is necessary for those concerned to recognize the behavior and to reward a person when a job is done well. As Mager and Pipe put it: " 'You oughta wanna' does *not* qualify as a universal incentive…" (p. 71), and this applies to performance appraisal as well as to any other behavior. To recognize and reward performance appraisal that is done well, it is necessary to *evaluate* this behavior; that is, it is necessary to "appraise the appraisers."

The performance appraisal literature has much to say about the ability, or lack of ability, of raters to produce ratings free from certain distribution errors. But it has little to say about differences in (a) the effort raters put into collecting relevant information (making observations) for the appraisal task, (b) the time they take to do the evaluation carefully, or (c) the use they make of the results to help subordinates improve their performance. And it has nothing at all to say about rewarding those who collect the information, take the time to do the appraisal well, then work with subordinates on evaluated strengths and weaknesses in the time period between appraisals.

The general lack of attention to appraising the performance appraisal behaviors of raters and to reinforcing those who do it well probably stems from the difficulty of differentiating good from poor performance on this complex task. If so, finding ways around this difficulty is a significant challenge to I/O psychologists. Until attention is given to this important issue, there is no way to make good performance appraisal matter because there is no way to define "good." And until it matters to those who must do it, there is unlikely to be any significant overall improvement in the quality of this critical organizational activity.

REFERENCES

BAIRD, L. S. Self and superior rating of performance: As related to self-esteem and satisfaction with supervision. *Academy of Management Journal,* 1977, *20*(2), 291–300.

BASSETT, G. A., & MEYER, H. H. Performance appraisal based on self review. *Personnel Psychology,* 1968, *21,* 421–430.

BERNARDIN, H. J., & BUCKLEY, M. R. Strategies in rater training. *Academy of Management Review,* 1981, *6*(2), 205–212.

BERNARDIN, H. J., & PENCE, E. C. Effects of rater training: Creating new response sets and decreasing accuracy. *Journal of Applied Psychology,* 1980, *65*(1), 60–66.

BERNARDIN, H. J., & SMITH, P. C. A clarification of some issues regarding the development and use of behaviorally anchored rating scales (BARS). *Journal of Applied Psychology,* 1981, *66*(4), 458–463.

BLANZ, F., & GHISELLI, E. The Mixed Standard Scale: A new rating system. *Personnel Psychology,* 1972, *25*(2), 155–199.

BLUMBERG, M., & PRINGLE, C. D. The missing opportunity in organizational research: Some implications for a theory of work performance. *Academy of Management Review,* 1982, *7*(4), 560–569.

BROGDEN, H. E., & TAYLOR, E. K. The dollar criterion—Applying the cost accounting concept to criterion construction. *Personnel Psychology,* 1950, *3*(1), 133–154.

CASCIO, W. F., & VALENZI, E. R. Relations among criteria of police performance. *Journal of Applied Psychology,* 1978, *63*(1), 22–28.

CEDERBLOM, D. The performance appraisal interview: A review, implications, and suggestions. *Academy of Management Review,* 1982, *7*(2), 219–227.

COOPER, W. H. "Ubiquitous Halo." *Psychological Bulletin,* 1981, *90*(2), 218–244.

CUMMINGS, L. L., & SCHWAB, D. P. *Performance in Organizations: Determinants and Appraisal.* Glenview, IL: Scott, Foresman, 1973.

DeNISI, A. S., RANDOLPH, W. A., & BLENCOE, A. G. Potential problems with peer ratings. *Academy of Management Journal,* 1983, *26*(3), 457–464.

DIPBOYE, R. L., & dePONTBRIAD, R. Correlates of employee reactions to performance appraisals and appraisal systems. *Journal of Applied Psychology,* 1981, *66*(2), 248–251.

DUNNETTE, M. D., & BORMAN, W. C. Personnel selection and classification systems. In M. R. Rosenzweig and L. W. Porter (Eds.), *Annual Review of Psychology* (Vol. 30). Palo Alto, CA: Annual Reviews, Inc., 1979, 477–525.

FAY, C. H., & LATHAM, G. P. Effects of training and rating scales on rating errors. *Personnel Psychology,* 1982, *35*(1), 105–116.

FEILD, M. S., & HOLLEY, W. H. The relationship of performance appraisal system characteristics to verdicts in selected employment discrimination cases. *Academy of Management Journal,* 1982, *25*(2), 392–406.

FISHER, C. Transmission of positive and negative feedback to subordinates: A laboratory investigation. *Journal of Applied Psychology,* 1979, *64,* 533–540.

FLANAGAN, J. C. The critical incident technique. *Psychological Bulletin,* 1954, *51,* 327–358.

GANDZ, J., & MURRAY, V. V. The experience of workplace politics. *Academy of Management Journal,* 1980, *23*(2), 237–251.

GOODALE, J. G., & BURKE, R. J. Behaviorally based rating scales need not be job specific. *Journal of Applied Psychology,* 1975, *60*(3), 389–391.

HENEMAN, R. L., & WEXLEY, K. N. The effects of time delay in rating and amount of information observed on performance rating accuracy. *Academy of Management Journal,* 1983, *26*(4), 677–686.

ILGEN, D. R., PETERSON, R. B., MARTIN, B. A., & BOESCHEN, D. A. Supervisor and subordinate reactions to performance appraisal sessions. *Organizational Behavior and Human Performance,* 1981, *28*(3), 311–330.

IVANCEVICH, J. M. Longitudinal study of the effects of rater training on psychometric error in ratings. *Journal of Applied Psychology,* 1979, *64*(5), 502–508.

KANE, J. S., & BERNARDIN, H. J. Behavioral observation scales and the evaluation of performance appraisal effectiveness. *Personnel Psychology,* 1982, *35*(3), 635–641.

KANE, J. S., & LAWLER, E. E. Methods of peer assessment. *Psychological Bulletin,* 1978, *85*(3), 555–586.

KANE, J. S., & LAWLER, E. E. Performance appraisal effectiveness: Its assessment and determinants. In B. M. Staw (Ed.), *Research In Organizational Behavior,* 1979, *1*, 425–478.

KAY, E., MEYER, H. H., & FRENCH, J. R. P. Effects of threat in a performance appraisal interview. *Journal of Applied Psychology,* 1965, *49*, 311–317.

KINGSTROM, P. O., & BASS, A. R. A critical analysis of studies comparing behaviorally anchored rating scales (BARS) and other rating formats. *Personnel Psychology,* 1981, *34*(2), 263–289.

LANDY, F. J., & TRUMBO, D. A. *Psychology of Work Behavior* (rev. ed.). Homewood, IL: Dorsey Press, 1980.

LATHAM, G. P., FAY, C., & SAARI, L. M. The development of behavioral observation scales for appraising the performance of foremen. *Personnel Psychology,* 1979, *32*(2), 299–311.

LATHAM, G. P., & WEXLEY, R. N. *Increasing Productivity Through Performance Appraisal.* Reading, MA: Addison-Wesley, 1981.

LAZER, R. I., & WIKSTROM, W. S. *Appraising Managerial Performance: Current Practices and Future Directions.* New York: The Conference Board, 1977.

LOVE, K. G. Comparison of peer assessment methods: Reliability, validity, friendship bias, and user reaction. *Journal of Applied Psychology,* 1981, *66*(4), 451–457.

MAGER, R. F., & PIPE, P. *Analyzing Performance Problems or ''You Really Oughta Wanna!''* Belmont, CA: Fearon, 1970.

MITCHELL, T. R., & KALB, L. S. Effects of outcome knowledge and outcome valence on supervisors' evaluations. *Journal of Applied Psychology,* 1981, *66*(5), 604–612.

MITCHELL, T. R., & LIDEN, R. C. The effects of social context on performance evaluations. *Organizational Behavior and Human Performance,* 1982, *29*(2), 241–256.

MURRAY, R. S. Managerial perceptions of two appraisal systems. *California Management Review,* 1981, *23*(3), 92–96.

NIEVA, V. F., & GUTEK, B. A. Sex effects on evaluation. *Academy of Management Review,* 1980, *5*(2), 267–276.

PETERS, L. H., & O'CONNOR, E. J. Situational constraints and work outcomes: The influence of a frequently overlooked construct. *Academy of Management Review,* 1980, *5*(3), 391–397.

PORTER, L. W., LAWLER, E. E., III., & HACKMAN, R. J. *Behavior in Organizations.* New York: McGraw-Hill, 1975.

PURSELL, E. D., DOSSETT, D. L., & LATHAM, G. P. Obtaining valid predictors by minimizing rating errors in the criterion. *Personnel Psychology,* 1980, *33*(1), 91–96.

ROSINGER, G., MYERS, L. B., LEVY, G. W., LOAR, M., MOHRMAN, S. A., & STOCK, J. R. Development of a behaviorally based performance appraisal system. *Personnel Psychology,* 1982, *35*(1), 75–88.

ROSS, J., & FERRIS, K. R. Interpersonal attraction and organizational outcomes: A field examination. *Administrative Science Quarterly,* 1980, *26*(4), 617–632.

SAAL, F. E., & LANDY, F. J. The mixed standard rating scale; An evaluation. *Organizational Behavior and Human Performance,* 1977, *18*(1), 19–35.

SASHKIN, M. Appraising appraisal: Ten lessons from research for practice. *Organizational Dynamics,* 1981, *9*(3), 37–50.

SCHMIDT, F. L., & JOHNSON, R. H. Effect of race on peer ratings in an industrial situation. *Journal of Applied Psychology,* 1973, *57*(3), 237–241.

SHRAUGER, J. S., & OSBERG, T. M. The relative accuracy of self-predictions and judgements by others in psychological assessment. *Psychological Bulletin,* 1981, *90*(2), 322–351.

SMITH, P. C., & KENDALL, L. M. Retranslation of expectations: An approach to the construction of unambiguous anchors for rating scales. *Journal of Applied Psychology,* 1963, *47*(2), 149–155.

THORNDIKE, E. L. A constant error in psychological ratings. *Journal of Applied Psychology,* 1920, *4*(1), 25–29.

THORNTON, G. C., III. Psychometric properties of self-appraisals of job performance. *Personnel Psychology,* 1980, *33*(2), 263–271.

WENDELKEN, D. J., & INN, A. Nonperformance influences on performance evaluations: A laboratory phenomenon? *Journal of Applied Psychology,* 1981, *66*(2), 149–158.

WHERRY, R. J., & BARTLETT, C. J. The control of bias in ratings: A theory of rating. *Personnel Psychology,* 1982, *35*(3), 521–551.

WHITE, G., HARTLEY, W. D., PETERSON, S., & LANIER, L. K. A drive to put quality back into U.S. goods. *U.S. News & World Report,* 1982, (September 20), pp. 49–50.

WYER, R. S., JR., & SRULL, T. K. Category accessability: Some theoretical and empirical issues concerning the processing of social stimulus information. In E. T. Higgins, C. P. Herman, and M. P. Zanna (Eds.), *Social Cognition: The Ontario Symposium on Personality and Social Psychology.* Hillsdale, NJ: Erlbaum, 1980.

ZAMMUTO, R. F., LONDON, M., & ROWLAND, K. M. Organization and rater differences in performance appraisals. *Personnel Psychology,* 1982, *35*(3), 643–658.

CHAPTER 14

Absenteeism, Turnover, and Job Commitment

I/O PSYCHOLOGY AT WORK

Gold Handcuffs

Even for the cash-flush oil industry, employees of Mitchell Energy & Development Co. near Houston enjoy some unusually lucrative benefits. Mitchell will finance homes for new workers through its own mortgage company at subsidized rates for up to six years. Executives marked for promotion can receive stock options worth as much as $500,000—without investing a penny of their own—that are fully redeemed by the company in six years. Some top employees may also receive shares in a company-sponsored oil-well drilling program. In fact, working at Mitchell has become so profitable that many employees would not even consider leaving.

This is precisely the company's goal. With corporate loyalty as outmoded as the 3¢ postage stamp, Mitchell Energy and many other American companies are examining ways to cut down on job hopping. According to Deutsch, Shea & Evans, a New York executive search firm, most companies expect half of their new employees to leave within five years. Booming industries like energy and computers are among the hardest hit, and some oil companies lose 30% or more of their exploration geologists each year.

The key ingredient of all the new plans is that they give money to employees several years in the future and only if they stay with the company. These ties that bind have become known in industry as "golden handcuffs." While they have long been common for very top executives, the programs are now routinely used for lower-ranking scientists or technicians. "We do not think in terms of locking someone in," says Ed Boches, public affairs director of Data General, a Massachusetts computer manufacturer. "We think that we'd like this person to stay, and this means we have to do something for him."

Management is understandably unhappy when trained productive employees want to leave the company, and often the company will offer incentives to reduce such turnover. "Golden handcuffs" are something of a new wrinkle—a turnover preventative measure put into effect before an employee begins work. So far, as the experience at Mitchell Energy and Development Company suggests, such programs seem to be successful.

Turnover is one of the two most frequently-used nonperformance behavioral criteria in I/O psychology research. The other is absenteeism. Both behavioral responses to a work situation are employed as measures of the success of recruiting, screening, selection, training and other activities designed to increase the fit between individuals, jobs, and organizations.

In Chapter 14, the meaning and measurement of turnover and absenteeism, along with reviews of the major lines of research into the determinants of these behaviors, are explored. Job commitment, the psychological state associated with regular work attendance and staying with the company, is also discussed.

ABSENTEEISM

Estimates of the cost of absenteeism to American organizations vary considerably, but fully-loaded costs are believed to be as high as $25 billion a year. The term *fully-loaded* means that indirect costs are included in the estimate as well as direct pay and benefits to employees who are not productive because they are not at work. Among the indirect costs of absenteeism are:

- administrative time to reorganize around an absent employee;
- costs of temporary replacement employees;
- performance losses due to a shorthanded staff or to employees not as well trained doing a job.

Whatever the true cost of absenteeism, it is undoubtedly high, and I/O psychologists have been studying this behavior for some time. Until recently, however, this interest has taken a rather narrow focus. There has been wide acceptance of the view that absenteeism is a ''. . . pain reductive response on the part of the worker to his work experience . . .'' (Nicholson, Brown, Chadwick-Jones, 1976, p. 735). In other words, absenteeism long has been believed to be a behavioral response to job dissatisfaction.

The premise that most absenteeism is caused by job dissatisfaction is based on a large number of studies in which questionnaire measures of job satisfaction were correlated with company records of absenteeism. The trend of these data shows a negative relationship between job satisfaction and absenteeism.

Correlation: See pages 61 to 63.

Despite the consistency of the findings, Locke (1976) and others have pointed out that measures of job satisfaction account for only a small amount of the variance in absenteeism. More recently, it also has been suggested that the causality might even go the other way; that is, absenteeism might have aversive consequences that promote job dissatisfaction (Clegg, 1983). This interesting hypothesis is discussed further in Chapter 15.

Variance explained: See pages 64 to 66.

Hypothesis: See page 47.

A closer examination of long-held assumptions about absenteeism has served to open up the study of this behavior considerably in the past 10 years. Three directions in which this research is moving may be identified as:

- investigations of absenteeism itself, its meaning and its measurement;
- investigations of the correlates of absenteeism, including, but not limited to, job satisfaction;
- investigations of the control of absenteeism.

Correlates: See pages 63 to 64.

Some recent representative research from each of these three categories is discussed here. The job satisfaction-absenteeism research is discussed in detail in Chapter 15.

The Meaning and Measurement of Absenteeism

Dependent variable: See page 52.

Operational definition: See page 48.

Although absenteeism seems to be a self-evident behavioral dependent variable, there are actually a number of ways in which it can be measured, or operationalized. The two most frequently-employed measures are (a) total days (or sometimes hours) lost and (b) frequency of absence occurrences. Further complicating matters is the issue of excused versus unexcused absences. If no such distinction is made, an absence for jury duty will be "thrown into the same data pot" with an absence for which no reason is given. If such a distinction *is* made, someone must make the decision concerning which absences are excused and which are not.

Organizations differ considerably in their policies about excused versus unexcused absences and whether or not anyone records absence reasons at all. Many companies simply allow for some number of "personal days" per month or year and do not question reasons for absence (unless the number of absences exceeds this figure). There is also considerable variation in supervisory accuracy in recording absence information. As Hammer and Landau (1981) note: ". . . criterion contamination can occur during the initial classification of absences, before a researcher ever touches the raw data" (p. 578).

Contamination: See page 402.

Initial criterion contamination, combined with differences in operational definitions of absenteeism, cast doubt on the wisdom of drawing any firm conclusions from absenteeism research as a whole. Both amount and kind of error is likely to be different in each study. A graphic illustration of the problem is shown in Exhibit 14–1.

Histogram: See page 161.

The histograms in Exhibit 14–1 illustrate the differences in obtained data distributions when six different measures of absenteeism were made on the same data (Hammer & Landau, 1981). Three of these measures were based on unexcused absences (voluntary) and three on excused (involuntary). Not only do these distributions differ from one another, every one has a significant deviation from the normal curve. And normality is a basic assumption underlying correlation and regression analysis.

Normal curve: See pages 59 to 60.

Most statistical analysis techniques can be used when there are mild deviations from normality. Hammer and Landau's data, however, are a very useful illustration of the inherent problems when absenteeism is used as a research variable. One of the more interesting suggestions to date for getting around these problems was made by Latham and Pursell (1975). These authors recommended that *attendance*, rather than absenteeism, be measured.

Reliability: See page 67.

Latham and Pursell cite dramatic increases in data reliability when attendance data were substituted for absence data, but their suggestion has not gained widespread acceptance. Even though all absences are not the same (and all attendances are), most researchers have concluded

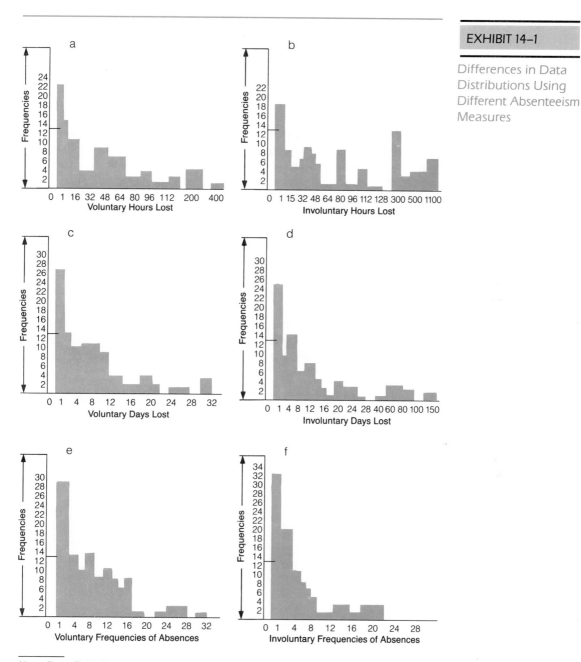

EXHIBIT 14–1

Differences in Data
Distributions Using
Different Absenteeism
Measures

Note. From T. H. Hammer and J. Landau. ''Methodological Issues in the Use of Absence Data.'' *Journal of Applied Psychology,* 1981, *66*(5), pp. 574–581. Copyright 1981 by the American Psychological Association. P. 569 adapted by permission of the authors and the publisher.

that absenteeism measures are preferable to attendance measures. A discussion of this issue may be found in Smulders (1980).

Latham and Pursell suggest a *standardized operational definition* as a solution to some of the problems researchers have in defining and measuring

Utility: See pages 92 to 95.

absenteeism. A different approach is to use more than one measure and compare the relative utility for research purposes, much as Hammer and Landau (1981) compared statistical properties. A study by Popp and Belohlav (1982) of absenteeism among all male, predominantly black employees of the City of Cincinnati's Solid Waste Collection Division illustrates this approach.

There were 19 predictor variables used in the Popp and Belohlav study. Only two of these variables, time with the Division and service in the Armed Forces, had a significant correlation (negative) with absenteeism as measured by total days lost. An additional three variables—job satisfaction, marital status, and perceived supervisory attitude toward absenteeism—were significantly correlated with absence frequency. In this organization, then, more could be learned about the correlates of absenteeism if it were defined in terms of absence frequency than in terms of total days absent.

Significance: See pages 58 to 59.

A different slant on the question of the measurement of absenteeism is taken by those who point out that global measures fail to address the issue of time-related trends in absenteeism. For example, differences in absenteeism over the five standard work days have been observed frequently. The typical pattern, as illustrated by the graph in Exhibit 14–2, is characterized by somewhat higher absenteeism on Mondays than on Tuesdays through Thursdays, and much higher absenteeism on Fridays than on other days.

EXHIBIT 14–2

Daily Trends in Absenteeism

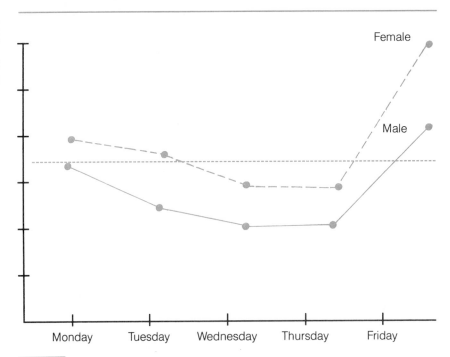

Note. From S. E. Markham, F. Dansereau Jr., and J. A. Alutto, "Female vs. Male Absence Rates: A Temporal Analysis." *Personnel Psychology*, 1982, *35*(2), pp. 371–382. P. 379 reprinted by permission of the authors and the publisher.

The study from which the graph in Exhibit 14–2 is taken was an investigation into the possible differences between male and female absence patterns in a large manufacturing plant (Markham, Dansereau, & Alutto, 1982). While such daily trends in absenteeism may be circumvented by collecting data for longer time periods, Markham and his colleagues also found strong seasonal trends. For example, six months is a fairly common minimum data collection period in absenteeism research. As Exhibit 14–3 illustrates, however, very different conclusions might be drawn from January to June data as opposed to July to December data.

Taken as a whole, the problems and issues discussed regarding the meaning and measurement of absenteeism suggest that caution should be taken when inferences are drawn from the research literature. Different ways of measuring absenteeism yield different results and can lead to different conclusions. Accordingly, any detailed comparative analysis of absenteeism studies should be undertaken only if the measures used are similar.

Inference: See page 58.

EXHIBIT 14–3

Seasonal Trends in Absenteeism

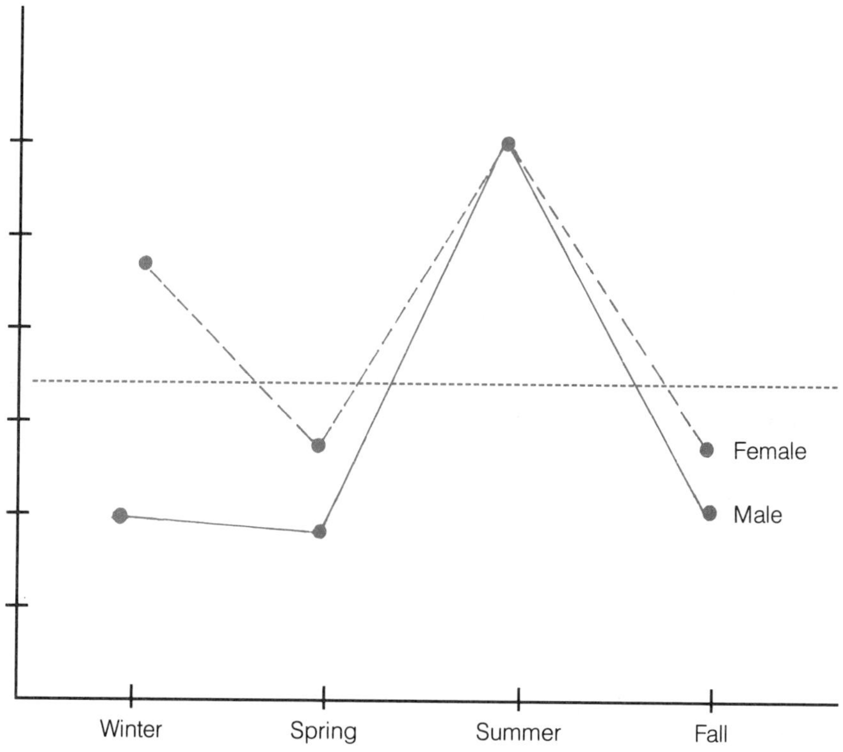

Female

Male

Winter   Spring   Summer   Fall

Note. From S. E. Markham, F. Dansereau Jr., and J. A. Alutto, "Female vs. Male Absence Rates: A Temporal Analysis." *Personnel Psychology,* 1982, *35*(2), pp. 371–382. P. 377 reprinted by permission of the authors and the publisher.

Research finds consistent differences between male and female employees in both absenteeism and turnover rates.

The Determinants of Absenteeism

Determinant: See page 64.

The search for personal characteristics and organizational variables associated with employees' tendencies to be absent from work has developed partially out of the realization that job dissatisfaction alone is an insufficient explanation. It must be noted, however, that proponents of the "job dissatisfaction causes absenteeism" hypothesis have made significant contributions to this research. By attempting to identify characteristics and variables associated with dissatisfaction (and so, with greater absenteeism), they have generated a meshing body of data.

Personal Variables and Absenteeism

Individual characteristics: See pages 28 to 33.

Among the personal characteristics most frequently investigated in connection with absenteeism are the following:

- age
- education
- marital status
- number of dependents
- race
- sex

Job tenure and level of position in the organization also are considered by some researchers to be personal characteristics (others define these variables as situational). All of these characteristics have been found to correlate with absenteeism, but the trend of the findings is not consistent and the variance explained is not large.

The least ambiguous relationship to emerge from investigations of the role of personal characteristics in absenteeism is the relationship between absenteeism and sex. The results of most of the studies of this variable show that women have a higher rate of absenteeism than men (e.g., Fitzgibbons & Moch, 1980; Markham, et al., 1982; Spencer & Steers, 1980). This trend may be observed in Exhibits 14-2 and 14-3.

A variety of explanations have been advanced for the finding that women are absent more from work than men. Most of these explanations center around the role conflict that can be generated by the special demands placed on women who work and also have families to take care of. The fact that women, in general, hold lower-level jobs than men, in general, (Semyonov, 1980) also is believed to be a relevant factor.

Organizational Variables and Absenteeism

A number of different aspects of the organizational job situation have been investigated in the search for the determinants of absenteeism. One that has received considerable attention is the *nature of the work* that an individual performs. Much of this research is based on the hypothesis that boring, unfulfilling work leads to job dissatisfaction, which in turn leads to increased absenteeism (see, for example, Maier & Verser, 1982). Some of this research supports this hypothesis and some does not; individual differences appear to be substantial.

A second organizational variable whose possible relationship to absenteeism has interested researchers is *size*, both size of the organization (e.g., Cleland, 1955) and size of the individual's work group (e.g., Markham, Dansereau, & Alutto, 1982). A general trend toward less absenteeism in smaller organizations and groups may be postulated on the basis on this research. This inference must be made with caution, however, because different studies in this line of research are difficult to compare directly.

Other organizational variables whose possible correlation with absenteeism have been investigated include:

- leader behavior (e.g., Johns, 1978)
- company ownership (e.g., Hammer, Landau, & Stern, 1981)
- employee shift (e.g., Watson, 1981)

Significant correlations have been found with all of these variables, but far more research is needed before conclusions may be drawn about their importance as general determinants of absenteeism.

A Model of Employee Attendance

Steers and Rhodes (1978) combine a variety of situational and individual variables into the employee attendance model shown in Exhibit 14-4.

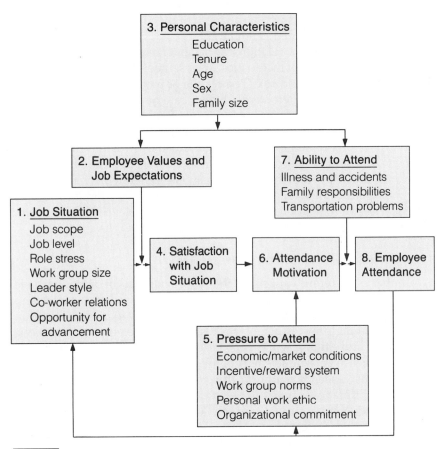

EXHIBIT 14–4

The Steers and
Rhodes Model of
Employee Attendance

Note. From R. M. Steers and S. R. Rhodes, "Major Influences on Employee Attendance: A Process Model." *Journal of Applied Psychology*, 1978, 63(4), pp. 391–407. Copyright 1978 by the American Psychological Association. P. 393 reprinted by permission of the authors and the publisher.

This model, although based to a considerable degree on the correlational relationships found in the absenteeism literature, is a process model. Some variables (e.g., ability to attend) are postulated to have a direct effect on attendance. Other variables (e.g., job expectations and aspects of the job situation) interact to affect the process by which the relevant attitudes and motivation of employees produce attendance or absence.

The complexity of the process hypothesized in the model in Exhibit 14–4 makes it difficult to test in its entirety. Research has yielded support for certain of the relationships, however. For example, Watson (1981) found age, marital status, shift, and tenure to be related to a time-lost measure of absenteeism; however, the postulated effect of job satisfaction was not confirmed.

Controlling Absenteeism

Absenteeism in organizations is a problem; one reason why it has received so much research attention is the expectation that a better understanding of absenteeism will offer guidelines for corrective action. The most obvious use of such research is to "select out" at the beginning job applicants with characteristics known to be associated with greater absenteeism.

Unfortunately, the practicality of refusing to hire people who are statistically more likely to be absent from work because of certain traits is limited. For example, sex is the most stable personal correlate of absenteeism, but discrimination in hiring on the basis of sex is prohibited by law. The finding of Breaugh (1981) that the best predictor of absenteeism is past absenteeism is more promising because this is a behavior and not a personal trait. The extent to which Breaugh's result, which is based on a study in one organization, can be generalized from one job to the next is not yet established, however.

EEO and hiring: See pages 126 to 127.

Generalization: See page 67.

If it is not practical to select out job applicants more likely to be absent, it is necessary to change something in the work situation to reduce absenteeism. This is one rationale behind some psychologists' attempts to establish situational correlates of absenteeism. An effective approach to controlling absenteeism has been available for some time, however, and has been used successfully in a variety of settings. This approach, positive reinforcement, is discussed in Chapter 12 in connection with motivation. A recent study by Carlson and Hill (1982) illustrates its application to controlling absenteeism.

Positive reinforcement: See pages 360 to 364.

Carlson and Hill used an application of positive reinforcement principles called *gaming* in a longitudinal study of absenteeism in a small California manufacturing plant. Eligibility to play a bingo-type game for immediate cash prizes was made contingent on work attendance. Absenteeism for one pregame, three game, and two hiatus (no game) periods over an 18-month period are shown in Exhibit 14–5.

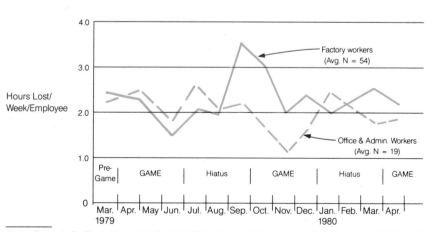

EXHIBIT 14–5

Reducing Absenteeism by Positive Reinforcement

Note. From J. G. Carlson and K. D. Hill, "The Effect of Gaming on Attendance and Attitude." *Personnel Psychology*, 1982, *35*(1), pp. 63–73. P. 69 reprinted by permission of the authors and the publisher.

As may be seen in Exhibit 14–5, gaming was associated with a dramatic drop in absenteeism for office and administrative workers. The factory workers' pattern, while less impressive, is similar. In addition, questionnaires administered before the gaming was instituted, and again one year later, showed significant improvements in expressed attitudes about the company even though nothing had actually changed.

Much of the improvement in employees' attitudes expressed after the positive reinforcement program for attendance was instituted at the California plant was attributed to the better communication that grew out of the program. Specifically, in the course of weekly meetings to determine game winners, employees got to know one another and to interact with management. The president of the company also used this opportunity to make announcements concerning such matters of interest as new employees, sales data, and upcoming company events.

Despite positive results, such as those reported by Carlson and Hill, it would not be accurate to say that the problem of absenteeism is solved. Such techniques do not always fit a particular situation. In addition, there can be considerable resistance to this approach. Some perceive it as too manipulative; others object to rewarding people for something they "should" do anyway (i.e., come to work).

Absenteeism in Perspective

Another objection to the reinforcement approach to reducing absenteeism is put forth by Staw and Oldham (1978) who raise the question of whether or not reducing absenteeism is always an appropriate goal. In an interesting study of the relationship between absenteeism and job performance (as evaluated by management), these authors found support for the following two hypotheses:

1. There will be a *positive* correlation between absenteeism and performance for individuals who perceive their jobs to be either too challenging or not challenging enough.
2. There will be a *negative* correlation between absenteeism and performance for individuals who perceive their jobs to offer about the right amount of challenge for their needs.

In other words, Staw and Oldham found that employees who are absent from work more are not necessarily poorer performers. They suggest that absenteeism may be the way that some workers cope with the pressures of jobs that do not fit their needs, desires, or abilities and still perform satisfactorily. If this is true, then comprehensive absenteeism-reduction programs could give rise to other problems. In the words of Staw and Oldham (1978):

> . . . *programs designed specifically to reduce absenteeism without changing more basic aspects of the job may carry some dysfunctional side effects. For example, when a contingent monetary reward . . . is provided for job*

attendance, the individual will probably reduce his absenteeism. However, if the job still remains psychologically incompatible with the individual, he may find it even more difficult to maintain his performance (p. 556).

Whether attempts to reduce absenteeism can backfire and lead to performance decrements is an empirical question as yet unresearched. Staw and Oldham, however, raise a valid issue when they question the assumption that absenteeism is always an "organizational bad." Their research also adds additional weight to the argument for efforts to match individual needs and abilities with job rewards and requirements at the selection and placement stage.

Matching model: See page 133.

TURNOVER

Until the last 10 years or so, the study of absenteeism and the study of turnover usually have been quite firmly linked. Absenteeism generally was seen as a safety valve for employees who were dissatisfied with their jobs; turnover was the last resort when pressures got too great. This view was supported by the number of studies finding positive correlations between absenteeism and turnover.

General recognition that absenteeism and turnover are separate behaviors warranting separate analyses seems to have begun in the middle 1970s. Despite the trend of empirical findings, which suggested a positive relationship between the two, many of the correlation coefficients were small. In addition, there were studies in which no relationship was found. Mobley (1982) offers a helpful summary of the range of plausible conditions under which no correlation between these behaviors would be expected. This summary is shown in Exhibit 14-6.

---

a) when turnover is a function of the positive attraction of an alternative job rather than escape, avoidance, or "withdrawal" from an unsatisfying or stressful current job;

b) when absenteeism is a function of the need to attend to nonjob role demands (e.g., parent, sports person);

c) when the consequences of quitting relative to the consequences of being absent have little in common;

d) when absenteeism or turnover is constrained, for example, a monetarily enforced absenteeism control policy and no job alternatives, respectively;

e) when absenteeism or turnover is a spontaneous or impulsive act;

f) when the work role is structured so as to permit discretionary, nonrecorded time away from the job, for example, professional, managerial positions;

g) when nonused days of absence are "vested" and can be taken with pay at the time of termination;

h) when absenteeism serves as a "safety valve" to dissipate work pressures that otherwise might precipiate turnover.

EXHIBIT 14-6

Conditions under which No Correlation between Absenteeism and Turnover Would be Expected

---

Note. From W. H. Mobley, "Some Unanswered Questions in Turnover and Withdrawal Research." *Academy of Management Review*, 1982, 7(1), pp. 111–116. P. 114 reprinted by permission of the author and the publisher.

It is indeed likely that there are cases in which absenteeism and turnover are positively related. An examination of the conditions listed in Exhibit 14–6, however, reveals the variety of situational factors that can separate the decision to be absent from work from the decision to leave a job. Although absenteeism and turnover still are investigated frequently within the context of the same research design, they have been separated conceptually to a considerable extent. Turnover research, even more than absenteeism research, has been expanded considerably.

The Classification of Turnover

Position: See page 247.

Turnover, like absenteeism, seems a simpler concept than it is. Bluedorn (1978) points out at least two different uses of the term in the literature. In the *generic* sense, turnover refers to a change in the membership of an organization; that is, a *position* turns over with an outgoing incumbent being replaced by a newcomer. In the *specific* use of the term, turnover refers to outgoing organizational *members*.

When used in the specific sense, it is usual to further divide turnover into *voluntary* and *involuntary* separations (Price, 1977); that is, to distinguish between employees who leave of their own accord and those who are terminated. Although most organizations define their turnover problems in terms of the number of voluntary separations, these are only part of turnover in the generic sense.

The voluntary-involuntary turnover distinction has been a basic one for some time, but as turnover research has expanded, it has become apparent that this distinction may be oversimplified. Some voluntary turnover occurs with employees an organization does not mind losing; in other cases, the organization would prefer to retain the services of those who are leaving. In other words, from the organization's point of view, some voluntary turnover is *functional* and some *dysfunctional* (Dalton, Todor, & Krackhardt, 1982).

A case of dysfunctional turnover occurs when an employee a company wishes to keep leaves. There are any number of reasons this might occur, and some have little to do with the organization. Among these reasons are:

- a spouse's job opportunity in another location
- illness
- a decision to resume an interrupted education
- a decision to make a change in lifestyle

There is little an organization can do to reduce voluntary turnover among employees who leave for reasons such as those listed. Accordingly, such turnover may be called *unavoidable dysfunctional turnover.* The remainder of the dysfunctional voluntary turnover group, employees who leave for job- or organization-related reasons, is the *avoidable dysfunctional turnover.*

Increasingly refined classifications of turnover have utility both for understanding this behavior and for applied efforts to reduce turnover. The "turnover problem" of an organization can be separated into a number of distinct groups that begins with the *voluntary-involuntary* distinction. This dichotomy can further be separated into *functional* and *dysfunctional* turnover, which in turn can be divided into *avoidable* and *unavoidable* turnover.

To the extent that there are different dynamics underlying turnover for different classifications, researchers' efforts to understand this behavior will be enhanced if these distinctions are made. For example, separating out the unavoidable voluntary turnover group should increase the success of research into the organizational variables associated with turnover because these variables have little relevance for the unavoidable group.

The practical utility of a more detailed analysis of turnover is illustrated in Exhibit 14–7. Based on the older simple classification of *voluntary-involuntary* turnover, an organization attempting to reduce turnover must try to sort out the relevant factors in the entire voluntary group (a hypothetical 30% in Exhibit 14–7). A more refined classification shrinks the actual size of the group toward which efforts to reduce turnover should be directed to less than one-fourth of that number.

The percentages used by Dalton and his colleagues (1982) in Exhibit 14–7 are hypothetical, but consistent with estimates in actual situations. For example, in one western bank, about half of the voluntary turnover

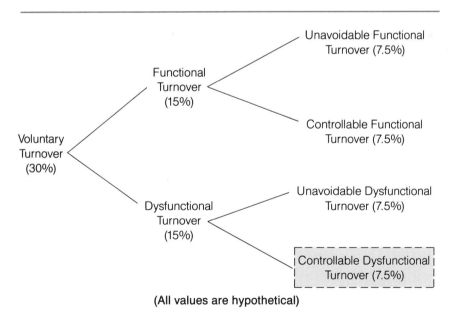

EXHIBIT 14–7

A Taxonomy of
Voluntary Turnover

(All values are hypothetical)

Note. From D. R. Dalton, W. D. Todor, and D. M. Krackhardt, "Turnover Overstated: The Functional Taxonomy." *Academy of Management Review*, 1982, 7(1), pp. 117–123. P. 122 reprinted by permission of the authors and the publisher.

was estimated to be functional, and about half of the dysfunctional turnover was judged to have been unavoidable (Dalton, Krackhardt, & Porter, 1981).

It is too soon to speculate about the extent to which new perspectives on turnover classification will lead to the reevaluation of conclusions from the existing body of turnover research. This possibility should be kept in mind as that research is reviewed here, however. Refer to Abelson and Baysinger (1984) for more detail on new approaches to turnover.

The Determinants of Turnover

As in the absenteeism research, there is considerable emphasis in the turnover literature on the personal and organizational variables that are associated with an individual's tendency to leave the employing organization voluntarily. Trends from this research are summarized here. A comprehensive review may be found in Bluedorn (1982).

Personal Variables and Turnover

Research into individual variables associated with turnover is dominated by investigations of employee job satisfaction; but other individual characteristics that are possibly related to turnover have been investigated. These include:

- sex
- age
- education
- professionalism
- job training
- job tenure
- expressed needs for personal growth on the job
- expressed intention to stay with the organization

Of the variables listed, *tenure* and *expressed intention to stay with a company* have been found to be the most consistently related to employee turnover (Mobley, Griffeth, Hand, & Meglino, 1979). Both relationships are negative; less turnover is associated with longer tenure and greater expressed intentions to stay. The extent to which these findings are useful in reducing turnover is limited, however.

Neither job tenure nor intention to stay with a company can be used at the selection stage to reject job applicants more likely to leave the organization soon after they have been hired because both are contingent upon being hired. In addition, both of these variables have been found to have significant positive correlations with other variables, such as age (Zey-Ferrell, 1982). Without research specifically addressed to the question, it is difficult for researchers to sort out these relationships in a meaningful fashion.

Turnover and Job Performance

A personal variable whose possible relationship to turnover has interested a number of researchers is job performance. Findings from this line of research are mixed. Some of the relevant literature suggests that it is better performers who leave an organization voluntarily (e.g., Bassett, 1967; Martin, Price, & Mueller, 1981). In other cases, no relationship has been found, and a number of investigations indicate that it is *poorer* performers who are more likely to leave their jobs. A long-term study by Dreher (1982) illustrates this line of research.

In a 15-year study of turnover in a large national oil company, Dreher found no evidence that it was the better performers who left the company. Multiple measures of (a) performance, (b) aptitude, (c) potential, and (d) promotional success supported the opposite hypothesis for the 500-plus employees who voluntarily left the company. Performance ratings and career advancement for "stayers" and "leavers" taken near the end of the 15-year data collection period are shown in Exhibit 14–8.

The "stayers" and "leavers" in the data chart in Exhibit 14–8 all entered the company at about the same time. As may be seen, "stayers" received significantly more promotions per year and significantly higher final performance evaluations than "leavers." Keller (1984) found a similar pattern with respect to performance in a medium-sized manufacturing plant.

Although findings are mixed, the conclusion that there is some relationship between job performance and job tenure seems warranted. One possibility that researchers have suggested for reconciling the different obtained empirical results lies in considering the level of performance as information to an employee about his or her job-related abilities. Jackofsky and Peters (1983) suggest that these abilities are important determinants of both (a) the perceived desirability and (b) the perceived ease of seeking alternative employment (March & Simon, 1958). Their model of this process is shown in Exhibit 14–9.

There is as yet little direct empirical evidence for the model in Exhibit 14–9 although Jackofsky and Peters (1980) report a study in which some preliminary support was found. Certain aspects of other research are

Variable	Stayers		Leavers		
	M	S.D.	M	S.D.	t
Rate of career advancement (number of promotions per year)	.43	.20	.31	.31	4.63*
Final performance appraisal	3.78	.62	3.15	.68	9.76*

*p < .01

Note. From G. F. Dreher, "The Role of Performance in the Turnover Process." *Academy of Management Journal*, 1982, *25*(1), pp. 137–147. Page 144 reprinted by permission of the author and the publisher.

EXHIBIT 14–8

Performance and Career Advancement Differences between "Leavers" and "Stayers"

The Role of Ability
in the Turnover
Process

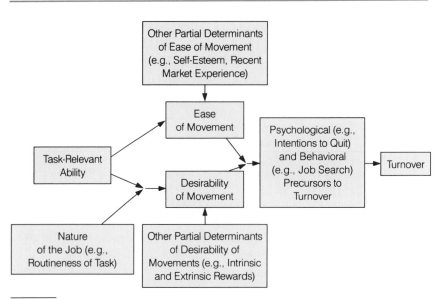

Note. From E. F. Jackofsky and L. H. Peters, ''The Hypothesized Effects of Ability in the Turnover Process.'' *Academy of Management Review*, 1983, *8*(1), pp. 46–49. P. 48 reprinted by permission of the authors and the publisher.

supportive of some of the model's components, however. For example, Keller (1983) found turnover higher for low performers, but he also noted that local employment opportunities at the time of his study were plentiful. Consistent with Jackofsky and Peters' conceptualization, this situation (relevant to ''recent market experience'' in the model) could have increased perceived *ease of movement* sufficiently to cause low performers to seek alternative employment.

Dreher (1982) also found turnover to be higher among poorer performers, but in this case the organization involved was one with a firm commitment to rewarding superior performance. In terms taken from the model in Exhibit 14–9, this reward system may have acted to reduce *desirability of turnover* for good performers (since intrinsic and extrinsic rewards are partial determinants of this factor).

Organizational Variables and Turnover

The reward system of an organization is an organizational, or situational, influence on turnover. Other situational variables that have been studied in this context include *pay, extent to which the job is routine,* and *promotion opportunities.* Both pay and promotion opportunities have been found to have negative correlations with turnover while routinization usually has a positive correlation with turnover (see Bluedorn, 1982).

The search for organizational variables related to turnover, like the search for personal variables, has yielded a number of simple relationships that account for a modest amount of variance. McCain, O'Reilly, and Pfeffer (1983) have suggested that this approach may be too narrow to capture the relationship between turnover and the organizational system. They argue that turnover may be in part a characteristic of the composition of the social system itself.

Organizational system: See pages 282 to 285.

McCain and his colleagues studied turnover in 32 departments of two universities. The particular composition, or *demographic*, variables of interest were (a) the proportion of faculty who entered a department at about the same time (called *cohorts*) and (b) the length of the time gap between groups of cohorts. As expected, they found both characteristics related to turnover. The authors concluded that the distribution within a department of the length of service of its members is related to turnover at almost every faculty rank.

Turnover as a Process

The study by McCain, O'Reilly, and Pfeffer is a complex one reflecting what appears to be a shift in turnover research. Specifically, there seems to be less emphasis on turnover as an *event* that occurs at one point in time and more on turnover as a *process* involving time, change, and individual-organization interactions (e.g., Mobley, 1982).

One of the newer conceptual approaches that emphasize the process view of turnover is an *investment model* somewhat similar in dynamics to the equity theory of motivation discussed in Chapter 12. For example, Farrell and Rusbult (1981) view turnover as stemming from low job commitment. Job commitment, in turn, is believed to be a function of an individual's perceptions of:

Equity theory: See pages 356 to 357.

- his or her relative investments in the job
- the rewards and costs of staying with the company
- perceived viable employment alternatives

The process aspect of Farrell and Rusbult's proposition lies in the fact that the relevant variables and the relationships between them are not static in a correlational sense; they shift over time. Turnover is most likely to occur under that particular combination of circumstances when:

- investments in the job are perceived to be low; *and*
- costs of staying in the organization are perceived to be high; *and*
- rewards for staying in the organization are perceived to be low; *and*
- there are attractive viable alternative employment opportunities.

The investment model suggests that an individual's intention to quit a job develops over time, and any number of factors may intervene to increase his or her job commitment before the act of leaving is carried out. It is not uncommon, for example, for a company to offer an employee who plans to leave inducements (more money, promotion, better working hours, and so on). In terms of the investment model, such inducements may increase the value of the *reward* term and shift the balance back toward job commitment and away from turnover.

Evidence for the investment model of turnover is as yet fragmented.

Farell and Rusbult (see also Rusbult & Farrell, 1983) offer support for their use of job commitment as the dependent variable, finding this variable to be more closely related to turnover than a measure of job satisfaction. There is also suggestive evidence in the results of studies not designed to test the model. For example, Matilla (1974) found that a large percentage of people make arrangements for new employment before they leave the current job. In terms from the model, they have viable alternative employment opportunities.

To what degree the more complex process approach to turnover will increase understanding of this behavior remains to be seen, but there does appear to be a growing movement in this direction. Other process models of turnover have been offered by Bluedorn (1982) and Green-halgh (1980). Similar shifts away from simple correlational relationships to dynamic interrelationships also may be observed in other areas of I/O psychology, such as communication and job performance research.

Turnover in Perspective

Just as some are now beginning to question the assumption that absenteeism in organizations must be eliminated, others are building a case for the idea that turnover can be beneficial as well as harmful to both individuals and organizations. Most of this work has been done by Dalton and his colleagues who argue that turnover has organizational, economic, sociological, and psychological benefits as well as costs (Dalton & Todor, 1979). Some of these benefits are difficult to demonstrate, but there is no such problem with economic benefits.

As illustrated by the story that opened Chapter 14, some organizations are willing to go to great lengths to avoid losing employees and incurring the costs of replacing and training new ones. But Dalton and Todor (1982) have presented convincing evidence that, under certain conditions, these costs are actually offset by savings. For example, in one subunit of a large western public utility, a 15% turnover rate resulted in a one-year savings of over $375,000.

The documented savings in the public utility stemmed largely from the fact that the employees replacing those who left were paid at lower entry-level salaries with associated lower benefit plan costs. This, of course, is not always the case, but such figures do undermine the basic conviction of many that turnover always *costs* money. As Dalton and Todor (1982) note:

The responsible analysis of the impact of turnover on the organization requires a careful examination of both its costs and benefits. Such an analysis may lend credence to those . . . who have suggested that turnover may not be an inexorably dysfunctional phenomenon for the organization (p. 217).

JOB COMMITMENT

The behavioral opposite of leaving an organization (turnover in the specific sense of an individual) is staying with it. The psychological state believed to be associated with staying is job commitment. Job commitment is a variable—it exists in different degrees. At one extreme is *alienation*, a condition under which there is no perceived connection or link at all with the job and the company. At the other extreme of this variable is *identification*; the individual's perception of connection is so strong that his or her self-descriptions tend to be primarily in terms of work role in a particular company (Guion, 1958).

Interest in the variable of job commitment has been stimulated by reports of some relatively strong empirical relationships between this variable and absenteeism (e.g., Cheloha & Farr, 1980) and turnover (e.g., Bartol, 1979; Farrell & Rusbult, 1981). The relationship between job commitment and turnover is supported further by the positive correlation between turnover and an individual's expressed intention to stay with a company as discussed earlier.

Job commitment is a variable reflecting the degree of connection an individual perceives himself or herself to have with a particular job in a particular organization.

The Determinants of Job Commitment

Most researchers agree that strong job commitment comes about through an interaction of (a) personal demographic variables, such as age and sex, (b) personal psychological variables, such as needs and values, and (c) characteristics of the specific work situation. In one recent study, for example, Morris and Sherman (1981) found the following to make significant contributions to predicting responses to a questionnaire measure of job commitment:

- Age and Education (personal demographic variables)
- Sense of competence (personal psychological variable)
- Supervisory Behavior and perceived Job Role Conflict (aspects of the work situation)

Of the many variables proposed as determinants of job commitment, perhaps the one that appears most frequently is the personal *value* system of an individual. More specifically, the literature strongly suggests that people with a high degree of job commitment also place a high value on work for its own sake (Chusmir, 1982).

There are a number of ways to assess the value of work to an individual. One question that gets to the heart of the matter is whether or not people would continue working if they were able to live as they wished without doing so. The classic study in this area is that of Morse and Weiss (1955).

Morse and Weiss reported that some 80% of their sample of 400 male workers would want to keep working even if they had no financial need to do so. These results have been replicated many times with all manner of subjects. As illustrated by the findings of the recent study of this

Survey research: See pages 57 to 58.

SPOTLIGHT ON RESEARCH

The Function and Meaning of Work and the Job: Morse and Weiss (1955) Revisited

Research question: How do present-day attitudes of people toward work compare with the results of Morse and Weiss?

Type of study: Field survey research.

Subjects: One thousand ninety-nine full-time male workers were identified through a quota sampling procedure based on U.S. census information. Average subjects age was 40; average education in years, 12.75; and 92% of the sample was white.

General Procedure: Subjects were interviewed in their homes by full-time professional interviewers. As part of a larger opinion survey, they were asked the following question: "If you were to get enough money to live as comfortably as you would like for the rest of your life, would you continue to work or would you stop working?" Subjects were also asked about their satisfaction with their current jobs.

Results: More than seventy-two percent of the men surveyed said they would continue to work, and just under 28% said they would quit if they became wealthy. Statistically, these results are significantly different from those of Morse and Weiss.

In other analyses, subject age and reported job satisfaction were found to be the strongest predictors of disposition to stop working if it were possible. In general, the older the subject and the less the job satisfaction, the less likely the subject to report he would continue working.

Conclusions: "The present findings underscore significant differences in the predispositions of the labor force of the mid-1970's relative to the labor force of the 1950's. There are several alternative explanations for the observed differences. . . . Excluding [question format and sampling procedures], one is left with the conclusion that an attitudinal shift in the male labor force has occurred over an approximate 20-year period. The shift is best summarized as a 39 percent increase in the number of male workers who would stop working if given the opportunity." (p. 365–366)

Summarized from R. P. Vecchio, "The Function and Meaning of Work and the Job: Morse and Weiss (1955) Revisited." *Academy of Management Journal,* 1980, 23(2), pp. 361–367.

question summarized in "Spotlight on Research," however, things appear to be changing.

The results of Vecchio's (1980) study, together with others of a similar but less comprehensive nature, suggest that the percentage of people who would keep working if they did not have to do so is dropping. Nevertheless, work remains a *central life interest* (Dubin, 1956) for a significant number of people. This is an encouraging finding if valuing work is in fact a necessary condition for job commitment.

A Model of Job Commitment

A number of authors have proposed models incorporating variables found to be correlated with job commitment or hypothesized to be partial determinants of commitment. One such conceptualization (Chusmir, 1982) is shown in Exhibit 14–10.

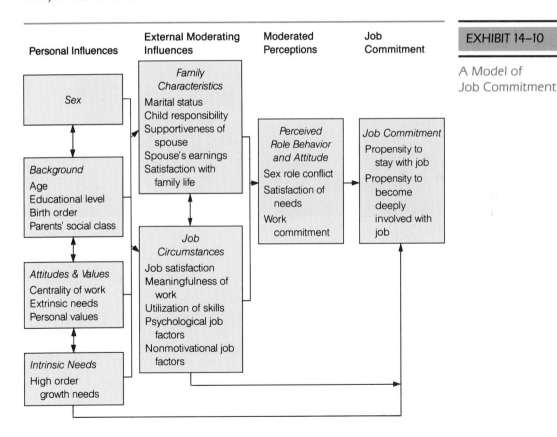

EXHIBIT 14–10

A Model of Job Commitment

Note. From L. H. Chusmir, "Job Commitment and the Organizational Woman." *Academy of Management Review*, 1982, 7(4), pp. 595–602. P. 597 reprinted by permission of the author and publisher.

Many men and women are highly committed to police work despite low pay and stressful working conditions.

Chusmir's model shows job commitment to be the product of three sets of influences—personal, external or situational, and perceptual. Personal and situational variables have a direct influence on degree of job commitment and also interact to produce an individual's moderated perceptions of himself or herself with respect to work and the job.

All of the variables in Chusmir's model have been found to be correlated with job commitment in previous research. This is the first formal model, however, that includes factors outside of the work environment (family characteristics). Chusmir argues that these factors are critical if the model is to be equally applicable to women and men.

Nonwork factors, Chusmir believes, have conceptual relevance to the job commitment of both sexes. Their influence is especially strong on women, however, because nonwork factors are the source of sex-role conflict that working men seldom experience. If this conflict is strong enough, even women who prefer to work outside the home and hold jobs they feel are satisfying may leave the organization, a situation very unlikely for a man.

The work of Chusmir and others in a similar vein is useful in two ways. First it organizes the job commitment research into an identifable unit. Second, it reveals what may be a major weakness in this research —disagreement or confusion about the definition of job commitment.

Reviews of the relevant literature, including that of Chusmir, reveal that the terms *job commitment* and *job involvement* often are used interchangeably. Thus, some of the research used in discussions of job commitment is based on a variable that was actually defined as job involvement. Conceptually, however, these may be separate phenomena, and if so, inferences based on a mixture of research will be misleading. This problem is explored further in ''At Issue.''

SUMMARY

Although separate behaviors, absenteeism and turnover long have been linked in the I/O psychology literature. The assumption that both are caused by job dissatisfaction, with turnover being the final resolution of the problem, was accepted by most as valid. The inadequacy of this conceptualization has become increasingly clear, and research on both behaviors has begun to progress independently. Some investigators also are beginning to doubt that absenteeism and turnover are always detrimental to organizational functioning; this doubt is serving to open up explorations of these phenomena still further.

Job commitment may be defined as the degree of connection an individual perceives himself or herself to have with a job in a particular organization. Less commitment has been found to be correlated with greater absenteeism and with higher rates of turnover. Among the variables believed to be associated with degree of job commitment are personal values, characteristics of the job itself, and outside pressures.

AT ISSUE

Job Commitment—Is the Cart in Front of the Horse?

Job commitment is a variable that has come to interest a number of researchers who study behavior in organizations. Potentially at least, it appears to be a better predictor of certain behaviors, such as absenteeism and turnover, than the more frequently-used job satisfaction predictor. To date, however, this research is marked by a lack of clarity about the definition of job commitment that has important theoretical and research implications.

Morrow (1983) has identified some 30 formulations of the job, or work, commitment concept that have appeared in the literature over the last 15 years. Labels attached to these formulations include all combinations of the words *commitment, involvement, job, work, career,* and *organization,* plus a variety of specialized terms.

While it is not unusual to find some disagreement about the meaning and measurement of certain constructs in I/O psychology, it certainly is not common to find over two dozen different names for the construct. It may be argued that each of these terms is intended to define a different concept, but Morrow's analysis shows substantial overlap. More to the point, many of these terms are *used* interchangeably in the literature. A case in point is the use of the terms *job commitment* and *job involvement.*

Most reviews and discussions of job commitment combine the research related to job commitment and job involvement. Yet it is by no means self-evident that these concepts are redundant. Most definitions of job commitment are organization-specific (e.g., Bateman & Strasser, 1984), that is, the commitment is to a job in a particular organization. By contrast, job involvement more often is defined in terms of a personal investment in work (e.g., Lodahl & Kejner, 1965). While involve-

ment in work may seem to *imply* a person's commitment to the organization in which the work is performed, no one to date has presented any convincing evidence that this is so.

The theoretical significance of mixing what may be the end products of very different psychological processes in an analysis of job commitment lies in our ability to understand the determinants and behavioral correlates of this concept. For example, research finds job commitment to be negatively correlated with absenteeism and turnover. Efforts to establish a relationship between job commitment and job performance, however, have been almost entirely unsuccessful (e.g., Rambo, 1982).

Conceptually, the pattern of results described above seems more logical if job commitment and job involvement are viewed as separate phenomena. Job commitment implies that an individual desires to remain in a particular job; hence, the negative correlation with voluntary turnover. But remaining with that job means not getting fired as well as not quitting. Coming to work regularly may be perceived by a person as instrumental to keeping his or her job; hence, reduced absenteeism with greater job commitment.

What may not be relevant to keeping one's job in a particular organization is performing at a level above average or even above minimally acceptable standards. If this is true, then there is no reason to expect a positive correlation between job commitment and job performance. Job involvement would seem to be a far more promising candidate for such a relationship because, as usually defined, it speaks more directly to effort.

This analysis is speculative, and that is entirely the point. The current state of confusion about the extent to which job commitment is or is not redundant with 29 similar formulations is as encouraging of speculation as it is of reliable inference. As Morrow (1983) phrases it:

"Work commitment has consumed an inordinate amount of researchers' attention without a commensurate increase in the understanding of its fundamental nature" (p. 498).

To put it another way, the horse (job commitment concept) seems to have gotten rather far behind the cart (job commitment research). The result, as might be expected, is reduced forward progress in understanding this aspect of the behavior of people at work.

REFERENCES

ABELSON, M. A., & BAYSINGER, B. D. Optimal and dysfunctional turnover: Toward an organization level model. *Academy of Management Review,* 1984, *9*(2), 331–341.

BARTOL, K. M. Professionalism as a predictor of organizational commitment, role stress, and turnover: A multi-dimensional approach. *Academy of Management Journal,* 1979, *22*(4), 815–821.

BASSETT, G. A. *A Study of Factors Associated with Turnover of Exempt Personnel.* Crotonville, NY: Personnel and Industrial Relations Service, General Electric, 1967.

BATEMAN, T. S., & STRASSER, S. A longitudinal analysis of the antecedents of organizational commitment. *Academy of Management Journal,* 1984, *27*(1), 95–112.

BLUEDORN, A. C. A taxonomy of turnover. *Academy of Management Review,* 1978, *3*(3), 647–651.

BLUEDORN, A. C. A unified model of turnover from organizations. *Human Relations,* 1982, *35*(2), 135–153.

BREAUGH, J. A. Predicting absenteeism from prior absenteeism and work attitudes. *Journal of Applied Psychology,* 1981, *66*(5), 555–560.

CARLSON, J. G., & HILL, K. D. The effect of gaming on attendance and attitude. *Personnel Psychology,* 1982, *35*(1), 63–73.

CHELOHA, R. S., & FARR, J. L. Absenteeism, job involvement, and job satisfaction in an organizational setting. *Journal of Applied Psychology,* 1980, *65*(4), 467–473.

CHUSMIR, L. H. Job commitment and the organizational woman. *Academy of Management Review,* 1982, *7*(4), 595–602.

CLEGG, C. W. Psychology of employee lateness, absence, and turnover: A methodological critique and an empirical study. *Journal of Applied Psychology,* 1983, *68*(1), 88–101.

CLELAND, S. *The Influence of Plant Size on Industrial Relations.* Princeton, NJ: Princeton University Press, 1955.

DALTON, D. R., & TODOR, W. D. Turnover turned over: An expanded and positive perspective. *Academy of Management Review,* 1979, *4*(2), 225–235.

DALTON, D. R., & TODOR, W. D. Turnover: A lucrative hard dollar phenomenon. *Academy of Management Review,* 1982, *7*(2), 212–218.

DALTON, D. R., KRACKHARDT, D. M., & PORTER, L. W. Functional turnover: An empirical assessment. *Journal of Applied Psychology,* 1981, *66*(6), 716–721.

DALTON, D. R., TODOR, W. D., & KRACKHARDT, D. M. Turnover overstated: The functional taxonomy. *Academy of Management Review,* 1982, *7*(1), 117–123.

DREHER, G. F. The role of performance in the turnover process. *Academy of Management Journal,* 1982, *25*(1), 137–147.

DUBIN, R. S. Industrial workers' worlds: A study of the central life interests of industrial workers. *Social Problems,* 1956, *3*, 131–142.

FARRELL, D., & RUSBULT, C. E. Exchange variables as predictors of job satisfaction, job commitment, and turnover: The impact of rewards, costs, alternatives, and investments. *Organizational Behavior and Human Performance,* 1981, *28*(1), 78–95.

FITZGIBBONS, D., & MOCH, M. Employee absenteeism: A multivariate analysis with replication. *Organizational Behavior and Human Performance,* 1980, *26*(3), 349–372.

GREENHALGH, L. A process model of organizational turnover: The relationship with job security as a case in point. *Academy of Management Review,* 1980, *5*(2), 299–303.

GUION, R. F. Industrial morale: The problem of terminology. *Personnel Psychology,* 1958, *11*(1), 59–64.

HAMMER, T. H., & LANDAU, J. Methodological issues in the use of absence data. *Journal of Applied Psychology,* 1981, *66*(5), 574–581.

HAMMER, T. H., LANDAU, J. C., & STERN, R. N. Absenteeism when workers have a voice: The case of employee ownership. *Journal of Applied Psychology,* 1981, *66*(5), 561–573.

JACKOFSKY, E. F., & PETERS, L. H. Task-relevant ability and turnover: Test of a model. *Southwest Academy of Management Proceedings,* 1980, 161–165.

JACKOFSKY, E. F., & PETERS, L. H. The hypothesized effects of ability in the turnover process. *Academy of Management Review,* 1983, *8,*(1), 46–49.

JOHNS, G. Task moderators of the relationship between leader style and subordinate responses. *Academy of Management Journal,* 1978, *21*(2), 319–325.

KELLER, R. T. The role of performance and absenteeism in the prediction of turnover. *Academy of Management Journal,* 1984, *27*(1), 176–183.

LATHAM, G. P., & PURSELL, E. D. Measuring absenteeism from the opposite side of the coin. *Journal of Applied Psychology,* 1975, *60*(3), 369–371.

LOCKE, E. A. The nature and causes of job dissatisfaction. In M. D. Dunnette (Ed.), *Handbook of Industrial and Organizational Psychology.* Chicago: Rand McNally, 1976, 1297–1349.

LODAHL, T. M., & KEJNER, M. The definition and measurement of job involvement. *Journal of Applied Psychology,* 1965, *49*(1), 24–33.

MAIER, N. R. F., & VERSER, G. C. *Psychology in Industrial Organizations* (5th ed.). Boston: Houghton Mifflin, 1982.

MARCH, J. G., & SIMON, H. A. *Organizations.* New York: John Wiley & Sons, 1958.

MARKHAM, S. E., DANSEREAU, F., JR., & ALUTTO, J. A. Female vs. male absence rates: A temporal analysis. *Personnel Psychology,* 1982, *35*(2), 371–382.

MARKHAM, S. E., DANSEREAU, F., JR., & ALUTTO, J. A. Group size and absenteeism rates: A longitudinal analysis. *Academy of Management Journal,* 1982, *25*(4), 921–927.

MARTIN, T. N., PRICE, J. J., & MUELLER, C. W. Research note on job performance and turnover. *Journal of Applied Psychology,* 1981, *66*(1), 116–119.

MATTILA, J. P. Job quitting and frictional unemployment. *American Economic Review,* 1974, *64*(1), 235–239.

McCAIN, B. E., O'REILLY, C., & PFEFFER, J. The effects of departmental demography on turnover: The case of a university. *Academy of Management Journal,* 1983, *26*(4), 626–641.

MOBLEY, W. H. Some unanswered questions in turnover and withdrawal research. *Academy of Management Review,* 1982, *7*(1), 111–116.

MOBLEY, W. H., GRIFFETH, R. W., HAND, H. H., & MEGLINO, B. M. Review and conceptual analysis of the employee turnover process. *Psychological Bulletin,* 1979, *86*(3), 493–522.

MORRIS, J. H., & SHERMAN, J. D. Generalizability of an organizational commitment model. *Academy of Management Journal,* 1981, *24*(3), 512–526.

MORROW, P. C. Concept redundancy in organizational research: The case of work commitment. *Academy of Management Review,* 1983, 8(3), 486–500.

MORSE, N. C., & WEISS, R. S. The function and meaning of work and the job. *American Sociological Review,* 1955, *20*(2), 191–198.

NICHOLSON, N., BROWN, C. A., & CHADWICK-JONES, J. K. Absence from work and job satisfaction. *Journal of Applied Psychology,* 1976, *61*(6), 728–737.

POPP, P. O., & BELOHLAV, J. A. Absenteeism in a low status work environment. *Academy of Management Journal,* 1982, *25*(3), 677–683.

PRICE, J. L. *The Study of Turnover.* Ames, IA: Iowa State University Press, 1977.

RAMBO, W. W. *Work and Organizational Behavior.* New York: Holt, Rinehart & Winston, 1982.

RUSBULT, C. E., & FARRELL, D. A longitudinal test of the investment model: The impact of job satisfaction, job commitment, and turnover on variations in rewards, costs, alternatives, and investments. *Journal of Applied Psychology,* 1983, *68*(3), 429–438.

SEMYONOV, M. The social context of women's labor force participation: A comparative analysis. *American Journal of Sociology,* 1980, *86*(3), 534–550.

SMULDERS, P. G. W. Comments on employee absence/attendance as a dependent variable in organizational research. *Journal of Applied Psychology,* 1980, *65*(3), 368–371.

SPENCER, D. G., & STEERS, R. M. The influence of personal factors and perceived work experiences on employee turnover and absenteeism. *Academy of Management Journal,* 1980, *23*(3), 567–572.

STAW, B. M., & OLDHAM, G. R. Reconsidering our dependent variables: A critique and empirical study. *Academy of Management Journal,* 1978, *21*(4), 539–559.

STEERS, R. M., & RHODES, S. R. Major influences on employee attendance: A process model. *Journal of Applied Psychology,* 1978, *63*(4), 391–407.

TIME. Gold handcuffs: New perks keep workers loyal. *Time,* 1981, (July 27), p. 58.

VECCHIO, R. P. The function and meaning of work: Morse and Weiss (1955) revisited. *Academy of Management Journal,* 1980, *23*(2), 361–367.

WATSON, C. J. An evaluation of some aspects of the Steers and Rhodes model of employee attendance. *Journal of Applied Psychology,* 1981, *66*(3), 385–389.

ZEY-FERRELL, M. Predictors of faculty intent to exit the organization: Potential turnover in a large university. *Human Relations,* 1982, *35*(5), 349–372.

CHAPTER 15

Job Satisfaction, Employee Development, and the Quality of Work Life

I/O PSYCHOLOGY AT WORK

How Citibank Rehabilitates Those It Fires

NEW YORK—Citibank fired a marketing vice-president last August, but the former manager is still hard at work in a special 26th-floor office at bank headquarters.

It's the placement department—or, in corporate jargon, the "outplacement" department—where he continues a process of counseling, making telephone calls, getting job referrals, and arranging for a new job elsewhere. He'll be paid through this month.

Although many companies long have employed independent firms to ease the departure of executives, only two dozen or so big companies have created their own departments to do such work. Besides Citibank, a unit of Citicorp, they include Celanese Corp., and General Electric Co.

Daniel McAneny, senior vice-president of Performance Dynamics International, a placement firm, thinks more major companies will start their own departments. David Switkin, the industrial psychologist who runs Citibank's, says direct employer help gives more individual counseling and provides "visible evidence to the people who stay that the corporation cares."

Citibank's Mr. Switkin tries to emphasize to fired executives that dismissal doesn't mean failure and can often lead to better jobs. He says that former employees who took other corporate jobs, after placement help, raised their pay an average of 25.3%. Mr. Switkin, who has shepherded more than 80 former executives through the program in two years, can handle five new ones in a month.

Although they are relatively new, "outplacement programs" may be seen as a logical extension of employee development efforts in an organization. With more and more people losing jobs, not because they did not perform satisfactorily, but because the jobs were eliminated by technology, mergers, or general corporate "belt tightening," outplacement may come to be a more standard personnel function.

As the opening story in "I/O Psychology at Work" suggests, the focus in Chapter 15 shifts away from outcomes of the individual-organization interactions, such as performance, absenteeism, and turnover, that are of primary concern to organizations. Here, this interaction is viewed from the other end of the telescope; that is, outcomes of primary concern to the employee are examined.

The major topics to be covered in Chapter 15 include job satisfaction, employee development, and the quality of work life. These outcomes of the individual-organization interaction are important to everyone, but they have *primary significance* for the individual employee. For example, however job dissatisfaction may affect an employee's work behavior, it remains the employee for whom dissatisfaction has the most extensive and long-term effects.

JOB SATISFACTION

Job satisfaction has been defined in many ways, but all definitions incorporate the idea that it is an attitude based on an *affective* (feeling) evaluative response to a job situation. In simple terms:

> *A satisfied employee finds more to like about his or her job situation than to dislike.*

The scientific investigation of job satisfaction has revolved around several questions: (a) How does job satisfaction come about? (b) How is it measured? (c) Who is relatively more satisfied, and (d) What does this mean for an individual's work behavior and attitudes?

Theories of Job Satisfaction

The interest that I/O psychologists have in job satisfaction goes back some 50 years. Job satisfaction is one of the single most researched topics in the field. Locke's (1976) frequently-cited estimate of over 3,000 articles and dissertations on the subject now probably can be accurately doubled.

Despite the volume of research on the subject, theories of job satisfaction—what causes it and how this causal process works—are not well developed. Most are offshoots of more general motivation theories. As these theories are discussed in some detail in Chapter 12, the closely related theoretical statements concerning job satisfaction are not described in detail here. A summary table of the basic tenets of the major approaches and the consensus of opinion as to the general empirical standing of each is provided in Exhibit 15-1.

The reader interested in more detail on job satisfaction theories may refer to the references in Exhibit 15-1 or to Locke's 1976 review. For practical purposes, job satisfaction is as it is measured, or operationally defined, and it is that measurement that is examined here.

Operational definition: See page 48.

Measuring Job Satisfaction

Job satisfaction is an attitude and, therefore, an hypothetical construct— something that cannot be seen, but whose presence or absence is believed to be associated with certain behavior patterns. As with all hypothetical

Construct: See page 80.

EXHIBIT 15-1

A Summary Table of
Theories of Job
Satisfaction

Name/Description	Related Theory of Work Motivation	Basic Tenent	Empirical Support
Two-Factor or Motivation/Hygiene (Herzberg, Mausner, & Snyderman, 1959)	Need Theory	Job satisfaction and job dissatisfaction are separate issues; satisfaction comes only from factors intrinsic to work itself.	Negative
Facet Satisfaction (Lawler, 1973)	Cognitive Theories	Satisfaction depends on perception of job inputs, job characteristics, and job outputs relative to other people.	Little
Value Theory (Locke, 1976)	Need Theory	Satisfaction comes from being able to achieve things one values by means of job.	Insufficient Research
Opponent Process (Landy, 1978)	None directly related	Satisfaction varies over time; forces always acting to reduce it.	Insufficient Research
Need-Discrepancy (Porter, 1961)	Need Theory	Satisfaction results from low discrepancy between what person needs and what job gives.	Little
Instrumentality (Porter & Lawler, 1968)	Expectancy Theory	Satisfaction depends on match between expected and obtained rewards.	Little

constructs, there is room for considerable disagreement as to how job satisfaction is defined and measured.

Three basic approaches to the measurement of job satisfaction are discussed—job satisfaction as a global concept, as a faceted concept, and as a function of fulfilled needs. Each approach is based on self-report questionnaires.

Job Satisfaction as a Global Concept

Job satisfaction was described as a positive evaluation of a job situation. This implies that job satisfaction is a one-dimensional concept—a sort of psychological summary of all of the liked and disliked aspects of a job. This, in fact, has been and remains a common approach to the measurement of job satisfaction. While such an overall measure can be obtained by summing the scales of instruments to be discussed, the focus here is on the single-item measures used frequently in research. For example, Vecchio (1980) used the following question in a recent investigation of the job quality–job satisfaction relationship:

The belief that the work they are doing is important is a source of job satisfaction for many people.

On the whole, how satisfied are you with the work you do—would you say you are very satisfied, moderately satisfied, a little dissatisfied, or very dissatisfied? (p. 481)

The single-item job satisfaction questionnaire has a number of advantages.

- It has no development costs.
- It is quick and easy to administer and score.
- It makes sense to those questioned.

On the other hand, single-item job questionnaire measures leave considerable room for individual interpretation of the question. Some respondents will reply on the basis of pay, some on the basis of the nature of the work itself, some on the basis of the climate of the organization, and so on down the line. In other words, the respondents in any particular sample may not be answering the "same" question, thus raising both reliability and validity questions.

Sample: See pages 49 to 50. Reliability / validity: See page 67.

Job Satisfaction as a Faceted Concept

An alternative to the single-dimension concept of job satisfaction is a multi-dimensional concept. This approach often is called the *facet,* or *component,* approach. It assumes that worker satisfaction with different aspects of a job situation can vary independently and should be measured independently. Opinions as to what and how many of these facets to include in a job satisfaction measure, however, vary. Among the possibilities are:

- compensation
- working conditions
- supervisor-employee relations
- opportunity for growth/development
- congeniality of coworkers
- opportunity to use knowledge/skills
- status/prestige of job
- job security
- company evaluation policies
- autonomy and responsibility on job
- general management practices
- work load

The measurement of job satisfaction tends to vary from one study to the next, and most of the possible components listed have been used at one time or another. Recently, however, there appears to be some move toward standardization as an increasing number of researchers use the Job Descriptive Index (JDI; Smith, Kendall, & Hulin, 1969), to measure job satisfaction.

The JDI is a five-facet scale used to measure employee satisfaction or dissatisfaction with *work, supervision, pay, promotions,* and *coworkers.* The instrument consists of a series of descriptive adjectives or phrases relevant to each of these five job facets. The respondent is asked to reply "yes," "no," or "don't know/can't decide" to each. Two items from each of the five scales are shown in Exhibit 15–2.

EXHIBIT 15–2	**Work**
	_____ Useful
	_____ Frustrating
Sample Items from the Job Descriptive Index	**Supervision**
	_____ Impolite
	_____ Intelligent
	Promotions
	_____ Dead-end job
	_____ Regular promotions
	Pay
	_____ Bad
	_____ Highly paid
	Coworkers
	_____ Smart
	_____ Hard to meet

_____

Note. From *The Job Descriptive Index* © 1975, Bowling Green State University. Information concerning this instrument may be obtained by writing to Dr. Patricia C. Smith, Department of Psychology, Bowling Green State University, Bowling Green, OH 43403.

The JDI now has some 20 years of use and development behind it. The literature in general supports its reliability (e.g., Bhagat, 1982) and its applicability to different demographic groups, such as blacks/whites, males/females, and managers/nonmanagers (e.g., Golembiewski & Yeager, 1978). The JDI is not without its problems, however. There seems to be some question as to whether it is actually five facets that the scale is measuring. For example, there is research suggesting that the *satisfaction with work* scale may be measuring several different aspects of job satisfaction, not one (e.g., Yeager, 1981).

Another problem with the JDI is more basic than how many facets it is measuring. As its name implies, the JDI is a *description* of a job situation. A person's *feelings* about that description, that is, the extent to which it is evaluated as personally satisfying or dissatisfying, must be inferred from this description.

As an example of the descriptive/evaluative problem, consider the description "dead-end job" under "promotions" in Exhibit 15–2. It is assumed that a reply of "yes" to this question indicates some job dissatisfaction, but such may not be the case. The job may be indisputably a dead end, but the current incumbent may not put a negative evaluation on this feature. Thus, to the extent that it actually measures job satisfaction, the JDI is dependent on the assumption that people are alike in their evaluations of certain characteristics of work situations.

Job Satisfaction as Fulfilled Needs

There is an approach that can be taken to measuring job satisfaction that does not require the assumption that all people feel a particular way about certain aspects of their job situations (such as a dead-end job is dissatisfying). The most well-known job satisfaction measure that takes this approach was developed by Porter and reported in a series of studies beginning in 1961.

Porter's job satisfaction questionnaire is based on a need theory approach to job satisfaction. It consists of 15 statements related to security, esteem, autonomy, self-actualization, and social needs. Based on his or her own needs and perceptions of the job, each respondent answers three questions about each statement: (a) How much is there now? (b) How much should there be? (c) How important is this to me? One sample item from this questionnaire as described by Porter (1961) is shown in Exhibit 15–3.

Need theories: See pages 348 to 352.

Perception: See page 36.

On the basis of the responses to questions about need fulfillment at work, such as that shown in Exhibit 15–3, job satisfaction is measured by the discrepancy between "How much is there now?" and "How much should there be?" The smaller this discrepancy, the greater the satisfaction. Separate scores are calculated for each of the need categories. The question, "How important is this to me?" allows for a measure of the relative strength of each need for the individual respondent.

Although it was once very popular, the need-discrepancy approach to measuring job satisfaction appears to have disappeared almost entirely from the literature. Porter's questionnaire is difficult to score relative to

EXHIBIT 15–3

A Need-Discrepancy
Approach to
Measuring Job
Satisfaction

Security Needs

The *feeling of security* in my management position

1. How much is there now?
   (min) 1 2 3 4 5 6 7 (max)
2. How much should there be?
   (min) 1 2 3 4 5 6 7 (max)
3. How important is this to me?
   (min) 1 2 3 4 5 6 7 (max)

Note. From L. W. Porter, "A Study of Perceived Need Satisfaction in Bottom and Middle Management Jobs. *Journal of Applied Psychology,* 1961, *45*(1), pp. 1–10. Copyright 1961 by the American Psychological Association.

other measures, but the individuality of this approach seems to have much to recommend it. In particular, the idea that job satisfaction is, to a considerable degree, a relative matter seems worthy of further pursuit.

Problems in Measuring Job Satisfaction

As noted, virtually all job satisfaction research is based on questionnaire measures of job satisfaction. Since job satisfaction is an individual subjective phenomenon, this may be the most appropriate measure. Nevertheless, it is important to be aware of certain limitations this approach places on job satisfaction research.

One set of problems created by questionnaire measures has to do with the accuracy of the responses. Respondents do not necessarily give misleading answers intentionally, but there is a host of situational variables that can affect both the extent to which they understand the questions and the extent to which they are candid in their answers. Among the relevant factors reviewed by Giles and Feild (1978) are the following:

- where the questionnaire is administered (at home, on the job, in the personnel office)
- the form taken by the cover letter and/or directions
- whether or not respondents are asked to identify themselves

In their own study, Giles and Feild also found job satisfaction scores to be influenced significantly by what they call *item sensitivity,* that is, the degree of concern the respondent has that others might learn how he or she answered the question. For example, items about working conditions were generally of low sensitivity, while those concerning supervision had high sensitivity. On the basis of their analysis, Giles and Feild suggest that job satisfaction questionnaires with specifically focused "depersonalized" questions (questions with no particular person, such as supervisor, as a referent) are more likely to elicit candid responses.

Measurement error: See pages 78 to 79.

The factors listed by Giles and Feild add error to the measurement of job satisfaction. As discussed in Chapter 4, they increase the discrepancy between the "true" degree of job satisfaction and the obtained measurement for any particular individual. When individual responses are combined or compared in some way, more error can be added. As discussed earlier, different people may use quite different frames of reference in answering such questions.

The problems described are not specific to the measurement of job satisfaction; to a greater or lesser degree they plague all questionnaire-based research. Although the associated measurement error cannot be eliminated, there are certain steps that may be taken to reduce it.

- Use a questionnaire with established reliability.
- Pretest directions for clarity.
- Guarantee subject anonymity.
- Use a sample size sufficiently large to assume that response bias is distributed randomly.

The Incidence and Parameters of Job Satisfaction

The extent to which workers in general are satisfied or dissatisfied with their jobs is a question that has been addressed at regular intervals for many years by means of surveys, both local and national. Most such surveys are based on the single-item global measure of job satisfaction discussed earlier and most find more workers satisfied than dissatisfied. Furthermore, as measured in this way, there is no evidence that job dissatisfaction is growing; rather it seems to be diminishing somewhat. The data in Exhibit 15–4 illustrate both findings.

The figures in Exhibit 15–4 come from annual national surveys of employee job satisfaction; each sample was drawn independently of the others each year. These figures show little evidence of the much-discussed worker alienation and dissatisfaction of recent years. They are, however, average figures and the question of whether such averages obscure differences in job satisfaction among different groups of employees is a valid one.

Reported Job Satisfaction Among Full-Time Workers
in the United States, 1972–1978

EXHIBIT 15–4

Job Satisfaction in the United States

Attitudes	Year of survey						
	1972	1973	1974	1975	1976	1977	1978
N	744	642	632	607	611	761	712
% Very satisfied	48.8	50.0	51.2	56.8	55.8	49.5	52.0
% Somewhat satisfied	36.6	37.4	36.7	31.8	32.6	39.2	37.2
% A little dissatisfied	11.2	9.0	8.5	8.1	8.5	9.6	7.9
% Very dissatisfied	3.4	3.6	3.6	3.3	3.1	1.7	2.9
Total	100.0	100.0	100.0	100.0	100.0	100.0	100.0

Note. From C. N. Weaver, "Job Satisfaction in the United States in the 1970s." *Journal of Applied Psychology*, 1980, *65*(3), pp. 364–367. Copyright 1980 by the American Psychological Association. P. 365 reprinted by permission of the author and the publisher.

Who Is Satisfied?

The question of possible differences in job satisfaction among various groupings of employees, such as male/female, white/nonwhite, and older/younger, has been investigated many times, and a number of stable findings have emerged. One is a positive correlation between *age* and reported job satisfaction—older workers in general report greater job satisfaction than do younger workers (e.g., Quinn & Shepard, 1974).

Correlation: See pages 61 to 63.

Other variables found to have a positive relationship with job satisfaction include *income level, occupation,* and *level in the organizational hierarchy.* No reliable correlation with sex has emerged, and the relationship between job satisfaction and race is consistently negative; nonwhites continue to report lower satisfaction with their jobs than whites. All of these trends may be observed in Exhibit 15–5.

The figures in Exhibit 15–5 are averages based on a maximum satisfaction score of "3." They show a consistent tendency over a seven-year period for job satisfaction to be higher for whites, older employees, employees with higher incomes, and people in sales, managerial, and professional occupations. Weaver (1980) notes that this pattern is essentially the same as that reported by Quinn, Staines, and McCollough (1974) for the period 1958 to 1973. Weaver concludes that job satisfaction in the global sense appears to have a stable pattern that is "somewhat unresponsive to changes in society" (p. 367).

The Special Case of Satisfaction with Pay

Data based on global measures of job satisfaction, such as that provided by Weaver (1980), show that overall reported satisfaction is higher as a person goes up the income scale. Individual satisfaction with level of income, however, appears to be a more complex matter. While a primary determinant of this satisfaction is absolute amount of pay received (e.g., Ronan & Organt, 1973), satisfaction also appears to have a *relative* component based on perceptions of its fairness (e.g., Dyer & Theriault, 1976).

The literature on satisfaction with pay suggests at least two basic determinants of perceptions of fairness. One is the extent to which pay is perceived to be related to level of performance (Cherrington, Reitz, and Scott, 1971; Lawler, 1966). A second is the extent to which pay is perceived to be equitable relative to what other people in similar jobs with similar qualifications are making (Adams, 1963).

Equity theory: See pages 356 to 357.

The question of whether pay is perceived to be fair relative to what other people are paid is taking on larger dimensions as disputes over what is called *comparable worth* multiply. The issue is one of equal pay for jobs judged to be about equal in terms of the qualifications required and the contributions the job makes to the organization (and/or society).

Job evaluation: See pages 270 to 272.

The basis for determining the worth of a job is the job evaluation process discussed in Chapter 9. Results of this process can be surprising. In a recent job evaluation study in Washington state, for example, the following pairs of jobs were judged of comparable worth: carpenter/social service worker, mechanic/medical record analyst, highway engi-

Mean Job Satisfaction Among Full-Time Workers in the United States, 1972–1978, by Selected Demographic Variables

EXHIBIT 15–5

Who Is Satisfied? Job Satisfaction by Various Demographic Groupings

Variable	Year of survey						
	1972	1973	1974	1975	1976	1977	1978
Race							
White	2.36	2.34	2.38	2.43	2.44	2.37	2.43
Black	2.09	2.32	2.17	2.34	2.13	2.36	2.01
Sex							
Male	2.32	2.31	2.35	2.44	2.41	2.33	2.38
Female	2.28	2.40	2.36	2.40	2.42	2.42	2.39
Education							
Grade School	2.32	2.22	2.28	2.32	2.32	2.33	2.35
High School	2.25	2.28	2.38	2.46	2.39	2.38	2.37
Some college	2.26	2.45	2.35	2.52	2.38	2.36	2.31
College degree or more	2.44	2.52	2.41	2.37	2.54	2.46	2.49
Age							
Less than 20	1.43	1.95	2.25	2.08	1.73	2.17	2.14
20–29	2.06	2.18	2.18	2.24	2.25	2.19	2.67
30–39	2.37	2.39	2.26	2.48	2.53	2.33	2.35
40–49	2.36	2.34	2.41	2.48	2.45	2.39	2.43
50 or more	2.51	2.46	2.55	2.55	2.53	2.55	2.55
Personal income[a]							
Less than $5,000	—	—	2.23	2.23	2.21	2.21	2.21
$5,000–$6,999	—	—	2.21	2.47	2.44	2.46	2.14
$7,000–9,999	—	—	2.26	2.38	2.37	2.32	2.31
$10,000–$14,999	—	—	2.42	2.44	2.47	2.35	2.43
$15,000 or more	—	—	2.58	2.60	2.55	2.48	2.50
Occupation							
Professional-technical	2.48	2.45	2.48	2.50	2.61	2.46	2.55
Managerial-administrative	2.51	2.65	2.59	2.64	2.56	2.52	2.55
Sales	2.24	2.35	2.33	2.71	2.41	1.96	2.48
Clerical	2.27	2.32	2.25	2.47	2.37	2.33	2.28
Craftsmen-foremen	2.34	2.19	2.44	2.33	2.56	2.42	2.50
Operatives	2.13	1.99	2.12	2.15	2.14	2.26	2.18
Laborers	1.89	2.21	2.29	2.50	2.16	2.36	1.89
Service	2.20	2.42	2.24	2.42	2.30	2.41	2.31

[a]Not available for 1972 and 1973.

Note. From C. N. Weaver, "Job Satisfaction in the United States in the 1970s." *Journal of Applied Psychology,* 1980, *65*(3), pp. 364–367. Copyright 1980 by the American Psychological Association. P. 366 reprinted by permission of the author and the publisher.

neer/registered nurse. The study did not find that those holding such jobs were receiving comparable pay, however; average compensation for those in the first-named jobs was from 16% to 42% higher (Gest, 1984).

The higher-paid jobs in the Washington state study were male-dominated jobs and the lower-paid jobs were female-dominated. Similar patterns have been found in other states. As such findings become more general knowledge, the number of court cases relating to pay discrimination based on comparable worth allegations grows. The Equal Employment Opportunity Commission estimated that over 75% of its pending cases in early 1984 fell into this category (Bales, 1984).

There are many reports and studies of pay discrimination in I/O psychology and related literature (e.g., Burstein, 1979; Sigelman, Milwards & Shepard, 1982). Both findings and opinions about the extent of the problem are mixed. To date, however, no one has presented any research relating to the more specific question of how the comparable worth issue affects job satisfaction in general and pay satisfaction in particular.

Job Satisfaction and Work Behavior and Attitudes

As Locke (1976) noted, the job satisfaction literature is vast and characterized by a belief that employees who are more satisfied with their jobs will stay with them longer, be absent less, and perform better. These relationships are explored in more detail here.

Job Satisfaction and Absenteeism/Turnover

As discussed briefly in Chapter 14, the relevant literature generally supports the hypothesis that there is an inverse relationship between reported job satisfaction and absenteeism and turnover. It does *not* support the claim, however, that job dissatisfaction accounts for a major portion of the variance in either behavior.

Variance explained: See pages 64 to 66.

Many studies might be cited to support the conclusion that job dissatisfaction, while related to absenteeism and turnover, is not a powerful predictor of either behavior. For example, Breaugh (1981) found that none of the three attitude measures in his longitudinal study of absenteeism among research scientists added anything to the predictability made possible by knowing their attendance records. Watson (1981) reached a similar conclusion, as did Popp and Belohlav (1982).

Predictor variable: See pages 64 to 65.

One of the more interesting analyses of the job satisfaction-absenteeism literature is reported by Clegg (1983). In his review of some 17 relevant studies, Clegg points out that the most obvious alternative hypothesis to ''job dissatisfaction causes more absenteeism'' was not investigated at all. Specifically, Clegg suggests that the causality may work the other way; that is, absenteeism may lead to greater job dissatisfaction.

Hypothesis: See page 47.

Clegg's suggestion makes sense at the intuitive level. For example, if absenteeism is followed by supervisory disapproval, wage docking, having to work late to catch up, or other unattractive consequences, job satisfaction may be reduced accordingly. In his own study involving some 2,500 employees, Clegg found support for this reverse causality. While one study does not establish the validity of this position, Clegg presents a strong case for additional investigations of this hypothesis.

Research finds a weak, but consistent, positive correlation between job satisfaction and job attendance.

Findings with respect to job satisfaction and job turnover mirror those of the job satisfaction-absenteeism research. In their comprehensive review of the satisfaction-turnover relationship, Mobley, Griffeth, Hand, and Meglino (1979) conclude that job dissatisfaction accounts for less than 16% of the variance in turnover.

Some of the other variables found to be associated with an employee's decision to leave an organization voluntarily are reviewed in Chapter 14, One of those factors is performance. It is suggested in that discussion that level of performance may have relatively direct effects on turnover because it offers employees information relevant to both ease and desirability of changing jobs.

A recent study (Spencer & Steers, 1981) suggests that performance also may have indirect effects on turnover by acting as a *moderator* of the satisfaction-performance relationship. As shown in Exhibit 15–6, Spencer and Steers found that turnover decreased as satisfaction increased, but *only for poor performers* (dotted line). Turnover rates for good performers (solid line) change little as job satisfaction increases.

Moderator variable: See pages 97 to 99.

The idea that performance level is central to employee attitudes and behavior is not new. For example, Miles (1965) raised the issue some 20 years ago in his discussion of employee participation in decision making and problem solving. Miles suggested that, far from being merely a mechanism for improving employee morale (what he called the *human relations view* of participative management), participation is a way of

EXHIBIT 15–6

Job Satisfaction,
Turnover, and
Job Performance

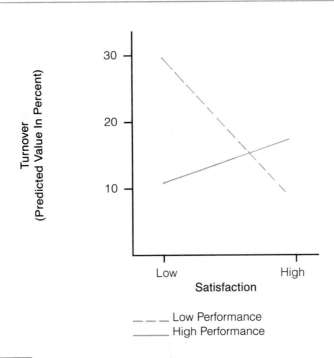

_ _ _ Low Performance
_____ High Performance

Note. From D. G. Spencer and R. M. Steers, "Performance as a Moderator of the Job Satisfaction-Turnover Relationship." *Journal of Applied Psychology*, 1981, *66*(4), pp. 511–514.
Copyright 1981 by the American Psychological Association. P. 513 reprinted by permission of
the authors and the publisher.

actually improving a work unit's performance (the *human resources view*).
Increased job satisfaction, if any, will result from employee contributions
to, and rewards from, this improvement.

To recapitulate, many years of research have yielded stable, but small,
negative correlations between reported job satisfaction and absenteeism
and turnover. Evidence suggests that one important moderator of this
relationship may be level of employee performance. It now is time to
turn attention more closely to the relationship between job satisfaction
and job performance.

Job Satisfaction and Job Performance

For at least 50 years, I/O psychologists have been wrestling with the
question of the relationship between job satisfaction and job performance. Researchers have put a considerable amount of effort into attempts
to show that the two are positively related in a particular fashion, specifically, to demonstrate the validity of the popular slogan: "A happy
worker is a good worker."

Results from the empirical literature are too mixed to support the
hypothesis that job satisfaction leads to better performance or even that

there is a reliable positive correlation between the two variables (e.g. Fisher, 1980). Many believe, however, that these results are equally inconclusive with respect to inferring that there is *no* such relationship (e.g., Organ, 1977). As a result, this continues to be an active line of research although it has changed somewhat in character.

The early job satisfaction-performance research was almost exclusively a search for simple correlations between measures of job performance and measures of job satisfaction. Recent studies of this relationship are characterized by a search for relevant moderator variables. The rationale is that certain personal and situational variables affect the nature of the job satisfaction-job performance relationship. When these are not identified and controlled, it would appear (statistically) that there is no relationship.

Among the possible moderators of the job satisfaction-job performance relationship that have been investigated recently are the following:

- nature of the work performed (e.g., Ivancevich, 1979)
- organizational pressures for performance (e.g., Bhagat, 1982)
- individual career stage (e.g., Gould & Hawkins, 1978)
- time pressures (e.g., Bhagat, 1982)

In general, such research has produced stronger correlations than those found in older research, but to date these findings cannot be regarded as generalizable to any significant degree.

One difficulty researchers have with drawing inferences about the satisfaction-performance relationship is that much of the relevant research is based on simple correlational analysis. As discussed in Chapter 2, this procedure does not lend itself to cause-effect inference. As far as evidence from simple correlations between job satisfaction and job performance may be taken, the causality may well go the other way; that is, it may not be that "a happy worker is a good worker," but that "a good worker is a happy worker."

Generalization: See page 67.

Inference: See page 58.

Porter and Lawler (1968) appear to have been the first formally to include job performance as a cause rather than an effect of job satisfaction in a model of work performance. The idea was carried one step further by Cherrington, Reitz and Scott (1971). In their experiment, which has become a classic in the area, these researchers found evidence to suggest that there is *no* inherent causal relationship between job satisfaction and job performance. Rather, results indicated that relationship between the two depends on a third variable—rewards. This study is summarized in "Spotlight on Research."

As noted, results of the job satisfaction-job performance research are mixed. In some studies, a positive relationship has been observed. In many, no significant relationship has been found. A few studies have shown what appears to be a negative relationship—higher levels of job satisfaction associated with lower levels of job performance. Cherrington and his colleagues produced both positive and negative correlations in the laboratory by manipulating the connection between job performance and formal rewards for that performance (in this case, a financial bonus).

Under the hypothesis of an inherent causal relationship between job

SPOTLIGHT ON RESEARCH

Effects of Contingent and Noncontingent Reward on the Relationship between Satisfaction and Task Performance

Research question: Is there a causal relationship between job satisfaction and job performance?

Research hypothesis: By selective manipulation of reward conditions, any empirical relationship between reported satisfaction and performance may be produced.

Laboratory experiment: See pages 52 to 54.

Type of study: Laboratory experiment.

Subjects: Ninety volunteer male and female junior-level business students.

Independent / dependent variables: See page 52.

Independent variable: Performance-reward contingency. Operational definition: (a) Appropriately rewarded—good performers got a bonus, poor performers did not; (b) Inappropriately rewarded—good performers did not get bonus, poor performers did. One half of good and poor performers were in each condition.

Dependent variable: Performance on experimental task. Operational definition: Total number of rows of figures scored as per instructions.

General procedure: Subjects were paid $1.00/hour to score tests they believed were taken by paper mill employees. They were told they had a 50:50 chance of receiving a bonus for performance quantity and quality, but these bonuses actually were distributed on a random basis to half of the high performers and half of the low performers.

Subjects worked for two hours. At the end of each hour they (a) answered questions about their performance and the perceived likelihood that they would receive a bonus, (b) were paid according to the experimental plan, and (c) answered a job satisfaction questionnaire.

Results: The hypothesis was supported. There was a positive correlation between performance and satisfaction for appropriately-rewarded subjects and a negative correlation for inappropriately-rewarded subjects. The performance of the appropriately-rewarded subjects also improved from the first hour to the next, while that of the other subjects did not.

Conclusion: ''The results of this study support the hypothesis that the nature and magnitude of the relationship between satisfaction and performance depend heavily upon the performance reward contingencies that have been arranged" (p. 535).

Summarized from D. J. Cherrington, H. J. Reitz, and W. E. Scott, Jr., "Effects of Contingent and Noncontingent Reward on the Relationship Between Satisfaction and Task Performance." *Journal of Applied Psychology*, 1971, *55*(6), pp. 531–536.

satisfaction and job performance, those subjects in the study who reported the greatest job satisfaction at the end of the first hour should have been the subjects whose performance went up during the second hour. Instead, better second-hour performance was turned in by those subjects who "learned" from the bonuses paid at the end of the first hour that there was a connection between their performance and the bonus.

The hypothesis confirmed in the findings from the study summarized in "Spotlight on Research" implies that observed correlations between job satisfaction and job performance depend upon the extent to which the same rewards are involved. If worker satisfaction depends considerably on being rewarded at a level that seems consistent with performance, satisfaction and performance will be positively related under appropriate reward systems. It must be recognized, however, that some people may not define job satisfaction in terms of rewards that depend upon their job performance. Exhibit 15–7 clarifies this concept.

In Exhibit 15–7, a number of factors that have been identified as possible sources of job satisfaction for employees are listed (left column). As may be seen, when it is necessary to do the job well in order to achieve these conditions (as for the first five on the list), a positive correlation between job satisfaction and job performance is observed.

When conditions that produce job satisfaction for an individual have nothing to do with job performance (as with the second five items listed

Possible Source of Job Satisfaction	Relationship of this Source to Job Performance	Observed Job Satisfaction-Job Performance Correlation
Pride Accomplishment Recognition Advancement Challenge	Depends on Performance	Positive
Location of Company Prestige of Company Hours Worked Benefits Working Conditions	Irrelevant to Performance	None
Opportunity to Socialize Light Work Load Job Security	Interferes with Performance	Negative

EXHIBIT 15–7

Conditions under which Different Job Satisfaction/Job Performance Relationships May be Observed

in Exhibit 15–7), no relationship between the two is obtained in a correlational study. Finally, when the primary sources of job satisfaction actually can *interfere* with job performance (as "opportunity to socialize"), an inverse relationship can be observed; that is, the employees reporting greater satisfaction will be among the poorer performers.

Expectancy theory: See pages 353 to 356.

In terms from the general expectancy theory of motivation discussed in Chapter 12, Exhibit 15–7 may be interpreted to mean that when good job performance is *instrumental* to achieving job satisfaction, the two will appear to be related. It may be, then, that some of the confusion about "a happy worker is a good worker" is a definitional problem having to do with the way that different people define job satisfaction.

Job Satisfaction and Other Behaviors and Attitudes

To a considerable degree, the job satisfaction literature is dominated by investigations of its possible relationships with absenteeism, turnover, and job performance. Studies of the relationship of satisfaction to other employee behaviors and attitudes appear less frequently, but some interesting findings have been reported. A brief review of some of this research is presented.

Lateness.   Adler and Golan (1981) found "coming to work late" to be a relatively stable pattern of behavior among some female telephone operators. Job satisfaction measures were predictive of this behavior, but not of absenteeism.

Perceptions of reasons others leave jobs.   Mowday (1981) found a negative relationship between job satisfaction and the tendency to attribute the cause of coworkers leaving the company to job dissatisfaction. This is, those who were dissatisfied were more likely to believe that those who left the company did so because they also were dissatisfied.

Correlate: See pages 63 to 64.

Significance: See pages 58 to 59.

Physiological states.   One of the more interesting correlates of job satisfaction is reported by Khaleque (1981). This author found the heart rates of female cigar factory employees reporting greater job satisfaction to be significantly lower than the heart rates of other subjects. There was no correlation between heart rate and perceived physical effort.

The decision to retire.   In a study of the variables relating to civil service employee decisions to retire from the job before it became mandatory (so-called "early retirement"), Schmitt and McCune (1981) found that attitudinal variables added little to predictability. Retirees and nonretirees reported being equally satisfied with their jobs although those who retired early tended to see their jobs as less involving and challenging.

Life satisfaction.   A number of I/O psychologists have been interested in the relationship between job satisfaction and general life satisfaction, or life adjustment. There are two theories about this relationship.

One, the *compensation hypothesis*, postulates that people who do not find work satisfying will compensate by taking actions to make the rest of life more satisfying.

The other hypothesis about the relationship between job satisfaction and general life satisfaction is the *generalization hypothesis*, sometimes called the "spillover" hypothesis. From this perspective, job satisfaction (or dissatisfaction) generalizes, or "spills over" into nonwork activities. Kabanoff (1980) finds support for both models in a review of the literature, but believes there are too many conceptual and methodological problems to draw any conclusions about which is more accurate.

Recent research into the relationship between job satisfaction and life satisfaction suggests that it is similar to the relationship between job satisfaction and performance found by Cherrington, Reitz, and Scott (1971); that is, job satisfaction and life satisfaction may be determined by some of the same factors, but they are not causally related (e.g., Keon & McDonald, 1982).

Concluding Remarks Concerning Job Satisfaction

Job satisfaction is an affective response to a job situation. There is some disagreement as to what causes it and how the process works and a number of alternative approaches to its measurement. However it is measured, surveys consistently find some degree of satisfaction to be the rule, rather than the exception, in American organizations.

Many years of research have yielded modest correlations between job satisfaction measures and a variety of work behaviors. In no case, however, has job satisfaction been found to be a *major* determinant of behavior. This conclusion is consistent with reviews of the general relationship between attitudes and behavior. Erlich's (1969) conclusion is representative: "Studies on the relation of attitudes and behavior have almost consistently resulted in the conclusion that attitudes are a poor predictor of behavior" (p. 29). Thus, while there seems little doubt that job satisfaction is important, its implications are probably greater for the individual than for the organization employing him or her.

To say that job satisfaction is relatively more important to the individual than to the organization is not to say that all people who work put job satisfaction high on their list of priorities. Results from research into the ways people perceive the roles of work and nonwork activities as fitting into their need and value systems suggest that this is not true (see Near, Rice, & Hunt, 1980).

For some people, work is a necessity that they accept without any particular expectations for deriving satisfaction from it. Nevertheless, it seems safe to assume that, other things being equal, they would prefer to receive some satisfaction from the experience. It also seems safe to assume, on the basis of the general job satisfaction literature, that employees differ in their definitions of job satisfaction. Whatever job satisfaction means to the individual, however, a group of activities usually called *employee development* may be one means by which a work situation can become more satisfying.

EMPLOYEE DEVELOPMENT

Employee development refers to all of those activities on the part of an organization that are for the purpose of helping a particular individual to be successful in his or her job and/or to achieve career goals.

The variety of ways that people define the conditions producing personal job satisfaction have different implications for what they must do to achieve it. For example, if a person defines job satisfaction primarily in terms of having a steady job that is not too demanding and that provides a comfortable social environment, adequate attendance and performance is required in order for that person to keep the job.

If the major source of job satisfaction for another person is the feelings of accomplishment derived from performing the job, then it is necessary for this person to be able to perform it well. Finally, if job satisfaction depends on recognition from others and/or achieving high-level career goals, it may be necessary to make a steady advancement upward. In all cases, some assistance may be required. Formal organizational activities that provide this assistance are called employee development.

While some may argue the point, the position taken here is that true employee development is individual and specific in nature. From this perspective, sending all supervisors to a communications workshop on the premise that "everyone could be a better communicator" does not really qualify. Such programs undoubtedly are helpful to some participants, but they are not based on an assessment of the development needs of the individuals involved.

For employee development to be individual it must be based on an analysis of what an individual employee wants or needs to be more successful in the current job and/or to pursue career ambitions. The results of this analysis may reveal obstacles to these goals in the form of insufficient or outdated skills/knowledge, personal problems, health problems, or merely a lack of relevant information about career possibilities and how to pursue them. Three broadly defined sets of employee development activities for helping to overcome these obstacles are career planning and development, skill/knowledge development, and personal counseling.

Career Planning and Development

In an organizational context, career development and planning refers to activities designed to assist employees in defining and meeting their career goals. Among these activities are *career counseling* (as for high-potential employees who are in dead-end jobs), *career pathing* (as job progression planned for employees who wish to advance), and *career information distribution* (as job posting for current or upcoming organizational vacancies).

It seems likely that many activities falling into the category of career planning and development are carried out informally on the basis of individual relationships. In the formal sense, reported surveys of organizational practices suggest that there is more verbal support for such activities than there are actual programs (e.g., Cairo, 1983; Seybolt, 1979). The recent interest of I/O psychologists in the determinants and effects of career-related variables (e.g., Mihal, Sorce, & Comte, 1984; Von Glinow, Driver, Brousseau, & Prince, 1983), however, may stimulate more applied activities in this area.

Driver (1979) offers a thorough analysis and review of the literature of career planning and development. One of the ideas put forth in this discussion is that effective career development is based on understanding individual differences in *career concept.* The four basic concepts identified by Driver are as follows:

- *Steady state*—Career choice is made early and remains constant—change is not desired.
- *Transitory*—Career choice is never fixed—major desire is to move on.
- *Spiral*—Career choice changes at 5 to 7 year intervals—emphasis is on creative change.
- *Linear* — Career choice is made early—emphasis is on upward movement.

From Driver's perspective, effective career development is based on helping employees to identify and follow their career concepts. In some cases, this may be a matter merely of providing information. For example, a ''linear type'' engineer would need to know the career paths available for an engineer in the organization. Two such paths are shown in Exhibit 15–8.

Exhibit 15–8 shows two *promotion ladders.* An engineer who has a ''steady state'' career concept may not be interested in climbing either ladder. One with a ''spiral'' concept may be interested in moving from

Job Level	Managerial Ladder	Professional Ladder
6	Manager of Engineering	Research Engineer
5	Senior Engineering Manager	Senior Engineer
4	Engineering Manager	Advisory Engineer
3	Supervisory Engineer	Staff Engineer
2	Engineer	
1	Associate Engineer	

EXHIBIT 15–8

Two Promotion Ladders for Engineers

one to the other at some point. According to Driver's analysis, appropriate career development activities for these types would differ.

Driver believes that the most important application of his idea of career concept lies in striving for a fit between an individual's type and the organization in which he or she is employed. Although there is no empirical work of this nature to date, the concept is consistent with the growing importance in I/O psychology of the idea of *matching* individuals to jobs and to organizations to the ultimate benefit of both parties.

Matching model: See page 133.

Employee Skill and Knowledge Development

Training activities in organizations have been expanding considerably in recent years. A great deal of this expansion is accounted for by a variety of training programs that are called employee development. Not all such programs are consistent with the individual approach advocated here; however, opportunities for skill and knowledge development do appear to be more readily available than at any time in the past.

One measure of the increased emphasis on employee development is the growing number of organizations that will pay for employees to attend conferences, workshops, and special job-related courses in local colleges and universities. Some also will pay part or all of the costs of an undergraduate or graduate education in a job-related field.

Not all employee development training takes place outside the organization. Some is conducted on site by special training personnel or by outside consultants. Eligibility standards for these as well as for off-site programs vary. Although they traditionally have been more available to managerial and professional employees, reports in personnel and business-related publications suggest that this is changing. A good source of information about the variety of programs now in use is the *Training and Development Journal* published by the American Society for Training and Development.

Although skill and knowledge training for employee development reaches more employees than formerly, the oldest and most familiar form of such programs is *management development* programs. Many such programs are not based on an assessment of individual manager needs, but are oriented toward a general improvement of "the management" in an organization. (This is where strategies such as organizations sending all of their supervisors to a communications workshop fit into the concept of employee development.)

Probably the most comprehensive and coordinated approach to *individual* management development is to be found in connection with the use of assessment centers. These centers are broadbased evaluative programs staffed by professionals. They have been found to be useful for screening for certain upper-management and executive positions (see Chapter 5), but they also serve an important diagnostic function for employees already in such roles.

Assessment center: See page 125.

Assessment centers evaluate a wide variety of skills and abilities relevant to the performance of managerial jobs. Among these are decision making, organization and planning, communication, and social skills and abilities. Most such centers also do attitude, value, and personality assessments as well. Among the characteristics evaluated at the well-known AT&T center, for example, are need for achievement, self-objectivity, and Bell value system orientation (Bray, Campbell, & Grant, 1974).

Evaluation by an assessment center is not a prerequisite for effective management development. There are other ways to assess individual strengths and weaknesses in order to identify development needs of employees. Two of these ways that have appeared in other contexts are Management by Objectives and the Team Selection Process used by Graphic Controls (see Chapter 5).

MBO: See pages 267 to 268.

Although evaluations by assessment centers are not critical to management development, the kinds of reports that typically come out of these evaluations provide good examples of an individual approach to such development. Part of one sample report, together with center recommendations relating to weaknesses that need developing, appears in Exhibit 15–9. A thorough review of the issues and research relating to traditional management development is provided by Campbell, Dunnette, Lawler, and Weick (1970).

EXHIBIT 15–9

A Sample Assessment Center Report

Strengths

Work standards: Tried hard in every exercise; works very hard on job; does not want to personally settle for less than the best. Was disappointed by own performance as indicated by his self-evaluation.

Intelligence: Fast reader, catches on fast.

Corporate Thinking: A company man, very loyal.

Integrity: Will not compromise convictions, e.g., copy machine discussion.

Energy: Active in all exercises.

Stress Tolerance: Except for management game, showed little stress.

Interest in Self-Development: Welcomes help; worked his way through college, willing to move. While interest seemed very high, there was some doubt about strength of drive for self-development.

Level of Aspiration: Seems to be unhappy without winning or doing the best possible.

Weaknesses

Creativity: Not seen in approach to current job or in exercises—nothing shown in creative writing exercise.

Leadership: After an initial positive impact, he could not influence group.

Independence: In present job, seems to do what his boss wants; same attitude expressed in in-basket where he tended to delegate up and to follow "what boss wants."

Use of Delegation: Average in in-basket. He reports he does mail that should be done by subordinates.

Problem Analysis: Didn't understand "conglomerate"; didn't see many of the major problems in in-basket; background interview indicates a lack of problem definition in job; did not see all facets of Pretzel Company problem.

Financial Analytical Ability: Below average on financial problems, e.g., missed opportunity to change product mix.

Range of Interest: Seems to be restricted to marketing.

Flexibility: Seemed to approach every case and every situation the same way (was flexible in accepting ideas of others).

Temper: When did not get his way in compensation committee discussion, he became an obstruction to the leader's efforts.

Recommendations

While Harris did poorly in many areas, it was felt that he is definitely trainable. He was seen as needing a lot of support and guidance and a supportive, understanding, "fatherly" supervisor, but one that would force him to make decisions. It was felt he would develop best in a highly structured job with slowly increasing planning and organizing responsibility as his skills develop. An assignment in Illinois as a product manager might be good.

Some priority development challenges: —management through others
                                            —problem analysis
                                            —organization
                                            —administrative skills

Harris should be easy to communicate with regarding his assessment. He is extremely open and was accurate in his self-appraisals. A potential difficulty may be his insecurity causing him to view "help" as a threat.

Note. From Richard Beatty and Craig E. Schneier, *Personnel Administration: An Experiential Skill-Building Approach.* Copyright 1977, Addison-Wesley, Reading, Massachusetts. Pages 239–240. Reprinted with permission.

Personal Counseling in Organizations

A group of mixed services for assisting individual employee development falls under the heading of personal employee counseling. The oldest and most extensive of such programs are for employees with alcohol and other drug-abuse problems. Estimates vary, but well over 1,000 companies are known to offer personal counseling services to employees.

In addition to alcohol and drug-abuse programs, some companies offer personal counseling services for marital, legal, financial, and psychological difficulties. There is also a growing trend to offer preretirement counseling and planning services to all employees. A few companies, like Citibank, extend such assistance to employees who have been terminated.

Some organizations have full- or part-time specialists on the premises for employee counseling. Others use outside professionals on a contract basis or have regular referral services to various agencies. A comprehensive review of the nature and extent of the use of counseling in industry, together with relevant research, is offered by Cairo (1983). On the basis of this review, he offers five conclusions and recommendations.

1.   There is no consistent use of the word *counseling* among the studies reported. The term is used to describe anything from a short conversation with a supervisor to extended sessions with a trained professional.

2. The objectives of counseling and how its effectiveness will be evaluated need more careful consideration.
3. There is a need for more studies comparing different counseling approaches and counseling compared with other helping activities.
4. More precise and detailed information about the use of counseling in industry is needed.
5. Much of the counseling literature available is in how-to-do-it form. Program developers in industry should assume a greater responsibility for balancing such prescriptions with an evaluation of their effectiveness.

Concluding Remarks on Employee Development

In the broadest sense, employee development includes all of those activities by which an organization can assist a particular individual in performing well in the current job and/or moving along a desired career path. This is a big commitment, but there is nothing altruistic about it. Employee development programs can help employees become more skillful on the job, less hindered by personal problems, more knowledgeable about their potential, and more aware of and interested in the opportunities for growth with the company. All of these outcomes should work toward supporting the three employee behaviors identified by Katz (1964) as essential to organizational survival and effectiveness:

1. staying with the company
2. performing jobs dependably
3. engaging in innovative and creative behaviors that go beyond minimally acceptable job performance standards

THE QUALITY OF WORK LIFE

Various components of general employee well-being have been discussed throughout this text. Among these are:

- a safe and healthy work environment
- work that suits the abilities and needs of the employee
- the support and friendship of coworkers
- a good relationship with supervisors
- a degree of satisfaction with the work situation
- opportunity for personal growth and development if desired

The term being used in the literature to describe this global and multidimensional individual/job/organization interaction outcome is *quality of work life.*

Quality of work life (QWL) refers to the impact of an entire work situation on an individual: Is it a "force for good" in that person's life or not? This concept may be easier to illustrate in a negative fashion by means of two frequently-discussed symptoms of a *low* QWL—boredom and burnout.

Boredom

Traditional research into boredom with work and/or a work situation focused on the variety of responses to boredom, such as daydreaming, that hinder job performance (e.g., Smith, 1953). There also has been considerable interest in the type of individual who appears to be more susceptible to boredom (e.g., Stagner, 1975).

Other researchers have investigated mechanisms by which employees can cope with boredom (e.g., McBain, 1970) and the working conditions more likely to produce it. *Constraint, unpleasantness,* and *repetitiousness* in work tasks or the work environment have been found to be associated with greater reported boredom (e.g., Geiwitz, 1966). Such conditions, then, work against the quality of work life. A complete review of the boredom research may be found in Smith (1981).

Burnout

A great deal has been heard about "burnout" in recent years. In their comprehensive review of this literature, Pearlman and Hartman (1982) conclude that burnout may be defined reliably as *a response to chronic emotional stress that is characterized by:*

Stress: See pages 240 to 241.

- physical and/or emotional exhaustion
- lowered job productivity
- a tendency to think in impersonal terms, even of oneself

More picturesquely, Morrow (1981) writes that burnout can be detected by "the smell of psychological wiring on fire" (p. 84).

There is some question as to whether or not burnout is something new, but no question that the trendy label has served to call attention to the plight of those who suffer from this syndrome. There are now scales for measuring burnout (e.g., Maslach & Jackson, 1981), a number of formal courses to deal with burnout, and a variety of self-help articles on the subject.

The causes of the reaction to work now being called burnout are understood only generally at this time. Those employed in certain professions—police work, social work, and nursing, to take three examples—seem to be more vulnerable, but more traditional business organizations also see their share of this reaction.

"Cures" for burnout range from personal counseling to extended leave, to transfer, to termination. Prevention is even less well organized. To the extent, however, that the job stress leading to burnout is aggravated by a poor physical condition and poor health habits, the growing trend toward formal organizational health programs may be a step in the right direction.

It is estimated that about 50,000 U.S. firms now have some form of formal employee wellness program. Control Data Corporation's Stay-Well program is one well-known example. This program includes stress management, fitness and weight control, and stop-smoking components among others. A similar program, called Live for Life, is available to employees of the Johnson & Johnson companies. Such undertakings can cost up to $1,000 per year per participant, but many psychologists and company executives express a belief that these costs are more than offset by the benefits (Wolinsky, 1983). Documentation of these benefits is still in the very early stages, however.

Improving the Quality of Work Life

One of the most persistent voices calling for organizations to improve the quality of work life for their employees is I/O psychologist Edward Lawler. In a recent article on the subject, Lawler (1982) discusses two strategies for this improvement. One is for organizations to take steps to improve quality on a voluntary basis. These steps would be based on research and shared information as to effective approaches.

An alternative strategy for improving the quality of work life in organizations is for the government to set standards and use incentives, controls, and regulations to enforce them, much as OHSA has done in the more specific area of employee health and safety. The major problem with either approach is finding guidelines; no organization can create the perfect work environment.

OSHA: See page 231.

The reason no organization can create a perfect quality work environment is, of course, that people are different. Certain conditions—overcrowding, understaffing, inadequate materials, unpleasant surroundings,

An increasing number of organizations are offering programs and facilities to help promote employee health, fitness, and general well-being.

and the like—probably are perceived by almost everyone as lowering the quality of work life. Past such basic quality standards, however, things begin to get more complicated. For example, some people seem to thrive on the very conditions that are overstressful to others—too much to do and too little time in which to do it.

Many other examples may be cited of the practical difficulties to be encountered when those concerned set out to create a quality work environment. Conceptually, as Lawler (1974) pointed out some time ago, the problem is how to achieve a balance between individual differences among employees and forces, such as finite resources and the need for standard practices, that push toward emphasis of individual similarities.

Lawler (1974) believes that quality of work life is more likely to be improved by a movement toward what he calls the ''individualized organization.'' He describes this organization as follows:

> . . . an organization based on individual differences assumptions would have a job environment for each person which fits his or her unique skills and abilities. It would accomplish this by a combination of good selection and self-placement choices in the areas of fringe benefits, job design, hours of work, style of supervision, and training programs (p. 37).

The theory, research, and practice reviewed in this book suggests that I/O psychology is moving in a direction consistent with an emphasis on individual differences among employees. Evidence for this trend may be seen in (a) the gradual rejection of ''one best way'' approaches to such activities as job design, selection, and placement, (b) the questioning of such standard assumptions as those that absenteeism and turnover always have negative consequences, and (c) greater interest in the effects of nonwork variables on the behavior and attitudes of people at work.

To the extent that greater recognition of, and emphasis on, individual differences will improve the quality of work life in organizations, I/O psychology seems to be on the right track. There is only so much that psychologists, managers, executives, or anyone else can do in this regard, however. The responses of employees to a work setting are only partially a function of the decisions and actions of others. In the last analysis, employees must share the responsibility for making the outcomes of individual/job/organization interactions more positive.

SUMMARY

Job satisfaction is an attitude determined by an individual's affective evaluation of a work situation. Job satisfaction research finds question-naire measures of satisfaction to have modest negative correlations with absenteeism and turnover. Correlations also have been reported with such behaviors as lateness and with perceptions of why other people leave their jobs. Evidence regarding the relationship between job satis-faction and job performance is mixed, and the hypothesis that there is no inherent causal relationship between these two variables seems viable.

Employee development is a term encompassing a variety of activities that will help employees overcome problems or skill deficiencies that may be inhibiting present performance or acquire new skills and knowledge to work toward future goals. Among these activities are career planning and development, skill training, and personal counseling. Such programs are one way that the quality of work life in an organization may be improved. Other determinants of work life quality include a safe and healthy work environment, good working relationships, and work and work rewards that suit an individual's abilities and needs.

AT ISSUE

What If It Were True?

The "job satisfaction causes good performance" hypothesis is easily the hardiest hypothesis in all of I/O psychology. Fifty years of research have failed to confirm it, yet the question continues to fascinate. This raises an interesting point: "What if it were true?"

The story used to be told of a child who asked a car-chasing dog's owner: "What will he do with it if he catches it?" The same question might be asked of those searching for a causal link between job satisfaction and better job performance: "What will you do with it if you find it?"

Organizations can give people many things. They can give them jobs and security and status and money and parking places and free child care, and so on down a long list. They can do their bests to create the *conditions* under which employees can be successful and happy. But they cannot give employees job satisfaction. Job satisfaction is an individual affective response to a particular job situation. It depends upon individual values, expectations, needs, and perceptions, as well as upon the characteristics of the work situation.

People's values, expectations, needs, and perceptions differ and so employees differ significantly in the kinds of job situations they find satisfying. If one went into a company and changed every single aspect of it to what five employees said would give them great job satisfaction, at least five others would quit the next day. What, then, would we do with the knowledge if some unexpected research breakthrough suddenly proved that job satisfaction is an important cause of good performance?

There is nothing at all in this discussion to suggest that I/O psychologists should drop their concern for job satisfaction; quite the contrary. As a student once wrote in reply to an exam question about the importance of job satisfaction: "Job satisfaction is a good thing." There are few, in organizations or out, who would disagree with this statement. Perhaps it is time for I/O psychologists to put less effort into trying to prove that job satisfaction is directly and significantly related to higher job performance and to give more attention to trying to understand job satisfaction better in its own right.

REFERENCES

ADAMS, J. S. Wage inequities, productivity, and work quality. *Industrial Relations*, 1963, *3*, 9–16.

ADLER, S., & GOLAN, J. Lateness as a withdrawal behavior. *Journal of Applied Psychology*, 1981, *66*(5), 544–554.

BALES, J. Dispute over comparable worth places burden on evaluators. *APA Monitor*, 1984, *15*(3), 17–18.

BEATTY, R. W., & SCHNEIER, C. E. *Personnel Administration: An Experiential Skill-Building Approach*. Reading, MA: Addison-Wesley, 1977.

BHAGAT, R. S. Conditions under which stronger job performance-job satisfaction relationships may be observed: A closer look at situational contingencies. *Academy of Management Journal*, 1982, *25*(4), 772–789.

BRAY, D. W., CAMPBELL, R. J., & GRANT, D. L. *Formative Years in Business*. New York: John Wiley & Sons, 1974.

BREAUGH, J. A. Predicting absenteeism from prior absenteeism and work attitudes. *Journal of Applied Psychology*, 1981, *66*(5), 555–560.

BURNSTEIN, P. Equal employment opportunity legislation and the income of women and nonwhites. *American Sociological Review*, 1979, *44*(3), 367–391.

CAIRO, P. C. Counseling in industry: A selected review of the literature. *Personnel Psychology*, 1983, *36*(1), 1–18.

CAMPBELL, J. P., DUNNETTE, M. D., LAWLER, E. E., & WEICK, K. E. *Managerial Behavior, Performance, and Effectiveness*. New York: McGraw-Hill, 1970.

CLEGG, C. W. Psychology of employee lateness, absence, and turnover: A methodological critique and an empirical study. *Jounal of Applied Psychology*, 1983, *68*(1), 88–101.

CHERRINGTON, D. J., REITZ, H. J., & SCOTT, W. E., JR. Effects of contingent and non-contingent reward on the relationship between satisfaction and performance. *Journal of Applied Psychology*, 1971, *55*(6), 531–536.

DAVIS, K. *Human Relations and Organizational Behavior* (4th ed.). New York: McGraw-Hill, 1972.

DRIVER, M. J. Career concepts and career management in organizations. In G. L. Cooper (Ed.), *Behavioral Problems in Organizations*. Englewood Cliffs, NJ: Prentice-Hall, 1979, 79–139.

DYER, L., & THERIAULT, R. The determination of pay satisfaction. *Journal of Applied Psychology*, 1976, *61*, 596–604.

ERLICH, H. J. Attitudes, behavior, and the intervening variables. *American Sociologist*, 1969, *4*(1), 29–34.

FISHER, C. D. On the dubious wisdom of expecting job satisfaction to correlate with performance. *Academy of Management Review*, 1980, *5*(4), 607–612.

GEIWITZ, P. J. Structure of boredom. *Journal of Personality and Social Psychology*, 1966, *3*, 592–600.

GEST, T. Battle of the sexes over comparable worth. *U.S. News & World Report*, 1984, (February 20), pp. 73–74.

GILES, W. F., & FEILD, H. S. The relationship of satisfaction level and content of job satisfaction questionnaire items to item sensitivity. *Academy of Management Journal*, 1978, *21*(2), 295–301.

GOLEMBIEWSKI, R. T., & YEAGER, S. Testing the applicability of the JDI to various demographic groupings. *Academy of Management Journal*, 1978, *21*(3), 514–519.

GOULD, S., & HAWKINS, B. C. Organizational career stage as a moderator of the satisfaction-performance relationship. *Academy of Management Journal*, 1978, *21*(3), 434–450.

GREENBERGER, R. S. How Citibank rehabilitates those it fires. *The Wall Street Journal*, 1980, (November 10), p. 1.

HERZBERG, F., MAUSNER, B., & SNYDERMAN, B. B. *The Motivation to Work*. New York: John Wiley & Sons, 1959.

IVANCEVICH, J. M. High and low task stimulation jobs: A causal analysis of performance-satisfaction relationships. *Academy of Management Journal*, 1979, *22*(2), 206–222.

KABANOFF, B. Work and nonwork: A review of models, methods, and findings. *Psychological Bulletin*, 1980, *88*(1), 60–77.

KATZ, D. The motivational basis of organizational behavior. *Behavioral Science*, 1964, *9*(2), 131–146.

KEON, T. L., & McDONALD, B. Job satisfaction and life satisfaction: An empirical evaluation of their interrelationship. *Human Relations*, 1982, *35*(3), 167–180.

KHALEQUE, A. Job satisfaction, perceived effort, and heart rate in light industrial work. *Ergonomics*, 1981, *24*(9), 735–742.

LANDY, F. J. An opponent process theory of job satisfaction. *Journal of Applied Psychology*, 1978, *63*(5), 533–547.

LAWLER, E. E. The mythology of management compensation. *California Management Review*, 1966, *9*, 11–22.

LAWLER, E. E. *Motivation in Work Organizations*. Monterey, CA: Brooks/Cole, 1973.

LAWLER, E. E., III. The individual organization: Problems and promise. *California Management Review*, 1974, *16*(2), 31–39.

LAWLER, E. E., III. Strategies for improving the quality of work life. *American Psychologist*, 1982, *37*(5), 486–493.

LOCKE, E. A. The nature and causes of job satisfaction. In M. D. Dunnette (Ed.), *Handbook of Industrial and Organizational Psychology*. Chicago: Rand McNally & Co., 1976, 1297–1349.

MASLACH, C., & JACKSON, S. E. The measurement of experienced burnout. *Journal of Occupational Behavior*, 1981, *2*(1), 99–113.

McBAIN, W. N. Arousal, monotony, and accidents in line driving. *Journal of Applied Psychology*, 1970, *54*(6), 509–519.

MIHAL, W. L., SORCE, P. A., & COMTE, T. E. A process model of individual career decision making. *Academy of Management Review*, 1984, *9*(1), 95–103.

MILES, R. E. Human relations or human resources? *Harvard Business Review*, 1965, *43*(4), 148–163.

MOBLEY, W. H., GRIFFETH, R. W., HAND, H. H., & MEGLINO, B. M. Review and conceptual analysis of the employee turnover process. *Psychological Bulletin*, 1979, *86*(3), 493–522.

MORROW, L. The burnout of almost everyone. *Time*, 1981, (September 21), p. 84.

MOWDAY, R. T. Viewing turnover from the perspective of those who remain: The relationship of job attitudes to attributions of the causes of behavior. *Journal of Applied Psychology*, 1981, *66*(1), 120–123.

NEAR, J. P., RICE, R. W., & HUNT, P. C. The relationship between work and nonwork domains: A review of empirical research. *Academy of Management Review*, 1980, *5*(3), 415–429.

ORGAN, D. W. A reappraisal and reinterpretation of the satisfaction-causes-performance hypothesis. *Academy of Management Review*, 1977, *2*(1), 46–53.

PERLMAN, B., & HARTMAN, E. A. Burnout: Summary and future research. *Human Relations*, 1982, *35*(4), 283–305.

POPP, P. O., & BELOHLAV, J. A. Absenteeism in a low status work environment. *Academy of Management Journal*, 1982, *25*(3), 677–683.

PORTER, L. W. A study of perceived need satisfaction in bottom and middle management jobs. *Journal of Applied Psychology*, 1961, *45*(1), 1–10.

PORTER, L. W., & LAWLER, E. E. *Managerial Attitudes and Performance*. Homewood, IL: Richard D. Irwin, 1968.

QUINN, R. P., & SHEPARD, L. J. *The 1972–73 Quality of Employment Survey: Descriptive Statistics With Comparison Data From the 1969–70 Survey of Working Conditions*. Ann Arbor: University of Michigan, Institute for Social Research, 1974.

QUINN, R. P., STAINES, G. S., & McCOLLOUGH, M. R. *Job Satisfaction: Is There a Trend?* Washington, DC: U.S. Department of Labor, 1974.

RONAN, W. W., & ORGANT, G. J. Determinants of pay and pay satisfaction. *Personnel Psychology*, 1973, *26*, 503–520.

SCHMITT, N., & McCUNE, J. T. The relationship between job attitudes and the decision to retire. *Academy of Management Journal*, 1981, *24*(4), 795–802.

SEYBOLT, J. W. Career development: The state of the art among the grass roots. *Training and Development Journal*, 1979, *33*(4), 16–20.

SIGELMAN, L., MILWARD, H. B., & SHEPARD, J. M. The salary differential between male and female administrators: Equal pay for equal work. *Academy of Management Journal*, 1982, *25*(3), 664–671.

SMITH, P. C. The curve of output as a criterion of boredom. *Journal of Applied Psychology,* 1953, *37*(1), 69–74.

SMITH, P. C., KENDALL, L. M., & HULIN, C. L. *The Measurement of Satisfaction in Work and Retirement.* Chicago: Rank-McNally, 1969.

SMITH, R. P. Boredom: A review. *Human Factors,* 1981, *23*(3), 329–340.

SPENCER, D. G., & STEERS, R. M. Performance as a moderator of the job satisfaction-turnover relationship. *Journal of Applied Psychology,* 1981, *66*(4), 511–514.

STAGNER, R. Boredom on the assembly line: Age and personality variables. *Industrial Gerontology,* 1975, *2*(1), 23–44.

VECCHIO, R. P. Worker alienation as a moderator of the job quality-job satisfaction relationship: The case of racial differences. *Academy of Management Journal,* 1980, *23*(3), 479–486.

VON GLINOW, M. A., DRIVER, M. J., BROUSSEAU, K., & PRINCE, J. B. The design of a career oriented human resource system. *Academy of Management Review,* 1983, *8*(1), 23–32.

WATSON, C. J. An evaluation of some aspects of the Steers and Rhodes model of employee attendance. *Journal of Applied Psychology,* 1981, *66*(3), 385–389.

WEAVER, C. N. Job satisfaction in the United States in the 1970's. *Journal of Applied Psychology,* 1980, *65*(3), 364–367.

WOLINSKY, J. Companies find wellness pays, but it's hard to assess costs. *APA Monitor,* 1983, *14*(1), 17.

YEAGER, S. J. Dimensionality of the Job Descriptive Index. *Academy of Management Journal,* 1981, *24*(1), 205–212.

APPENDIX A

Useful Addresses

American Psychological Association
1200 17th. Street NW
Washington, DC 20036

American Board of Professional Psychology
2025 Eye Street NW
Suite 405
Washington, DC 20006

American Association of State Psychology Boards
100 Corporate Square
555 S. Perry Street
P.O. Box 4389
Montgomery, AL 36101

APA Committee on Professional Practice
4545 42nd Street NW
#304
Washington, DC 20016

APPENDIX B

APA Divisions of Particular Interest to I/O Psychologists*

Division 5
Division of Evaluation and Measurement

Division 13
Division of Consulting Psychology

Division 14
The Society for Industrial and Organizational Psychology, Inc.—A Division of the APA

Division 19
Division of Military Psychology

Division 21
Division of Applied Experimental and Engineering Psychologists

Division 23
Division of Consumer Psychology

Division 42
Division of Psychologists in Independent Practice

---

*Addresses for any of the divisions may be obtained from APA.

APPENDIX C

Selected List of Professional Journals of Particular Interest to I/O Psychologists

Academy of Management Journal

Academy of Management Review

Administrative Science Quarterly

American Psychologist

Ergonomics

Human Factors

Human Relations

Industrial Engineering

Journal of Applied Psychology

Journal of Experimental Psychology: Human Perception and Performance

Journal of Industrial Psychology

Organizational Behavior and Human Performance

Organizational Dynamics

Personnel Psychology

Psychological Bulletin

INDEX

A

ß